International Kierkegaard Commentary

International Kierkegaard Commentary

Stages on Life's Way

edited by
Robert L. Perkins

MERCER UNIVERSITY PRESS

MUP/ P533

Published by Mercer University Press
1501 Mercer University Drive
Macon, Georgia 31207

9 8 7 6 5 4 3 2 1

Books published by Mercer University Press are printed on acid-free paper that meets the requirements of the American National Standard for Information Sciences—Permanence of Paper for Printed Library Materials.

Cataloging-in-Publication Data
Stages on life's way / edited by Robert L. Perkins.
xx+xxxpp. 6x9" (15x22 cm.)—(International Kierkegaard commentary; 11)
Includes bibliographical references and index.
ISBN 978-0-88146-577-8
1. Kierkegaard, Søren, 1813–1855. Stadier paa livets vej.
I. Perkins, Robert L., 1930–. II. Series
[B4376.S833]
198'.9s—dc21]
[198'.0]

Contents

Acknowledgments

All the contributors to the volume would wish to make acknowledgments, but that privilege is reserved for the editor. Those whom contributors would have named will be content to have served their friends and colleagues.

I also have the privilege of thanking a number of persons at Stetson University who have supported my work in general and the *International Kierkegaard Commentary* in particular: H. Douglas Lee, president of Stetson University; Grady Ballenger, dean of the College of Arts and Sciences; Donna Schick, secretary to the Department of Philosophy; and Mindy Cecil and P. Albert Vogel, student assistants.

The advisory board and the volume consultant read all the contributions, offered valuable insights into the articles, and also made some recommendations for changes. Julia Watkin of the University of Tasmania continues to be particularly helpful in suggesting possible authors and tracking down obscure allusions in Kierkegaard's texts. The interest of Mercer University Press and especially the efforts of Senior Editor Edmon L. Rowell, Jr. are deeply appreciated. Princeton University Press gave permission to quote from *Stages on Life's Way* and other translations to which they hold copyright.

The several contributors and I also thank our families for the lost evenings and other scattered hours while we pursued these tasks. Finally, I wish to thank my wife, Sylvia Walsh, for assistance at every stage of this project and for making our life together an unutterable joy.

Robert L. Perkins

In Memoriam

Masaru Otani
19 October 1911–1 December 1999

Sixtus Scholtens
27 August 1925–14 February 2000

Sigla

AN	"Armed Neutrality." See PV.
BA	*The Book on Adler*, trans. Howard V. Hong and Edna H. Hong. Princeton NJ: Princeton University Press, 1995.
C	*The Crisis and a Crisis in the Life of an Actress*. See *Christian Discourses*.
CA	*The Concept of Anxiety*, trans. Reidar Thomte in collaboration with Albert B. Anderson. Princeton NJ: Princeton University Press, 1980.
CD C	*Christian Discourses* and *The Crisis and a Crisis in the Life of an Actress*, trans. Howard V. Hong and Edna H. Hong. Princeton NJ: Princeton University Press, 1997.
CI NSBL	*The Concept of Irony* together with "Notes on Schelling's Berlin Lectures" trans. Howard V. Hong and Edna H. Hong. Princeton NJ: Princeton University Press, 1989.
COR	*The Corsair Affair*, trans. Howard V. Hong and Edna H. Hong. Princeton NJ: Princeton University Press, 1982.
CUP	*Concluding Unscientific Postscript to 'Philosophical Fragments'*, two vols. trans. Howard V. Hong and Edna H. Hong. Princeton NJ: Princeton University Press, 1992.
EO, 1 EO, 2	*Either/Or*, 2 vols., trans. Howard V. Hong and Edna H. Hong. Princeton NJ: Princeton University Press, 1987.
EPW FPOSL	*Early Polemical Writings*, trans. Julia Watkin. Princeton NJ: Princeton University Press, 1990.
EUD	*Eighteen Upbuilding Discourses*, trans. Howard H. Hong and Edna H. Hong. Princeton NJ: Princeton University Press, 1990.
FPOSL	*From the Papers of One Still Living*. See EPW.
FSE JFY	*For Self-Examination* and *Judge for Yourself!*, trans. Howard V. Hong and Edna H. Hong. Princeton NJ: Princeton University Press, 1990.
FT R	*Fear and Trembling* and *Repetition*, trans. Howard V. Hong and Edna H. Hong. Princeton NJ: Princeton University Press, 1983.
JC	Johannes Climacus or De omnibus dubitandum est, See PF.
JFY	*Judge for Yourself!* See FSE.

JP	*Søren Kierkegaard's Journals and Papers,* Ed. and trans. Howard V. Hong and Edna H. Hong, assisted by Gregor Malantschuk. Bloomington: Indiana University Press, 1, 1967; 2, 1970; 3 and 4, 1975; 5-7, 1978.
LD	*Letters and Documents,* trans. Hendrik Rosenmeier. Princeton NJ: Princeton University Press, 1978.
NA	Newspaper Articles, 1854-1855. See TM.
NSBL	"Notes on Schelling's Berlin Lectures." See CI.
OMWA	On My Work as an Author. See PV.
P WS	*Prefaces* and "Writing Sampler", trans. Todd W. Nichol. Princeton NJ: Princeton University Press, 1998.
PC	*Practice in Christianity,* trans. Howard V. Hong and Edna H. Hong. Princeton NJ: Princeton University Press, 1991.
PF JC	*Philosophical Fragments* and "Johannes Climacus," trans. Howard V. Hong and Edna H. Hong. Princeton NJ: Princeton University Press, 1985.
PV AN	*On My Work as an Author,* "The Point of View for My Work as an Author" and "Armed Neutrality", trans. Howard V. Hong and Edna H. Hong. Princeton NJ: Princeton University Press, 1998.
R	*Repetition*. See FT.
SLW	*Stages on Life's Way,* trans. Howard V. Hong and Edna H. Hong. Princeton NJ: Princeton University Press, 1988.
SUD	*The Sickness unto Death,* trans. Howard V. Hong and Edna Hong. Princeton NJ: Princeton University Press, 1980.
TA	*Two Ages: the Age of Revolution and the Present Age.* A Literary *Review,* trans. Howard V. Hong and Edna H. Hong. Princeton NJ: Princeton University Press, 1978.
TDIO	*Three Discourses on Imagined Occasions,* trans. Howard V. Hong and Edna H. Hong. Princeton NJ: Princeton University Press, 1993.
TM	*'The Moment' and Late Writings,* trans. Howard V. Hong and Edna H. Hong. Princeton NJ: Princeton University Press, 1998.
UDVS	*Upbuilding Discourses in Various Spirits,* trans. Howard V. Hong and Edna H.Hong. Princeton NJ: Princeton University Press, 1993.
WA	*Without Authority,* trans. Howard V. Hong and Edna H. Hong. Princeton NJ: Princeton University Press, 1997.
WL	*Works of Love,* trans. Howard V. Hong and Edna H. Hong. Princeton NJ: Princeton University Press, 1995.
WS	"Writing Sampler" See P.

Introduction

With the title *Stages on Life's Way* Kierkegaard gave a new phrase to many languages and offered a tentative solution to a major conundrum of both modernist and postmodernist sensibility—the question of human identity. Conceding nothing to modernist and postmodernist fashions, he asks how we can put our lives together so we can find some inner coherence and happiness. The title suggests the volume is a *Bildungsroman*. It is that and more. The subject/hero of the novel is not, however, the character around whom a plot episodically weaves; nor is there a cast of characters who are defined through their relation to the hero or antihero. Rather the subject/hero of the novel is the reader himself or herself. The volume is then an arabesque, a collection of apparently separate works followed by a commentary and interpretation of the collection, all of which is dedicated to the philosophical analysis of many facets of modern thought and the psychological investigation of the modern self or the lack thereof. The text becomes the interlocutor and the reader the respondent; the reader is read.

Both brilliant and dense, revealing and concealing, a repetition of earlier themes and completely new, Kierkegaard adds new insights to previously examined issues and radically changes the emphasis of the earlier pseudonymous writings in preparation for the next and central work of the authorship, *Concluding Unscientific Postscript to the "Philosophical Fragments." Stages on Life's Way* is both an intellectual challenge, a literary imbroglio, and a provocation to Socratic reflection.

This sense of incompleteness while yet ending and the concomitant sense the reader has that there must be more to be said account for the unusual, that is, the cool reception of the book that Kierkegaard himself predicted (SLW, 494). Of course, the great length is a common focus of much complaint from his literary superiors, but many think Kierkegaard used no more words than he needed. The real difficulties are, first, the repetitions and reinterpretations of a previously told story, the failed engagement, and second, the conflict with the cultural icons and idols of the time, from the self-assured confidence of bourgeois culture to its various intellectual and aesthetic underpinnings in romanticism, Hegelianism, and idealism more generally. Yet as one reads *Stages on Life's Way* one senses this is the last of the major literary diversions we will receive. There will be a few more such, but they will be minor compared to the giant tomes of *Either/Or* and *Stages on Life's Way*. In his journals Kierkegaard emphasized the finality when he notes that William Afham even promises that Constantius will never have to prepare another banquet nor will Victor Eremita ever again have to speak of Don Juan admiringly (JP, 5:5823). One also feels that Kierkegaard is finished with the engagement, and this feeling is not just hindsight. The last word in the book is *dixit*, "I have said it," but the remaining portion of the traditional closing words in Latin oratory are missing: *et liberavi cor meum*, all together meaning, "I have said it and delivered my heart" (SLW, 494, 742n.588). He has indeed delivered his heart, and the engagement will not again be the focus it has been through the pseudonymous literature. A different fate awaits the cultural and social matters.

Kierkegaard's disagreements with the intellectual currents and the social-political assumptions of the time are at least implicitly expressed in the pseudonymous literature, but there he has done little more than criticize. He had not worked out and presented a clear and comprehensive critique and alternative to the matters of the mind and, though those with hindsight can see the forthcoming storm over Christendom, he has not laid out the foundations of a comprehensive rational critique of its assumptions and presumption. The impotence and innocuousness of Christendom vis-á-vis the amorality and immorality of the speakers at the banquet, the certitudes of Judge William, and the despair of Quidam is apparent for all to see in *Stages on Life's Way*. Kierkegaard's understanding of the reasons for this powerlessness and his recommendations for the cure are soon to be delivered in *Concluding Unscientific Postscript to "Philosophical Fragments."* Kierkegaard did not suspect that working out the implications of this "concluding" volume would require a whole second literature. *Stages on Life's Way* is then both an end and a beginning.

There are three (or four) parts of this last novel, the most famous of which is "In Vino Veritas," a dialogue that invites comparison with Plato's *Symposium*. Plato's speakers praise love while Kierkegaard's bash women. Some symposiasts are familiar, they having previously appeared in one or another of the previously published pseudonymous works, though there are also new characters. The symposium is reported by William Afham. Judge William, the ethicist from *Either/Or* II, defends marriage with bold assurance and ethical insight against its contemporary critics, be they the aesthetes or some religious exception. The largest part of the novel is "Guilty?"/"Not Guilty?" a diary by a certain Quidam who reflects on his engagement to a certain Quaedam. The "Letter to the Reader," a commentary on and an explanation of "Guilty?"/"Not Guilty?" is a separate (and fourth) part that does not appear in the table of contents. Both the diary and the letter are written by Frater Taciturnus, who reflects in the last paragraph that "there is no reader who reads all the way through" (SLW, 494). Frater, however, is wrong. There are many such readers—the contributors to this volume and many others who have puzzled over this text and have attempted to answer its interrogation.

The contributions to this volume focus issues particular to the various parts of the book, for the most part, thus suggesting that the sequence of the commentary follows the sequence of the book itself. Three essays relate somewhat more pointedly to specific issues in *Stages on Life's Way* and are interspersed at proper points. This collection is perhaps the most contentious to appear in the International Kierkegaard Commentary to date, though some pretty onerous disagreements have previously been published.

Amy Laura Hall hurls down the gauntlet in a searing criticism of *Stages on Life's Way*, almost the complete authorship, and Kierkegaard himself. She reads *Stages on Life's Way* using *Works of Love* as providing the criteria by which to interpret and judge the moral worth of the complete authorship and its author. Hall claims the central theme to be the avoidance of the other, an avoidance she finds even in "Some Reflections of Marriage in Answer to Objections by a Married Man." For Hall, gender relations lie at the heart of *Stages on Life's Way*, and William Afham (whose name means "by himself") is the paradigm male as well as the appropriate collector of the pieces that make up the volume focused on the avoidance of deep and nonstereotypical gender relations.

Robert E. Wood accepts the several provocations inserted into the text to compare and contrast Plato's *Symposium* and "In Vino Veritas." He analyzes the theme of recollection, which is basic to both dialogues. The deep irony in Plato's dialogue is that, after having been excluded by common consent, wine is reintroduced into the party by the drunken, dissolute, and soon to be traitorous Alcibiades. One would not expect the truth from Alcibiades, but he is the truth teller, gaining Socrates' consent to every detail of the sordid tale he tells. Irony metamorphoses the story of his failed seduction of Socrates into a recollection of his misfired desire for wisdom. Kierkegaard's symposiasts, by contrast, begin drinking early and are required to feel the affects of the alcohol before speaking. Perhaps their "recollection" shows the deficiency of contemplation, the first hint of which occurs at the end of the dialogue when Judge William, in an episode separated by time, place, and company from the symposium itself, refuses to participate in a speculation, though teasingly urged to do so by his beloved wife.

Adriaan van Heerden takes a completely different approach to "In Vino Veritas" from that of Wood, focusing on the issue of the unity of the comic and the tragic. Plato and Kierkegaard approach the relationship through a questioning of the adequacy of immediacy, in Plato called the "great nonsense of mortality" (*Symposium*, 211e) and in Kierkegaard, the aesthetic. In both Plato and Kierkegaard the tragic is the same, the neglect of one's soul. The care of the soul in Plato is expressed in the metaphor of erotic ascent (in Diotima's speech). In *Stages on Life's Way* the care of the soul is also expressed through a figure of movement, a transition from the immediate through ethical responsibility to religious subjectivity. The recognition of the human tragedy transforms it from an irreparable one into, potentially at least, a reparable one through the comic, the comic and the tragic becoming united in the existence of the person. Van Heerden does not think that the resolution of the problem of the relation of the comic and the tragic is satisfactorily resolved in *Stages on Life's Way*, with the result that we must look further, to *Works of Love*, for the complete resolution. Looking into this last text suggests a new theme to be used in the critical interpretation of *Stages on Life's Way*: the full equivalence of the ethical and the religious.

Paul Martens' article, "The Equivocal Judge William: Comparing the Ethical in Kierkegaard's *Stages on Life's Way* and *Either/Or*," takes into consideration Johannes Climacus's claim that the latter ends with the ethical while the former proceeds to the religious. Martens addresses such questions as: Does *Either/Or* actually end with the ethical? What role does the ethical play in *Stages on Life's Way* in defining the proper understanding of the religious? Is the transition from the aesthetic to the ethical the same in both books? To answer these questions, Martens presents a detailed analysis of several changes in the life-view of Judge William between his earlier letters and the later essay. The other pseudonymous works published between 1843 and 1845 account for the differences in Judge William's views and his development.

George Connell argues that Judge William's contribution, "Some Reflections on Marriage in Answer to Objections by A Married Man," is no rehash of positions previously presented in *Either/Or*. The judge uses a new form, the essay, which contains and exhibits the judge's concern for seriousness, the fundamental mood of the ethical stage and the antithesis of the irony of the aesthetes that was clearly shown in "In Vino Veritas." Defending a narrow pass (SLW, 169) between the aesthetes and the "religious exception," Judge William comes off very well. Following a detailed and important discussion of our ambivalence toward seriousness, Connell examines Judge William's critique of the religious exception, and finds him lacking in a fundamental way. Arguing that Judge William is only an example of the concept of seriousness, we are urged to look elsewhere for another and even more serious concept and example, to *Fear and Trembling*.

Vincent McCarthy extends his study of moods using Freudian categories in his essay, "Morning and Melancholia in 'Quidam's Diary,' " to question the adequacy of Kierkegaard's concept of "enclosing reserve" and whether his explanation of the love affair, so overanalyzed in the pseudonymous literature even before we arrive at "Guilty?" / "Not Guilty?" opens the way to the religious. McCarthy concludes that "the theory that enclosing reserve is a symptom of religiously directed melancholia (*Tungsind*) is never argued, only asserted, and is finally to be rejected." Enclosing reserve is then a danger to the religious, not one attendant condition, among other possible ones. McCarthy concludes that the fixation on the engagement does not undercut the larger concept of subjectivity that is necessary in Kierkegaard's understanding of the religious.

Darío González in his article, "Suspended Reflections: The Dialectic of Self-Enclosure in Kierkegaard's 'Guilty?'/'Not Guilty?' " argues that the "contradiction defined by immediate and reflective existence is . . . linked to the tension between the immediate and religious categories." This tension is shown between the female, who is "immediate," and the male, who is "reflective." When objectified by reflection, his fiance becomes an image before Quidam's imagination and/or mind, much as Cordelia was also transformed into an image by Johannes the Seducer's reflection in *Either/Or* I. This likeness does not suggest any affinity between Johannes and Quidam so much as it suggests the fundamental characteristic of the activity of reflection—that it cannot grasp the existential but only its image. After showing several applications of this characteristic, each one becoming more and more abstract from existence until the object is an unknown X, the way out is offered by communication, the word. The word breaks the solipsism and enclosing reserve of reflection and the image.

Louise Carroll Keeley excavates the importance of possibility for Quidam and for the religious life generally in her essay, "Living the Possibility of a Religious Existence: Quidam in Kierkegaard's *Stages on Life's Way*." Quidam, unfortunately, remains always a possibility, never undergoes the necessity of repentance, and never enters the actuality of the religious life. Keeley interestingly relates possibility to enclosing reserve. The reason is that enclosing reserve is as much a product of the imagination as of reflection, both of which have infinite elasticity. The way out is repentance, that is, claiming oneself, which though founded in Socratic self-knowledge is more conceptually complex. However, both imagination and reflection militate against repentance and self-knowledge because neither can grasp or express existence.

John J. Davenport turns his attention to "The Ethical and Religious Significance of Taciturnus's Letter in Kierkegaard's *Stages on Life's Way*." "The Letter to the Reader" is perhaps the most philosophically important part of the volume, for there Taciturnus argues what he has just shown in Quidam's diary. Discussing many important themes in moral psychology, this rich philosophic epistolary essay is concerned with the logic of volition, character, ground projects, well-placed and misplaced love, and intrinsic values. All these themes fit snugly with Kierkegaard's moral psychology as expressed not only in *Stages on Life's Way* but also in the complete authorship. Davenport also puts Taciturnus in conversation primarily with Bernard Williams and Harry Frankfurt, and to a somewhat lesser extent with Alastair MacIntyre, Charles Taylor, and C. S. Lewis (in the footnotes).

Grethe Kjær examines the concepts of fate and providence in the authorship but particularly in *Either/Or*, *The Concept of Anxiety*, *Stages on Life's Way*, and *The Sickness unto Death*. After discussing fate in paganism, Kjær explains its relation to Christianity, contrasting it to providence, and its relation to the stages on life's way. These latter connections are not as linguistically casual and obvious as it may appear at first sight. The difference between fate and Christian providence lies in personal experience, in the possibility of becoming a religious exception, not perhaps in the stature of an Abraham, but within the limits of one's own gifts, that is, within a personal providence.

Andrew J. Burgess examines the relations between *Stages on Life's Way* and *Three Discourses on Imagined Occasions* which were published on successive days. The relation between the two is not at all as clear as one would think. There are three stages in one and three imagined occasions in the other. There is, however, no neat conceptual fit between the books and the relation of the two in terms of the writing history is far from clear. Burgess's own contribution to the clarification of the relation between the two books is his detailed examination of the concept of the stages on life's way itself. After a finely nuanced analysis of the concept Burgess concludes that "reading *Stages on Life's Way* can itself be a powerful antidote to an overly simplistic grasp of what the stages are." Building on previous contributions to the International Kierkegaard Commentary, Burgess enriches our understanding of the texture and inner organization of Kierkegaard's works and the authorship as a whole. In the present context, his "The Bilateral Symmetry of Kierkegaard's *Postscript*" is of particular interest,[1] for it is easier to read backwards from the *Concluding Unscientific Postscript to "Philosophical Fragments"* to understand *Stages on Life's Way* than vice versa.

Not only has Kierkegaard in *Stages on Life's Way* offered a new phrase to many languages, he has refocused the major complexities of his pseudonymous literature before revealing the depth of human subjectivity upon which it is based. In *Concluding Unscientific Postscript to "Philosophical Fragments"* Kierkegaard shows the ontological and epistemological basis of the pseudonymous literature and lays the foundations for the second literature and the social and political polemic that will follow.

This volume of essays is offered to our readers, who by criticism and better thinking we invite to become our teachers.

Robert L. Perkins

---

[1]See *International Kierkegaard Commentary: Concluding Unscientific Postscript to "Philosophical Fragments,"* IKC 12 (Macon GA: Mercer University Press, 1997) 329-47.

1

Stages on the Wrong Way: Love and the Other in Kierkegaard's Stage's on Life's Way *and* Works of Love

Amy Laura Hall

> [T]he lover has with his beloved the most priceless amusement and the most interesting subject of study in his life. (SLW, 52)

> As far as I am concerned, the emphasis must be placed elsewhere—whether I was actually capable of giving my life the kind of expression that a marriage requires. (SLW, 195)

> This mode of answering, to swing away from the direction of the question . . . in order instantaneously to press the task as close as possible to the questioner, what he has to do—this is characteristic of the essentially Christian. (WL, 96)

Introduction

William Afham prefaces his tale of wine and truth, "In Vino Veritas," with an enigmatic discussion of reflection and seclusion, wondering, "how can the beaten and frequented be reconciled with the out-of-the-way and the hidden" (SLW, 16). Existence, "the essential," "the idea," all require that the self be adept at the "art" of critically reflected memory, an ability to "conjure away the present" and be "absent" even while in the presence of another (SLW, 13). How can life's demand for reflective solitude cohere with the ineluctably relational facets of existence? How can the frequented be reconciled with the hidden? William Afham, whose name indicates that he is resolutely "by himself," gives thanks to a "friendly spirit" who has "protect[ed his] stillness" and granted him "a hiding place" all his own (SLW, 17). But, as he suggests, "recollection's bookkeeping is a curious thing" (SLW, 11), and the protective spirit who grants secrecy may not be benign; it may rather be malevolent. An individual's motives for seeking a solitary place in which to reflect and write do matter. One may eschew the influence of others on one's own "reflective bookkeeping" in order to attend to the truth, in order to perpetuate self-delusion, or for even more sinister purposes. William Afham, who is alone, thanks his friendly spirit for preventing the "interruption" of another into his own silent retreat and notes, "only someone who sought solitude unworthily can benefit" from such a disturbance (SLW, 18). William Afham thus mentions fleetingly that the "surprise" of another's voice, intruding on an individual's self-inclosed reflection, may correctively "disturb" the invidious "secret" bookkeeping with which an individual becomes preoccupied. By reading *Stages on Life's Way* with *Works of Love* in view, we here attempt to provide such an interruption.

In this collection of papers, *Stages on Life's Way*, a "fraternity" of men (as the bookbinder's "learned friend" calls them) considers in various ways that "beaten and frequented" institution of marriage and whether life may accommodate contact with that other who truly interrupts a man's reclusive bookkeeping—that is, with a woman (SLW, 6). The stages along these divergently deviant ways well depict several means by which a man may avoid a true encounter with the female other.[1] The banquet revelers explicitly exclude anyone lacking the requisite tool ("cigar," "pipe," "divining rod") thus ensuring that no one "impertinently insists on being an actuality" over and against their manhood (SLW, 23). Judge William the Married, unlike William Alone, believes himself joined to an other, but in the course of his treatise reveals his dependence on a

---

[1]Drawing upon French feminism, Céline Léon offers another reading of *Stages* as a text on the negation of otherness in her excellent essay "The No Woman's Land of Kierkegaardian Exceptions" in *Feminist Interpretations of Søren Kierkegaard*, ed. Céline Léon and Sylvia Walsh (University Park: Pennsylvania State University Press, 1997) 147-73. Reading *Stages on Life's Way* with *Works of Love* allows us not only to indict Kierkegaard for his own painful evasions (as does Léon) but, more to the point, to find *ourselves* implicated in the multiple narratives of *Stages on Life's Way*. We here use Kierkegaard's own critique, in *Works of Love*, of the deception, use, and avoidance of the other to crack open this fraternal text. To do so also allows us to hear in *Works of Love* Kierkegaard's call to a Christian alternative only glimpsed through the fissures of *Stages on Life's Way*.

feminine fabrication of his own spinning. Finally, the Diarist, in his earnest reflection upon life, acknowledges the genuine otherness of the beloved but, in mistrust of himself and her, chooses to seek solitude through an elaborate deception of self and other. Although the way of each man is mistaken, their missteps are instructive. Especially in the Diary we have occasion to note the close resemblance between one man's apprehensive retreat from reality and the sober self-examination Christianity requires. By interrupting each man's thoughts on marriage with the command to love, we may insert the other back into the text and spoil the inappropriately inclosed reserve of each. When the actual (female) neighbor thus enters this fraternal discourse, each reflection reveals each man to be, as the epigraph suggests, more simian than saintly (SLW, 8).[2]

Every mistaken stage in this book of wrong ways begs for Christian correction. By reading *Stages on Life's Way* with *Works of Love* we may hear God rudely interrupt Constantin's carefully orchestrated feast, insist that Judge William's "sickness unto death" is beyond his wife's recuperative power, and call the dear Diarist out of his idea and into an authentic encounter through self-disclosure.[3] In *Works of Love*, Kierkegaard seeks to bring God's command so close to the reader as to avoid any possible diversion or excuse for not loving the other. While bona fide engagement is a fragile possibility for many objective and subjective reasons, the one task on which the individual is to focus is: "to acquire the true conception of love" (WL, 236). Constantin and his guests speak of the misrelation between men and "woman" that precludes involvement, and the Diarist tortures himself over the inherent, intractable misunderstanding between himself and his beloved. In *Works of Love* we have

---

[2]"Such works are mirrors: when an ape looks in, no apostle can look out" (SLW, 8). The idealistic Young Man, Judge William, and the Diarist are less apish than the others, but, as Kierkegaard asserts, "To become better or seem to be better by means of comparison with the badness of others is, after all, a bad way to become better" (WL, 286). No stage in this pseudonymous book of mistaken ways unambiguously depicts the path of discipleship.

[3]See Judge William's section on this "sickness" SLW, 129-30. Again, in naming each necessarily interrupted discourse, I do not want to separate the reader from the vicious or mistaken character. Kierkegaard intends for the careful reader to find him or herself similarly indicted.

Kierkegaard's urgent reminder that the only impediment to our engagements with which we should be concerned is the "misrelation" or "inversion" in our own understanding of love (WL, 31, 40, 162). Because their inquiry is more blatantly vicious than that of the Diarist, the celebratory misogynists of "In Vino Veritas" may be expelled with less attention than either William or the Diarist. The Diarist's missteps are most difficult to dismiss; his self-scrutinizing reflection is askew, but almost imperceptibly so. The contrast between the Diarist's recurring apprehension and Judge William's unshakable confidence may instruct us as we attempt to meet Kierkegaard's call in *Works of Love* for a genuine, honest construal of love. The Diarist seeks seclusion in part because he, in his own disoriented manner, rightly recognizes that true love with another requires both self-examination and a sober acknowledgment that the beloved is a stranger. Although Judge William bypasses the Diarist's temptation to flee, he does so largely by virtue of amorous luck, idealizing the other and underestimating the treachery of intimacy.[4] After interrupting each man's evasive treatise with God's command, we will consider how God's presence as a confidant (rather than as an idea) might facilitate an (albeit arduous) marriage for the Diarist, and for those of us who similarly struggle.

Divining Rods and Unmentionable Cravings

> It is a sad but all too common inversion to go on talking continually about how the object of love must be so it can be loveworthy. . . . (WL, 159)
>
> [T]he idea of woman is only a workshop of possibilities. (SLW, 76)

To spend any time distinguishing a true construal of love from the words of Constantin and his cronies may seem like overkill.[5] But,

---

[4]Judge William also has intimations of true love in his passages against comparison (SLW, 122, 123). This truth slips through his hands, however, when he suggests that love can be based on his admiration of the maternal and sustained by woman's inherent goodness (SLW, 131,134).

[5]Although these men's divergence from Kierkegaard's norm in *Works of Love* is obvious, the nuances of their distortions are worth attention. For a much more in-depth look at "woman bashing" in this portion of the text, see Robert L. Perkins,

as the narrator explains, these "nocturnal revelers seen in the morning light" may have "an almost *unheimlich* [disquieting] effect," and Kierkegaard intends for the reader to be alarmed by this first set of stages. It is not incidental to Kierkegaard's purposes that we enter this text through the stark depiction of vice at the banquet. If the bookbinder's tutor is right, these men's words are "stitched together" with the treatise on marriage and the Diary because "In Vino Veritas" is associated in some way with what follows (SLW, 6). The celebrants' explicit attempts to shield themselves from the reality of the other, to avoid the "frequented" while musing on intimacy, introduces blatantly the fear and avoidance of otherness more implicit in William's marriage and the Diary. In this way, Kierkegaard introduces an issue that is central to the text: the avoidance of real interaction with an other.

As Johannes asserts, there is "nothing more nauseating" than to have one's fantasies broken by "immediate" and "impertinent" actuality (SLW, 23), and the whole banquet is set up to allow each man to reach climax without interaction. Every "worthy member brings with him" an "unmentionable craving," and Constantin's intent is to "awaken and incite" that craving with no threat of surprise (SLW, 25). Smoking his own cigar, Victor notes that "there should never be any women at a banquet," and our resolutely solitary narrator cheers (SLW, 24). The absence of contingency is crucial, for who "has not sensed the anxiety that something might suddenly happen, the most trifling thing" that would "upset everything" (SLW, 27). Keeping their "wrist[s] flexible" so as best each to serve "the lamp in his hand," they begin their masturbatory musings on "the relation between man and woman" (SLW, 27, 31). Each with his "divining rod" may enjoy the evening, for "all one needs to do is wish" (SLW, 27, 28). The entire setting is constructed to provide for male pleasure by ruling out interaction, interruption, and consequence. The content of each man's speech follows according to this form, precluding a time "when men and women banqueted together" and portraying with extremity the evasion of genuine intimacy (SLW, 30).

"Woman Bashing in Kierkegaard's 'In Vino Veritas': A Reinscription of Plato's *Symposium*," in Léon and Walsh, *Feminist Interpretations of Søren Kierkegaard*, 83-102.

There is one among them who fails to enjoy himself, at least in the way intended. Our narrator recalls that the first speaker in this lineup, the Young Man, had a "loving sympathetic demeanor" that "involved no one" (SLW, 21). This description points to a problem in the Young Man's way: his manner of loving the other, while seemingly innocuous, involves no one. There is no other to whom he gives his love. Unlike those who follow him, the Young Man does not seek to construe "woman" in order to deny her reality. Rather, the love to which he attests is "pure," self-enclosed in his "thought" and independent of actuality (SLW, 46). His reasons for remaining alone reflect his refusal to infer the other as merely of interest for his fulfillment. The other with whom an individual is to interact is, as a human being, "a complete entity" herself, and thus intimate interaction cannot be merely a game of finding a complementary piece (SLW, 43). The Young Man explains that actively to take note of such an other involves risk; apprehending "the impression" of another requires a "surrender" of "control" (SLW, 32). Before such a venture, he explains, one should be aware of the multiple "fox traps" of erotic love (SLW, 38).

Through the Young Man's voice, Kierkegaard introduces an important facet of the Diarist's apt apprehension regarding his engagement with another. The stakes facing the lover and the beloved are perilously high. While others may bumble through this very "narrow path" as if it were instead a "broad way," the Young Man refuses to ignore the "spiritual trials" inherent to the endeavor (SLW, 46). He thus "does not dare to walk or put his foot on the ground" or, as he also puts it, smoke his pipe (SLW, 38, 33). Rather than walk confidently, wielding his "divining rod" or smoking his pipe, the Young Man resolves to remain above the route altogether. This first speaker of wine and truth commends a stance subtly askew from Kierkegaard's requirement that the individual take serious note of love's danger. If he is to love, the Young Man explains, he must know well the task (SLW, 35). By acknowledging the traps and trials involved, the Young Man reveals his acuity, but his solitary resolution in *Stages on Life's Way* is no more loving than it is at the close of

Repetition.[6] While Kierkegaard also seeks earnestly, throughout *Works of Love*, to point out the dangers inherent to engagement, he insists that one must put his foot to the ground and commence walking the quite narrow way of loving well on earth. We will return later to this precarious, pedestrian love.

While the Young Man keeps himself afloat in the clouds rather than harm himself or others, the speakers who follow him assert that reality, in the form of "woman," may be tricked, consumed, subsumed, and negated. The Young Man flees the consequence of love by remaining alone; his fellow banqueters deny the other's consequence by systematically barring her from the colloquy. Insisting again that "between two such different entities no real interaction can take place," Constantin steers the men back to the trajectory set when he excluded women from the occasion (SLW, 48). Constantin proclaims that women exist to the extent that they relate to men, and the speakers proceed to work off this assumption (SLW, 48). He construes "woman" as a man's "most priceless amusement"—an opportunity for men's "jest"—because she is in her youth "a demure miss . . . constructed in one's imagination" and, later, a "broken-in horse" who still may be "teased" (SLW, 52, 53). Joking to his "fellow conspirators," the fashion designer scathingly suggests that "woman does have spirit" and is quite "reflective," for, he continues, is she not able infinitely to transform all that is sacred into that which is "suitable for adornment" (SLW, 67)? As the "high priest" of a sustained hoax at the expense of women, the fashion designer vows that eventually "she is going to wear a ring in her nose" (SLW, 71).

For his part, Johannes commends another use of "woman," who is "a whim from a man's brain, a daydream" to be enjoyed craftily in order to avoid repercussion (SLW, 73, 75). It is imperative, he explains, that a man not become entangled with an actual woman; she must be handled carefully so as to "evaporate and dissolve into that indefinable something" that is her essential form, "like a temporary character whose time is up" (SLW, 80). The Fashion Designer's task in life is to materialize Constantin's and Johannes's

---

[6]We should note that the young man shudders at the thought that he might find a woman who likewise understood the dangers involved in intimacy, for this would "betray alarming foreknowledge" and thus taint "her lovableness" (SLW, 47).

imaginary construction: woman exists for men to view, enjoy, and "prostitute" (SLW, 71). Victor Eremita considers the matter by suggesting that woman is "an undefinable quantity" made "blissful in fantasy," and asserts that this simultaneously "being 'hurrah' and nothing" is a fate worse than being a slave and therefore something (SLW, 59, 56). Ultimately, both he and Johannes sum the discussion up by noting that, really, in order to be of any use to her lover, a woman must, in effect, be dead (SLW, 61, 80).

Thus, over their wine and mutton, these men reveal the many means by which we may avoid and even slay the reality that is the other. By envisioning the other in this manner, as nothing of real ethical consequence, and by reconstructing meticulously every potential interaction as "only forgery," an individual may be, as Victor puts it, "better safeguarded than if he entered the monastery" (SLW, 65). In their patriarchal construction of intimacy, there is no need for the Young Man's abstinence; we may imagine ourselves alone even while embracing another. By willing the theoretical exclusion of the other from reality, the banqueters may take with them, as a memento of the occasion, their host's carefully constructed gift of seclusion. Each may imagine himself alone holding his "lamp," able to grant himself every "wish" without interruption, even after exiting Constantin's banquet hall.

Objections to the Married Man's Answer

> Thus woman has a possibility that no man has, an enormous possibility . . . and the most terrible of all is the witchcraft of the illusion in which she feels so happy. (SLW, 62)
>
> [J]esting aside, marriage in many ways really is a venture in natural magic. (SLW, 90)

Judge William's "Reflections on Marriage in Answer to Objections" is, while less overtly contemptible than "In Vino Veritas," still objectionable. Our narrator relates that these "nocturnal revelers" come upon William and his wife while the two are hidden away in an enclosed arbor, "much too secure to think of themselves as objects of observation by anyone but the morning sun" (SLW, 82). Kierkegaard's narrative segue provides an interpretive link from "In Vino Veritas" to William's "Reflections." Although the banqueters in word and deed exclude the other from the table while William shares tea with his wife, William's treatise also betrays an attempt to exclude the other's real, disturbing, presence. Not taking sufficient account of God's command and the self-critical humility that is to result from an encounter with God, William's defense of intimacy is built on overly buoyant suppositions. His "venture in natural magic" at times touches tangentially the love Kierkegaard describes in *Works of Love*, but it is William's wizardry, not his acknowledgment of God's presence, that keeps his domestic situation happily "humming" (SLW, 159). As William explains, "a married man who writes about marriage writes least of all to be criticized," and the trees which shelter his marriage from observation metaphorically imply precisely that problem (SLW, 94).

Kierkegaard indicates again through this essay, as through William's contribution to *Either/Or*, the small but quite significant missteps that occur, to the detriment of self and other, when one loves without God as the intrusive third party to one's marriage. Only when God enters that sheltered *tete á tete* with the command that William acknowledge his wife first and continually as his neighbor, and thus set apart from him, may William perceive the extent to which he himself is fallen and unable to get up, even strengthened on the milk of her kindness.[7] William's parasitic understanding of "womanhood" denies his wife's existence as distinguishable from her role as his nurse, and his subsequent advice to "Cheer up!," be "courageous" and accept the "assured blessedness" of marriage is reckless, considering the gravity of his and our condition (SLW, 111, 112, 161). Given that we who come to the arbor are stumbling because we have inherited a severe "sickness unto death" rather than a tendency toward foot callouses, we need divine help, not natural magic (SLW, 129-30).[8]

---

[7]For a different interpretation of the narrative transition from "In Vino Veritas" to Judge William's treatise, see Robert L. Perkins, "Woman Bashing in Kierkegaard's 'In Vino Veritas'." Perkins understands Kierkegaard here (1) to underscore the extent to which "the Judge and his wife are far closer to the ethical" than the banqueters and (2) to undermine subtly the banqueters' underestimation of female intelligence (100).

[8]N.B.: I say "our condition" rather than merely "his" in order to involve us all in this critique. If we at any point in Kierkegaard's poetics find ourselves peeking

But before finding fault with Judge William, we should note the extent to which his problematic call to love resembles Kierkegaard's own in *Works of Love*. William speaks almost with Kierkegaard's own voice when he insists that, in true love, "resolution is present from the beginning" (SLW, 103). If the lover instead allows his resolve to "tag along behind" while he tests out "probability" and seeks to determine "outcome," the lover is "lost" (SLW, 103, 105, 110). This "mirage of perdition" that "frequently prowls around when the making of a resolution is at stake" leads a person to chase after chance rather than love (SLW, 110). As God "always does business *en gros*," love is insecure unless sealed from the onset against change (SLW, 110). A lover must thus avoid assiduously the tendency to "inspect whether the beloved meets the abstract conception of an ideal" (SLW, 158). Any "reflection of this sort" is "an offense" to the resolution that secures one's love (SLW, 158). William thus concludes that a lover must "always [be] in love," or else he will never at any point truly love; love must be "a given," must be "assumed" in order to be lived (SLW, 122-23). Even a husband's periodic, "adoring admiration" of his beloved betrays a kind of inappropriate "separation" from his love whereby he stands back and appraises (SLW, 158). There is "a criticism dormant in this admiration," and it is thus "an affront," a "kind of unfaithfulness to the beloved" (SLW, 158). Much here could be transposed onto Kierkegaard's own insistence in *Works of Love* that we "abide in love," "avoid comparison," and refuse to appraise the other.[9]

Even though William here addresses the problems of mistrustful appraisal and comparison, the love William defends is significantly off-kilter from Kierkegaard's. There are traces in the treatise of the resolute, noncomparative love to which Kierkegaard calls us in *Works of Love*, but undergirding William's system is a self-serving ideal of womanhood. This ideal, to which he holds his wife, collapses the

---

in self-righteously at others, we have missed (and also illustrated) his point. While Kierkegaard satirizes patriarchal domesticity by use of William, the allegation implied is more generally applicable than merely to the oblivious, married man. Relationships between women or between women and children may be fraught with assumptions similar to William's.

[9]See, e.g., WL, 228, 139, 36.

distance between his needs and her existence (SLW, 91, 133-34) William immediately, unfortunately amends his prohibition on a husband's appraisal of his beloved: *"on the other hand* there is a feminine lovableness"—"essentially that of the wife and mother"—which "dares to be admired," for it is "the lovable substance of her nature" (SLW, 158-59; emphasis mine). Through the "incorruptible humming of quiet joy" that is marriage, a woman is "transfigured" to reflect the true "beauty of [her] soul," and a man may rightly appreciate her for this maternal, solicitous beauty (SLW, 159, 160). With this maternal beauty, woman "has the joy of continually equipping" and "strengthening" her husband (SLW, 144). Although a husband is not otherwise to stand back and evaluate the extent to which his wife meets the ideal that best fits his own desires and needs, he is allowed this type of appraisal. The problem of the beloved's otherness is bypassed because a wife becomes, in marriage, *essentially* and continually that which conforms to her husband's "abstract conception of an ideal" (SLW, 158). This is not appraisal, William implies, this is merely a husband's recognition of a married woman's natural aptitude.

William has advanced little beyond his advice in *Either/Or,* with his continued refusal seriously to consider the possibility that the circle of faith, marriage, maternal solicitude, and husbandly joy will hit a significant hurdle. As he has construed the situation, a husband is to have resilient faith in the state of marriage (not, we note, faith in God). While the composition that is marriage may "contain a very difficult passage," William himself has only a "presentiment of the terror" that might prompt him to flee (SLW, 111, 92). This married man's explicit advice (the implicit later) is for the lover to be of good "cheer" and to keep plowing ahead with his faith in domestic harmony (SLW, 111, 161, 163.) There is no need for ponderous worry about this or that transgression. A man's earnest conviction is his justification, and thus at the altar, "the church will proclaim him to be a lawful husband" (SLW, 91). That we might find ourselves in, or will ourselves into, a situation that is unjustifiable and out of which we cannot resolve ourselves is a possibility beyond the scope of William's immediate concern.

An instructive refrain runs through the last pages of his treatise: "that a young man in love is happy goes without saying" (SLW,

161,164). If one is uncertain about his love, his justification, his resolve, he should take "comfort" in knowing that "he is just like other human beings" (SLW, 164). And here William ever so briefly considers that a person might be "singular" in a way that does not "promptly come off in the washing of resolution." It might, possibly, be the case that someone is soiled beyond the scope of such laundering. This exception should not be his, or our, concern, however. William states "I shall not pursue this here." For, as he explains, "difficulties of that sort have no place in a general consideration" (SLW, 164). We who resemble other human beings need not worry. "Hip, hip hurrah!" The "exception" to his rule of happy marriage "vanishes" (SLW, 164, 165). While there may in fact be the genuinely exceptional one who "has attired himself in misunderstanding" and is thus in "a void from which mankind shrinks," William declares that "the terror is now far removed," and he departs to "have lawfully as [his] own" she whom he has been "authorized" to take (SLW, 183). For he knows well that what a husband has with a wife is "infinitely more precious" than what a husband has while alone with his "pen" (SLW, 184).

Explicitly, William advises a prospective husband first to take "resolution's bath of purification" and marry (SLW, 164). The subsequent step, he implies, is to bathe oneself in the "mother love" of one's wife (SLW, 134). In this implicit advice, William both underestimates the depth of our estrangement, which prevents our easy use of another as a salve, and ignores the import of God's command, which precludes such use. In noting an advertisement hocking a cure for foot corns, William indirectly reveals his inability seriously to regard our fallen predicament.[10] He considers "humor-

[10]We should note that William does directly address the issue of original sin in *Either/Or* II. But he there suggests that hereditary sin leaves merely "a little depression," a remnant that need not unduly become the focus of one's concern (EO, 2:190). What Victor Eremita says of William in *Either/Or* applies as well to William in *Stages on Life's Way*: "When B supposes that out of a hundred people who go astray in the world ninety-nine are saved by women and one by divine grace, it is easy to see that he is not very good in mathematics, inasmuch as he gives no place to those who are actually lost" (EO, 1:11). In both texts, William underestimates the extent to which he and his reader are "actually lost," and he thus can posit matronly love as the antidote to his "sickness unto death" (SLW, 131).

ously": what if the lover or his betrothed suffers an intractable illness that cannot be easily detected? For example, what if one has inherited foot corns? "Yes, it is difficult, it is difficult . . . no one can know for sure about them, whether someone has them or has had them or is going to have them" (SLW, 129). What might this mean for an afflicted woman and her blissfully unsuspecting lover, for a flawed husband and his unwitting wife? After briefly thinking on the potential for one's carrying an illness that would infect a marriage, he quickly shakes off this way of thinking and gathers his confident wits about him. Similar to the manner with which he ends his consideration of the "singular exception" to his call to wash in resolution's tub, William here insists to himself, "But enough of this" (SLW, 129). William transforms the serious into the trifling by musing comically on the advertisement, rendering our hidden potential for error and for harm virtually inconsequential, and stops himself before detecting a crack in his system.

In part due to his trivialization of that which is hidden, he is able to cling securely to the immediate, human comfort he has in his wife. Connecting William's light-minded treatment of the advertisement with his subsequent discussion of his wife's work on him, the reader may note the interlocking errors in William's advice. With his sanguine estimation of his own plight and her goodness, he shifts quickly to her redemptive work on him. Because he deems that neither he nor she may have an undetectable and significant fault, he is able to keep operative their magical domesticity. Evidence, whether of his wife's inherent goodness or of his own confident resolve, is unnecessary: "For I know what I knew and what I am repeatedly convinced of—that there within my wife's breast beats a heart, quietly and humbly, but steadily and smoothly, I know that it beats for me and for my welfare" (SLW, 129-30). She not only breathes for him, she also transmits vitality. That same feminine breast in which her heart beats dispenses a balm which "natural scientists maintain is lifesaving for someone who is sick unto death" (SLW, 130). Indeed, he attests, her "tenderness" has "many times" saved him "from the death of despondency and evil torment of vexation of spirit." The "sickness unto death" to which William refers twice in this section can be cured through the rejuvenating powers of "woman" (SLW, 131). She "provides the solution for the worried person" and is "the best eulogy on existence by being life's beautiful solution" (SLW, 134).[11]

It is this "mother's milk" of life, solicitude and security that distinguishes the young flirtatious girl from a woman like William's own wife and that allows his domestic life to cohere (SLW, 134). Through marriage, a woman is able to become "life's beautiful solution," a lover from whose being flows life-giving sustenance not only for her children but also, importantly, for her husband. William's implicit advice on marriage here meets up with his explicit call for each potential husband to remain resolute. In order for the "natural magic" of marriage to work, a man must believe securely that marriage can "transform" his wife into one who can cure him of his "sickness unto death" (SLW, 134). By both dismissing as an "exception" a serious impediment to matrimonial harmony and treating with levity the potential for undisclosed barriers to domestic bliss, William is able to posit "woman" as the tie binding together a man's resolution and his happiness.[12]

Stages on Love's Way?

When compared to the slimy seducer, the flamboyant designer or the caustic cynic at the banquet, William seems to approximate, much more closely than they do, Kierkegaard's description of the faithful lover in *Works of Love*. Does not Kierkegaard there commend a love that "believes all things," that resolutely hopes in the good-

---

[11]Kierkegaard's imagery here is quite provocative; he implies through this extended metaphor that Judge William parasitically partakes of his wife's very being. While Judge William clearly notes that his wife rightly sustains her children physically, he metaphorically extends her lactation as providing sustenance for himself as well. But William is not a child. Because Kierkegaard here links, in the voice of Judge William, the idea of a "sickness unto death" and the "beautiful solution" of womanhood, he is implying a strong, theological critique of such a view of marriage (SLW, 131-34). While other readings are plausible, I believe there is strong textual warrant for suspecting Judge William and all of us who similarly err.

[12]As one reader suggests, at least William recognizes that he needs his wife, rather than thinking himself an independent entity. Yet I believe Kierkegaard implies in the text a critique of the husband who relies on his wife for what God alone can give. As Kierkegaard suggests in *Works of Love*, William's mistake is not merely his own, but indicative of a condition besetting us all (WL, 58).

ness of the other, that "presupposes" that love is continually present in the other?[13] There are two crucial distinctions between Kierkegaard's and William's conceptions of love. First, Kierkegaard warns from the onset and throughout *Works of Love* that the faithful lover must assiduously avoid the temptation to see the other as an extension of himself, as an appendage created to serve his needs. The term "neighbor" is to act as a conceptual wedge between the lover and the beloved, reminding him that she is indeed an other self, unto herself (WL, 21). William's estimation of "woman" is not carnal (as is Johannes') or sardonically comic (as is Constantin's or the designer's) but it is based on an understanding of his wife as "essentially" for another, namely him. He presupposes that her heart beats for his sake (SLW, 130). "Woman" is, in William's treatise, a "hurrah and nothing," to use Victor's perceptive phrase. Woman is a "hurrah" in that she is the one who sustains William, but woman is in a significant sense "nothing" in that her defining role is to sustain William. Her existence as an entity apart from their domestic life together, her existence as an individual fallen and redeemed before another to whom she is *ultimately* accountable, is obscured in William's treatise.

The second distinction between William's and Kierkegaard's advice on love involves the basis of William's ability to abide in his love for his wife. For Kierkegaard, our ability to love generously is united inextricably to the proper context of love: our debt. Through a happy coincidence of his own resolve and his wife's indulgence, William is able to continue believing that she is "life's beautiful solution" (SLW, 134).[14] In *Works of Love* Kierkegaard explains that one is only able to abide in love if one remains fixedly in the knowledge of one's own debt before God (WL, 180). To put a critical Christian twist on William's assertion: we are to disturb, rather than reassure, ourselves with the fact that we are "just like other human beings," that is, irre-

---

[13]See much of the first five chapters of the second series of *Works of Love*, to which we will return again below.

[14]One reader rightly notes that William's wife may willingly choose this arrangement. Kierkegaard recognizes that a woman is capable of choosing to make her lover's happiness the measure of her existence (see, e.g., the "Silhouettes" of *Either/Or* I) but he warns against this tendency even in the supposedly safe confines of an ethical marriage, likening such a relationship to an "ingrown toenail" (WL, 272).

solute sinners before a forgiving God (SLW, 164). This "certain transformation of attitude and mind" that Kierkegaard describes involves our recognition of the debt we each owe, infinitely to God (WL, 177). We who are fallen and indebted are consequently forbidden to evaluate the other's worth, whether that evaluation leads us to dismiss her (as do the banqueters) or to idolize her (as does William). To state the matter shockingly (as I believe it is Kierkegaard's intent to do), love is no more in its element in William's defense of marriage than it is at the banquet. William's underestimation of his own predicament and his overestimation of his wife's purity provide a brittle foundation for marriage. His inability to understand his wife as a separate person (herself fallen and redeemed before God alone) and to acknowledge forthrightly his debt to God indicate, according to *Works of Love,* the false assumptions undergirding his present affection. On the other side of the Diarist's pertinent fear of self and other we will return to a more sober, Christian, conception of a love that can endure our realization of our own and the other's errors.

Interlude

The ways in which each reflection up to this point in *Stages on Life's Way* differs from Kierkegaard's reveals the hazards of thinking alone. While the crowds are maddening, solitude may also warp. As William Afham observes, "recollection's bookkeeping is a curious thing" (SLW, 11), and although authentic understanding requires that we each ponder in stillness, for each and every moment of reflection there is an occasion for self-delusion. This is why, for Kierkegaard, a treatise on love must continually ricochet the question of the other back to the potentially delusive questioner himself (WL, 14, 90, 96). The reflective reckoning of engagement must take place with the love command in view, lest we become preoccupied with our own hunger and transform love into a matter of the coherence between our taste and the object's fare. Each of our previous speakers (excepting the young man) makes use of the "stillness," "secrecy," and "hiddenness" of recollection to his own advantage. During their clandestine caucus on erotic love, Constantin and his guests swerve away from love itself to reflect on the factor preventing "real interaction," that is, "woman" (SLW, 48). By excluding the other from the conversation and focusing on the extent to which she satisfies each man's craving, these men construct a hermetically sealed space for their iniquitous deliberation. The other may not enter. For his own part, Judge William is wed, but not suitably engaged. The "life immersion" that is his domestic existence (SLW, 89) negates his wife as an other who exists apart from him, leaving him safely alone with his thoughts, needs, and wishes.[15] Up to this point, it is only the Young Man who seems to have sat earnestly with the disturbing thought that an individual is not alone when he is with another. His apt fear compels him to be truly, unthreateningly alone. As we move to the reflections of the Young Man's close cousin, the Diarist, we consider whether an individual's solitary self-disclosure before God may transform reflection itself.[16]

The Diarist's Retreat

> Might it be possible, might my whole attitude to life be askew, might I have run into something here in which secretiveness is forbidden. . . . (SLW, 223)

After prying open the Diarist's buried box and finding the key inside, the narrator comments that "inclosing reserve is always turned inward in that way" (SLW, 189). The Diarist entrusts his tormented reflections on his engagement to paper alone; his reflections on himself, love and his beloved remain locked inside his head and within this sunken container. Of all the men who hide in this stitched together collection of papers, the Diarist is the most adept. Yet it is also commendably the case that his secretive avoidance of frank discourse reflects more his apt appraisal of his predicament than his desire invulnerably to enjoy (Johannes), mock (Constantin), or use (William) his beloved. The Diarist's self-inclosure and broken vow are the result of his terror before the great responsibility that is engagement. From the beginning, he understands himself to be "the

[15]Indeed, if she refuses to cohere to these wishes he may by law, as he notes, "go out to the forest and cut the switches white" (SLW, 85).

[16]For a more in depth discussion of the difference between the Young Man and the Diarist, see again Céline Léon, "The No Woman's Land of Kierkegaardian Exceptions."

one acting"; the success or failure of his engagement is a question posed to him alone. But, unlike William (who deems himself as actor but also justified) the Diarist deeply suspects himself as "the guilty one" (SLW, 198).[17] The others avoid their accountability and thus this apprehension from the onset by construing the other either as an infinitely malleable trifle (the banqueters) or as gloriously, "essentially," for the man to whom she is "lawfully" wedded (William).

The Diarist refuses both the seducer's and the husband's option, but neither will he disclose himself to this other who binds him and before whom he is responsible. Recognizing the numerous dangers to both her and himself, the Diarist vows to "flee back into my interior being and leave nothing, not a trace, in the outer world" (SLW, 201). The Diarist's stages are along yet another wrong way, subtly distinguishable from the way of honest and fragile intimacy in *Works of Love*. He explains that he wishes to retreat to the "monastery" in order to "find peace" (SLW, 198). Kierkegaard will not let him escape so easily God's vexatious call to love the other. By shedding light on the Diarist's self-reflection using God's command for honesty, we may illumine the slip of space between fear and faith. We may note the difference between the walk of an individual who, due to fear, is alone with his idea and an individual who is alone, in faith, before God.

Within the first few entries of his long, painful account, the Diarist manifests several clues to his secretive existence.[18] At the point in time when he is forced to face the possibility of interaction, the Diarist is already quite gifted at deception (SLW, 195-96). He explains that he is able convincingly to emulate "a candid face and an openhearted nature" even while involved in an elaborate

---

[17]This distinguishes the Diarist also from the Young Man of *Repetition* and Constantin's banquet. It is not incidental either that the Young Man is at the banquet or that he chooses Constantin as his confidant. The Young Man, unlike the Diarist, maintains his own purity and innocence in both texts. We will further discuss this necessarily prior step of guilt and confession below.

[18]Here the reader should be forewarned. As one of my students exclaimed, "The Diarist will NOT shut up!" At the risk of evoking the same response regarding this section of the paper, I will trudge us through the almost interminable terrain of the Diarist's passages. I believe Kierkegaard forces us through this prolonged section for a reason, and to skim it would threaten to undermine his rhetorical aim.

"sleepless and thousand-tongued reflection" (SLW, 196). We should note here that he calls the generic one with whom he converses on such deceptive occasions "the opponent," who must be kept uncertain as to whether she "is coming or going" (SLW, 196). In this way, the Diarist explains, "one attains one's security" (SLW, 196). This apprehension and this pretense is at the heart of his initial feelings for her ("I have secretly and clandestinely been absorbed in this love" SLW, 202) and continues throughout the affair. Dodging the other's potentially keen gaze, the Diarist flips through multiple possibilities while leaving the beloved ignorant of the turmoil within him. She must not be allowed to know his "suffering," his "suspicion," or the "craftiness of [his] understanding," and, to this end, the Diarist is able to mimic both reassuring confidence and disarming confusion (SLW, 196, 198, 199). Although he is, halfway through, unmasked in a fencing game, the young man is incapable, from the onset, of bare and vulnerable engagement (SLW, 300). By considering the multiple reasons for and ramifications of his frightened maneuvers, we may better perceive the fault line between love's apt caution and doubt's refusal to disclose.[19]

The Diarist explains from the beginning that "the reason [he is] so cautious, cautious to the very last moment" is the manifold possibility for error in his engagement (SLW, 202). Purposefully imagining "many a terror," he determines "not to do the slightest thing without calculation" lest he underestimate "the storms" ahead for him and his beloved (SLW, 202, 203). Along the way, his realization that he is "almost happier in [his] hiding place" seeps into the crevices of his presentiments and, ultimately, wins out (SLW, 206). In his engagement, the Diarist has "come so close to actuality," but accurately perceives that—between the work of time, her error, and his frailty—there is also an insurmountable "distance" intrinsic to such involvement (SLW, 205). He finds himself therefore "happier in the distance of possibility"; and, in the end, this is where he resides (SLW, 206).

---

[19]Céline Léon, in "The No Woman's Land of Kierkegaardian Exceptions," judges the Diarist more harshly than do I, reading his break with the girl primarily as evidence of his fear of her rather than as evidence of his fear of his own potential for harming her or of his fear of the rough road ahead of them.

It is important we parse his calculations. For while his apprehensions overlap, we may differentiate and evaluate several of his central concerns. First, although he claims that his "soul is resolved" to "imagine everything lovable about her," one cause of the Diarist's caution is his sneaking suspicion that his beloved is less than he had first hoped (SLW, 206). Second, the Diarist suspects that he himself is damaged beyond marriageability. His own sternly willed resolve to "earn a livelihood of joy for her" may not, he speculates, be sufficient to sustain them both (SLW, 197). Finally, and related to the first two, he surmises a fundamental "misrelation" between his and her conception of existence and, subsequently, of love itself (SLW, 244). Each of his misgivings are, to some extent, apt, but the resolution he chooses is wrought from the stuff of further calculation, deception, and fear. We will first read through his fears, on to his elaborate plan to deceive his betrothed, and slowly forward in the direction of a "third position" whereby he and she both may be "remade" as each alone before God (SLW, 220, 320).

In order to get an inkling as to why the Diarist begins to look askance at himself and his beloved we should note the absurd ideal to which he, at least initially, holds their love: "when I belong to her, I shall be able to concentrate my whole soul on making her as happy as it is possible for me. I ask no more in the world than that my soul might still have one abode where joy is at home, one object upon which I can concentrate in order to make happy and to be made happy" (SLW, 206). In order for his hope and joy to be realized, the Diarist must be single-minded and she must be perfectly receptive. He must "concentrate" his "whole soul," and she must be capable of returning his concentration with perceptible levels of euphoria. The Diarist's quite perceptive concern that each of them may not be up to this colossal task comes to bear on his vision of his betrothed. The "demon of laughter" and the "craftiness of the understanding" combine in his scrutiny of her as an individual who cannot secure a safe and jubilant abode (SLW, 198, 199). Interspersed throughout the entries is this appraisal of her behavior and her motives. She must indeed not be loving, given her behavior; she seems to wish "to wound someone who is tortured to death" (SLW, 212). He allows himself to consider that "she fancies herself to have become commonsensical," that she may be "thinking" and herself "reflecting" on their relationship, that she may in fact be "proud," and then orders himself to "Stop!" for he has "no factual information that justifies" his suspicions (SLW, 214, 216, 235).

But the suspicions take hold. As he explains, what he most wants is for her to "express herself a little more so that [he] can see what is taking place within her" (SLW, 235). (We will return to the hypocrisy of this project.) Even though he has worked arduously to conceal his tendency to judge, he guesses that she trenchantly "regards [him] as a very sharp critic" and that she in turn "stifles" her thoughts (SLW, 235). Regardless of what she does or does not reveal, midway through the engagement he concludes his "report": the one to whom he is engaged is "only an ordinary dollar," "a little miss," who "lacks the integration that beautifies," who has "a secret pride," and whose "fidelity is of a dubious kind" (SLW, 237, 268, 308, 356). Trying on a guise of indifference, he vows to "steal her [untainted] image" as he is free to "see it in [his] imagination," gazing at his hope of her rather than what he has discovered (SLW, 334). He progressively determines that "externally she cannot now be [his]" and, finally, that, by "playing false in the religious," she is the one to "blame" for the whole mess (SLW, 239, 393).

But, to his credit, the Diarist also places himself under the microscope. The other Young Man argues vehemently (here and in *Repetition*) for his purity. And the banqueters and Judge William deflect self-criticism by speaking (in various ways) of "woman." But the Diarist faces head-on the task of self-examination. He retreats from her with his pen and his paper, but does not thereby avoid self-inspection. The early passage wherein he confesses, "I fear no one as I fear myself," sets the tone for much of what follows (SLW, 207). He continues, "Oh, that I do not make a false step," and pledges to detect in himself any sign of "deceit" (SLW, 207, 208). His tangle of apprehensions includes his general fear that she will be "far happier without [him]," that he will in particular use his art of deception "to prevail upon her," and that his tendency toward "calculation" will spoil the whole affair (SLW, 206, 207, 208). Throughout, he is anxious not to "make a false step!" and thereby injure her and indict himself (SLW, 208).

The Diarist's assessment of the many potentially false steps leads him to walk in a strange way indeed, as he attempts simultaneously to avoid fraudulent deception *and* reckless candor, cruel detection *and* irresponsible ignorance, undue distance *and* inappropriate familiarity. That, in spite of all his efforts, the engagement spins recklessly out of his control propels him repeatedly to his room where he may reflect on the affair in the form of the Diary itself. He finds himself "sleepless" in the maddening confusion of his motives, "because I cannot know for sure whether I love or do not love" (SLW, 232). "Perhaps," he thinks, "I have not loved her at all; perhaps on the whole I am too reflective to be able to love?" (SLW, 231). He attempts to deliberate back upon himself to distinguish "corruption" and "hypocrisy" from "chivalry," wondering whether he may be "even to the point of nausea ensnared in self-deception" (SLW, 317). When his beloved perceives his impending retreat and more passionately "surrenders" herself to him, the matter becomes ever more perilous. The "narrow pass" of "responsibility" becomes more than he can bear, and he determines over time that he must use his wits and his powers of subterfuge to set her free, and, not incidentally, free himself of her (SLW, 316). It is in the midst of this engagement that the Diarist finds himself most vulnerable to his own scrutiny, and he vows, with increasing resolve, to get himself back to the monastery.

In "A Leper's Self-Contemplation," the Diarist reveals two significant clues for understanding the despair ensuing from his estimation of himself and of her (SLW, 233). First, whereas Judge William flippantly jests about an undetectable proclivity for foot sores, the Diarist imagines himself narratively as Simon, who is literally covered with infectious sores and therefore should rightly "fill the desert with [his] shrieking and keep company [only] with wild animals" (SLW, 233). The Diarist accurately perceives the depth of his disorder and quickly recognizes that he is beyond his beloved's curative powers. The entry following their first kiss finds the Diarist initially seeking in her a salve for what plagues him:

> A girl with a joyful temperament, happy in her youth! And she is mine. What are all dark thoughts and fancies but a cobweb, and what is depression but a fog that flies before this actuality, a sickness that is healed and is being healed by the sight of this health that is mine since it is hers . . . she can say, as an apostle said to the paralytic, "Silver and gold I do not have, but what I have I give you; stand up and be well! (SLW, 211)

His beloved must be pure joy, happiness, and well-being in order through the union to impart health to this leper. The Diarist's hope in this frail, human other is taut to the point of breaking precisely because he is more acutely aware of his dire straits than is William. Unlike William's faith in "natural" marital "magic," the Diarist's anticipation of conferred health is ephemeral. He finds that his "dark thoughts" return with a vengeance and that she is not, in fact, an apostolic redemptress. Even in love, the Diarist remains a leper.

But, unlike Simon, the Diarist is not yet alone in the desert; his beloved is still with him. This story of infectious disease is also about the individual's courageous disclosure, before an other, of that communicable disease. The Diarist as Simon condemns Manasse, who uses a salve to render his infection invisible and then runs to the city, thereby secretly endangering everyone with whom he interacts. Simon instead remains in the desert, holding fast to his hope eventually to sup with friends who know his disease and yet do not fear him (SLW, 233). Simon's resolve in this story not only stands in contrast to William's willed ignorance of his plight, but also implicitly indicts the Diarist's own behavior. The Diarist, unlike Simon, opts to deceive his beloved rather than believe her able to sup with one who is unclean. Appropriately recognizing that she is not the other who may effectively say to him "Stand up and be well," the Diarist continues to hide from her the gravity of his affliction. Not finding in her a salve that would cure him and currently unable to live alone, the Diarist does in fact accept a path similar to Manesse's, hiding his affliction from a beloved he cannot trust. When we return below to *Works of Love* and to the only other who may enable the sinfully paralyzed to walk, we find warrant for Simon's hope that a leper may uncover his face before his friends.

The tangled, deceptive web the Diarist instead weaves around himself and his beloved ensnares them both. The entire relationship becomes ever more snarled in a mess as the Diarist attempts to construct a way to work her free from him. In his entries, the Diarist conveys his growing resolve to preclude her receiving a "reliable conception of [him] and of [their] relationship." She is under no circumstance to receive an "authentic interpretation" of his hopes, plans or fears (SLW, 246). Indeed, those very plans and fears become a piece with his deception. Although he complains that it is a "torment to have to observe a phenomenon when the phenomenon itself changes in relation to the observer," the Diarist overlooks this pivotal moment for reflecting on the effect of his dishonesty on his engagement (SLW, 234). His machinations infect his observation and their interaction. He wonders at her "circumspect reticence" and wishes that he might know "what her state is in a deeper sense," but his otherwise discerning mind is unable to make the connection between his deceit and her own determined impenetrability (SLW, 250). As quoted before, the Diarist's most fervent wish is that she would "express herself a little more so that [he] can see what is taking place within her," that she would "sit still" while he examines her relation to him, but he himself sets up the affair to be an elaborate artifice, precluding the revelation of truth (SLW, 235). Her "stifle[d] freedom of expression," as he words it, is hardly accidental (SLW, 335).

Whether the beloved also actively chooses the pretense fundamental to their interaction the reader cannot know, but the Diarist takes up that question as an undercover detective accepts a perplexing case. Claiming that he is using "ingenuity in the service of righteousness" rather than "in the service of deceit," the Diarist carefully orders his feet not to "leave a betraying clue" and his hand not to betray what is "hidden" in his "heart" (SLW, 267, 265). She must not know that he is monitoring her, nor is she to know the "sympathy," "fear," and "suspicion" that motivate his surveillance (SLW, 273, 372, 198). There is, in all this, scarcely any chance for real intimacy. We barely catch sight of a missed opportunity in the story when the Diarist is literally "unmasked" and wounded while fencing (SLW, 300).[20] But, he concludes, "the whole thing does not count if the mask falls off," and he quickly returns to the game, cloaking himself "at [her] entryway" in order to "renounce every expression," daring not to "alter [his] features," and offering instead "a cold and callous front" (SLW, 300, 336, 349, 350) He regulates every minute facet of his behavior to ensure that "no truth glimmers through the deception" (SLW, 332).

---

[20]Although he dismisses his beloved's poignant response as sheer sentimentality, the reader may guess that the irony of the moment is not lost on her.

This young lover, in a myriad of ways and for various apt reasons, does not trust himself, his beloved, or their love. Before proceeding, however, we should note that in finding himself on this intractable patch of space the Diarist has refused at least three other wrong paths on the way. First, while he wistfully glances momentarily at a marital ideal (similar to William's) which neither of them can approximate, he refuses to remain poetically, romantically duped. His scrutiny of himself and of her, although at times masochistic or cruel, is preferable to an illusive, fragile overestimation of their ability each to make the other unremittingly "happy." A second path which the Diarist refuses is that of the seducer or spoiled husband. Though the Diarist cannot trust his beloved, she is for him a separate entity to whom he is responsible. He refuses, from the onset, to "whirl her off like an abracadabra" (SLW, 198) or use his deception in order to create "a magic word" or "a rune" that would transform her into an extension of himself (SLW, 202). Neither will he allow her to fashion herself into a devoted, submissive wife. The type of marriage wherein she thinks herself "indebted" to him—where she is "devoted" to the point of prostrating herself (figuratively and literally) before him—is not an option (SLW, 226, 312). He would rather cause her suicide by breaking their engagement than allow her to think him her benefactor (SLW, 370). The only one under whom a person should surrender herself is, he insists, God (SLW, 235). Like the Young Man at the banquet, the Diarist holds as a prior assumption the fact that in the calculation of responsible intimacy, she counts in and of herself; interaction is not the meeting of one and a half (SLW, 43).[21] Finally, the third, erroneous, option which the Diarist will not choose is a marriage built on deceit. He refuses to pretend that she is not a stranger to him or that there is not a deep "misunderstanding" between them. And he will not countenance a marriage plagued by her confusion and his mistrust (SLW, 351, 355). It would be a "profanation" of marriage for him to "vow" to love her while not simultaneously bringing her into his confidence, "for it is a deception that marriage does not tolerate" (SLW, 355, 375). It is here that he finds himself: unwilling to dismiss her,

[21]Yet, as we will relate, the Diarist does, to some extent, believe himself to be one and a half to her one.

loath to dominate her, unable to understand her, incapable of making himself comprehensible, and, quite sadly, "stranded" (SLW, 375).

The Prayer of a Diarist

> In other words, the Pharisee thinks he is speaking with God, whereas from what he says it is clear and distinct enough that he is speaking with himself or with another Pharisee. (SLW, 238)

At one point the Diarist wishes but that his "pen were a living thing" (SLW, 307). The form of his (lack of) communication, among himself and his mute paper and pen, fits the content of his account. His text is not a discourse, his engagement is not, ultimately an interaction, and his prayer is not, finally, a prayer. It is only through accident and against his fervent wish that the Diarist reveals his thoughts to the reader at all. Through various evasions, the Diarist escapes from revealing himself to his beloved. And his concluding resolution with his "idea" of God is not a revelatory encounter. Although the Diarist thinks he is speaking with God, it is clear enough that his "religious" resolution is consistent with what has come before. Standing alone in the midst of the whirl of guilt and suspicion, he seeks alternative ways to answer his fundamental question, guilty or not, and finds in the "idea" an apt escape clause. But along his mistaken route, the Diarist catches sight of an alternative manner of being whereby he may, with courage, reveal his reflections, speak honestly to her, as well as receive and accept true forgiveness. He at one point surmises that he has indeed "run into something" in which "secretiveness is forbidden," and he transiently realizes that he must "break [himself] of the habit of walking in this way" if his "journey" is to be "pleasing to heaven" (SLW, 223). He who has "with most extreme effort" become "a master in [the] art" of deception must take to heart that his "method is completely wrong" (SLW, 223). While true prayer and self-revelation do not, by any estimation, make one a "yodeling saint" who proclaims that life is "wonderful," they thwart our solitary bookkeeping and may enable each of us to "persevere" in our engagements (SLW, 259).

From early on in his engagement, the Diarist surmises that there are "religious crises" at stake (SLW, 216). As his relationship to his beloved renders his "life-view ambiguous," he casts about to find some reliable mooring, and his search does indeed hold implications for the state of his soul (SLW, 216). Unable to "advance," not knowing with certainty of what he should repent and how best he may "recant," the Diarist finds himself *in suspenso* (SLW, 261). He hopes that it will soon be "resolved," and he will thus be "free again" (SLW, 261). One way in which he attempts initially to secure himself is through a careful assessment and arrangement of his intentions toward her. The fact that he gives her only snippets of the truth and reveals nothing of himself is justifiable, he determines, only if his fabrications are for her own good. "Inclosing reserve, silence," is a legitimate "teleological suspension of the duty to speak the truth" if the liar has the hearer's care in view (SLW, 230). Because the Diarist believes that his deception is only licit if he does indeed practice it out of love for her (SLW, 230), he sets the details of his life in order logistically to make room for her: "Everything I buy, I buy double. My table is set for two; coffee is served for two . . . for me it is a matter of integrity, which I take with the greatest earnestness" (SLW, 295). In his taking note of her existence and his responsibility toward her, he hopes to make his "balance sheet balance down to the last penny" (SLW, 295). Through this careful accounting, he seeks to reassure himself that, in his clandestine scheming, he has "not [his own] welfare in mind but hers," as his Lutheran rule book requires (SLW, 230).

The narrative interlude on a tortured man from Christianhavn, who may have sired children but cannot know for sure, sets the tone for the Diarist's struggle to rectify his own yearly ledger with his beloved (SLW, 276). Even while giving vast amounts to the children of Christianhavn, the potential father finds his efforts tragically comical, given "his own enormous account" (SLW, 284). Just so, the Diarist discovers the "solidarity between guilt and innocence," in his own life, and cannot make his column of figures tally up to a indisputable sum of integrity or culpability (SLW, 301). When an individual goes about detecting "life's pathological elements absolutely, clearly, legibly," he begins to perceive the distorting prevalence of "sin" rather than disjunctive "bungles," and it is difficult for him continually to maintain that existence is a clear, decipherable "system" (SLW, 291, 292). If the Diarist is to find shelter from the whirl of confusion around him, he cannot do so by counting, cutting, computing, and pasting his (or her) portion of virtue or vice. While he continues intermittently to "demand" that life will "make clear whether [he] was trapped in self-delusion or [he] loved faithfully," he ultimately chooses another route (SLW, 384).

Several months into the engagement, the Diarist confesses: "What I have shaped myself to be with all my passion appears to me to be an error," and then continues, "I cannot be remade now" (SLW, 320). If his intentions toward her are not pure sufficiently to warrant indisputably his passionately deceptive shape, he must find another route out of the mess. If there is hope for him, by his estimation, there must be a defensible "third position" in the "theological proceeding" against him (SLW, 220). The Diarist relies increasingly on his detective "report" of his beloved: "with regard to the religious, " she is "only an ordinary dollar" (SLW, 237). Returning again and again to the difference between her "buoyancy," and "childlike happiness," and his own depth, the Diarist determines that he must "chose the religious" (SLW, 222). Judging her own reflection to be "only single," whereas he adequately grasps their situation, he is able to justify his working out matters above her, so to speak, hidden behind "the category" or "idea" to which she cannot aspire (SLW, 303, 304). Because he "has the category and the idea" on his side," he must make himself impervious to her pleading (SLW, 356). The "third position" he fashions for himself, beyond guilt or innocence, is that of the justified religious martyr, forced to deceive and desert his beloved for the sake of his own religious conscience. With this solution, what is good or ill for her does not, ultimately, matter. Carrying with him a "divine counterorder," the Diarist must "retreat," regardless of the cost to him or to her, and take upon himself the task of going "through repentance" toward "freedom" (SLW, 261). As he eventually concludes, he may not justify his broken "ethical commitment" to her by means of "any calculation of probability." Rather, he must assume "the ultimate possibility of responsibility" (SLW, 394).

In repentance, the Diarist hopes to make his "way back over the chiasmic abyss that separates good and evil in time," to transform himself into "nothing, nothing at all" (SLW, 353). Whereas the Young Man at the banquet (and in *Repetition*) makes his escape from actuality to eternity through innocence, the Diarist finds freedom through a hybrid of resolute repentance and religious self-justification. He is justified in leaving her; after all, "she does not have infinite passion but only to a certain degree" (SLW, 349). His deception is warranted, given that "there is a language difference between" (SLW, 312). But, nevertheless, he finds himself whirled backward into a pit of "misunderstanding," and the only way out is repentance (SLW, 351). This movement is the final stage in the Diarist's irreligious way, and it bears the marks of his previous pattern of evasion. He confesses, immediately prior to the "religious structur[ing]" of his existence: "When the right thing becomes doubtful to me, I have usually said my name aloud to myself, with the addition: One may die, one may become unhappy, but one can still preserve meaning in one's life and faithfulness to the idea" (SLW, 346). The Diarist explains that he has, "lost the very substance of [his] existence," the "secure place of resort behind [his] deceptive appearance," and the "religious" method he employs is akin to his repeating his name "aloud" to himself, with the addition of an "understanding" that vindicates his "honor" (SLW, 351, 353). "Only religiously" is he able to "become intelligible to [himself] before God," he surmises, but the religious communication he finds is akin to an inverse tower of babel (SLW, 351).

He burrows deeper and deeper into himself in order to find that which is not "acquired" from another but rather his own. Unable "to structure [his] life ethically in [his] innermost being," the Diarist is "forced back further into" himself and there, utterly apart from actuality, he finds "religious" truth (SLW, 351). He may rest here assured that his new self-understanding is not "chattering blabbing," for, he asks, "to whom should I speak?" (SLW, 351). Following the lead of his own, hidden, untranslatable "reminders," he is able to reach an "eternal certitude of the infinite" (SLW, 378). While it is true that burrowed deep into himself and his Diary he is no longer able to deceive another or to be deceived by another, the Diarist is still capable of self-deception. In his attempt to become "nothing at all," turned inward to such a degree that his existence leaves no footprints, he is safe but deluded.

From Diary to Dispatch

> When does eternity begin? What language is spoken there? Or is there perhaps no speaking at all? Could there not be a little intervening time? Is it always high noon in eternity? *Could there not be a dawn in which we found understanding in intimacy*? (SLW, 390, my emphasis)

Given that the Diarist has not found God's confidentiality to be the determining encounter for all subsequent encounters, the Diarist continues to judge his beloved, deceive the world, and proceed with his withdrawal. We may surmise that the Diarist's conversion is askew from what follows it. The "understanding" he has with God is but his deeper intrenchment into a self-inclosed monologue, and it thus issues forth in yet more secrecy with his beloved (SLW, 351). At this crucial juncture wherein he is forced to cease his efforts at ethical calculation, the Diarist comes ever so close to the possibility of an "understanding in intimacy." Moving from the "starting point of knowledge" that is "wonder," he tangentially brushes the prospect of real prayer (SLW, 348). Where "wonder shipwrecks one's understanding," he explains, one may begin to speak to God as "the only one who does not become weary of listening to a human being" (SLW, 348). It is this shift that the Diarist cannot make. He cannot take even God into his confidence. His "method" for reaching the "holy city" is still "completely wrong" even though he is still walking "with most extreme effort" (SLW, 23). Although he deems his life to be "religiously structured," he does not encounter God as an other to whom he must reveal himself, as he is, in "actuality" (SLW, 351).

This follows the trajectory of his inclosing apprehensions. In entries scattered throughout the Diary, the Diarist considers then despairs of real disclosure to another. Not able to trust even the one he supposedly loves, he despairs of finding any other in whom truly to "confide" (SLW, 219). Given that every possible "third party" with whom he could consult regarding his predicament would judge his acts as "villainy," the Diarist cannot possibly speak (SLW, 224). He later "assure[s]" himself "how absurd it would be if [he] sought out any confidant" (SLW, 347). Finally, "realiz[ing] clearly that [his] depression makes it impossible for [him] to have a confidant," he determines that he cannot possibly marry his beloved, for marriage requires the truth (SLW, 374). In the midst of this last resignation, the Diarist envisages that if he "did have a confidant," that intimate would advise him to "constrain himself and thereby show that he is a man" (SLW, 375). It is imperative, he imagines the third party insisting, that he conceal his "depressing idea" before his beloved (SLW, 375). Having not truly found God in his inward turn, having not risked the truth before God as his confidant, the Diarist cannot risk the truth before her.

There is an alternative way not chosen but woven discretely through the Diarist's text. Soon after reflecting on the occasion when his fencing mask fell off, the Diarist comes face to face with his betrothed at church. There, surrounded by reminders of God's presence, he is "so easily tempted to regard the matter eternally" and almost finds himself therefore capable of "speak[ing] the truth." But he wishes anxiously, "not in time . . . not yet" (SLW, 301). In worship, having recently recalled the experience of being laid bare in a fencing match, he glimpses an alternative implication of "the eternal" whereby one is able vulnerably to unveil oneself. But he continues rather to say to himself, "the truth . . . [but] not yet" (SLW, 301). Whether "arrang[ing] occasion[s] and pos[ing] situational question[s]," "dropp[ing] a few hints in a joking or chatty tone," or sending a missive indirectly through mutual friends, the Diarist continues guardedly to evade the possibility of truth, giving her instead "little dose[s] of untruth" (SLW, 267, 272, 338). Not trusting her ability to comprehend, and progressively determining that "her fidelity is of a dubious kind," he disguises himself and precludes honesty (SLW, 356).

If the Diarist had connected the moment of being unmasked and the moment of insight at the church with a previous moment wherein he contemplates forgiveness, he might have started on the (narrow and precipitous) path toward intimacy: "what if the word 'forgiveness' between us were to be earnest, the earnestness of judgment, and not a ball we both hit in the game of erotic love while fidelity jubilated over its victory" (SLW, 227-28). Deeming his beloved to be "out of step" and thus incapable of grasping "that it is being faithful to reject illusory relief," the Diarist does not himself embark on the hard work of self-revelation, confession, and forgiveness (SLW, 228). Fearing that she will not understand him in his "entire makeup," he decides that forgiveness between them would be hollow, "dubious," and merely "illusory relief" (SLW, 383, 228).

If the Diarist's repentance before God had been a dispatch rather than a journal entry, he might have caught sight of that "little intervening time" in eternity that makes a narrow path for intimacy: God's forgiveness (SLW, 390). Turning inward to the point of oblivion, the Diarist does not repent before an other; he does not repent before one who may offer remission. Within both "Solomon's Dream" and the "Leper's Self-Contemplation" are key clues to the Diarist's inability to accept this route of forgiveness. Solomon, who "was able to separate truth from deception" finds himself struck dumb by the possibility that "to be singled out by God one has to be an ungodly person" (SLW, 251). But Solomon's dream stops with the image of his father, David, crying out in "despair from the penitent's soul" (SLW, 251). For Solomon and for the Diarist, there is no debt paid or sinner redeemed. Rather, there is one "rejected by God" (SLW, 251). Or, as is more the case for the Diarist, there is one who preemptively avoids coming before God in fear of the encounter and its consequence. As we have above noted regarding the Diarist's dialogue as a leper, he himself is unable to trust his beloved to sit and sup with him regardless of his dangerous, infectious malady. It is also the case that here, as in Solomon's dream, the Diarist's vision of the soul before God is aslant. Praying that God would "hear him if his heart is still not infected," the Diarist/Leper imagines himself as "blessed" precisely in his willingness to suffer his disease righteously, with an uninfected heart (SLW, 234, 233). In both stories and in the Diarist's eventual "religious" repentance, there is not the possibility of one's beseeching God while infected, duplicitous, and malformed and then receiving God's pardon. It is not surprising that the Diarist, in turn, cannot free himself to speak the truth of his culpable affliction before his own fallen beloved.

Loving the Leper Within

> When, however, the God-relationship determines what is love between human beings, the love is prevented from stopping in any self-deception or illusion, while in turn the requirement of self-denial and sacrifice is certainly made infinite. (WL 113)
>
> Ah, it is enough to make one lose one's mind. (SLW, 312)

As is implied by the quotes opening this study, the Diarist's self-critical turn resembles much more closely the "essentially Christian" than either the revelers' self-serving, other-negating speeches or Judge William's confident, cheerful charge forward. Given that "the God-requirement" is "infinite," the way of faithful intimacy requires of us our sober, somber estimation of our own incapacity to love. Before correcting the Diarist's way, first we must note that the Christian stages on life's way are excruciatingly difficult—a point William blithely misses and we may be tempted to overlook. The Diarist insightfully likens our relation to God to a Syrian hermit's effort to stand on a small platform upon a tall pillar. The man's life consisted of "bending himself into the most difficult positions and frightening away sleep and searching for terror in the crises of balance" (SLW, 253). Whether the best metaphor is the Young Man's "fox traps" or the Diarist's wavering platform, our attempt to exist honestly before God requires not only stamina, but our ability to reflect earnestly on our own resilient tendency toward sin (WL, 18). As Kierkegaard depicts in *Works of Love* with meticulous detail, "divine authority . . . fastens its piercing look" upon each one of us and is "as if all eyes," finding within us every small and great evasion of God's command that we acknowledge and love the other (WL, 97).

We are "in fear and trembling before God" to fear ourselves, detect our own "crises of balance" and with effort and grace attempt to adjust accordingly (WL, 15). In *Stages on Life's Way* Kierkegaard narratively depicts a myriad of ways that love can go awry when the lover evades the command to acknowledge, see, and forgive the other. With the interruption of God's command, we are able to detect the self-deception and danger in the text, but we are moreover to note the ways that we too swerve off balance or step flat into a snare.

We are, like the banqueters, often tempted to consume the other in a secluded, solitary lair. We are, like the Happily Married Man, tempted both to underestimate our sin and use the beloved as the felicitous resolution of our own crises. And therefore, with the Diarist, we are called to reflect piercingly on our own incapacity even to approximate the infinitude of God's command. This is, by Kierkegaard's estimation, a requisite and continuing task for the Christian. Is it, indeed, enough to make one lose one's mind.

But, as the Diarist inadvertently reveals, such reflective self-inspection, when divorced from an encounter with the God who shoulders our debt, may dangerously lead us either to seek self-justification through a careful calculation of the beloved's own faults or to escape God's call altogether in a frantic burrowing inward, away from actuality. As Kierkegaard characterizes a true encounter with God, one perceives together the overpowering magnitude of love's task *and* the well from which all love must draw strength (WL, 9). One clear way Kierkegaard describes this, our dependence on God's love, is with the metaphor of "infinite debt" (WL, 102). If we attempt to remain engaged without our immeasurable debt before God constantly in view, love "wastes away and dies" (WL, 180). Incapable of the hope that enables courage that enables disclosure, we who inadvertently or willfully remain on the other side of redemption watch our love trickle out or become murky with distortion.

Love's demise may take many forms, but the Diarist manifests two obvious symptoms which Kierkegaard links to our lacking a sense of indebtedness. First, the Diarist "commits treachery," as Kierkegaard puts it, by bringing a criterion to bear on his beloved: "Life certainly has tests enough, and these tests should find the lovers, find friend and friend, united in order to pass the test. But if the test is dragged into the relationship, treachery has been committed. Indeed, this secretive inclosing reserve is the most dangerous kind of faithlessness" (WL, 166).

Kierkegaard describes this "secretive inclosing reserve," whereby one examines the other, as a sometimes subtle but destructive "lack of honesty" and as a definitive sign that love has gone awry (WL, 151). As if speaking specifically about the Diary, Kierkegaard notes "how mistrustingly one must conduct oneself in order the make the discoveries" about one's beloved(WL, 283). Hoping to save ourselves from the fox traps or secure our footing on the pedestal, we go about calculating the probability of the lover's fidelity, worth, or beauty (WL, 254). Second, the Diarist and we are tempted, if we perceive accurately the treachery of intimacy, to escape. Not knowing the one to whom we can turn for sustenance, not perceiving grace simultaneous with the command, he and we may burrow deep or, as Kierkegaard puts it, attempt to fly "above the world" (WL, 84). Noting that the beloved is ineluctably untrustworthy (after all, she too is fallen), recognizing that we are not up to the task of love, we may, like the Diarist, decide that "none of us is worth loving" and flee (WL, 158).

That the Diarist is not adept at the "strange way of speaking" and has not experienced the "transformation of attitude and mind" that accompanies the realization of God's infinitely excessive forgiveness is clear (WL, 178). Perhaps fearing that his fate would be that of David in Solomon's dream, he does not truly reveal himself before God or unmask himself before his beloved. His self-inspection leads him instead to ever more elaborate scheming to detect her faults, clear himself, and find a "religious" way out. For Kierkegaard, Christian self-reflection is inextricably linked to our faithful self-disclosure in prayer, and it is to enable our taking the risk of vulnerability before another. Kierkegaard depicts by way of the Diarist what plagues many of us who, finding ourselves unforgiven, suspect others and hide from God. In a strange way, the Diarist's and our frequent determination that "like loves only like"—and that thus we should find a lover whom we can "understand" and whose way in the world is one with which we may "deeply and essentially sympathize"—is a warped inversion of Kierkegaard's insistence that we forgive the sinner before us because we know well our iniquity (SLW, 222; WL, 386). But rather than find himself a sinner in the hands of a forgiving God, the Diarist persuades himself that he is a religious martyr temporarily engaged to a shallow girl. His "religious" method of escape is especially pernicious at the point where he justifies his deception of her by determining that he has "the category and the idea on [his] side" (SLW, 356). Finding no way out of the whirling confusion around him, finding that these two who are to wed are instead strangers, he falsely pulls rank on her. Unable to know God as the confidant to whom he may disclose all, he continues to dwell on her misunderstanding and to remain silent.

In the context of our infinite debt before God, it is as if the beloved is let off the perilous hook, so to speak. She need not be expected to act as that confidant who understands one fully and whose forgiveness has eternal significance, because there is another to whom we are instead accountable and on whom we are to rely. Kierkegaard explains that, when the lover recognizes his debt to God, God himself "lovingly assumes love's requirement," as a "guardian for the beloved" (WL, 189). This facet of Kierkegaard's description has many implications, one of which is that the heat is turned down on our relationship with this fallen stranger to whom we are ourselves engaged. Our debt assumed by God, we are enabled to venture self-disclosure even while simultaneously praying that the beloved will treat our honesty with care. Living in the midst of God's grand, eternal abundance and our infinite gratitude, the love that we show another is not contingent upon the minute or large particulars of the beloved herself (WL, 157). Kierkegaard speaks of this similarly when discussing the "belief" in love consequent to our recognition of our debt. If we know ourselves as existing in the midst of a radical gift, we may perceive the love we show another as also within this context of free, gracious bestowal (WL, 242). This is to free the lover to love regardless of the potential outcome of his gift. If reciprocity is required, the love bestowed is not a true bestowal and we betray ourselves as outside the proper framework for love. The Diarist's arduous attempt to "imagine many a terror" and to gain an exhaustive list of the "storms in which" his love will be tested, all prior even to his risking a meeting with her is here exposed as a significant misunderstanding of love's task (SLW, 202). His meticulous efforts to gauge her reliability and religious depth before committing to her, wanting a "defect removed" or a "perfection added . . . as if the bargain were not yet concluded," are exposed by Kierkegaard as symptoms of a mistaken way (WL, 165).

What rightly troubles the Diarist is that he *is* truthfully alienated from his beloved and that she *is*, as a person, to be held to the same requirement of faith. Although the Diarist is culpable, from the onset, for bringing mistrust into the relationship from the onset, he is likely correct that his beloved would not fully understand him even if he did truly unmask himself. But when the Diarist asserts that he has the religious on his side against her, figuring himself as one and a half to her individuality, he betrays a culpable confusion. Although he correctly perceives, unlike the misogynist banqueters or Judge William, that his beloved is truly a stranger to whom he is nevertheless responsible, he exacerbates their alienation by considering his religious reflection superior to her own. Her "reflection is only single," he reports, and he wonders at the difference between woman and man, toying with the idea that perhaps "infinite reflection is not essential for a woman" (SLW, 302, 303, 306). To his credit, he is not long willing to be "consoled" by this option whereby she would remain "beautiful" even though inferior (SLW, 306, 307). He rejects the "illusory relief" that would ensue were she not also expected to meet the requirement of faith (SLW, 228).

The Diarist is right not to excuse his beloved metaphysically from "the requirement," but he betrays his religious error when he decides that he himself cannot "exist intellectually" in his "category," unless she "is able to exist in the same thing" (SLW, 305). Believing that his existence itself is an "indirect judgement" on her, he finds marriage to his beloved impossible (SLW, 305). Again, for him "like loves only like," and marriage requires intrinsic compatibility (SLW, 222). He missteps here in the text (and we misstep here in this life) in at least two related ways: according to Kierkegaard's words in *Works of Love*, the fitting consideration for the Diarist and for us is not the other's faith but his and our own, and, we are always wrong to think that faith tips the balance in any one's favor. Regarding true love's refusal to compare, genuine faith is to turn the lover inward again to inspect himself, not outward to discern his beloved's depth or lack thereof. The assumption about the other properly coincident with faith is that the other is "equal" to oneself "before God" (WL, 60). She is not worthy to the extent that she has similarly probed the depths that brought him to the (so called) religious. Rather, she is worthy in her own right, before God: "unconditionally every person [even his buoyant beloved] has this equality and has it unconditionally" (WL, 60).

It is for a reason that Kierkegaard forces us past William's insistence that love is "happy" and through the Diarist's anguish. It would be to invite yet another form of self-delusion were we to think that interrupting the Diarist's treatise with God's command loops him and us back to William's beautiful, enclosed garden. Self-disclosing, self-reflective prayer before God may enable us to know ourselves as indebted and to risk the dangers of intimacy, but our beloved remains, to some extent, a stranger. And our love for the one to whom we are engaged remains, to every extent, dependent on grace. Only the uniquely blessed or, what is more likely, the happily oblivious, find themselves intertwined in marriage with another whose understanding is daily and ultimately compatible with their own. As herself fallen and also called by God in a way undetectable to others, the other continues, even in faithful intimacy, to prevent by means of her very existence a "union" between self and human other.[22]

Living simultaneously with an other and with God is, by Kierkegaard's very apt estimation, less like William's "solution to the worried person" and more akin to Frater Taciturnus's image of "lying out on 70,000 fathoms of water" (SLW, 134, 445). By noting what Taciturnus calls the Diarist's "dialectical treading water," we are to resist any notion that faithful love "goes so smoothly" that "Point 18 follows upon or after Point 17" (SLW, 452). When faced with the prospect of supping regularly and "having daily arguing from" the other we may note, with the Diarist, "how dangerous it is for a thinker to be in love" (SLW, 305). The occasions for error within marriage are inexhaustible, from evading self-disclosure to judging the other, from believing ourselves despicable to thinking the divine balance tipped in our favor. Taciturnus hence suggests: "From the religious point of view, the greatest danger is that one does not discover, that one is not always discovering, that one is in danger" (SLW, 469). But, Kierkegaard insists, just as there are 70,000 fathoms of water or 70,000 fox traps and only seven square inches on the

---

[22]See Judge William on this: "neither of us is anything by oneself, but we are what we are in union" (SLW, 93). Again, while William's treatise may, by some readings, make a strong claim for mutuality, the truly Christian mutuality Kierkegaard describes in *Works of Love* requires God as the "third party" to whom both man and woman are finally, individually, accountable. To quote, "God in this way not only becomes the third party in every relationship of love but really becomes the sole object of love, so that it is not the husband who is the wife's beloved, but it is God . . . this is beyond mutuality" (WL, 121).

Syrian hermit's high pedestal, God's love is infinite. Only as we self-reflect before this God are we enabled to keep afloat, to heed the most treacherous of traps, and to approximate the vexatious balance that is loving the other.

2

Recollection and Two Banquets: Plato's and Kierkegaard's

Robert E. Wood

In *The Concept of Irony*, Kierkegaard's dissertation, Socrates is the key figure. Developing the concept of irony around Socrates, Kierkegaard spends some pages giving an account of Socrates in Plato's *Symposium*.[1] That dialogue between a group of homosexuals takes place at a banquet following a banquet celebrating Agathon's having received the equivalent of the Academy Award for the best tragedy of the year. Several years after his dissertation in the first part of *Stages on Life's Way*, "In Vino Veritas," Kierkegaard produced his own imitation of Plato's *Symposium* about another banquet some twenty-three hundred years later. The occasion is a sumptuous banquet, replete with wine, for five aesthetes, not, as their ancient Greek counterparts, clearly homosexual, but rather preoccupied with the nature of women.

In this paper I will compare the main features of the two dialogues, centering attention upon the several meanings of recollection basic to each dialogue. Recollection is linked up to the use of wine, a background theme in Plato's work, but the central metaphor for recollection in Kierkegaard's work. In Kierkegaard's piece there is a contrast between recollection as simple memory and as transformative vision; in Plato's there is a distinction between recollection as the linking together of eternal truths and as the attempt to gather the past of memorable events or venerable opinions. In each case, "the erotic" is closely tied to certain types of recollection. In keeping with the pseudonymous author of Kierkegaard's dialogue, William

---

[1]Kierkegaard first gives a sort of overview with a focus on irony (CI, 41-52); later (CI, 78-79) he returns for a few paragraphs to Diotima. All internal references to the *Symposium* are to the standard Stephanus numbers only; references to the other dialogues are indicated by name.

Afham, for whom recollection is a matter of getting one's life as a whole into focus by grasping what is essential (SLW, 11), my own recollection will first attempt to survey each dialogue in terms of what is essential.

1

Both dialogues deal with love: Plato's focally, but not exclusively, with homosexual love, Kierkegaard's with heterosexual love and with a special focus on the nature of woman. Both dialogues consist of a series of speeches, both by men in the absence of women; but in both, a woman appears late and with terminal significance in the work. In both works there are seven speakers. In Plato's they are, in order, Phaedrus, Pausanias, Eryximachus, Aristophanes, Agathon, Socrates, and Alcibiades, with Aristodemos as first, Apollodoros as second oral narrator of the event, and Plato himself a third narrator in writing. In Kierkegaard's work there are also seven speakers: the Young Man, Constantin Constantius, Victor Eremita, the Ladies' Tailor, and Johannes the Seducer, each of whom gives a speech, followed by Judge William and his wife whose conversation is observed by the group. There is one mediator, the writer William Afham, who, in addition to recording the event, offers a preface on recollection, with Kierkegaard himself as the author behind the pseudonym.

Plato's work presents a kind of ascending order to the speakers, the first two recollecting traditional views, with Pausanias offering a higher view. Eryximachus, Aristophanes, and Agathon create new traditions as cosmologist, comic, and tragic writer respectively. Socrates functions as critic of the previous speakers and mediator of *doxa*[2] (here 'opinion') about a Ladder of

---

[2]In classical Greek, *doxa* carried a set of related meanings central to my interpretation of the dialogue. Lidell-Scott's dictionary of classical Greek usage roots *doxa* in *dokeo*, "I seem." It has the following meanings: I. 1. notion, opinion, expectation; 2. sentiment, judgment; 3. mere opinion; 4. fancy, vision; II. 1. opinion others have of one, one' reputation; 2. glory, splendour. Plato's Ring of Gyges has as its function to "do away with the *doxa*," (*Republic*, II, 367B) understood here not simply as opinion but as one's appearance both to other men and to the gods. Further, the Cave in which we live our lives is referred to as the realm of *doxa*, which should thus be taken in a larger sense than simply 'opinion' (*Republic*, VII, 534A). I am currently working on an attempt to show in some detail "*Doxa* as a Key to Plato's *Symposium*" by working out the relations between Eros as the love of the mortal for the immortal, the relative immortality of famous men, events, and opinions secured by recollection as well as the peculiar recollection of the immortal

Ascent out of the Cave of *doxa* (as comprehensive lifeworld) to the highest object of Eros taught him by Diotima the prophetess. Alcibiades locates the highest in his recollection of the life of Socrates, bringing it back down to the Cave of everyday encounters.

Phaedrus and Pausanias recall traditional thought and homosexual practice. Phaedrus recollects the teaching of philosophers and poets to support his absolutizing of Eros as a god, an assumption shared by all the speakers prior to Socrates. He proposes an army of homosexual lovers whose Eros motivates courage in battle inspired by the presence of the beloved whose *doxa* governs the lover (178A-180B). From Pausianias we have a recollection of the customs of various Greek cities regarding the sexual relationship of men and boys, culminating in a distinction between heavenly and earthly love based upon love of the mind versus love of the body (180C-185).

Eryximachus the physician gives the discussion cosmic extension by seeing the duality of Eros in all things, recollecting and refocusing the medical tradition (186A-189B). As poets, Aristophanes and Agathon help form a new tradition. From Aristophanes we get a view of three original natures, heterosexual and homosexual (the latter both male and female), and also the notion of Eros as the striving for wholeness, bodily and psychic, caused by a primordial split in the original natures (189C-193D). From Agathon, we get a focus upon creativity and the governing power of Eros (195A-197E).

Socrates functions as critic of the old and new traditions, attacking the notion that Eros is a god by getting them to recollect from their own experience the essential lack that belongs to Eros by nature (198B-201C). He goes on to relate what he was taught by Diotima, a woman intruded into the hitherto all-male discussion from which the women had deliberately been excluded. Mythically expressed, Eros was born on Aphrodite's feast day from Poros as craftiness seeking fulfillment because of his linkage with Penia or emptiness, on account of which Eros their offspring is simultaneously always lacking and always seeking fulfillment. Eros is in all the living as the striving of the mortal for the immortal through reproduction. In addition, because human beings have minds which can deliberately recollect the past and anticipate the future, they seek to live on in *doxa*, in the glory realized in the eyes of others who recollect "immortal" works and deeds.

---

eidetic features involved in the lifeworld. We will pick this up later in this essay.

More deeply still, minds can arise from the Cave of *doxa* through the Ladder of Ascent from the beauty of an attractive body to the beauty of soul, of customs shaping souls, and of the sciences of cosmic and human order, culminating in the vision of Beauty Itself. In his recollection of Diotima's teaching Socrates builds up the *doxa* of his interlocutors regarding Diotima's teaching but thereby puts them and us as readers in the position to recollect the essential truths from our own experience (201D-212C).

Finally, Alcibiades recollects the stories of his own personal erotic experiences with Socrates which help establish the basis for Socrates' glory (215A-222B). And, of course, Plato writes the dialogue to aid in keeping the glory of Socrates as immortal as temporal transmission will allow. The dialogue is built as a series of recollections which produce the subsequent *doxa*, ultimately for us, regarding the banquet event and regarding Eros, and providing, in Diotima's account, a way from the Cave of *doxa* to *episteme* through another mode of recollection.

"In Vino Veritas" is also a recollection of an event, in fact it is subtitled "A Recollection." Like the *Symposium*, the characters recollect famous opinions, the later speakers those of the earlier as well, and recollect their own experience in order to develop their opinions. Afham as narrator reflects upon recollection in the beginning of the work and at the end Judge William's wife raises a question which provokes the Judge's recollection about marriage in the essay following the dialogue in *Stages on Life's Way* (or at least that is how I interpret the origin of the second piece). The core of the dialogue recounts how five unmarried male aesthetes gathered at a banquet to enjoy a sumptuous feast and each other's company. Contrary to the *Symposium*, there seems to be no order of progression in the speakers. Paralleling in Plato's dialogue the common view of all but Socrates that Eros is a god, Victor, as a consummate aesthete, represents the view common to the five symposiasts that the aim of nature is to be taken up in the service of the senses and arranged into an integral whole. Their "god" is their own refined enjoyment. For Victor the event has to be unique and the whole beautiful setting must be destroyed after the banquet is over (SLW, 22-25). Flux is king: what is important is to enjoy the immediate. The traces of the past are actively erased as the aesthetes look for new occasions for enjoyment.

The first speaker is a Young Man (presumably not named because he has not yet made a name for himself) who has deliberately kept himself from being involved with women.[3] This, he claims, gives him a relation in thought to all and not simply to one or a few women (SLW, 32). He is able to recollect all that he has been able to observe of women is a purely detached mode. As Phaedrus basis his opinions on Eros upon recollection of the opinions of famous men, so the Young Man, in explicit recollection of Plato's *Symposium*, praises Plato's exaltation of "Eros in the Greek sense," which is not that between man and woman—a possible discreetly ambiguous praise of homosexuality and/or of "Platonic love" (SLW, 33). He also recollects Aristophanes' division of the sexes, a comic state which amused the gods (SLW, 35). Love itself is a comedy. Comic he finds it that the matter of falling in love, taken to be so important by an epoch that requires reflectiveness before action, renders a man blind and unable to give reasons why one particular woman would be the object of his being so attracted (SLW, 36, 41). Thus women, for whom reflection is impossible, entice men to become ridiculous (SLW, 46). Furthermore, rendering the whole matter contradictory, the egoism of pleasure leads to a total regard for another, only to establish a mutual egoism, itself overcome in reproduction (SLW, 42-43).

Constantin Constantius is a detached psychological observer.[4] In his view man expresses the absolute, that is, what is self-subsistent and thus at base absolved from all relation; woman can only exist in relationship (SLW, 48). He recollects the opinions of Plato and Aristotle (and in this they are followed by Aquinas),[5] that woman is incomplete man (SLW, 55). She is the weaker sex who lives in imaginary illusion (SLW, 48, 52). She regularly dies of love and then is reborn with the next love (SLW, 55). Since she continually falls into contradiction, she needs to be corrected by the male

---

[3]Compare the nameless young man of *Repetition*.

[4]Perkins sees him, consistent with his name, as one who is so locked into his egoism that he is unable to undergo the changes required by existence. See Robert Perkins, "Woman Bashing in 'In Vino Veritas'," in C. Léon and S. Walsh (eds.), *Feminist Interpretations of Søren Kierkegaard* (University Park: Pennsylvania State University Press, 1997) 93-94. In the piece following "In Vino Veritas," that is, "Reflections on Marriage," the anonymous author refers to one who does not view marriage as a higher expression of love and remains unmarried as "a scoffer, a seducer, a hermit" or one who remains thoughtless in marriage (SLW, 100). The three speakers who have names are Johannes the Seducer, Victor Emerita, and Constantin. One could suppose then that Constantin is the scoffer, as his speech also indicates.

[5]Plato, *Timaeus*, 91a, and see also *Laws* XII, 944d; Aristotle, *On the Generation of Animals*, IV, 2; Aquinas, *Summa theologiae*, I, q. 91, ad 1.

(SLW, 52). To become, like Othello, jealous of her falling to another man makes a man comic, something one cannot imagine in the case of Socrates (SLW, 49-50).

Victor Emerita is the consummate aesthete: he describes the aesthetic conditions for the banquet; he is thrilled at the music of Mozart.[6] He has achieved the victory of a life of enjoyment of the senses and stands in an ultimate eremetical solitude, for his supreme joy does not presuppose the presence of others. He continues the snowballing denigration of woman, whose value he sees as inflated through gallantry (SLW, 56-57), and whose higher function, totally subservient, consists in inspiring the works of the spirit in the creative male. Ideality comes into the world and poets receive their inspiration through woman (SLW, 59). However, it is not the girl he gets but the girl he does not get that inspires the genius, the hero, the poet, and the saint, a privilege secured by a wife only through early death (SLW, 61). Through recollecting his relation to her, a man produces inspired work. She inspires the striving and yearning which leads a man to the consciousness of immortality (SLW, 60).

The Ladies' Tailor, like the Young Man also nameless except in his special functional relation to women, experiences women everyday close by in their vainest moments. Recollecting his experiences, he concludes that woman lives by her nature in an unreflective mode of the aesthetic life, immersed in the immediacy of relation to other likewise immersed females, caught up in the flow of novelty and addicted to fashion in all things (SLW, 66-71).

Johannes the Seducer plays a role similar to that of Diotima: he recollects, corrects, and grounds the views expressed in the previous speeches. In contrast to the Young Man, he knows first hand and intimately an ever-increasing number of women. He detaches himself from the familial function (and thus has no surname). He is simultaneously the most egoistically manipulative and the most philosophic of the group, suggesting that philosophy itself is a kind of aesthetic seduction.[7] Like Aristophanes and Diotima he creates a myth: originally there was only man; but the gods became envious and, desiring to weaken him, created woman in order to trap him into the complexities of the finite through marriage (SLW, 75, 79).

---

[6]Croxall sees Victor as one who stands ironically apart from life. See T. H. Croxall, *Kierkegaard Commentary* (New York: Harper, 1956) 108.

[7]See "Reflections on Marriage," SLW, 170-71, for a confirmation of this view from the anonymous author.

Recollecting the two bases of Western thought, he claims that creation of woman occurred either in the Hebrew way by removing a part from man as in *Genesis* or in the Greek way, as in Plato's Aristophantic view, by slicing man in two (190D). In his pithy, densely expressed Hegelian view and relating back to Constantin's speech, Johannes presents woman as the finite, which involves both "living in the genus" as reproductive and being accidental, that is, dependent upon the male. The male, on the other hand, is the infinite, detached from the finite and thus a free and substantial individual.[8] In the male the essence of the species is found as an individual. Relating back to Victor's view, Johannes sees woman's inspiration cynically as the source of "the delusive infinity of all divine and human illusions" (SLW, 76). Seeing through the trap set by the gods (SLW, 75), the Seducer understands that he can relate to an inexhaustible number of women and thus learns to maximize his gratification. He knows how to break off relationships at their consummation in order to go on to still further conquests (SLW, 75-79). Both he and Victor transcend the masses who pursue sensuous immediacy. The two aesthetes seek the reflective cultivation of the senses. Victor Eremita lives the life of quiet and ultimately private aesthetic cultivation, while Johannes pursues the most intense of all sensual pleasures, sexual enjoyment. They live the height of the aesthetic life, mediated by reflection, one in the quiet, solitary mode, the other in the more intense pleasurable mode of sexual relation to members of the opposite sex.[9]

At dawn Constantin brings the event to a close by commanding one last libation followed by the breaking of the glasses as the crew arrives to dismantle the banquet setting, leaving no trace of the event (SLW, 80-81). This parallels the Seducer's requirement of breaking off relationships at their consummation. The past is destroyed so that a new immediate, a new occasion for enjoyment, can come to be.

The banqueteers are driven together some distance where they await their individual carriages. In the interim they stroll through the woods and happen upon Judge William and his wife taking morning tea in their garden.

---

[8]Hegel sees the infinity of the human to lie in the ability to detach oneself from every finite content, to say "I" as over against everything finite, even within oneself, and thus to choose freely among the finite options. The System thus situates rather than absorbs the individual precisely in his/her subjectivity. See *Hegel's Philosophy of Mind*, trans. William Wallace and A. Miller (Oxford: Clarendon Press, 1971) #381, *Zusatz*, 21.

[9]Cf. "The Seducer's Diary," EO, 1.

The line of Afham's recollection culminates in Judge William and his wife, the former named by his function and the latter only by her functional relation to him, thus without any personal name at all. Of all the males in the dialogue, the Judge has the most intimate knowledge of what a woman can be. Detached observers who have no personal knowledge of marital relations, the group observes the couple in secret, the Judge and his wife oblivious of their presence (SLW, 82). Contrary to the insecure clinging that characterizes lovers, the married people move securely in each other's presence. The wife remarks to her husband that if he had not married her he would have become a much greater person in the world, confirming the Seducer's view of woman as the occasion for the fall of man (SLW, 84). The Judge does not reply directly but playfully hums the tune to a ballad about a husband cutting a cudgel for his wife, indicating the essentially subservient role of women in Danish practice and establishing the background for the negative view of women expressed by the symposiasts. After she complains that he never takes her seriously, playfully again he tells her to forget her remark. In effect, she should not bother her pretty little head about it but simply live in the immediacy of her functional relationship to him.[10]

The dialogue ends with Victor Eremita pilfering a manuscript from the Judge's study, only to have it taken from him, in turn, by Afham. The manuscript is presumably the piece which follows, "Reflections on Marriage," the result of the Judge's having recollected the question posed him, no doubt several times before, by his wife.

Having sketched the most general content and progression of the speeches in each dialogue, I will go on to consider the theme of wine, contained in the title of Kierkegaard's work. He explicitly ties it to the theme of recollection, which I will then consider in each of the dialogues.

2

Kierkegaard's title, "In Vino Veritas," indicates the special role of what may seem to be a purely accidental theme, namely wine. In Plato's work it serves to distinguish the Dionysian element, focally present in the discussion of Eros, from the Apollonian, ironically setting up, by the intrusion of nature in the form of hiccups, an accidental but measured, perfect Apollonian

---

[10]Perkins suggests that the morning tea of the Judge and his wife and not the evening wine is the source of truth about woman ("Woman Bashing," 100).

alternation in the arranged order of those present at the banquet between Dionysiac drinkers and Apollonian nondrinkers. And on this occasion the initial deliberate Apollonian abstinence of all the speakers, drinkers and nondrinkers alike, is overcome by the entry of the drunken Alcibiades and the heavy imbibing which follows. Socrates rises above it all, drinking them under the table in Dionysian darkness, and rising with the sun to bathe in the grove of Apollo, god of light. This is setting for the proclamation of Dionysian ascent of Eros up the Ladder to Apollonian contemplation of the order of the cosmos and beyond to its Source in Beauty Itself, the occasion for the highest level of intoxication.

In Kierkegaard's work wine is present as a feature of the banquet, but it serves a more important function in the preface as the fundamental metaphor of the work. The password to the banquet is *In vino veritas*, "In wine there is truth," an adage which recalls a statement by Alcibiades in the *Symposium* (217E). Contrary to stipulation for the speakers in Plato's piece, the speakers in Kierkegaard's work *must* feel the power of wine in order to speak, just as the culmination of the whole of the *Symposium* comes in the testimony of the drunken Alcibiades. But, much more important, the preface to Kierkegaard's work first introduces wine as a metaphor for the theme of the subtitle, *recollection*. Recollection transforms the grapes of experience into wine (SLW, 9), grapes raised to a higher power, as it were.[11] The work aims to provoke recollection in the special sense in which Kierkegaard employs it. Wine thus serves as symbol for transformed consciousness.

Following out the clue in Kierkegaard's title, what I want especially to attend to is the claim that, although the focal topic of each dialogue concerns sexual relations, the key to each lies in the notion of recollection and the "erotic understanding" it entails. The immediate theme of Plato's dialogue is Eros, the Dionysiac element *par excellence* and object of the after-dinner speeches. However, one often gains a clue for reflection upon the inner significance of a Platonic dialogue by attending to the first words.[12] The

---

[11]Schopenhauer uses the same metaphor for philosophy: philosophy transforms the grapes of experience into wine. See *The World as Will and Representation*, II, supplement to book 3, chap. 34, 407.

[12]The *Republic*, for example, begins with *kateben*, "I went down," giving us the central metaphoric opposition of down and up linked to the opposition of darkness and light initiating the search for what is "up" or "down" in human experience and finding it in ascending from the darkness of the Cave to the sunlight of the Good. See my "Image, Structure and Content: A Remark on a Passage in Plato's *Republic*,"

Symposium begins with *Doko moi*, "It seems to me," employing a cognate to the term *doxa* that is a constant in Plato's dialogues. *Doxa* is usually translated as 'opinion', but its meaning is much broader. In addition to 'seeming' and 'opinion', it also means 'glory', as in the liturgical doxology. As glory, it is the maximum state of how one seems to others and how one secures a measure of immortality by living on in the memory of others. The banquet is a celebration of the glory of Agathon's victory; the *Symposium* itself as a literary work is a celebration of the glory of Socrates. The *doxa* of Diotima's account notes how doing great deeds and producing great works is a way to achieve the glory of living on in the memory of others, one of the "minor mysteries" of Eros as the desire of the mortal for immortality. Alcibiades' concluding speech helps establish the immortal *doxa* of Socrates.

Plato uses *doxa* as the comprehensive term for the state of mind we are constantly in before the discovery of *episteme*. Comprehensively taken, it means 'opining/appearing' or how things are present to us in ordinary life as appearing through the senses and mediated both by others and by the intrusion of the past into the present. In response to an inquiry about an event that took place many years ago, the very beginning of the dialogue asks for a recollection. It goes on to construct a path of recollection about the famous banquet. The process terminates in the building up of *doxa*, the seeming that constitutes a community, both with regard to past events generally and with regard to the theme of Eros. The dialogue shows the workings of *doxa* as the residue of recollection regarding that theme. From the dialogue as a whole we gain some insight into the way *doxa* operates.

Apollodoros ("the gift of Apollo") recollects to an unnamed group of people (including us as readers) what he had narrated yesterday to Glaucon about what happened at a banquet when he and Glaucon were infants. Glaucon had asked Apollodoros to fill in what he had heard from an unnamed source who got it from Phoenix who, in turn, got it from the eyewitness Aristodemos, the same who had recounted it to Apollodoros. The initial focus of the dialogue is upon weaving the web of *doxa* within which members of a community live. The narrator, Apollodoros, recollects the process of the transmission of the *doxa* about the banquet held a long time ago. The dialogue itself fixes the transmission in writing, and both *Phaedrus* and *Theaetetus* reflect upon writing and reading as vehicles of building up

---

The Review of Metaphysics 40 (1987): 495-514.

doxa.[13] Seeming is dependent upon recollection and fixation either in memory or in writing, passed on by various pathways to constitute what Quine has called "the web of belief."[14]

Apollodoros tells us that Aristodemos cannot recall everything, but only the memorable (178A). Memory is not a neutral recorder, but operates in function of interest. What is important remains, and much that occurs is not judged important and is thus forgotten. Memory works automatically, but it can also be deliberately cultivated. And language can be employed to seek actively to reconstruct the past through the aid of others as well as, with the rise of literate culture, through fixation on the page. Interest sustains the past by helping to weave the web of *doxa*. Plato is reflecting upon the construction of the Cave of human dwelling. The dialogue is thus in a significant way about recollection as the building up of a community's *doxa*.

Kierkegaard's subtitle indicates that the work itself is a recollection (*Erindring*). And his preface is really a prerecollection (*Vor-erindring*) or a recollection about recollection.[15] This shows that he has grasped what is at the center of Plato's work generally: the notion of recollection. The distinctively human does not consist in living in immediacy like an animal; it lives off of recollection. For Kierkegaard the truth attained through the wine of recollection is what the *Concluding Unscientific Postscript* calls "subjective truth," truth held in the passion of inwardness (CUP, 1:203, 242). The narrator aims at promoting what he calls "recollection's erotic understanding" (SLW, 15). Though he does not explain what he means by that expression, the qualification of understanding as "erotic" suggests a kind of heightened awareness and thus something more than clear insight into essential connections. It is a matter of intensified presence parallel to Diotima's description of the sudden epiphany of Beauty Itself.

In "In Vino Veritas" William Afham is the reporter who subsequently relates the incident. How is he able to relate it? He is not described as an eyewitness the way Aristodemos, the original reporter of the *Symposium*, was. In the preface Afham says that he sometimes feels as though he had not experienced it, but had poetically invented it (SLW, 15). In this way he

---

[13]See my treatment of this in "Self-Reflexivity in the *Theaetetus*: On the Lifeworld of a Platonic Dialogue," *The Review of Metaphysics* (January 2000).

[14]W. V. O. Quine and J. S. Ulliam, *The Web of Belief* (New York: McGraw Hill, 1978).

[15]See Walter Lowrie's note to his translation of *Stages on Life's Way* (New York: Schocken, 1967) 27.

participated in the banquet without being a participant: he made it up. Of course, we should not forget that the author is Søren Kierkegaard who knows nothing experientially of the secret of marital love, being himself unmarried. In this case, he is underscoring the need for experience to understand the depths of subjectivity by pointing to something he himself could not fully understand: the secret mentioned in the very first sentence of the work (SLW, 9)—although, as real author of the anonymously authored "Reflections on Marriage," he presents himself indirectly as understanding matrimonial intimacy.

Having indicated the central notion of recollection in both thinkers, what I want to do from this point on is to examine that notion in greater detail, beginning with Plato.

3

Platonic recollection, the notion of *anamnesis*, is part of philosophic *doxa*, of the opinions passed on in the academic community. What it really entails may not be so well known. Baldly put, according to conventional *doxa*, Plato is said to handle "the problem of universals" by claiming that the Forms, the ground of language in the universals whereby we come to identify individuals as being of a certain type, are innate in the soul from a previous existence. Experience of individuals in the sensory world reminds one of the preexistent Forms appropriate to understanding the specific individuals involved.

The "doctrine" is introduced in the *Meno* in conjunction with an exploration in geometry which is itself introduced in a *prima facie* improbable attempt to ground Pindar's poetic proclamation that the soul is immortal.[16] Socrates leads a slaveboy to a geometric insight which is the solution to the problem of squaring a given square while retaining the square figure. However, Socrates claims that the boy only has *alethes doxa*, manifest opinion or insight. This is a step higher than *orthe doxa* or correct opinion guessed at or memorized without insight. But it is lower than *anamnesis*, which consists, Socrates says, in tethering the insight by reasoning. Such tethering (*desei* from *deo*, I bind) would consist in developing the axiomatic system within which the insight could be demonstrated. Reflected upon, this furnishes a basic insight into the distinction between *episteme* and *doxa*, which Socrates, who claimed in the

---

[16]*Meno*, 81B-D.

Apology that his wisdom consisted in knowing that he does not know, claims in the *Meno* to be among the things he knows.[17]

Anamnesis is clearly distinguished from *mneme* or simple memory by its ability to gather together, axiomatize, deduce and thus systematize what appears haphazard in experience. The geometric example is meant to be a regional demonstration of this ability. It begins the verification of Socrates' first introduction of the notion of *anamnesis* in the *Meno* by his proclamation that all nature is akin, and that, this being so, if one could recollect one universal truth, one could go on to recollect all.[18] *Anamnesis* is tied in with our ability to gather the whole of being together in a unified way, to re-collect it at the level of the togetherness of the eidetic features found in experience.

In the treatment of the Line of Knowledge in the *Republic*, Socrates uses a geometric theorem again, this time in order to lead us to a meta-reflection upon the eidetic features of the "play of the fourfold"—sensible and intelligible, sense and intellect—presupposed in all wakeful life. And that in turn leads us by "the upward way" to consider the Good as the source of unity and as the term of aspiration for intellect which operates in the light of a sought-after unity. Ultimately what we recollect is our founding reference to the whole of being, and this leads us to re-collect experience into a systematic eidetic whole.[19]

What is crucial to notice is that the Platonic dialogues deal with recollection on two levels: the active recollection of things past (retained in a more fixed and universally available way in writing), especially those connected with glory, and the active re-collection of our place in the cosmos. Both operations are moved by a kind of Eros as the desire of the mortal for immortality, the desire to fix forever what perishes. Before it is tied into a theoretical claim to a recollection of previous existence or an anticipation of an afterlife, the *anamnesis* Plato is after is a matter of experience: it has to do with gathering the eidetic features of the eternal order of the cosmic whole in relation to the things we experience in the Cave of *doxa*, the communally based recollections of concrete events and judgments about things-in-general. But it also has to do with what Kierkegaard would call "the How" of that recollection. For Plato it is suffused by an erotic

---

[17]*Apology*, 23B; *Meno*, 98B.

[18]*Meno*, 81B-D.

[19]*Republic* VI, 509D. See my "Plato's Line Revisited: The Pedagogy of Complete Reflection," *The Review of Metaphysics* 46 (1991): 525-47.

intoxication with what Diotima calls "Beauty Itself," linked to the Good as the origin and end of the cosmos.[20]

4

"In Vino Veritas" presents a substantial retrieval of the notion of recollection, adding a new dimension to it.[21] William Afham's *Forerindring* to the *Erindring*, his prerecollection to the recollection, begins by focusing upon the recollection of an unnamed secret which requires total recollection as a matter of obligation. One wonders immediately what the secret is. It turns out to be any true recollection which can only happen in the secrecy of one's own subjectivity (SLW, 14). One wonders also what "total recollection" is. It appears to be a grasping of what is essential to holding one's life together as a whole in the mode of "passionate inwardness." That is, it involves concern for the whole of one's life in a mode which involves the whole of one's awareness and not simply some recognitional or intellectually explanatory mode.

The wine theme of the title appears in the second paragraph: "The bottling of the recollection must have preserved the fragrance of the experience before it is sealed" (SLW, 9). This is immediately followed by a distinction between recollection and remembrance. Remembrance is only a minimal condition. Mere memory leaves one unconcerned (SLW, 10) and what is merely memorized or what might float up in reverie might easily be forgotten subsequently. But what is truly recollected cannot be forgotten because it is a matter of concern (SLW, 13).

Recollection "consecrates" the experience. The wine metaphor is significant here: it indicates a transformation in the How of our relation to things. According to Afham, an old man has poor memory but recollection is his best faculty, giving him poetic far-sight. The opposite is the case for the child: good memory, poor ability to recollect, and thus no "poetic farsightedness" (SLW, 10). Furthermore, "the grape must not be pressed at

---

[20]*Republic*, VI, 506E.

[21]There seems to be a change of meaning for 'recollection' here from that in *Repetition*. There it is set in contrast with the title word and indicates a fixation which closes the openness of the future emphasized in repetition. See John Caputo, "Kierkegaard, Heidegger, and the Foundering of Metaphysics," 201-24, and Stephen Crites, "'The Blissful Security of the Moment': Recollection, Repetition, and Eternal Recurrence," 225-46, in *International Kierkegaard Commentary: Fear and Trembling and Repetition*, ed. Robert L. Perkins (Macon GA: Mercer University Press, 1993).

every season" (SLW, 10); a certain ripening of experience is required. For the child, both spontaneous experience and memory are matters of "immediacy." Memory itself only recalls immediately (SLW, 12); recollection is reflection which produces a relation mediated by distance. This allows the old man to see things near at hand, whereas the child sees them from afar. This last turn in the metaphor should not be taken to mean that the child sees farther, for Kierkegaard has just said the opposite: it is the old man who has poetic far-sight. Too close to life at the level of immediacy, one is unable to see it properly. In fact, living in immediacy, one is *not* close to things; living through recollection, one can in fact draw nearer to existent things. We see the former exhibited in the Young Man who has had no experience whatsoever with women in the erotic sense. But we see it also in each of the speakers who have not had the inner experience of marriage. They remain outside the experience within which alone one can understand woman at her best.[22] Their disposition looks only to the present and the future of enjoyment with no attempt to hold it in continuity with the recollected past.

In a strange turn, Afham says that recollection is indifferent to past and present. One would have thought that it is concerned only with the past. Memory of the past is a necessary condition. The work of recording here is a setting free for recollection of what has been lying perfected in memory (SLW, 15). Drawing upon past experience through memory, one is able "to conjure away the present for the sake of recollection" (SLW, 13). The nearness here is the nearness of familiarity, of what Heidegger would call "average everydayness" (*Alltäglichkeit*).[23] There is a deeper sort of nearness grounded in the achievement of the distance of reflection which presupposes memory's gathering as its precondition. It requires a second or "double reflection."[24] The symposiasts recollect both their past experience and the opinions of others, but they do not practice the requisite reflection upon the recollection which deepens the experience. The deepening occurs by way of

---

[22]"Reflections on Marriage" is based upon a shift in perspective. See especially SLW, 124-25 and 143-44. One must not remain a mere connoisseur.

[23]Martin Heidegger, *Being and Time,* trans. John MacQuarrie and Edward Robinson (New York: Harper & Row, 1962) 149ff.

[24]CUP, 1:73. See Gabriel Marcel's parallel distinction in *The Mystery of Being,* trans. G. Fraser (Chicago: Regnery, 1960) 1:95-126, between first reflection as abstractive and second as "recuperative," recovering the concreteness of existence at a deeper level.

a kind of Heraclitean law of opposites: according to Afham it requires acquaintance with contrast in moods, situation, environments. What is at stake is an appreciative awareness involved in nearness. Thus Heraclitus claimed that by sickness we know health, by hunger and thirst satiety; and both Heidegger and Buber claimed that by anticipation of death we know the preciousness of life.[25]

But what is at stake is not simply the appreciation of some particular. Recollection, Afham further says, gives continuity to life. It is also not lost on Kierkegaard that the *Symposium* teaches a flux cosmology through the *doxa* Socrates hands on from Diotima (207D ff). Knowledge itself is in flux and has to be replaced by caring, by exercise, by study (*meletan*). Knowledge as recollection is the struggle to hold one's life together as a whole as time flows by and one, like a child, is immersed in the present moment. The distance provided by old age is what allows one to bind one's life together in recollection and to bring the relevant past to bear upon the deepening of our relation to what is present. "Actually, only the essential can be recollected" (SLW, 12). A mass of detail distracts recollection (SLW, 13). Here Kierkegaard's character joins Plato in focusing upon the essential, which Afham explicitly connects with the idea. The question of the dialogue then is, What is the essential matter with respect to a man and a woman and to the relation between them for the whole of their existence (SLW, 30)? Grasping the essential through recollection allows one distance from the flow of immediacy to bring it to significant presence and to give continuity to one's life as a whole. However, the characters in the dialogue do not undertake the requisite reflection. It is what his wife requires of Judge William, the conditions for which are given by Afham. One has to go on to the next piece in *Stages on Life's Way* (presumably the piece pifered from the Judge at the end of the dialogue) to secure the proper perspective for the actual recollection.

Afham, I said, lays out the conditions for recollection. He says that the sounds and tastes are recollected best in a place "quiet, remote and forgotten"—the solitude of the forest in the peace of late afternoon, in "the infinite sea of silence," in the holy quietness of solitude (SLW, 18). Quietness, remoteness, forgottenness, solitude, silence: all involve being set

---

[25]On Heraclitus, see fr. 204 in G. Kirk and J. Raven, *The Presocratic Philosophers* (Cambridge: Cambridge University Press, 1966) 189; on Heidegger, *Being and Time*, 278-311; on Buber, *Daniel: Dialogues on Realization* trans. Maurice Friedman (New York: McGraw-Hill, 1965), 91.

at a distance from others, not hearing their addresses, not receiving their attention. In a forest far removed from the city, in late afternoon when the tasks of the day are finished, the shadows lengthen, and darkness begins to descend. They all create external preconditions for the sense of the infinite that can open up in inner silence. Max Picard's wonderful little work, *The World of Silence*, ends with a quote from Kierkegaard: if he were a physician and were asked to cure the sickness of the age, he would have one prescription: Create silence.[26]

In the light of the early morning sun the Judge's wife poses the question about his life without her. At that time the Judge is silent. Presumably the process of recollection is setting in. Just as Diotima's teaching on the Ladder of erotic ascent may have provoked Socrates' own erotic recollection as he stood in rapt attention, so the Judge's wife as a kind of second Diotima provokes his recollection.[27] Presumably, as a good wife, she had asked the same question of him before, probably several times. Perhaps he found the full and requisite silence of solitude in the evening darkness where he composed his "Reflections on Marriage."

Afham attaches the notion of the holy to that silence found in solitude. One is reminded here of Kierkegaard's frequent remark that "we float on waters seventy thousand fathoms deep" and are scarcely aware of it (CUP, 1:232). The depth dimension to be attained by recollection is a secret growing in complete solitude, inaccessible from the outside. "The winepress of recollection every man must tread alone" (SLW, 15). One understands now why the first line of the work focuses upon the secret. There is a clear parallel in the *Symposium* which highlights in the beginning and in Alcibiades' speech at the end the frequent lapse of Socrates into prolonged periods of withdrawn silence and physical fixity (174D-175B, 220C).

Afham finds his retreat at the Nook of Eight Paths, located at the convergence of eight solitary paths upon which no one travels (SLW, 16). I suggest that the Eight Paths are the ways of life followed by each of the seven characters and by the narrator. No one really travels upon them because they are Kierkegaard's fictions, although they name essential possibilities. They are solitary because ultimately everyone travels alone in her/his heart of hearts. Quiet solitude is holy. This allows experience to be "consecrated" in recollection.

---

[26]Max Picard, *The World of Silence* (Chicago: Regnery, 1954).

[27]I owe this most helpful insight to a suggestion by Robert Perkins.

A long and very confusing penultimate paragraph (SLW, 17-19) parallels the intrusion of someone upon the quiet of an individual in solitude with the intrusion of someone upon lovers in solitude, seeing without being seen. It prefigures the penultimate scene of the dialogue when the group of aesthetes, seeing but unseen, comes upon a married couple in their solitary country home.

The prefatory remarks on recollection end thus: "anyone who has once understood what recollection is has been captured for all eternity and is captured in it; and anyone who possesses one recollection is richer than if he possessed the whole world; and not only the one about to give birth but above all the one who is recollecting is in blessed circumstances" (SLW, 19).

5

As I have attempted to show, both dialogues, Plato's and Kierkegaard's, deal centrally with recollection. Both play on a distinction between memory, which is a precondition, and recollection technically taken. For Plato's Socrates recollection (*anamnesis*) at its deepest consists in re-collecting the eidetic features of the cosmic order from the contingencies of experience by seeking the single principle of order for the whole in order to deduce the whole eidetic realm therefrom. Plato's own focus sets the theoretical cosmological, scientific, and theological project within the context of a lifeworld in encounter with other individuals. Hence the dialogue form that his thought takes. To that extent Plato's "essentialism," his focus upon essential Forms, plays in counterpoint with an "existentialism" in the dual sense of involving encounter with individual human existents and in calling for a peculiar modality of subjective inwardness. Hence the focus upon Socrates. But Plato also explores another sense of recollection, that which establishes the *doxa* in which a community lives, both spontaneously and in terms of the deliberate attempt to recollect the past. It is out of that web of *doxa* and back in relation to it that the erotic ascent takes place which lays bare the underlying kinship of things within the cosmos.

For Kierkegaard's Afham recollection consists in gaining distance from the flowing immediacy of the surface of life in order to draw near to what underlies that surface through bringing forward what is essential, drawn from the past into the present. This occurs in the secrecy of one's own subjectivity and has to do with the ineffability of the individual and the "erotic understanding," the transformation of awareness into passionate inwardness through the double reflection of recollection, fixing in memory and allowing what is thus fixed to draw near so as to affect one's life as a whole.

All the speakers in Kierkegaard's banquet live in a world from which the gods and the cosmic concern are absent. That would also seem to include Afham for whom "the holy" in the dialogue is not explicitly the divine. One has to go on to the next piece in *Stages on Life's Way*, "Reflections on Marriage," to find the religious dimension to marriage and perhaps the hidden secret behind the loving relation between the Judge and his wife: "If the individual has not in faith placed himself in the relationship with God as spirit, paganism haunts his brain as a fantastic reminiscence and he cannot enter into any marriage" (SLW, 100). Certainly in the dialogue in question, despite the parallels with and the deliberate invocation of Plato's *Symposium*, Diotima's cosmic interest is entirely absent. The world of "In Vino Veritas" is the narrow world of bourgeois individualism and aesthetic enjoyment with no cosmic sensibility whatsoever. William Afham has achieved a higher level of reflection than all the others as one who comprehensively reflects upon all the others. The Judge, however, is one who exhibits in his marriage and profession a form of life higher than the speakers and also higher, through his lifelong commitment, than the higher aesthetic of William Afham.

But at least as important in attending to what is present in the dialogue is what is absent from it. One has to look to *Stages on Life's Way* as a whole and beyond. There the equivalent of the cosmic and theological features of the *Symposium* lie in the stage of religion represented initially by the married author of "Reflections on Marriage," hence in all probability the Judge displaying his deeper side. And one has to look to Kierkegaard's work as a whole to see the extent to which the cosmic extension of the human quest for eternity enters into his work. It certainly takes center stage in relation to Christ as the Paradox, the Absurd, as the Infinite made finite (CUP, 1:209ff).

In an age increasingly dominated by specialized scientific and technical thinking, it is crucially important to recover the dimension of religious sensibility to which Kierkegaard constantly points. But it is also crucially important to recover the ability exhibited by Plato to recover the whole context of human existence and thus find a place both for scientific and philosophic discipline. Plato simultaneously leads us to reflection upon the building up of *doxa* as the tradition within which a given community lives.

Kierkegaard and Plato can thus be put into complementary relation with one another. And both together underscore the central import of "erotic understanding" in the recollective transformation of consciousness. Our reflection upon their two dialogues only opens up the beginning of a more comprehensive reflection which will learn to mine both thinkers simultaneously.

3

Does Love Cure the Tragic? Kierkegaardian Variations on a Platonic Theme

Adriaan van Heerden

> I think people have entirely missed the power of Love [Eros], because, if they had grasped it, they'd have built the greatest temples and altars to him and made the greatest sacrifices. But as it is, none of this is done for him, though it should be, more than anything else! For he loves the human race more than any other god, he stands by us in our troubles, and he cures those ills we humans are most happy to have mended. (Plato, *Symposium*[1])

Introduction

These words, spoken by Aristophanes as a prologue to his encomium of Eros, highlight an important theme in the *Symposium*, a theme that is taken over in *Stages on Life's Way*. The theme I have in mind here may be formulated as the question of whether love *cures* the tragic. In this article I will explore the relation between love and the tragic in *Stages on Life's Way* in the light of the thematic relation between *Stages on Life's Way* and *Symposium*. By doing so I hope to establish a new reading of *Stages on Life's Way* and to indicate the significance of this reading for the interpretation of the concept of "the religious" in the text.

Kierkegaard himself provides the main incentive for this intertextual comparison. The first section of *Stages on Life's Way* (entitled "In Vino Veritas") significantly takes its name from a latinized form of a phrase at *Symposium*, 217e (cf. JP, 3:2408 and 5:5699), and like the *Symposium* it tells the story of a number of men who come together in order to eat, drink and

[1]Plato, *Symposium*, 189c-d, trans. Alexander Nehamas and Paul Woodruff, in John M. Cooper, *Plato: Complete Works* (Indianapolis: Hackett Publishing Company, 1997).

deliver speeches on erotic love. It is important to note, however, that Kierkegaard's dialogical engagement with Plato's text doesn't end with "In Vino Veritas." It continues just as surely, albeit more subtly, throughout the rest of the book. A number of scholars have drawn attention to the fact that "In Vino Veritas" is some kind of parody or "reinscription" of the *Symposium*, but no one to my knowledge has grasped the full extent of Kierkegaard's rewriting of Plato's text.[2] One of my central claims—which forms an important part of the background to the question of whether love cures the tragic—is that the *whole* of *Stages on Life's Way* is in some sense a critical engagement with the *Symposium*. The reason for this claim will become clear once we have uncovered the thematic framework that connects the two texts.

As soon as one tries to answer the question of whether love cures the tragic, and when one asks what is *meant* by "love" and "the tragic" in the respective texts, it appears that these concepts are inextricably interwoven with a larger constellation of conceptual relations which are in themselves problematic. These issues are the following: (1) the relation between "the tragic" and "the comic"; (2) the movement from the realm of the "aesthetic" (which is alternatively referred to as the realm of the "poetic" or the "immediate"), through the realm of the "ethical" (which includes the philosophical or dialectical element), to the realm of the "religious"; (3) the tension between the "erotic ascent" and the "erotic descent"; and (4) the relation between man and woman.

Comparing *Stages on Life's Way* with *Symposium* we find that this constellation of relations is fully fledged only in Kierkegaard's text. The framework of *Stages on Life's Way* is layered in terms of the aesthetic, the

---

[2]Cf. Robert L. Perkins, "Woman Bashing in Kierkegaard's 'In Vino Veritas,' " in *Feminist Interpretations of Søren Kierkegaard*, ed. Céline Léon and Sylvia Walsh (University Park: Pennsylvania State University Press, 1997) 83-102, for an introduction to Kierkegaard's "reinscription" of the *Symposium*. Perkins, however, stops short of postulating a dialogue between the *Symposium* and *Stages on Life's Way* as a whole. Marie Mikulová Thulstrup, in "Plato's Vision and Its Interpretations," in *Bibliotheca Kierkegaardiana*, ed. Neils Thulstrup and Marie Mikulová Thulstrup, vol. 14 (Copenhagen: C. A. Reitzels Forlag, 1985) 100-101, writes that, in *Stages on Life's Way*, "reference is made to Plato in the same way as in *Either/Or*, but more vaguely and without any serious treatment of the Platonic themes." George E. Arbaugh and George B. Arbaugh, *Kierkegaard's Authorship* (London: George Allen & Unwin, 1968) 183, downplay the relation: " 'In Vino Veritas' [The Banquet] . . . is a work of great artistry, modelled slightly after Plato's *Symposium*, although in no sense being dependent upon it. The *Symposium* praises love; the Banquet derides woman."

ethical and the religious. A concomitant feature of this three-tiered structure is that there are three criteria in terms of which an answer to the question of whether love cures the tragic may be evaluated: the relation between the comic and the tragic, the relation between the erotic ascent and the erotic descent and the relation between man and woman will all appear differently depending on whether they are interpreted from the perspective of an aesthetic, an ethical or a religious life-view. Reading *Symposium* in the retrospective light of this framework reveals that only the first two categories (the aesthetic and the ethical) are present in Plato's text, which leads us to believe that Kierkegaard engages in dialogue with the *Symposium* in order to effect a revaluation of the "Platonic project". This revaluation proceeds by means of (implicitly) subjecting the "Platonic project" to the demands of the religious category.

Symposium maps onto *Stages on Life's Way* as follows. The first five speeches in *Symposium* correspond to the five speeches of "In Vino Veritas" insofar as they fall into the category of the aesthetic. The speech of Socrates/Diotima corresponds to Judge William's essay in *Stages on Life's Way* insofar as these communications signal a break with the aesthetic and initiate a movement in the direction of "the absolute." In Plato's text this movement is set in motion when the aspiring philosopher recognizes the inferior ontological and moral status of the "great nonsense of mortality" (*Symposium*, 211e); in Kierkegaard's text the movement is initiated when "the absolute in the ethical requirements" (SLW, 48) is taken infinitely seriously. The exchange between Socrates and Alcibiades prefigures the relationship between Quidam and Quaedam (sketched in Quidam's Diary and analyzed by Frater Taciturnus in his "Letter to the Reader") insofar as both these relationships are characterized by moral misrelation and misunderstanding. Frater Taciturnus develops the concept of the religious in the context of the unity of the tragic and the comic—a theme (i.e., the unity of the tragic and the comic) that is also suggested in *Symposium*.

In the light of this thematic correspondence between the two texts I suggest that the only way to give an adequate account of the question of whether love cures the tragic is to explore the underlying features of, and motivations behind, Kierkegaard's dialogical engagement with the *Symposium*, and to consider it in the full context of the constellation of relations described above. Conversely, the question of whether love cures the tragic provides a convenient point of access into both texts and their relation to each other. I shall begin with Plato's treatment of the question of whether love cures the tragic in the *Symposium*.

1. The Question of Whether Love Cures the Tragic in Plato's Symposium

Let us for the purposes of the present article play along with a traditional line of interpretation by acknowledging a philosophical phantom called "Plato's project."[3] And let us furthermore identify the purpose of this project as the critique and revaluation of tragedy (as literary genre, rhetorical instrument and cultural institution) in the light of "the absolute" and "the philosophical" (with its close ties to the "ethical"). By bringing the full force of his dialectic to bear on the traditional definitions(s) of tragedy (i.e., the received conception(s) of what it is that constitutes "the tragic"), Plato changes the meaning of this concept. The same method is also applied to concepts like "love" and "the comic" (or "the ridiculous").

In the *Republic* Socrates argues that (dramatic) tragedy is not the serious thing that people ordinarily think it is. According to Socrates tragedy cannot lay hold of the truth because it is an inferior imitation of what is *truly* serious.[4] What is truly serious according to Plato is "the way we're supposed to live,"[5] where this has both an individual and a collective dimension. In *Philebus* (48d-e) Socrates argues that a person can be self-ignorant (have a conceit of knowledge) about his external goods, his bodily goods, or the goods of his soul. The self-ignorance of the soul is the most common and usually takes the form of an overestimation of one's own virtue and wisdom.

---

[3]My skepticism at this point results from the fact that Plato is as much a master of "indirect communication" as is Kierkegaard himself. For a clear scholarly defense of an "open" (as opposed to a "doctrinal") reading of Plato—i.e., reading Plato as an indirect communicator concerned with certain recurring problems but with no particular doctrine of his own—cf. Robert Wardy, *The Birth of Rhetoric: Gorgias, Plato and their Successors* (London: Routledge, 1996) 52-56. Those who accept the authenticity of *Letter VII* may refer to it for some of Plato's own thoughts on this matter: cf. *Letter VII*, 340b-344d (trans. Glenn R. Morrow, in Cooper, *Plato: Complete Works*), where he insists that the most important truths of his philosophy cannot be communicated directly: "this knowledge is not something that can be put into words like other sciences; but after long-continued intercourse between teacher and pupil, in joint pursuit of the subject, suddenly, like light flashing forth when a fire is kindled, it is born in the soul and straightaway nourishes itself" (*Letter VII*, 341c). For a more traditional ("doctrinal") reading of Plato, cf. Gregory Vlastos, *Socrates: Ironist and Moral Philosopher* (Cambridge: Cambridge University Press, 1991).

[4]Plato, *Republic*, 608a, 602b, 603b.

[5]Plato, *Gorgias*, 500c, trans. Donald J. Zeyl, in Cooper, *Plato: Complete Works*.

Socrates links this self-ignorance explicitly to comedy and implicitly to tragedy: a self-ignorant person who is weak and powerless to retaliate when wronged is a comic character, while self-ignorance in one who is powerful makes him or her dangerous and consequently the kind of character found in tragedy.[6]

From this cursory tour of Plato's corpus we may postulate that Plato's redefinition of "the tragic" proceeds via two stages. *First*, a dualism of body and soul is introduced. The (lower) realm of the body is demarcated as the realm of earthly, human suffering, in contrast to the (higher) realm of the soul. The latter exists in a dimension separable from the body, and (given that the realm of the soul is immune to the onslaughts of "the tragic") its cultivation may consequently be said to raise one outside the domain of the tragic. *Second*, (poetic) tragedy and comedy are classed together (i.e., their unity is posited) on the grounds that (1) both are inferior imitations of the truly serious and ridiculous[7] and (2) both depict self-ignorant characters who, in one way or another, are overly and misguidedly concerned with worldly fortune. Philosophy, on the other hand, aims at the cultivation of the soul and hence *is* the only effective antidote to "the tragic."[8]

These themes are also active in *Symposium*. The dualism of body and soul is introduced by Diotima (*Symposium*, 206c), and she hails the goods of the soul as incomparably superior to those of the body (*Symposium*, 208e-209e); the unity of the tragic and the comic is suggested in the speeches of Aristophanes, Agathon and Alcibiades; and philosophy is variously affirmed (both explicitly and implicitly) as the only activity capable of identifying and improving the greatest goods of the soul. Redescribing the second stage of the "erotic ascent" (*Symposium*, 210a-212a) in terms of Kierkegaardian categories, we can say that the pursuit and love of wisdom is an activity that

---

[6]Plato, *Philebus*, 49a-c. Cf. Andrea Wilson Nightingale, *Genres in Dialogue: Plato and the Construct of Philosophy* (Cambridge: Cambridge University Press, 1995) 88-89.

[7]In *Gorgias*, 509a, Socrates argues that anyone who attempts to dismiss philosophy or argue against the philosopher will always appear "ridiculous."

[8]Insofar as there is at all room for a concept of "the tragic" in Plato's philosophy, this is the only place where it could occur. However, given the overall ontology and moral hierarchy we can see that no person can really be a "tragic" character in the traditional sense: someone who fails to live up to the demands of the philosophical way of life is simply pathetic (in the sense of deplorable, worthless, contemptible, feeble) and hence cannot be a figure of absolute significance or consequence. In a sense, then, Plato's whole philosophy is situated *outside* and *above* the phenomenon of "the tragic."

redirects one's existence away from the realm of the "immediate" (the aesthetic, the physical and the mortal) towards the "absolute" (the ethical, the psychical and the immortal).[9] Since the unity of the tragic and the comic is used as the basis for the distinction between the "immediate" and the "absolute" realms of existence, I shall begin by showing how this idea (the unity of the tragic and the comic) appears in the speeches of Aristophanes and Agathon before proceeding to a discussion of how the movement from the "immediate" to the "absolute" takes place.[10]

We have already seen that Aristophanes credits Eros with "[curing] those ills we humans are most happy to have mended" (*Symposium*, 189d)—in other words, love cures the tragic element in human existence. The nature of our most painful ills are described by Aristophanes in the famous myth of the divided globular beings. In terms reminiscent of the biblical myth of original sin, Aristophanes relates that "Human Nature" was different "in the beginning" (*Symposium*, 189d): each human being was completely round, with eight limbs, two faces, and two sets of sexual organs. Individually and collectively, the humans were terrible in strength and power (*Symposium*, 190b). However, this state of affairs was not to last. The humans had great ambitions and made an assault on the gods (*Symposium*, 190b); the assault was unsuccessful and as punishment Zeus divided each human being in two.

---

[9]At this point it is probably a good idea to remind ourselves that this sentence does serious violence to the Platonic text if it is presented as a piece of Platonic scholarship. The reason for this is that the aesthetic, the ethical, and the religious are all part of the same package deal in Plato's philosophy. It is precisely one of Kierkegaard's great contributions to have distinguished sharply between these different spheres of existence while simultaneously identifying the imperative of combining these elements dynamically in a higher form of existence.

[10]For Plato dialectic is defined negatively in contradistinction to poetry, rhetoric and other "aesthetic" forms of speech; it is only when the similarities between different kinds of poetry (and between poetry and other kinds of "aesthetic" speech) have been grasped that one can progress to a "higher" form of thought and communication. For Kierkegaard the "religious contradiction" emerges from the unity of the tragic and the comic: a situation or relation (e.g., the relationship between Quidam and Quaedam) that appears tragic from one perspective can appear comic from another perspective, and it is only when these divergent perspectives merge in one's own life-view that one acquires the ground for progression to the religious form of life. Religiousness begins in the "higher passion" which chooses the tragic part out of this unity, since the choice based on this understanding indicates that one moved beyond the realm of aesthetic immediacy—it is an expression (sign) of a deep existential interest.

This division is the cause of the great desire each person has to be reunited with his or her own other half (*Symposium*, 191a), and love is another name given to this desire: "Love is born into every human being; it calls back the halves of our original nature together; it tries to make one out of two and heal the wound of human nature" (*Symposium*, 191d). Our greatest desire is to be as we were in the beginning—completely undivided, sharing one life with our other half—and if Hephaestus offered to weld two halves (lovers) together they would certainly accept the offer. But such total healing is out of the question given the nature of our punishment (*Symposium*, 192c-193b).

Ostensibly, then, Aristophanes affirms that loves cures the tragic, but a tragic element remains in his vision of healing: as divided globular beings we are always engaged in a quest to find our other half in order to find ultimate happiness and wholeness, but such union—if it takes place—is necessarily only temporary, given that Hephaestus never *actually* welds two lovers together for all eternity (*Symposium*, 191a-193a). Although love may therefore be said to cure the tragic, it is only a temporary cure, and this lack of finality and permanence (with the concomitant frustrated desire which is a permanent feature of the human condition) indicates a fundamentally tragic strand in Aristophanes' otherwise comic vision.

In Agathon's speech love appears to be a permanent cure of the tragic. When Eros came to be king among the gods, he says, everlasting peace and brotherhood resulted for both gods and men (*Symposium*, 195c); the regime of Necessity was replaced by a regime of Love, and "all goods came to gods and men alike through love of beauty" (*Symposium*, 197c). In some sense, then, Agathon's speech is more "comic" than that of Aristophanes. The underlying metaphysics in Agathon's speech indicates a steady state which has all the characteristics of a "happy ending," since love provides a permanent solution to "those ills we humans are most happy to have mended."

Two important things happen in these speeches. First, a relation between love and the tragic is posited, and, second, the unity of the tragic and the comic is suggested. The latter theme comes into sharp focus at the end of *Symposium*[11] where Socrates tries to prove to Agathon and Aristophanes that "authors should be able to write both comedy and tragedy: the skilful tragic dramatist should also be a comic poet" (*Symposium*, 223d). We are not given

[11]There is also a hint of the unity of the tragic and the comic at the beginning of the dialogue, i.e., in Glaucon's failed joke at *Symposium*, 172a.

the explicit argument for this claim, but Robert Wardy[12] argues (to my mind correctly) that Plato has implicitly (by means of example) demonstrated the argument in the speeches of Aristophanes and Agathon (which here represent the realm of "immediacy"). Although the speeches of both poets contain tragic as well as comic elements, the comic poet (Aristophanes) delivers a speech that is more tragic than comic, whilst that of the tragic poet (Agathon) is more comic than tragic (the overall metaphysical view in Agathon's speech is positive while that of Aristophanes is negative). Aristophanes warns the other participants against taking his speech as a comedy (*Symposium*, 189b, 193c); Agathon, on the other hand, indicates at the end of his speech that his purpose is not entirely serious: "Let [my speech] be dedicated to the god, part of it in fun, part of it moderately serious . . . " (*Symposium*, 197e-198a).

We turn now to the progression from "the immediate" to "the absolute," and we may indicate at least four moments in *Symposium* in which this movement may be said to occur.

The first moment occurs at *Symposium*, 198d, where Socrates says that "I realized how ridiculous I'd been to agree to join with you in praising Love and to say that I was a master of the art of love, when I knew nothing whatever of this business, of how anything whatever ought to be praised. In my foolishness, I thought *you should tell the truth* about whatever you praise, that this should be your basis . . . " (my emphasis). Using Kierkegaardian categories we can say that what Plato does here is to contrast rhetorical speeches—i.e., the realm of the "immediate" and the "aesthetic"—with a higher passion and a higher rationality that is somehow not "immediate" or "aesthetic." For Plato this higher passion and rationality is the "love of wisdom," or philosophy. Philosophy as higher passion and rationality is driven by a strong ethical dimension that distinguishes it from art: the imperative and the virtue of always telling the truth and not misleading others with regard to the best way to live.

The second moment occurs at *Symposium*, 204d-205a. Diotima begins with a question: what is the point of loving beautiful things? Socrates answers that we love them because we want to possess them. But Diotima isn't satisfied with this answer; she prompts Socrates to distinguish between the beautiful and the good: "Suppose someone changes the question, putting

---

[12]In his lectures on *Symposium* delivered in the Classics Faculty at the University of Cambridge (in the Lent terms of 1998 and 1999).

'good' in place of 'beautiful.' . . . " The point of this distinction is that beauty is not good in itself, and it is only when one possesses the good that one has *eudaemonia* (i.e., that one has reached the pinnacle of human well-being, happiness, and flourishing). What we have in this moment is therefore a prioritisation of the good (the realm of the ethical) over the beautiful (the realm of the aesthetic). This is graphically illustrated in Diotima's reference to Aristophanes' speech at *Symposium*, 205e: "'Now there is a certain story,' she said, 'according to which lovers are those people who seek their other halves. But according to my story, a lover does not seek the half or the whole, unless, my friend, it turns out to be good as well.'"

The third moment occurs at *Symposium*, 201a-212a, in Diotima's account of the "erotic ascent." It is possible to discern two main phases in the "erotic ascent." In the first phase (*Symposium*, 208e-209e) erotic energy is directed away from the realm of the female (or physical) towards that of the male (or psychical). The second phase (*Symposium*, 210a-212a) is characterized by an increasing refinement in the measure of abstraction of "the beautiful," starting with one particular beautiful body and ending with a conception of beauty as it is "itself by itself with itself" (*Symposium*, 211b), that is, "absolute, pure, unmixed, not polluted by human flesh or colors or any other great nonsense of mortality" (*Symposium*, 211e). The most significant element in the first phase is that the lover of beauty turns his attention away from women towards young men, since the realm of the female represents a lower form of immortality than that of the male. In the second phase the focus shifts away from bodies altogether (whether male or female) and comes to rest on psychic qualifications (first virtue, or beauty of soul, then beautiful laws and customs, then beautiful *logoi*, and finally absolute Beauty).[13] It is here, then, that we find the clearest account of the concept of "the absolute," and we may gather that philosophy culminates in the soul's discovery of, and participation in, this concept.

The fourth moment occurs at *Symposium*, 212c-223b, with the interruption of Alcibiades. From his speech and interaction with Socrates we deduce that the comic and tragic elements are also united in Alcibiades, but in a lower form than they are in Socrates, because they are united in a lower passion and rationality. Socrates is the paradigm of the "higher man" (or "truly

[13]It is important to note that these psychic qualifications are all confined to the realm of the masculine.

good man"[14]) towards which Alcibiades aspires (or rather, towards which he thinks it is in principle a good idea to aspire), but he is easily led astray by worldly pleasures, and it is a sign of his chthonic ("immediate") nature that he thinks he can exchange physical pleasure for the virtue of Socrates.

Two important elements emerge from the picture sketched thus far of the "Platonic project" (as represented also in *Symposium*). First, the realm of the body is identified with mortality ("mortal rubbish") and the susceptibility to the tragic element, whereas the realm of the soul is associated with the idea of immortality (since the Forms are unitary, incorporeal, immutable and eternal[15]) and hence with the only real possibility of an antidote to the tragic (although, as mentioned before, it is an open question of whether "the tragic" is even recognized or recognizable as such in this philosophy). Second, and following from the first, it seems that "the (human) other" *disappears* in the "erotic ascent." It is in the soul's love of philosophical wisdom, goodness and Beauty—independent of mortal, suffering bodies—that Plato locates the cure of the tragic.[16] These elements

---

[14]Cf. *Symposium*, 222a.

[15]Cf. Gregory Vlastos, *Platonic Studies* (Princeton: Princeton University Press, 1973; 2nd ed., 1981) 23-24.

[16]Cf. Plato, *Philebus*, 66c-67b. On the issue of whether Plato abandons the love for an individual other in favor of the love for an abstract idea(l) (Form), cf. the debate between Gregory Vlastos, "The individual as object of love in Plato's dialogues," *Platonic Studies*, 1-34, and Martha Nussbaum, who responds to Vlastos's position in *The Fragility of Goodness: Luck and Ethics and Greek Tragedy and Philosophy* (Cambridge: Cambridge University Press, 1986; repr. 1988) 165-99. According to Vlastos, "Plato is scarcely aware of kindness, tenderness, compassion, concern for the freedom, respect for the integrity of the beloved, as essential ingredients of the highest type of interpersonal love"; and: "[Plato's theory] does not provide for love of whole persons, but only for love of that abstract version of persons which consists of the complex of their best qualities. This is the reason why personal affection ranks so low in Plato's *scala amoris*. When loved as congeries of valuable qualities, persons cannot compete with abstractions of universal significance, like schemes of social reform or scientific and philosophical truths, still less with the Idea of Beauty in its sublime transcendence. . . . The high climactic moment of fulfillment—the peak achievement for which all lesser loves are to be 'used as steps'—is the one farthest removed from affection for concrete human beings" ("The individual as object of love in Plato's dialogues," 32, 33). Nussbaum argues that this interpretation is wrong on the grounds that the "interruption of Alcibiades" is actually a vivid demonstration of how one person (Alcibiades) loves the whole being of another person (Socrates), and that Plato may actually be chastising his mentor (Socrates) for radically misunderstanding the nature of love. Personally I do not think that either Vlastos or Nussbaum is entirely correct in their interpretations. Vlastos fails to take Plato's use of indirect communication into account and hence is blind to the

are challenged and transfigured in Kierkegaard's treatment of our title question, to which we now turn.

3. The Question of Whether Love Cures the Tragic in Stages on Life's Way

In the previous section we saw that tragedy, and the realm of the "immediate" in general, is criticized and devalued in the "Platonic project" on the grounds of the (supposed) superiority of the categories of "the absolute" and the "philosophical" (or "ethical"). In this section we shall see Kierkegaard go one step further than Plato by exposing the shortcomings of the category of "the ethical" in the light of the category of "the religious." A "religious" response to the vulnerability and suffering of existing, temporal bodies requires that the soul not retreat (by means of the "erotic ascent") into its self-sufficient realm of "immortality" to the detriment and exclusion of "the (human) other" (or "neighbor"). Instead, the religious imperative commands that one pursue the "erotic ascent" (or what we may call the "love of God") and the "erotic descent" (i.e., the love of the other or neighbor) simultaneously towards the limit.

In the religious life-view it is no longer true that the soul's independent pursuit of the absolute implies total recovery (separation) from the tragic. Rather, the "religious contradiction" consists in the fact that one is suffering and yet joyful at the same time, as Frater Taciturnus explains:

> There are three existence-spheres: the aesthetic, the ethical, the religious. . . . The aesthetic sphere is the sphere of immediacy, the ethical the sphere of requirement (and this requirement is so infinite that the individual always goes bankrupt), the religious the sphere of fulfilment, but, please note, not a fulfilment such as when one fills an alms box or a sack with gold, for repentance has specifically

---

fact that Plato *problematizes* the nature of love and beauty (whether it is abstract—as Diotima would have us believe—or concretely present in the person of Socrates). Nussbaum gets part of the problematizing issue right but then errs in completely misunderstanding the figure of Alcibiades, whom she credits with loving Socrates as a particular, whole person, for what he is in himself. This is wrong because Alcibiades does *not* have a firm grip on what Socrates is really about, and it is clear from the dialogue that he cannot love Socrates as an equal. I even suspect that Alcibiades *cannot* do what Nussbaum credits him with: he does not *love* Socrates as a unique and exemplary human being *in the right way*, and this is part of what Plato is urging us to see. Alcibiades rather reminds us of the fickle figure of Dionysius (cf. Plato, *Letter VII*).

> created a boundless space, and as a consequence the religious contradiction: simultaneously to be out on 70,000 fathoms of water and yet be joyful. (SLW, 476-77)

We see here that the "religious contradiction" emerges from the unity of the tragic and the comic. This idea is explained further in our next passage, where Frater Taciturnus writes as follows about Quidam:

> The male character in the imaginary construction . . . sees the comic, but not as a seasoned observer sees it. He sees the comic and with this fortifies himself for the tragic. It is this in particular that engages me, for this serves to illuminate the religious. Paganism culminates in the mental fortitude to see the comic and the tragic simultaneously in the same thing. In the higher passion, which chooses the tragic part of this unity, religiousness begins—that is, the religiousness for which immediacy is over. . . . (SLW, 422)

According to Frater Taciturnus, then, Plato's *Symposium* in some sense represents the culmination of "paganism," for it is there that we witness for the first time "the mental fortitude to see the comic and the tragic simultaneously in the same thing." Furthermore, such mental fortitude is a necessary but not a sufficient condition to progress to true religiousness. In order to attain to true religiousness, it is also necessary to *choose the tragic* out of the unity of the tragic and the comic, and to do so in a "higher passion." (We may note that the "higher passion" of the "religious" is here explicitly posited as *higher* than the passionate love of wisdom that underlies the "mental fortitude" of the Platonic philosopher.)

The fact that "the mental fortitude to see the comic and the tragic simultaneously in the same thing" is not a sufficient condition for progression to true religiousness is clarified in the realization that the unity of the comic and the tragic is the point of departure for *all* the authors of *Stages on Life's Way*.[17] What differentiates them is their *reaction* to this unity, where each individual's response is determined by his position on the spectrum that stretches from "the aesthetic" ("the immediate"), through "the philosophical" (or "ethical"), to "the religious." Thus the aesthetes of "In Vino Veritas," who represent the realm of "immediacy," choose the comic out of the unity of the tragic and the comic; Judge William, who represents the ethical realm, lives in the unity of the tragic and the comic, as it were, and holds back from taking the leap into "the religious" (cf. SLW, 169-84); Quidam vacillates

[17]Cf. e.g. SLW, 38, 50-51.

between the tragic and the comic: although he tends in the direction of the tragic he fails to make the resolution of choosing the tragic, and consequently he identifies himself as a religious character, or, rather, as "a regular and perfectly constructed possibility of such a person" (SLW, 257; cf. SLW, 422). It is important to note, however, that each of these characters in some sense fails to conform completely to (or live up to the standards of) the category which he is supposed to (or tries to) instantiate.

Three preliminary observations are in order at this point. First, it must be remembered throughout that each author writes against the background of the unity of the tragic and the comic (and in a sense lives in this unity), so that when something is said about love we may legitimately ask whether what is said is presented as a *cure* for a (partly) tragic (modern) human condition. Second, it is to be expected that the question of whether love cures the tragic will appear quite differently depending on whether it is viewed from the aesthetic, the ethical or the religious perspective. Third, an important difference between *Symposium* and *Stages on Life's Way* appears in the fact that the question of whether love cures the tragic is in the latter text always considered in terms of the relation between man and woman.[18] This dimension (somewhat clouded in Plato's text) comes into focus as a result of the "erotic descent," which in turn is set in motion by the discovery of the category of "the religious."[19]

---

[18]Already in the speeches of the aesthetes we detect a reversal in the order of the "erotic ascent" as described by Diotima. Constantin Constantius proposes that the subject of the speeches be "erotic love or the relation between man and woman" (SLW, 30-31); the Young Man says that by "love," "I understand here the relation between man and woman and am not thinking of Eros in the Greek sense, for example, as so beautifully eulogized by Plato, but with him it was so far from being a matter of loving women that this is mentioned only in passing and is even considered to be imperfect in comparison with loving young men" (SLW, 33). Thus woman is placed back on the agenda of erotic, philosophic and religious discourse in *Stages on Life's Way*.

[19]The kind of "protofeminism" in evidence here is prefigured in *Symposium* by the fact that Diotima is a woman (not to mention a stranger and a prophetess). (I use "feminism" to refer only to that kind of consciousness that is minimally committed to questioning received conceptions concerning woman's—usually inferior—moral and political status in relation to man.) It is surely significant that philosophy receives its legitimizing *logos* (the vision of absolute Beauty that justifies its existence) from a woman. Gregory Vlastos adopts another definition of feminism in his treatment of the question "Was Plato a Feminist?" in *Feminist Interpretations of Plato,* ed. Nancy Tuana (University Park: Pennsylvania State University Press, 1994) 11-23.

Stages on Life's Way picks up on the question of whether love cures the tragic where the *Symposium* had left off (i.e., at the "erotic descent" which emerged from the unity of the tragic and the comic), but now there is no convergence on the result that love cures the tragic (as there had seemed to be in the latter text). The aesthetes of "In Vino Veritas" deny that love can cure the tragic (for various reasons); Judge William vows that it does and elaborates on the virtues and value of marriage; Quidam's Diary presents us with a complex situation in which love is avowed as a real possibility, but is then shown to manifest itself in different forms (the aesthetic and the religious), so that its inner experience (in the religious form) may ironically result in (or necessitate) the opposite outer expression, and so in one sense lead deeper into the tragic. Let us consider these in turn.

There are five speakers at the banquet: the Young Man, Constantin Constantius, Victor Eremita, the Fashion Designer, and Johannes the Seducer. The speeches of these "aesthetes" do not fit clearly into any of the categories outlined in *Stages on Life's Way*, however. We can see that the aesthetes of "In Vino Veritas" (as elsewhere in Kierkegaard's writings) are much too reflective simply to be classified as belonging to the category of "immediacy": they are themselves critical of many of the institutions, prejudices and presuppositions of "immediacy" and "finite common sense" as contained, for example, in "bourgeois-philistintism" (cf. FT, 38-39). Rather, they are hyper-reflective to the point of being "demonic" (cf. SLW, 436-37): they remain on the border between the aesthetic and the ethical spheres, and refrain from entering the ethical precisely in order to make fun of ethics. We can get a better idea of their position when we look forward to the *Concluding Unscientific Postscript* where Climacus writes that "The spheres are related as follows: immediacy, finite common sense; irony,

---

According to Vlastos, feminism consists in the requirement that "Equality in the [legal, social, economic and moral] rights of persons shall not be denied or abridged on account of sex," and on the grounds of this definition he argues that it would take at least four distinct propositions to formulate an answer to the question of whether Plato was a feminist: "(1) In the ideally best society outlined in books IV to VII of the *Republic* the position of the women in its ruling elite, the so-called guardians, is unambiguously feminist. (2) In that same society the position of the great majority of its free women, composing its industrial and agricultural class, is unambiguously antifeminist. (3) In the alternative, second-best society laid out in the *Laws*, the position of free women is a hybrid, feminist in some respects, antifeminist in others. (4) In his personal attitude to the women in his own contemporary Athens Plato is virulently antifeminist" ("Was Plato a Feminist?" 11-12).

ethics with irony as its incognito; humor; religiousness with humor as its incognito—and then, finally, the essentially Christian, distinguished by the paradoxical accentuation of existence, by the paradox, by the break with immanence, and by the absurd" (CUP, 1:531-32; cf. SLW, 476-77). We may gather from this that the aesthetes are *romantic ironists*: they are detached both from the world of immediate (traditional, received) morality as well as from the world of considered (reflected) moral commitment.

The aesthetes—as a company of confirmed, conspiratorial bachelors[20]—are all pessimists about love and thereby implicitly deny that it can cure the tragic. Fundamental to their understanding of the relation between man and woman is that woman has her existence in the realm of "immediacy" while the function of the man is to express "the absolute."[21] Woman is an aesthetic, relational and irrational creature and hence incapable of conceiving or expressing the absolute. This difference between man and woman is the cause of them fundamentally misunderstanding and misrelating to each other, which means that love is impossible.[22] It is ironic, however, and a token of their moral hypocrisy, that the aesthetes themselves fail to express "the absolute." Their failure in this regard is due to the fact that their existence is confined within the realm of their own narcissism. From the Young Man's speech we may infer that what he loves above all else is himself (perhaps he finally loves *only* himself), and this applies to the aesthetes *in toto*.[23] Consequently they remain stuck in "immediacy" insofar as they desire (in their nihilistic, romantic despair) to recapture the bliss of "immediacy" rather than to move to a higher level of existence which assumes the difficult task of expressing "the absolute" in existence.

For Judge William love finds fulfilment in the institution of marriage, where the immediate aesthetic erotic is transformed into a higher expression of love: the security of mutual care and sympathy (SLW, 93, 100). Marriage, according to the Judge, is the absolute meaning and highest *telos* of life (SLW, 101) because it is only in married love—which appears in the form of an absolute commitment to one's partner—that "the tragic" (understood here as suffering in solitude and wasting one's life in trivialities) is

---

[20]There is some suggestion that they are the same collection of individuals identified as the *Symparanekromenoi* in *Either/Or*, I. Cf. SLW, 49, 73, 82.

[21]Cf. e.g. SLW, 46, 48-49, 51-52, 60-62, 64-67, 71, 76, 79-80.

[22]Except, of course, in the case of the Seducer, but his conception of erotic love is the opposite of the ethical conception which demands transparency and equality.

[23]Cf. e.g. SLW, 45-46.

sufficiently and permanently cured. Marriage, he says, "rests in understanding of and feeling for the deep pain of all life" (SLW, 118), and it is precisely by virtue of the fact that in marriage the daily sufferings and burdens of life are *shared* (in like-mindedness and care) that the pain of both partners is alleviated and their joy increased (SLW, 183).

However, the Judge also fails to live up to the standards of the category ("the ethical") which he tries to instantiate. The reason for this conclusion can be traced to the fact that he posits no essential equality between the sexes in the *ethical* sphere, but only in the aesthetic and the religious spheres (SLW, 167-68). The Judge agrees with the aesthetes insofar as they all consider woman incapable of reflection (cf. SLW, 166), and it is this incapacity for reflection that defines her as essentially an *amoral* being. This understanding of woman's "nature" makes an entrenched patriarchal, patronizing attitude towards her obligatory and almost a virtue. No wonder, then, that the Judge's understanding of the religious begins to ring hollow when sounded against Quidam's understanding of it. Thus, although love may be said to cure the tragic in the Judge's life-view, it is a cure acquired ultimately at the expense of woman's ethical equality and spiritual development, and hence it fails the test of the ethical-religious.[24] Just as the Judge had implicitly indicted the aesthetes' hypocrisy by saying that "to use ethical categories to insult or at least to want to insult woman is not exactly the mark of an ethical individuality" (SLW, 145; cf. SLW, 48), so Quidam's conception and attempted implementation of the religious imperative

---

[24]That is to say, the criterion of what qualifies as truly ethical-religious in *Stages on Life's Way* develops in the direction of spiritual equality: everyone, regardless of sex, has the ability to become a self in the strong sense. This is seen retrospectively from Quidam's Diary where the inner dialectic of the book has worked itself into a dilemma in this regard: on the one hand Quidam believes that everyone is in principle capable of being spiritually equal; on the other hand he is confronted with the disquieting truth (which emerges when he tries to implement his ideal principle in the actual world and then realizes that there is a discontinuity between these two worlds) that spiritual development is not an inevitable fact but a strenuous, often painful, lifelong task which may not fit in with everyone's idea of a good life. The dilemma is whether it is justified to intervene in someone else's state of blissful ignorance (although the superficial appearance of happiness may belie a deeper state of inner despair), or whether it is better to make them as comfortable as possible in their state of "immediacy."

exposes the lacunae in the Judge's understanding, not only regarding the concept of the religious, but also in terms of the ethical.[25]

Quidam's understanding of the ethical-religious imperative may be illuminated with reference to Johannes Climacus's definition of the ethical task in *Concluding Unscientific Postscript*. Climacus defines the ethical task as "truly to exist," and this requires that one express the eternal and the temporal simultaneously in existence (CUP, 1:308). In order to give both these elements their due it is necessary to "die to immediacy," the reason being that the pull of "immediacy" leads one into the "deepest despair" and thereby prevents one from relating properly to both the eternal ("the absolute") and the temporal (CUP, 1:460-63, 499). The task, then, "is simultaneously to relate oneself absolutely to the absolute *telos* [i.e., one's eternal happiness] and relatively to relative ends" (CUP, 1:431). The absolute goal may therefore not be pursued to the detriment or exclusion of relative ends (i.e., the projects, relationships and values that identify us as temporal social-cultural and political-economic beings and direct our moral actions[26]). The most adequate expression for the ethical-religious imperative, therefore, is that *one must pursue the absolute end (absolutely) and the relative ends (relatively) simultaneously towards the limit.* And this is precisely what Quidam tries to do.

Quidam's situation is as follows: his "absolute *telos*" is his God-relationship (SLW, 222), and the most significant "relative end" he is pursuing is his relationship with Quaedam. We can see immediately why the Judge's template of "earthbound" absolute commitment will not fit the case of Quidam. For Quidam marriage isn't and cannot be the highest *telos* of life, because the highest purpose of life is to express "the absolute" in religious

---

[25]This is not to suggest that Quidam's concept of the religious passes the test of equality between the sexes, but only that spiritual equality—which Quidam identifies as the "vital force" of his existence (SLW, 315)—is noticeably absent in Judge William's conception of ethics. Sylvia Walsh, "Issues that Divide: Interpreting Kierkegaard on Woman and Gender," in *Kierkegaard Revisited*, ed. Niels Jørgen Cappelørn and Jon Stewart (Berlin: Walter de Gruyter, 1997) 203, argues that Quidam resembles the Judge and Johannes the Seducer in his deprecation of woman's reflective ability and that this compromises his claim of an essential equality between the sexes at the ethical-religious level. Later on in the article I will argue for a qualification of Walsh's argument.

[26]On the role and place of personal projects in Kierkegaard's moral philosophy, cf. Anthony Rudd, *Kierkegaard and the Limits of the Ethical* (Oxford: Clarendon Press, 1993; pbk. repr., 1997) 81-114.

passion and inwardness (i.e., in his relationship with God). Marriage in the context of the religious is possible only if it is contracted between "true minds," that is, if both individuals, in complete spiritual equality and mutual understanding, relate absolutely to their absolute ends and relatively to their relative ends. However, a problem arises if a dissymmetry exists between two lovers in this regard. If one person in a relationship endeavors to fulfil the religious demand whilst the other partner has no intimation of the existence of such a "higher life" (thus remaining in either the aesthetic or the ethical sphere), then this will create a fundamental misunderstanding between them.[27] This latter scenario applies in Quidam's relationship with Quaedam and constitutes the origin of his dilemma.

Quidam's ethical-religious task may be defined as follows: *pursue the "erotic ascent" and the "erotic descent" simultaneously towards the limit.* He endeavors to fulfil this task, but an obstacle appears in the form of the kind of fundamental misunderstanding described above. Consequently he is forced to make a tragic choice: *either* God *or* the woman he loves "religiously" (but who reciprocates his love in an "aesthetic" manner). Such a choice would be inconceivable to the Judge, but it happens in Quidam's case precisely because Quidam applies the ethical category to woman as though she were (or ought to be) a moral, intellectual and spiritual being of equal standing with himself. He considers it his duty to love her as he loves himself, but the fact that she has no religious presuppositions means that they cannot meet as equals in the religious sphere of existence (SLW, 239, 315). And since he cannot love her if he deceives her (i.e., if he lies about his own feelings and religious orientation), he decides to leave her in the hope that she will find happiness with someone else (SLW, 377-78).

But does this really indicate that there is a kind of "protofeminism" at work in the text? This question opens up a treacherous bit of territory and it is worth going on a short digression in order to get clarity of what is at stake. I will start by stating a view from the scholarship that differs from my own. In her overview of Kierkegaard's thoughts on woman and gender, Sylvia Walsh[28] claims that "Quidam's motive in *eliminating* woman's reflective capacity, like that of Johannes the Seducer's in *developing* it, may be

---

[27]It is worth noting that the model here needn't be defined in terms of the relation between man and woman, but may be generalized to any relationship in which there is ethical-religious disparity.

[28]Walsh, "Issues that Divide," 191-205.

suspected of being self-serving rather than self-sacrificing, enabling him to get out of a love relation that cannot be consummated in marriage. . . ."[29]

I want to suggest that we qualify Walsh's reading of Quidam. Quidam is not merely concerned about his own welfare (as the aesthetes are): he also wants what is best for Quaedam (cf. SLW, 246, 331-32, 339). However, he fears that the absolute best (religious reflectiveness) may be out of her reach since she doesn't possess the necessary predisposition to reflectiveness and concludes on this basis that she (and he, as far as she is concerned) would have to be content with second best: being as happy as she can in her "immediate" state of existence (his project of curing her of limited reflectiveness is aimed at bringing about this result). Although Quidam's belief that Quaedam doesn't possess the necessary predilection for reflection is arguably linked to her being a *woman*, I think it is closer to the truth to say that it has more to do with the *particular kind of individual* that Quaedam actually is. Thus, if the relationship had been a friendship between two men, rather than a proposed marriage between a man and a woman, a similar situation could have arisen, and this is why I have suggested that we would understand the whole situation better if we consider its analogy with the relation between Socrates and Alcibiades in *Symposium*. What is at stake is *the problem* of how to relate to someone who is on a different (lower) spiritual plane than oneself: whether it is patronizing to suppose that all should be equal in the religious sphere of existence, or patronizing *not* to, etc. A great anxiety attends Quidam's consideration of these problems—an anxiety which wouldn't have been present if he was *merely* self-serving. Ironically it is precisely the fact that these problems are considered in the context of the relation between the sexes that gives us the most reason to suppose that a kind of "protofeminism" is at work in the text: it was Kierkegaard, after all, who placed woman back on the map vis-à-vis the *Symposium*. This at least creates the problem of *how* woman is to be rewoven into the text of ethical-religious discourse, even if it does not (or cannot) ultimately solve this problem.[30]

---

[29]Walsh, "Issues that Divide," 204.

[30]Another way to view Kierkegaard's "protofeminism" in *Stages on Life's Way* is to juxtapose a few quotes from the text. Consider the motto (by Lichtenberg)—"Such works are mirrors: when an ape looks in, no apostle can look out" (SLW, 8)—in conjunction with a number of passages from the Fashion Designer's speech: "in a short time every woman is going to be made a fanatic by the demented and defiling mirrored image of fashion, which corrupts her in quite another way than

The ethical-religious misunderstanding and misrelation that results from Quidam's problematic attempt to implement the "erotic descent" creates a situation that is simultaneously tragic and comic and, as we have seen, it is the ability to see the comic and the tragic as simultaneously present in the same situation which constitutes the grounds for progression to the religious (via the "erotic ascent") (cf. SLW, 366-67).

"The comic" and "the tragic" are united in the relationship between Quidam and Quaedam (a situation, as mentioned already, that is prefigured in the relationship between Socrates and Alcibiades). As Frater Taciturnus explains, "The tragic is that two lovers do not understand each other; the comic is that two who do not understand each other love each other" (SLW, 421). From one perspective, then, it appears that "love" does not cure "the tragic" for Quidam. But from another perspective it appears that this was not real ("religious") love at all, the reason being that Quaedam is trapped in a similar kind of "aesthetic" self-love which characterized the aesthetes of "In Vino Veritas." She doesn't understand or care about the ethical-religious requirement of self-resignation which is a precondition for the emergence of

---

if she were seduced" (SLW, 70); "Do you understand my view of woman? Everything in life is a matter of fashion; the fear of God is a matter of fashion, and love and hoopskirts and a ring in the nose" (SLW, 71); "Woman does have spirit, but it is invested just about as well as the prodigal son's resources" (SLW, 67). I read this as Kierkegaard's way of holding up a mirror to woman and challenging her to see herself as an "ape" that is being led about (through a ring in the nose) by manipulative, immoral men, and that the task before her is to "invest" her "spirit" more wisely: to exist in the eminent sense and to become a self. Anyone with "spirit" in Kierkegaard's sense is bound to take up this challenge and this may have been part of his design/intention. What Kierkegaard also brings to our attention in the Fashion Designer's speech is the dissymmetry in the social substructures which inform the everyday interactions between men and women (which dissymmetry precipitates the emergence of a phenomenon like fashion), and this makes us realize that what may be required for women to achieve equality is precisely a revolution in these underlying structures (although the equality here would be formal rather than inevitable in one's spiritual progression). From Walsh's account it seems unlikely that Kierkegaard himself considered such a feminist revolution to be a good thing (although perhaps not going as far as Judge William, who threatened to weep in public if this ever occurred—cf. EO, 2:22, 311). However, the structure and presentation of the text as a whole seems to necessitate the asking of those very uncomfortable questions that Walsh indeed asks in her treatment of the question, which is why I would defend the appellation "*proto*feminism."

love in its authentic religious form (SLW, 435-36; cf. WL, 55-56; JP, 4:4603).

Quidam's sympathetic overidentification with Quaedam "[disturbs] his integration of himself in repentance" (SLW, 436), which means that he, like the other authors of *Stages on Life's Way*, fails to instantiate the category he aspires to. His failure is due to the fact that he does not make the religious resolution: at the point of decision he becomes dialectical because of Quaedam (SLW, 426, 436), and this defines him as a "demonic figure oriented to the religious" (SLW, 436, 484). As Frater Taciturnus points out, however, it is not the dialectical *per se* that makes a person "demonic," but *remaining* in the dialectical (SLW, 436-37).

Judged from the aesthetic perspective, then, love does not cure the tragic for Quidam. But from the religious perspective the "love" between Quidam and Quaedam was not really love at all. In the higher ("religious") perspective, love is reborn as the best *response* to the reality of the tragic. Love (in the religious sense) is the redemption *of* (not *from*) the tragic (i.e., it "buys back" the suffering of existence). This indicates a dialectic between "love" and "the tragic": since the choice of "the tragic" out of the unity of the tragic and the comic in a "higher passion" is a precondition for the emergence of true religiousness, it follows that (the choice *for*) the recognition of suffering is in an important sense a precondition for the emergence of authentic (religious) love.

Conclusion

In this article I have endeavored to trace the interpretation of the question of whether love cures the tragic in the framework of the constellation of relations described in the Introduction—a framework that is suggested by the intertextual relation between *Symposium* and *Stages on Life's Way*. We have seen that Plato and Kierkegaard agree insofar as both proceed from the unity of the tragic and the comic—which unity marks the break with the sphere of "immediacy"—in the direction of "the absolute." For Plato this "absolute" is attainable via philosophical dialectic and the "erotic ascent," and consequently the "love of wisdom" may be said to effect a cure for what is truly tragic: neglecting the greatest goods of one's soul. *Stages on Life's Way* goes through these two turns (the aesthetic and the ethical) and then adds a third: "the religious." The religious imperative commands the pursuit of the "erotic ascent" and the "erotic descent" simultaneously towards the limit.

The question of whether love cures the tragic appears as a problem in the ethical-religious sphere when the self discovers the (significant) other in his or her uniqueness, vulnerability and potential spiritual equality, but then at the same time encounters (1) a disparity in their spiritual development and (2) the demands of the absolute. This situation is simultaneously comic and tragic—that is, "comic-tragic" (SLW, 420)—and in the higher passion that chooses the tragic out of this unity, true religiousness begins, and with it, the possibility for the emergence of true (religious) love.

Another important question remains concerning the relation between man and woman. For all his good intentions, Quidam still conceives of woman as intellectually inferior, which is evidenced by the fact that he can find consolation in the thought that "infinite reflection is not essential for woman" (SLW, 306). We see, then, that Quidam is torn between viewing reflection as inessential to woman and wanting her to exist on an equal spiritual plane with himself, and in this "tornness" we can see the germ of a kind of "protofeminism" at work in the text.

A further important question that remains to be answered is whether one has a *duty* to disturb others in their "aesthetic immediacy" in order to awaken them to the possibility of living in a higher realm of existence, or whether Quidam is right in letting Quaedam remain in her ignorant, blissful—and yet (from the "higher" Socratic perspective) essentially "tragic"—state.

These problems—including the question of whether love cures the tragic—are not finally solved in the text of *Stages on Life's Way* itself, with the result that we have to look elsewhere—both to our own (ethical) reflections and to other Kierkegaardian texts (e.g. *Works of Love*)—for further possible clues. This lack of finality notwithstanding, what has been established in this article is the outline of a new paradigm for reading *Stages on Life's Way*. This paradigm is especially significant for the interpretation of Kierkegaard's concept of the religious, which is here seen to be directed not only towards "the absolute," but also towards the moral well-being of "the other" (or "neighbor").

4

The Equivocal Judge William: Comparing the Ethical in Kierkegaard's Stages on Life's Way *and* Either/Or

Paul Martens

Johannes Climacus, in an appendix in *Concluding Unscientific Postscript*, reviews the writings of Kierkegaard's previously published pseudonyms. He notices that, with the publication of *Stages on Life's Way*, there appears to be some sort of repetition of *Either/Or*. Although the apparent editors of these two books are not the same, the names of many of the characters within are the same, and on the surface it appears the characters are saying the same thing in both books. Climacus, however, is subtle enough to notice that this may have been a ploy by the author of the later book, *Stages on Life's Way*, to evade the "inquisitive public" (CUP, 1:284-86). Making the comparison to *Either/Or*, Climacus recognizes that many of the "inquisitive public" have concluded that the two books are essentially the same.

In reality, Climacus is not as foolish as the public. He concludes that the most attentive reader hardly will find "a single phrase, a single turn of thought or language, as it was in *Either/Or*" (CUP, 1:287). The differences are imbedded in the details, yet also obvious on the surface. For example, there are only two parts to *Either/Or*, while there are three in *Stages on Life's Way*. Stephen Crites, in the essay entitled "Pseudonymous Authorship as Art and as Act," succinctly affirms Climacus's judgement by stating, "If the matter were put to argument, though, I should wish to argue that the surface similarities of *Either/Or* and *Stages* are altogether deceptive, and that the dialectical tensions of the two works are in fact quite different."[1]

---

[1]Stephen Crites, "Pseudonymous Authorship as Art and as Act," in *Kierkegaard: A Collection of Critical Essays*, ed. Josiah Thompson (New York: Anchor Books, 1972) 203-204.

Kierkegaard's own cryptic remarks, however, do not seem to fully endorse a complete differentiation between the two books. In a journal entry from 1845, while considering specific aspects of *Stages on Life's Way*, he states, "It is exactly the same as *Either/Or*." Later in the same entry, he emphatically states, "*Three Stages and yet one Either/Or*" (JP, 5:5805). Certainly, it might be argued that this journal entry should not speak for the entirety of either book. However, it does remind us that Kierkegaard himself thought there were important parallels.

The question of the precise nature of the relationship between the two is left up to us, as readers, to ponder. The conclusion drawn by Climacus on this matter simply is that the inadequacy of *Either/Or* rests in the fact that it ends ethically. This is pointed out and resolved in *Stages on Life's Way* with the introduction of the religious in its own place (CUP, 1:294). Although this explanation appears sufficient at first, it does not really provide a harmonious resolution to the other differences that appear.[2] Despite Climacus's assurance, there are many questions that beg to be answered: Does *Either/Or*, in fact, end ethically? What role, in *Stages on Life's Way*, does the ethical have in putting the religious in its own place? Is the change from the aesthetic to the ethical the same in both writings? These, and many others, have not been answered by Climacus.

Although the following article cannot provide a comprehensive analysis of the relationship between the two books, it will focus on one of the stages of life, the ethical, to begin to illuminate the broader relationship; it will attempt to demonstrate a significant change within the life-view of Judge William between the writing of his first letters to A published as *Either/Or*, Part II, and the later "Reflections on Marriage" published in *Stages on Life's Way*. In order to accomplish this comparative task, the ethical point of view established in the latter will serve as the primary focus. Three subdivisions of the ethical stage will be posited to illuminate the fullness of the ethical in this consideration: (1) the relation between the aesthetic and the ethical; (2) the maintenance of the ethical life; and (3) the relation between the ethical and the religious.[3] The description of the ethical life in *Stages on Life's Way*, however, will continually be informed by, and compared to, the earlier

---

[2]Climacus goes on to attempt to explain the differences between the stages in terms of his own interests, that of existence-positions (CUP, 1:295).

[3]Obviously, many aspects of the ethical encompass more than one of these categories. However, examined in this way, the dynamic nature of the "intermediate" stage of existence will be highlighted.

writings of the Judge in *Either/Or*.[4] In this way, not only will a comprehensive analysis of the ethical stage of life as described in *Stages on Life's Way* be articulated, but the similarities and differences between the two sets of writings will also emerge sharply. From this analysis, it will become apparent that there are several pivotal differences that illustrate a change in the entire shape of the Judge's later life-view. I suggest that the best way to understand these changes is to see them as a narrowing of the ethical, particularly in its relation to the religious. To conclude, then, several questions will be posed regarding the possible link between the Judge's change of mind and the development, following 1843, of Kierkegaard's own understanding of the ethical life-view and its relation to the religious.

The Relation between the Aesthetic and the Ethical

For Judge William, the relationship between the aesthetic and ethical is a rather tumultuous affair. Right from the start, erotic love and marriage are shown in antithesis: erotic love has the god of Eros; marriage has the God of Christianity.[5] Rooted in the diverse relations to the divine are other serious differences: erotic love is poetic psychical immediacy; marriage is dutiful spiritual resolution (SLW, 99-101). A harsher juxtaposition is difficult to imagine. However, in familiar Kierkegaardian dialectical fashion, this is not the end of the relationship.

With the resounding clash of opposition still ringing in our ears, the Judge suggests another point of view on the aesthetic. Far from denigrating erotic love, it is assumed as a given (SLW, 123). The Judge accepts it as the god's gift and gives thanks to the god for the gift (SLW, 121-22), for "first

---

[4]Although I recognize that there is ongoing discussion surrounding the impact of Kant on Kierkegaard's ethics, only a sidelong (but nonetheless watchful) glance will be cast in that direction for the purposes of this paper. I intend to stick closely to the discussion between the "two Judges."

[5]It is important to note that the Judge usually speaks strictly of erotic love [*Elskov*] and marriage. These are somewhat equivocally related to the aesthetic and the ethical for there certainly are times when the Judge suggests that the aesthetic and the ethical categories encompass a much larger sphere than just love and marriage. Further, there are times when the Judge speaks particularly about marriage and not the ethical life, such as some of his comments on the specific roles of women and men. However, as is usually practiced, most references to the relation between erotic love (also called first or romantic love) and marriage will be understood metaphorically to illuminate the relationship between the broader categories of the aesthetic and the ethical.

things must still always come first" (SLW, 120). Similar sentiments are found in *Either/Or*. The Judge goes as far as to state that erotic love is the real constituting element of marriage (EO, 2:32). In fact, his task in writing to the aesthete is "to show that romantic love can be united with and exist in marriage—indeed, that marriage is its true transfiguration" (EO, 2:31).[6] Recognizing that the god of erotic love is still Eros, the Judge appears to affirm and appropriate love's goodness. He goes even as far as requiring erotic love as the antecedent to marriage.

Implicit in all the Judge's praise for erotic love, however, is the need for transformation. Erotic love cannot persist according to the aesthete's preferences; it must be baptized into marriage. For the Judge, marriage is the highest *telos* of individual life and it simply cannot be evaded (SLW, 101). Articulating the transition not only draws out the ethical failures of the aesthetic but also points to the positive content of the ethical life-view. In *Stages on Life's Way*, the key to moving into marriage is resolution. "[R]esolution is the triumphant victor who, like Orpheus, fetches the infatuation of falling in love to the light of day, for the resolution is the true form of love, the true explanation and transfiguration," exclaims the Judge in one of his more poetic moments (SLW, 117).

Marriage is not written on a blank slate. The resolution of marriage does not want to invalidate erotic love. It presupposes love (SLW, 147, 157). Marriage is based on resolution, but resolution is not the direct result of the immediacy of erotic love; it must be chosen freely (SLW, 102). Resolution is what is present from the beginning in marriage and its introduction into erotic love transforms everything. In the face of abstraction, it brings concretion (SLW, 104); in the face of suspense, it brings happiness (SLW, 108); in the face of necessity, it brings freedom (SLW, 111). When the abyss of the eternal opens, resolution spans the temporal and the eternal, securely embracing them both (SLW, 112). In short, a person's total ideality lies first and last in resolution (SLW, 108). The process and content of resolution will be more fully discussed in the next section addressing the ethical life itself,

---

[6]In *Either/Or*, the Judge makes use of the concept of "concentricity" as one of the ways to describe the relation between the aesthetic and the ethical. First love is drawn into the higher concentricity of marriage through the work of willing (EO, 2:47). Sylvia Walsh has excellently shown in detail how the aesthetic and the ethical are brought together in *Either/Or* by the Judge in *Living Poetically: Kierkegaard's Existential Aesthetics* (University Park: Pennsylvania State University Press, 1994) 99-125.

but for this discussion, it is important to recognize that there is only one path from the aesthetic to the ethical in *Stages on Life's Way*: resolution.

Implicit in the Judge's understanding of resolution is the notion of willful choice, yet when he once, and only once, describes the need "to choose oneself," he somewhat ironically includes the parenthetical comment that "it is my favorite category and encompasses an individual's existence" (SLW, 121). One is immediately directed back to *Either/Or* where the Judge often communicates that "to choose is an intrinsic and stringent term for the ethical" (EO, 2:166). Aside from this explicit link, however, the Judge's portrayal of the movement from the aesthetic to the ethical in *Either/Or* follows a somewhat different path than that of resolution alone.

In *Either/Or*, the aesthete is faced with the choice: either good and evil or rule them both out (EO, 2:169).[7] Despair is the state of existence that must be chosen, for only in choosing despair can the aesthete move into the ethical (EO, 2:211).[8] The aesthete must choose himself. At a basic functional level, resolution and self-choice are similar in that they are both energetic efforts undertaken by the will to facilitate the move from the aesthetic to the ethical.[9]

Challenging this apparent similarity, *Either/Or* also contains the idea of self-reception, a concept foreign to *Stages on Life's Way*. Not only is the aesthete challenged with radical self-determinative choice, he is also required to choose what he already is (EO, 2:270), and what has already been given (EO, 2:177). The choice itself serves to differentiate the aesthetic and the ethical,[10] yet the reception of oneself presupposes another Source which gives one one's self.[11] As we shall see, the Judge's later formulation

---

[7]The only thing described as evil by the Judge in *Stages on Life's Way* is the "ideality of evil" in the aesthetic love that does not arrive at marriage (SLW, 105). This is further clarified when the Judge describes the seducer, in his deliberate intention to make enjoyment as brief and as intense as possible, as maintaining demonic resolution. It surely is ethical, but ethically bad (SLW, 148-49).

[8]The Judge's development of despair in *Either/Or* is not as penetrating as Anti-Climacus's in *Sickness unto Death*, yet it is already possible to see hints of despair associated with willing to be oneself (SUD, 13-21).

[9]For a fuller discussion of the process of choosing and its importance for becoming a self, see Mark C. Taylor, *Kierkegaard's Pseudonymous Authorship: A Study of Time and the Self* (Princeton NJ: Princeton University Press, 1975) 185-216.

[10]Even here the aesthetic is still present in the ethical, though not as the absolute (EO, 2:177).

[11]Edward F. Mooney, "Kierkegaard on Self-Choice and Self-Reception: Judge

of resolution must formally take place before God, yet there does not seem to be any trace of *Either/Or*'s understanding of self-reception in the ethical sphere of *Stages on Life's Way*, except perhaps with the reception of the aesthetic as the gift from the god.

Finally, in *Either/Or*, repentance surfaces, to ease the dialectical tension between self-choice and self-reception. Repentance begins the way to "salvation;"[12] repentance is rooted in the recognition that God loved me first. The Judge states, "To this stipulation that to choose oneself is to repent oneself, however simple it is in and by itself, I cannot return frequently enough. In other words, everything revolves around this" (EO, 2:248).[13] Repentance is a volitional act rooted in a reality beyond itself and beyond one's control. Robert Perkins rightly alerts us to the fact that the Judge's use of "repentance" may not conform to the traditionally Christian, or at least Lutheran, understanding of the term.[14]

In Kierkegaard's own estimation, one similarity between *Either/Or* and *Stages on Life's Way* lies in the fact that the Judge is "unconditionally the winner" over the aesthetic stage (JP, 5:5804). However, as one can easily see, hardly a "single turn of thought or language" is repeated in the Judge's later articulation of the relation between the aesthetic and the ethical life. But, the transition into the ethical life is not the end of the discussion. It only serves as a preface to the contents of the ethical life itself. Perhaps the perceived differences between *Stages on Life's Way* and *Either/Or* will be resolved through scrutiny of the process of the maintenance of the ethical.

The Maintenance of the Ethical Life

The importance of the transition for the ethical is paramount. In *Either/Or*, the Judge poses a definition for the ethical: "that it is that whereby a person becomes what he becomes" (EO, 2:253). This process

---

William's Admonition," in *International Kierkegaard Commentary: Either/Or, Part II*, ed. Robert L. Perkins (Macon GA: Mercer University Press, 1995) 17.

[12]This is the Judge's own choice of term (EO, 2:216).

[13]See EO, 2:216, 224, 232, 239. In *Stages on Life's Way*, repentance takes on a much more dubious role for the Judge. Repentance is twice linked to the exception (singularity). In the first instance, love and repentance question one up and down in a "much too rigorous" manner (SLW, 164); in the second instance, repentance swings its whip over the wretchedness of the exception (SLW, 181).

[14]Robert L. Perkins, "Either/Or/Or: Giving the Parson His Due," in *IKC: Either/Or, Part II*, 217-18.

takes place in time, and once a person begins "becoming," that is, once a person has made the choice to become, the ethical life begins. As we have seen, the embrace of temporality is necessary for marriage. However, it is precisely time which is the married person's most dangerous enemy. A married person does not kill time, but rescues it and preserves it for eternity. Therefore, marital love has its enemy, its victory and its eternity in time (EO, 2:138-39). Further, time is not a linear progression for marriage. Time is more; it is the growing progression in which the original is preserved but also in which the original is increased (EO, 2:142).

George J. Stack has suggested that although the Judge does not use the language of habit, it can be argued that there are intimations that the security and repetition of resolution, at least in *Stages on Life's Way*, might resemble it to some extent.[15] For example, the Judge describes the life in resolution as one in which a person immerses oneself day after day in the original basis of the resolution (SLW, 108). Although this might look like habit, there can really be no mistaking of habit for the ethical life in either of Judge William's writings. The Judge states, "'Habit' is properly used only of evil" (EO, 2:127). Habit always designates something that is not free.[16] But just as one cannot do the good except in freedom, so also one cannot remain in it except by being in freedom. Therefore, one can never speak of habit in relation to the good (EO, 2:127). Habit, as it relates to concrete action in time, is different than the day-in, day-out ethical existence because concrete ethical expressions are rooted in inner qualifications that must be lured forth. Faithfulness, constancy, humbleness, patience, long-suffering, tolerance and other inner qualifications of marital love must be brought forth out of the individual in various circumstances at various times (EO, 2:139).[17] These inner qualifications make up the constancy of the ethical life, not the multifarious concrete actions that result from them. After all, the ethical life is not a linear repetition of ethical actions, but a growing progression.

---

[15]George J. Stack, *Kierkegaard's Existential Ethics* (University AL: University of Alabama Press, 1977) 105-106.

[16]Judge William also addresses two perceptions of marital habit from the aesthete's point of view, and in the process, shows that they are not really habits, but misunderstandings about the historical nature of marriage (EO, 2:140, 143).

[17]Somewhat similar sentiments are expressed in *Stages on Life's Way* where the Judge warns against looking at the outcome when making a resolution. He states, "the person who fastens his gaze on the outcome is bitten by a serpent . . . lost both for time and for eternity" (SLW, 110).

As we have already seen, the key to unlocking the entrance to the ethical life in *Stages on Life's Way* is resolution. The Judge appears to also suggest that resolution is a person's *ideality* and this statement implies that there is some sense of continuity and stability in resolution that moves beyond merely the transformation of the aesthetic. After all, it certainly looks like the Judge has remained continuously in the state of marriage for some amount of time, or at least long enough to claim that his knowledge of life is superior to anyone who has merely traveled the world, deeply learned foreign languages or discovered a new astronomical system (SLW, 89).

In order to clarify further his conception of resolution, the Judge suggests two differentiating descriptive adjectives that sharpen his understanding of resolution: positive and negative. According to the Judge, "positive resolution" is what is required for marriage. It is positive because it embraces the content of the world in its temporality and its concretion. Positive resolution is not based on probabilities and outcome because it has the "eternal" in it (SLW, 110). In the terms of the Church's wedding ceremony, it is an "eternal duty[18] that is the eye's delight and the heart's desire" (SLW, 111). Negative resolution, on the other hand, is negative only toward temporality but positive toward the eternal. Therein lies its difficulty and insecurity, for in negative resolution one only exists hypothetically or subjunctively (SLW, 108-11).[19] Before further examining the role of the eternal in the ethical life, a few comments on duty are in order.

In *Stages on Life's Way*, duty is linked only to a religious convention: the wedding ceremony. Later, it is also briefly mentioned with the intimation that the conception of resolution supercedes the role of duty. The Judge argues that when the lover "is bowed down under the imperative of duty," he is then "raised again in the optative of the resolution" (SLW, 163). In fact, resolution is its own best recommendation and justification, for it cannot be provided by a third person outside the marriage (SLW, 156). One is left with the conclusion that duty is a conceptual invasion from the religious

---

[18]In using the phrase "eternal duty," the Judge refers not so much to the natural movement of the ethical, but to the injunction of the pastor at a wedding with the *"You Shall"* (SLW, 111). This thought is picked up and rigorously examined in a distinctly Christian context by Kierkegaard in the corresponding discourse, "On the Occasion of a Wedding" (TDIO, 42-68), published simultaneously with *Stages on Life's Way*, and again later, and more fully, in *Works of Love*.

[19]The Judge later brings this charge, in the language of abstraction, against certain forms of the religious life (SLW, 172-75).

that cannot really serve to further the ethical life. In *Either/Or* the Judge also recognizes that the "You Shall" emerges from the Church (EO, 2:92-94). However, duty is assessed in a different, and more difficult, manner.

There is no question about the rigorousness of duty in married love, for the ethical and the religious have duty within. Therefore, duty is no stranger to marriage, whether it is the duty to love, the duty to have a calling or the duty to work for a living. Love and duty are consonant; love makes duty, and duty makes love, the true temperate climate (EO, 2:147). When love fears, duty is its divine nourishment, "for duty says, 'Fear not; you shall conquer'—says it not just in the future tense, for then it is only a hope, but in the imperative mood, and therein rests a conviction that nothing can shake" (EO, 2:146). In a manner reminiscent of the optative of resolution in *Stages on Life's Way*, the Judge also argues that duty commands, but the ethical individual takes the command of duty and translates it from the outer to the inner, thereby moving beyond duty (EO, 2:148). Stated even stronger, duty is not something that is laid upon, but something that lies within a person. The Judge goes as far as to affirm that the truly ethical person has an inner serenity and security, for he or she does not have duty from outside, but from within (EO, 2:254). Once inner serenity and security is achieved in one's personality, the ethical life bursts forth from its depth (EO, 2:257).

Duty, however, is not then discharged from the ethical life, for there are times when the only salvation possible is to let duty speak (EO, 2:152). In dialectical fashion, duty also serves as a key concept that illumines the positive relation between the eternal and the ethical life in *Either/Or*. According to the Judge, when individuals understand things right, they will see in duty only the sign that the road to eternity is prepared for them. They are not only permitted, but also commanded, to take this road. A divine providence watches over this road which continually shows them the prospect and places signposts at danger spots (EO, 2:149). On one hand, duty is immanent in the ethical life; on the other, it is spoken from outside, from the divine.[20] Far from seeing the ethical and divine providence as antithetical,

[20]The broad outlines of the consideration of duty really do not do justice to the complexity of the relationship of the external and internal as motivations for action. Further clarification on this topic is necessary, but cannot be done in this context. See George Schrader, "Kant and Kierkegaard on Duty and Inclination," in *Kierkegaard: A Collection of Critical Essays*, 324-41; Norman Lillegard, "Judge William in the Dock: MacIntyre on Kierkegaard's Ethics," in *IKC: Either/Or, Part II*, 83-111; John E. Hare, *The Moral Gap: Kantian Ethics, Human Limits and God's Assistance*

the Judge here appears to suggest that the eternal, and a rather personal eternal, is either necessary for, or at least compatible with, the ethical life. The question that obviously remains to be answered is whether the immanent and the divine are the same voice.

We shall now return to the eternal as it finds its way into *Stages on Life's Way*. How does the eternal work its way into the definition of resolution? Is it merely an ancillary comment, or does it have something in common with the "double-reflected" nature of traditional Christianity?[21] The Judge begins this complex process as follows:

> I have the resolution before I begin to act in virtue of this resolution. But how, then, have I come to the resolution? A resolution is always reflective. . . . In a perfectly ideal reflection the resolution has ideally emptied actuality, and the conclusion of this ideal reflection . . . is precisely the resolution: the resolution is the ideality brought about through a perfectly ideal reflection, which is the action's acquired working capital. . . . [Y]et resolution is the true beginning of freedom, but it is required of a beginning that it be timely, that it have a proper relation to that which is to be carried out. (SLW, 160-61)

Reflectiveness is a polyvalent term that does not inherently supply its own justification.[22] It can make one an unethical connoisseur; it can continue infinitely, and thus not lead to timely action. In order to cut reflection short, then, it is discharged into faith, ethical faith, "which is precisely the anticipation of the ideal infinity as resolution" (SLW, 162). Therefore, through the "purely ideally exhausted reflection," resolution gains a new immediacy, an immediacy far superior to that of falling in love.[23] And why

(Oxford: Clarendon Press, 1996) 194-97; and Ronald M. Green, *Kierkegaard and Kant: The Hidden Debt* (Albany: State University of New York Press, 1992).

[21]To address this charge in its broadest application, George B. Connell attempts to show that religious invocations are an integral part of the ethical life for the Judge. See "Judge William's Theonomous Ethics," in *Foundations of Kierkegaard's Vision of Community: Religion, Ethics and Politics in Kierkegaard*, ed. George B. Connell and C. Stephen Evans (Atlantic Highlands NJ: Humanities Press, 1992) 56-70.

[22]James Collins, "Faith and Reflection in Kierkegaard," in *A Kierkegaard Critique: An International Selection of Essays Interpreting Kierkegaard*, ed. Howard A. Johnson and Niels Thulstrup (Chicago: Henry Regnery Company, 1962) 144.

[23]It must be noted that, for the Judge, men and women take different courses to this new immediacy. What he has described above is the man's course. Women, on the other hand, skip reflection altogether. They come to resolution "swiftly as a bird;" they move immediately from aesthetic immediacy to religious immediacy

is it superior? Because it is a *religious* view of life "constructed upon ethical presuppositions" (SLW, 162).[24] The resolution is not a person's power, courage or ingenuity; it is a religious point of departure. Could this be another form of "repentance?" Perhaps, but in what sense? We will return to these questions later.

In the end, an ethical individual will place himself, through the universal, in relationship with God. According to the Judge, a person's "comfort is precisely that he is just like other human beings and in this common humanity is in relationship with God by faith and by the resolution" (SLW, 164). This is the resolution's bath of purification; this is how the eternal becomes an essential characteristic of resolution; this is the "holy beauty of the resolution" (SLW, 165). We have already seen how *Either/Or* incorporates the eternal into duty. The earlier text also includes a somewhat parallel passage to the above quotation from *Stages on Life's Way* that relates reflection and the eternal. The Judge states:

> It is now sufficiently clear that reflective love continually consumes itself and that it altogether arbitrarily takes one position and then another; it is clear that it points beyond itself to something higher. . . . This something higher is the religious, in which the reflection of the understanding ends, and just as nothing is impossible for God, so also nothing is impossible for the religious individual either. (EO, 2:30)

At this point, the Judge appears to be blending the ethical and the religious stages, but, as we shall see in the following section, the Judge also has

---

(SLW, 166-67). This immediacy is religious in the same way that resolution is located in a religious point of departure. Therefore, the Judge is really presenting a picture of the movement from the aesthetic to the religious that only males follow. For a more detailed analysis of the gender-specific nature of reflection and the movement between the stages, see Céline Léon, "(A) Woman's Place Within the Ethical," in *Feminist Interpretations of Søren Kierkegaard*, ed. Céline Léon and Sylvia Walsh (University Park: Pennsylvania State University Press, 1997) 112-14; and Wanda Warren Berry, "Judge William Judging Woman: Existentialism and Essentialism in Kierkegaard's *Either/Or*, part II," in *IKC: Either/Or, Part II*, 39-40.

[24]For all the Judge's divergences from Immanuel Kant, this comment looks very much like the central theme of *Religion within the Boundaries of Mere Reason*: "Morality thus inevitably leads to religion." See *Religion within the Boundaries of Mere Reason*, ed. and trans. Allen Wood and George di Giovanni (Cambridge: Cambridge University Press, 1998) 35. A similar expression is found in *Either/Or*, where the Judge suggests that marital love not only has its apriority in itself, but also its constancy (EO, 2:98).

several definitions of the religious. Therefore, to call the Judge's general position "ethicoreligious" is partially correct, but also partially misleading. The religious view employed in *Stages on Life's Way* finds its particular characteristic in defining one's relationship with God in the universal as common to all humanity; the religious view in *Either/Or* is a little more complex.

The religious will be addressed again shortly, but first some concluding comments regarding the ethical must be made. In sum, the Judge believes that he has articulated a comprehensive position of the ethical life which will continually and securely stand one in good stead within all spheres of life. The ethical individual must develop the personal, the civic, and the religious virtues (EO, 2:262). Personally and aesthetically, marriage becomes the fullness of time which is the beautiful focal point of life and existence. Religiously, marriage is sacred and blessed by God. Politically and socially, marriage ensures that lovers belong to the state and the fatherland and share the common concerns of their fellow citizens. Poetically, one conscientiously translates enthusiasm into reality through marriage (SLW, 117).[25]

The ethical life seems to emerge through a combination of inherent dispositions, willful choosing, and receiving; the ethical life seems to be defined by a combination of abstract categories and universal principles. Eventually there must be some way to bring cognitive cohesiveness to these various elements. Anthony Rudd has structured the Judge's ethical position as social morality, largely through the study of *Either/Or*, and he is not alone in his assessment.[26] Louis Mackey boils the ethical down to three propositions, aside from the obvious necessity of marriage: 1) it is every man's duty to work for a living; 2) it is every man's duty to have a calling; and 3) it is every man's duty to do his job and not fret himself about what he may have

---

[25]The Judge rhetorically articulates that marriage is the poetic culmination of the aesthetic. However, he does this by suggesting that the highest form of the poetic exists when it is brought into actuality. This method is employed in *Either/Or* with respect to the beautiful as well. He states:

> If one traces dialectically and just as much historically the development of the esthetically beautiful, one will find that the direction of this movement is from spatial categories to temporal categories, and that the perfecting of art is contingent upon the possibility of gradually detaching itself more and more from space and aiming towards time. (EO, 2:136)

[26]Anthony Rudd, *Kierkegaard and the Limits of the Ethical* (Oxford: Clarendon Press, 1993) 69-114. See also Merold Westphal, *Becoming A Self: A Reading of Kierkegaard's Concluding Unscientific Postscript* (West Lafayette LA: Purdue University Press, 1996) 24-29.

accomplished over and beyond the simple fulfillment of his duty.[27] This judgment seems appropriate when one gives special emphasis to some of the statements the Judge makes. For example: "Personal life as such was an isolation and therefore imperfect, but when he turns back into his personality through the civic life, the personal life appears in a higher form" (EO, 2:263).

I would like to suggest that even though, in *Stages on Life's Way*, social morality ends up being part, and maybe even a large part, of the ethical life, there just might be more, especially in *Either/Or*, to the ethical than accepting the moral requirements that one's performance in social roles entails.[28] The Judge's following account of the struggle of the day-in, day-out reality of the ethical life serves to demonstrate the problem with viewing the ethical only through the lens of social morality, and it again sharpens the importance of moving to the consideration of the religious and its relation to the ethical:

> And what struggle could be more educative than the struggle with the cares about the necessities of life! How much childlikeness it takes to be able almost to smile sometimes at the earthly toil and trouble an immortal spirit must have in order to live, how much humility to be content with the little that is gained with difficulty, how much faith to see the governance of a providence also in his life, for it is easy enough to say that God is greatest in the least, but to be able to see him there takes the strongest faith. . . . What grace and dignity it takes to turn away from them and yet not to run away from them! How often the weapons have to be changed—now it is a matter of working, then of waiting, then of holding one's own, then of praying! . . . He has no public; no one has time to look at him. No one has time, and, of course, this takes time, because his

---

[27]Louis Mackey, *Kierkegaard: A Kind of Poet* (Philadelphia: University of Pennsylvania Press, 1971) 67-69. Mackey's suggestion that it is one's duty to work for a living as a necessary concrete expression of the ethical life is complicated, however, by Judge William's own assertions. The Judge admits,

> I have never had cares about the necessities of life, for although up to a point I do have to work for a living, I nevertheless have always had my good income. Therefore I cannot speak from experience, but I have always kept my eyes open to the hardships involved, but have also kept my eyes open to the beauty in it, the educative and ennobling aspects of it. (EO, 2:283)

[28]The explicit rejection of the state as the highest, at least in the Aristotelian formulation, is a sign that the Judge may be moving in a different direction (EO, 2:322).

> performance is not a half-hour juggling act; his tricks are more subtle and require more than a cultured public to be understood. But he does not crave that either. (EO, 2:286)

So what does he crave? He craves the approval of an "umpire" with eyes who see in secret, and eyes that do not weary of watching; he craves the approval of an umpire who hears the working of his thoughts and who senses how his better nature extricates itself from the torture of spiritual trials. He craves the approval of this umpire, even though he knows he cannot deserve it (EO, 2:287).

The Relation between the Ethical and the Religious

Of course the Judge is a lay Christian, a Lutheran and a member of the Evangelical-Lutheran Church of Denmark. Therefore, when it actually comes right down to it, the Judge never suggests that the ethical is the highest life. In *Stages on Life's Way*, he acknowledges that there is a "higher" life. The ethical life is merely the narrow pass in which an interrogation checkpoint is established. It is in this pass that the Judge ensures that all individuals choose not pure spirit, but the human as well (SLW, 169). He is also quick to point out that the desire to find a true concretion for the religious is not easy; actually, it is nothing but a pious wish! (SLW, 172). Of course, it is good to ponder, but it is impossible to articulate, and even more difficult to imitate. In this way, the Judge actually digs a rather large ditch between himself and any sort of threatening religious life-view.

As we have noted, Judge William, in *Stages on Life's Way*, employs immanent religious concepts, such as the eternal and God which he believes arise out of the contemplation of the ethical life, especially if they provide ammunition for overcoming the aesthetic stage. Any sense of a transcendent divine Being is essentially useless. Although the religiousness of the Judge is not as fully developed as Religiousness A, there are some striking similarities.

However, there is also another religiousness which the Judge is familiar with, and which he strongly condemns: religiousness which is open to the infinite abyss of abstraction (SLW, 172). The desire to belong to God alone is not only inhumanity toward human beings, it is also importunity toward God. The religious person in this sense certainly lacks experience; he or she is also a threat to the socially accepted roles and morality of nineteenth century Denmark. The Judge has enough "imagination" to suggest that in order for an individual to become an exception to the universal, that person must have rather explicit orders from God (SLW, 181). He can also imagine that it would really be too much for any individual. He states, "For the person who has actually had sufficient inwardness to comprehend that the religious is the highest love, how heartbreaking, how annihilating it must be to discover that he has allowed himself too much" (SLW, 175).

Therefore, it is pretty clear, in *Stages on Life's Way*, what the relation between the ethical and the religious is: universal religiousness is embraced only if it can be drawn out immanently from the ethical; "exceptional religiousness" is rejected if it demands, or even suggests, that the universal must be breached.[29] There can be absolutely no thought of the teleological suspension of the ethical. Further, the ethical does not need to use imported theological terms, for its own are definitely sufficient. The relation can be summed up with the following observation of the Judge:

> The ethical is so incorruptible that if our Lord himself had been obliged to allow himself a little irregularity in creating the world, ethics would not let itself be disturbed, although heaven and earth and everything found therein is nevertheless a quite fine masterpiece. (SLW, 155)

The relation between the religious and the ethical in *Either/Or* is not nearly as straightforward.[30] Again, the Judge recognizes that the ethical is not the highest. He remarks that the religious, which can be combined with others, is the most beautiful (EO, 2:73). Even more cryptic is the Judge's description of himself as an unreliable articulator of the ethical, since he himself is trapped within it (EO, 2:179). Lastly, the Judge even invites a

---

[29]Sylvia Walsh helpfully points out Judge William's criteria for legitimate religious exception in *Living Poetically*, 183. The second criteria she suggests is that the exception must be married. Could this criteria not simply mean that the legitimate exception must not be an exception at all? Judge William, in *Stages on Life's Way* admits that finding a concrete expression of the religious is theoretically (and perhaps more accurately, literarily) possible, but then he goes on to almost mockingly suggest that it is a mere pious wish to find a proper religious expression for marriage (SLW, 172). The Judge's cavalier comments here seem to reinforce the idea in *Stages on Life's Way* that marriage and the religious cannot be joined in any real way, therefore negating the ethical legitimacy of any religious exception.

[30]Although the inclusion of the sermon at the end complicates this issue immensely, I will attempt to make my point through only the analysis of the Judge's own words. The inclusion of the sermon will be addressed shortly.

further movement from the ethical to the religious in pointing out where the jumping off point for the theological might be located (EO, 2:218).

Perkins, however, rightfully resists any easy transition from the ethical to the religious. He charges the Judge with moral ambiguity.[31] To very briefly summarize his argument, the Judge does his theology from below, and therefore he does so from the perspective of a bourgeois Lutheran Protestant. Moral responsibility is thus linked to marital earthiness and social decency. In the process of arriving at theological concepts, the Judge uses human feelings and the analogy of childlikeness.[32] This leads to conceptual slippage in the theological terms. Therefore, the Judge ends up being a moral and religious exemplar, but there is no radical need for divine grace in his formulation of the ethical.[33] It is up to the sermon by the parson at the close of *Either/Or*, Part II, to bring this into relief. Here, in the sermon, it becomes clear that "we are always in the wrong before God."

Every one of Perkins's assertions can be supported and what he says about the sermon resolving some of the problems of the ethical is absolutely correct. I would, however, like to suggest that there may be a few pieces missing from his description. I believe there are several indications that the Judge is already aware of the tension between the religious and the ethical in *Either/Or* before the sermon makes its appearance in the third letter to A. Certainly, the theological terms that the Judge uses do not mimic the use of the same terms under the condition of "double-reflected" Christianity. But, these are also not just mere terms which reflect intentional immanent categories, like those of *Stages on Life's Way*.[34] In fact, Julia Watkin strongly argues that Judge William, in *Either/Or*, "makes no secret of the fact that he holds and is helped by 'the Christian view.'"[35] Something outside mere ethical faith directly impinges upon actuality: God, the incarnation of Christ, and God's grace. Only by holding the tension between

---

[31]Perkins, "Either/Or/Or," 211.

[32]Perkins, "Either/Or/Or," 214-15. I realize that the recognition that Jesus also taught by using children as exemplars for entrance to the Kingdom of God (Mark 10:13-16) does not refute Perkins's conclusion. However, it raises contextual questions about what weight to place on the Judge's examples from childhood.

[33]Perkins, "Either/Or/Or," 219.

[34]Peter J. Mehl also alerts us to the important role the "theistic commitments" of Judge William play in the ethical self-realization recommended in *Either/Or*, II. See "Moral Virtue, Mental Health, and Happiness: The Moral Psychology of Kierkegaard's Judge William," in *IKC: Either/Or*, II, 182.

[35]Julia Watkin, "Judge William, A Christian?" in *IKC: Either/Or*, II, 120.

the use and misuse of theological terms in *Either/Or* does one embrace the fullness and complexity of the Judge's early formulation of an ethical life-view.

Before moving to any final conclusions about the Judge's perspective of the religious in *Either/Or*, a comparison to *Stages on Life's Way* is necessary. Rather than rejecting the necessity of "the third power" in marriage, the Judge suggests that the individuals themselves voluntarily turn to it in order to bind themselves to each other in faithfulness (EO, 2:55). Later, the Judge speaks of the difference between conquering and possessing love. Conquering takes pride, violence and greed and it requires eating and drinking, that is, living an earthly life; possessing takes humility, patience and requires contentment with little, prayer and fasting, that is, living the religious life. True greatness is not in conquering, but in possessing (EO, 2:131-32). As we have already seen in *Stages on Life's Way*, resolution looks a little more like conquering than possessing.

Further, *Either/Or* affirms the helpful Christian conclusions regarding sin (EO, 2:239).[36] In the face of suffering, the Judge portrays a position of an individual who is humbled and who feels the offense. There is only one word for the suffering: guilt; there is only one word for the pain: repentance; there is only one hope: forgiveness (EO, 2:237). Whether he is accurate or not, the Judge's description here is far from the later discussion in *Stages on Life's Way*. Also, the Judge's invocation of Scripture gives the argument a new tone. We are well aware that the Judge knows the Bible well enough to qualify for a theological degree (EO, 2:70). He also recognizes that ethics and the Bible provide us with diverse, yet compatible teaching. There are some things that the Bible reveals that ethics cannot, such as the fact that it is appointed for every human being to die and to face judgement; there are some things that ethics can reveal by themselves, such as the fact that it is the meaning of life and actuality that a person become open (EO, 2:322). Perhaps what reflection on the ethical life reveals is that it is only a trifle compared to Balle's catechism (EO, 2:323)?[37]

Finally, the treatment of the exception brings the difference between *Either/Or* and *Stages on Life's Way* to a head. As we have seen in the latter,

---

[36]The conception of sin, however, is not fully addressed until *The Concept of Anxiety*, and much later, in *The Sickness unto Death*.

[37]For an in-depth analysis of the importance of the references to Balle's catechism, see Julia Watkin, "Judge William, A Christian?" in *IKC: Either/Or, Part II*, 113-24.

the exception is one who can not incorporate himself into the universal. A similar conception is strongly presented in *Either/Or*, and those who are exceptions exist in a kind of purgatory (EO, 2:331). What is added by the Judge is the notion that every person is the universally human and also the exception (EO, 2:332). The ethical life has an inconsistency built into it; all people fall short of its ideal. Therefore, not only is it not a sin to remain single (though it does not fulfill the universal) (EO, 2:302), but a young person can be forgiven for adventurousness, and, in the end, all can be forgiven for their shortcomings. At worst, the relation between the religious and the ethical life presented in *Either/Or* is ambiguous; at best, it is conciliatory. These options rule out a strictly polemical relationship.

Do we need to move to the inclusion of the appended sermon to show that the Judge presents two rather distinct formulations of the ethical life? I do not think so. If we do move to affirm the Judge's endorsement of the sermon, the case made here is much stronger, but the argument's merit does not stand or fall on the sermon alone.[38] Certainly, many, if not all, of the concrete expressions of the ethical life will look the same to an external observer. But, so might the concrete expressions of the aesthetic, ethical, and religious life. What is fundamentally different between the earlier and the later formulation is the orientation of the ethical life in relation to the religious. In *Either/Or*, the Judge is not limited to only endorsing a religiousness which corresponds directly to the universal. The religious position that the Judge initially holds is one that also has the universal as its ideal, but it makes room for failure. In a very real sense, there is grace; there are gifts of grace for which one must thank God: cheerful boldness, trust, belief in actuality and in the eternal necessity whereby the beautiful triumphs. And finally, the gift of blessedness implicit in the freedom with which the individual offers God his assistance (EO, 2:123).

It is the ambiguous nature of the ethicoreligious formulation of the ethical life in *Either/Or* that has spawned a series of articles attempting to demonstrate how important the religious is to the Judge.[39] Although the

---

[38]An excellent description of the movement and content of the "Ultimatum" can be found in David R. Law's "The Place, Role, and Function of the 'Ultimatum' of *Either/Or*, Part II, in Kierkegaard's Pseudonymous Authorship," in *IKC: Either/Or, Part II*, 233-47.

[39]To those mentioned already can be added Michael Plekon, "Bourgeois Moralist, Knight of Faith, Teacher?" in *IKC: Either/Or, Part II*, 125-37. Plekon's suggestion that the Judge may be employing a type of indirect discourse in the first

sermon articulates clearly that "one is always in the wrong before God," and that "the truth which builds up is truth for you" (EO, 2:341-54), it is not absolutely necessary to include it in order to demonstrate that the role of the religious in *Either/Or* stands in rather sharp contrast to that found in *Stages on Life's Way*.

Conclusions

I do not want to overemphasize the difference between the ethical life-views articulated by the Judge. Both are, after all, still ethical views that battle the aesthetic and provide a context for the genesis of the religious. However, as the different relations to the religious are brought into view, the ethical differences between *Either/Or* and *Stages on Life's Way* begin to appear understandable. If there is no conception of a transcendent God who has a role in forming us, how could one receive, or even choose, oneself? This illuminates the move from self-choice and self-receptive language to the language of will and resolution in *Stages on Life's Way*. If the only position with regard to duty is that it is imposed externally, should it come as a surprise that there is room for it in *Either/Or* and that it is shut out of *Stages on Life's Way*? No. Would it then surprise the reader that *Stages on Life's Way* greatly increases the role of reflection in coming to resolution? No. If there is no theological rootedness for evaluation of actions, does it come as a surprise that the language of sin, good and evil is essentially dropped in *Stages on Life's Way*? Or, that nearly all other theological terminology, such as repentance and prayer, is dropped as well? The answer to both of these is no. Looking back from the relation between the two evaluations of the religious, the complex ethical positions held by the Judge on these two occasions seem much more internally consistent, and more dissonant with each other. One might guess that this was what Crites was partially referring to when he stated that the dialectical tensions of the two works are quite different.

In this paper, I have simply attempted to show how the two versions of the Judge's ethical life are similar, yet substantially different. Hopefully, it plays a small part in understanding the total relationship between the two books. However, it only leads to a further question, 'What does one make of the ambiguity of *Either/Or*?' This is immediately raised because the

---

two letters is an interesting, though slightly problematic, way to explain the transition to the endorsement of the sermon (129).

ethicoreligious position held by the Judge, even with the inclusion of the sermon, is still some distance from becoming a Christian sermon in the sense that it includes specifically Christian categories like the paradox, atonement or the forgiveness of sins.[40]

In a Journal entry of 1843, the same year as the publication of *Either/Or*, Kierkegaard poignantly asks, "But where is the boundary between worldly wisdom and religiousness" (JP, 5:5637). I believe this is the exact question he has posed, through the Judge, in *Either/Or*, Part II. There is no definitive line between worldly wisdom and religiousness. Saying this, I do not think that the religious language can be simply "explained" by arguing that the Judge is merely expounding worldly wisdom in another language. It is equally wrong to elevate the religious simplistically and explain the ethical language of the immanent in its terms. These must be held in tension as they are juxtaposed in the Judge's life-view. It seems that Climacus, in his comments on *Either/Or*, struggles with the same ambiguity. First, he says that it ends with the upbuilding truth; then he says that the book would need a religious, rather than an ethical orientation; then he moves to the discussion of *the leap*, and finally to the comment that everyone faces the collision of the ethical and the religious because the religious paradigm is irregular (CUP, 1:256-59).

In the pseudonymous work following *Either/Or*, Kierkegaard tackles this question head-on. *Fear and Trembling* poses the question that the Judge leaves begging to be asked: "How far does the ethical allow the exception to be forgiven?" Many direct connections to *Repetition*, *Fragments* and *The Concept of Anxiety* can also be made from *Either/Or*. Therefore, by the time the Judge is allowed to recount the ethical life again in *Stages on Life's Way*, much water has already flowed under the bridge, and there has been a great degree of conceptual clarification and differentiation.[41] If Climacus had written the *Postscript* in 1843, I am not convinced his reading of *Either/Or* would have looked the same as it does in 1845.

By the time of the writing of *Stages on Life's Way*, Kierkegaard, through his pseudonymous authorship, has narrowed the ethical considerably. Kierkegaard himself describes the Judge's later position as polemical. The Judge, in *Stages on Life's Way*, is grappling in existence because he cannot end

---

[40]David R. Law, "The 'Ultimatum' of Kierkegaard's *Either/Or*, Part II, and the Two Upbuilding Discourses of 16 May 1843," in *IKC: Either/Or, Part II*, 263.

[41]It is also important to note that the same type of clarification has happened in the religious life-view, although this process is not discussed here at all.

where he stands (JP, 5:5804). Further, I would also like to request that we, as readers, cannot accept the narrow view of *Stages on Life's Way* as Kierkegaard's final summation of the ethical just because Judge William has spoken his last. I believe the Judge never reappears in Kierkegaard's later writings because his version of the ethical has ultimately shown itself to be unstable, truncated, and polemical. Under his own name in 1847, Kierkegaard addresses the same issue that *Either/Or* presents for us in *Works of Love*. However, the conciliatory (or ambiguous) nature of the relation between the ethical and the religious has taken a different direction. Rather than the polemical stance found in *Stages on Life's Way*, *Works of Love*, from an explicitly Christian point of view, shows anew how the ethical has essentially been taken up into the "higher concentricity" of the religious (as Judge William intimated in *Either/Or*). Pointing to this alternative movement presents us with another potential option for the resolution of the question posed by the ethicoreligious position of the Judge in *Either/Or*.

5

The Importance of Being Earnest: Coming to Terms with Judge William's Seriousness[1]

George Connell

> These words [Either/Or] have always made a great impression on me and still do, especially when I say them this way plainly and by themselves. . . . They act upon me like an incantation formula, and my soul becomes exceedingly earnest, at times almost in a state of shock. I think of my early youth, when without really comprehending what it is to make a choice in life I listened in childish trust to the talk of my elders, and the moment of choice became a very solemn and momentous matter. . . . (EO, 2:157)

As he made abundantly clear in *Either/Or*, II, Judge William is a serious man. In contrast to A of *Either/Or*, I, who apparently evacuates every choice of ultimate significance and denies the seriousness of every either/or when he ecstatically proclaims, "Do it or don't do it, you'll regret it!" Judge William approaches every choice, both the trivial and the great, with gravity, resolve, and focus. He is the soul of seriousness. If with Vincent McCarthy we read Kierkegaard's writings as a sort of "phenomenology of moods," the various pseudonyms bringing vividly to life a variety of ideal emotional atunements, then clearly Judge William is a literary realization of the mood of seriousness.[2]

Although few readers of *Either/Or*, II have ever complained that the Judge's letters are too short, we are treated to another hundred

---

[1]I extend special thanks to Art Budyonny with whom I spent a semester-long independent study discussing *Stages on Life's Way* in general and the issues explored in this essay in particular.

[2]Vincent A. McCarthy, *The Phenomenology of Moods in Kierkegaard* (The Hague: Martinus Nijhoff, 1978).

pages of William's reflections in *Stages on Life's Way*. Thanks to the early morning thievery of the rogue's gallery from "In Vino Veritas," William's anonymous treatise, "Some Reflections on Marriage in Answer to Objections—By a Married Man," makes its way into Hilarius Bookbinder's compilation. And once again, Judge William is the soul of seriousness; once again, he defends the ethical life chiefly by defending marriage.

But what new insight does Kierkegaard provide us by this repetition of his earlier pseudonymous achievement? What do the Judge's reflections achieve here beyond showing the flag, beyond giving the ethical stage a somewhat desultory last expression before the text hurries on toward an existence that transcends it in "Guilty?"/"Not Guilty?" The comparative brevity of "Some Reflections on Marriage," the defensive quality of both the title and the text, and especially the epigram, "The deceived is wiser than one not deceived" (SLW, 88), raise questions about the Judge's conviction, that is, about how serious he really is in this text.

In the following essay, I will argue that "Some Reflections on Marriage" isn't just a rehashing of the Judge's letters from *Either/Or* but rather shines new light on the character and dilemmas of the ethical stage of existence. Specifically, this text significantly deepens and complicates the issue of the Judge's seriousness, the fundamental mood (*grund Stemning*) of the ethical stage. Where *Either/Or* tempts us to see an essentially dyadic picture, the aesthete's refusal of seriousness over against the Judge's seriousness, *Stages on Life's Way* places the Judge in what he calls a "narrow pass" (SLW, 169), his seriousness called into question by the sardonic laughter of the aesthetes in "In Vino Veritas" on the one side and the agonized self-examination of Quidam in "Guilty?"/"Not Guilty?" on the other. As we follow his rather cramped, beleaguered defense of this pass, we find that questions of the nature and value of seriousness are at the very center of both his and his polemical partners' concern. While I will argue that Judge William comes off surprisingly well in his confrontations with his cultured aesthetic despisers, he is clearly very, very anxious about the threat to his understanding of himself and his way of life posed by an oddly vague and hypothetical "religious exception," a category realized in the next section of *Stages on Life's Way*, "Guilty?"/"Not Guilty?" Looking into that anxiety raises interesting questions about what seriousness really is and whether the Judge is ultimately as serious as he seems at first blush.

In the interest of "good order and discipline," a virtue Judge William could not but approve even though he doesn't display it in composing his essay, I will first examine the *de facto* debate over the nature and value of seriousness waged by the aesthetes on the one hand and Judge William on the other before I move on to the religious challenge to the Judge's understanding of himself as serious. While it makes sense thus to treat the simpler, aesthetic vs. ethical contestation of seriousness before examining the Judge's troubled anticipations of the religious, it is important to note that, unlike in *Either/Or*, II, where the "Ultimatum" is a sort of religious question mark appended to the two long letters, Judge William begins and ends "Some Reflections on Marriage" worrying about the religious. But before going into the details of the Judge's two-front war, I will first show that Kierkegaard is onto something deep, widespread, and significant in dramatizing our conflicting ideas and opinions about seriousness.

A Serious Case of Ambivalence

Reading "Some Reflections on Marriage" with a sustained focus on seriousness is rewarding in part because of the rich and varied associations the concept carries. This is especially evident in the distinctive etymological backgrounds of words for seriousness in European languages. The Hongs translate the Danish *Alvor* sometimes as "seriousness," but more often as "earnestness," paralleling the German translation of the word as *Ernst*.[3] Where "serious" is etymologically associated with heaviness and weight (Old English *swaer* = heavy; also related to Greek *herma* = ballast), "earnest" carries connotations of battle (Old English *eornest*= combat or duel).[4] In contrast, the Danish *Alvor* signifies complete, unalloyed truth. (*al* =

---

[3]Earlier translators such as Walter Lowrie and Lee Capel prefer "seriousness"; Reidar Thomte follows the Hongs in using "earnestness."

[4]Eric Partridge, *Origins: A Short Etymological Dictionary of Modern English*, 1983 ed. [repr. of 1966 4th ed.] (New York: Greenwich House, 1983) 175, 609. In the prologue to *Henry the Eighth*, Shakespeare has his narrator tell the audience to expect not laughs but things "That bear a weighty and a serious brow."

all; *vor* = truth, related to the Latin *verus* and the German *wahr*).[5] Significantly, all of these senses and many more are evoked by Judge William in his paean to ethical existence. He speaks of the married man as bearing a weight of responsibility; he frequently uses images of battle to describe both his life and his essay; and he plays on the Danish word for husband (*ægtemand*, composed of *ægte* = genuine and *mand* = man) to bring out the suggestion of truth (SLW, 91, 93).

But the richest significance of seriousness, the consideration that makes it an especially revealing focal point as we read the Judge's essay, is that we—and that "we" includes Kierkegaard and his pseudonyms—have profoundly mixed thoughts and feelings about seriousness. On the one hand, seriousness carries a host of positive associations. It is honesty vs. imposture, concern vs. indifference, authenticity vs. inauthenticity, commitment vs. experimentation, weight vs. "unbearable lightness," significance vs. meaninglessness. On the other hand, seriousness carries equally strong negative and even ludicrous associations. It is pompous and pedantic, smug and self-content, pretentious and pharisaical, fatuous and finicky. Ironically, in its very humorlessness, this second seriousness is an inexhaustible source of humor. From Shakespeare's Polonius to the Marx Brothers' Margaret Dumont, the ponderously serious straight man or woman is the occasion of infinite mirth. As Oscar Wilde so clearly showed, there is almost nothing so funny as being earnest.[6]

Wilde is but one of a number of writers who have played on this equivocality, juxtaposing the positive and pejorative senses of seriousness, to vivid effect. In one of his characteristic paradoxes, he writes, "Life is much too important to be taken seriously."[7] More recently, Maria Lugones has written, "I am . . . scared of ending up a serious human being, someone with no multidimensionality, with no fun in life, someone who is just someone who has had the fun constructed out of her. I am seriously scared of getting stuck in a 'world' that constructs me in that way."[8] But it is especially writers

[5]Lis Jacobsen, ed., *Nudansk Ordbog* (Copenhagen: Politikens Forlag, 1979) 1:59.

[6]There is currently a comedy troupe that goes by the name "In All Seriousness."

[7]Quoted by Robert C. Roberts, "Sense of Humor as a Christian Virtue," *Faith and Philosophy* 7/2 (1990): 179.

[8]Maria Lugones, "Playfulness, 'World' Traveling, and Loving Perception," in

of the existentialist tradition who have played on this juxtaposition of senses. Nietzsche's first paragraph of *The Genealogy of Morals* is a brilliant case in point.

> We are unknown to ourselves, we knowers: and for a good reason. We have never sought ourselves—how then should it happen that we *find* ourselves one day? It has rightly been said: "where your treasure is, there will your heart be also"; *our* treasure is where the beehives of our knowledge stand. We are forever underway toward them, as born winged animals and honey-gatherers of the spirit, concerned with all our heart about only one thing—"bringing home" something. As for the rest of life, the so-called "experiences"—who of us even has enough seriousness for them? Or enough time? In such matters I'm afraid we were never really "with it": we just don't have our heart there—or even our ear![9]

Here, the serious, all-too-serious worker-bee scholars specifically lack the awareness, the availability to experience, the mindfulness, that Nietzsche identifies with true seriousness.

Sartre and de Beauvoir, in turn, stipulate a technical definition of seriousness as a bad faith postulation of objective values, evading the anguish of freedom and responsibility. Summarizing Sartre's thought, de Beauvoir writes,

> *Being and Nothingness* is in large part a description of the serious man and his universe. The serious man gets rid of his freedom by claiming to subordinate it to values which would be unconditioned. He imagines that the accession to these values likewise permanently confers value upon himself. Shielded with "rights," he fulfills himself as a *being* who is escaping from the stress of existence. . . . There is the serious from the moment that freedom denies itself to the advantage of ends which one claims are absolute.[10]

Even while these two typically utter the word, "seriousness," with a derisive scowl, they find themselves reaching for the positive

---

Women, Knowledge, and Reality: Explorations in Feminist Philosophy, ed. Ann Garry and Marilyn Pearsall (London: Routledge, 1996) 429-30. I thank my colleague Susan Poppe for calling my attention to this passage.

[9]Friedrich Nietzsche, *On the Genealogy of Morals*, trans. Maudemarie Clark and Alan J. Swensen (Indianapolis: Hackett, 1998) 1.

[10]Simone de Beauvoir, *The Ethics of Ambiguity*, trans. Bernard Frechtman (New York: Citadel, 1948) 46.

sense of the word in expressing what is lacking in seriousness in the pejorative sense. As de Beauvoir puts it, "Beyond the rejected seriousness is found a genuine seriousness."[11] For de Beauvoir, this "genuine seriousness" is the unflinching acceptance of one's own freedom and a corresponding commitment to the freedom of all others.

To lead our discussion back to Kierkegaard, we find a further striking example of this ambivalence about seriousness in Louis Mackey's preface to his *Points of View*, a collection of his articles on Kierkegaard over more than twenty years. After confessing an ironic "dirty old man's" embarrassment over the "earnest young man" of his earliest articles, and expressing the hope that "the grave young father of the early essays be corrupted by the feckless old scribbler who succeeds him," Mackey ruefully observes that, "there is, in this country and in these days, a group of writers—mostly young, mostly philosophers—determined (as I think they might put it) to 'take Kierkegaard seriously as a philosopher.'"[12] Though Mackey laments this sort of seriousness as producing "tidied up versions (repetitions)" of Kierkegaard, he counters it with a call for a true seriousness:

> [T]he way to "take Kierkegaard seriously" as a philosopher (or a theologian) is not to domesticate him but rather to magnify, as much as the case allows, the essential perversity of the texts.[13]

What is significant in these examples is not so much the particular changes on the theme of seriousness they each ring as their indication of a widespread and recurrent ambivalence about seriousness and a corresponding need to gainsay whatever one has said on that intriguingly dialectical concept. In each case, the critiqued and the standard of criticism are doubles of a sort, one a lugubrious and grave phony, the other the genuine article.

---

[11]de Beauvoir, *The Ethics of Ambiguity*, 60.

[12]Louis Mackey, *Points of View: Readings of Kierkegaard* (Talhassee: Florida State University Press, 1986) xvii-xviii.

[13]Mackey, *Points of View*, xviii-xix.

Some Versions of the Ethicist or Which William?

Under which aspect of seriousness should we view the Judge? That is the test Kierkegaard poses us in the two long letters in *Either/Or*, II and then in "Some Reflections on Marriage" in *Stages on Life's Way*. When we read the Judge's pleas for ethical life generally and marriage in particular, do we meet a paragon of appropriation, of existential reduplication, or a stodgy, long-winded, repetitive, thoroughly conventional bore?

Kierkegaard has provided us important help in addressing this question by formulating his theory of the stages. Where many other writers have simply played on our ambivalent feelings about and contrasting senses of seriousness, Kierkegaard's theory of the stages allows us to conceptualize the two aspects as functions of perspective and life-view.[14] At a basic level, the positive view of seriousness correlates to the Judge's sense of himself. It is the ethical person's self-satisfaction. Correspondingly, the negative take on seriousness correlates to an outsider perspective, here using "outsider" to mean both a third person perspective (even when one takes it on oneself) and a disengagement from the values and projects of the one critically observed. As the Judge notes, even when the aesthete, A, is with him and his family physically and socially, A preserves a disengaged, critical perspective (EO, 2:204). From that position, the Judge's seriousness is alternatively and even perhaps simultaneously boring and funny. In a memorable example in "Rotation of Crops," A tells how he discovered rich amusement in the thitherto tedious harangues of an acquaintance (surely the Judge) when A turned his attention to the droplets of sweat gathering at the end of the

---

[14]Jane Austen nicely dramatizes the role of perspective in determining which aspect of seriousness manifests itself. In *Sense and Sensibility*, the younger, rather romantic sister, Marianne, and her beau, Willoughby, see serious Colonel Brandon as "a very respectable man, who has every body's good word and nobody's notice," who "has neither genius, taste, nor spirit," whose "understanding has no brilliancy, his feelings no ardour, and his voice no expression." In contrast, her older and more serious sister, Elinor, finds him, "a sensible man, well bred, well informed, of gentle address, and I believe possessing an amiable heart." Jane Austen, *Sense and Sensibility* (Oxford: Oxford University Press, 1990) 44.

speaker's nose (EO, 1:299). As humorous as this story is, it represents a disturbing refusal of engagement and sympathy. So, Kierkegaard links the two senses of seriousness to two perspectives that are both a bit off-putting, one an attitude of moral self-contentment, the other of inhuman disengagement.

The obvious (and lazy) resolution of our question of how to regard seriousness in general and the Judge in particular would be to say that these two senses correlate to ultimately incommensurable viewpoints so there is no question of adjudicating between them. Besides representing a rather sterile reading, such a view neglects that both A and the Judge argue their cases, sometimes explicitly and rationally, sometimes rhetorically and emotionally. As we work our way into those arguments, we find that our simple assignment of the negative perspective on seriousness to the aesthete and the positive to the ethicist is far too simple. Just as it is too simple to see *Either/Or*, I as the "either" and *Either/Or*, II as the "or" because both the aesthetic and the ethical are distinctive ways of saying "either/or," so we can't assign a single, simple sense of seriousness to a single stage. On closer inspection, we find both critiques of and appeals to seriousness on the part of both A and Judge William as they carry out their polemics against each other.

Seriousness from the Aesthete's Perspective

Though the pathetic Edward from "The Seducer's Diary" is a memorable caricature of the serious, lovelorn young man, the most significant statements about seriousness in *Either/Or*, I are found in "Diapsalmata" and in "Rotation of Crops." At points, these texts issue an apparently total and unambivalent rejection of seriousness. But other bitterly humorous passages that critically depict the serious burghers of Copenhagen actually give us more insight into the nuances of A's attitude.

> The most ludicrous of all ludicrous things, it seems to me, is to be busy in the world, to be a man who is brisk at his meals and brisk at his work. Therefore, when I see a fly settle on the nose of one of those men of business in a decisive moment, or if he is splashed by a carriage that passes him in even greater haste, or Knippelsbro tilts up, or a roof tile falls and kills him, I laugh from the bottom of my heart. And who could keep from laughing? What,

> after all, do these busy bustlers achieve? Are they not just like that woman who, in a flurry because the house was on fire, rescued the fire tongs? What more, after all, do they salvage from the life's huge conflagration? (EO, 1:25)

> When I was very young, I forgot . . . how to laugh; when I became an adult, when I opened my eyes and saw actuality, then I started to laugh and have never stopped laughing since that time. I saw that the meaning of life was to make a living, its goal to become a councilor, that the rich delight of love was to acquire a well-to-do girl, that the blessedness of friendship was to help each other in financial difficulties, that wisdom was whatever the majority assumed it to be, that enthusiasm was to give a speech, that courage was to risk being fined ten dollars, that cordiality was to say "May it do you good" after a meal, that piety was to go to communion once a year. This I saw, and I laughed. (EO, 1:34)

> There is an indefatigable activity that shuts a person out of the world of spirit and places him in a class with the animals, which instinctively must always be in motion. There are people who have an extraordinary talent for transforming everything into a business operation, whose whole life is a business operation, who fall in love and are married, hear a joke, and admire a work of art with the same businesslike zeal with which they work at the office. (EO, 1:289)

Two motifs recur prominently in these passages: busyness and self-serving financial calculation, motifs interestingly joined in the English word, "business." A's indictment of seriousness pigeonholes it as the characteristic and contemptible mode of being-in-the-world for which Danes have the terrible-wonderful word, *Spidsborgerlighed,* a word translated by the Hongs as "bourgeois-philistine mentality" and as "bourgeois philistinsim." What makes bourgeois-philistine mentality so contemptible and laughable is, first, its paltriness, but, fundamentally, the inappropriateness of the object of its seriousness, typically some form of worldly advantage, especially of a financial character. Further, A targets the humorlessness of bourgeois-philistine mentality. A loathes the self-importance of his targets who have no critical distance on themselves, who fail to see the relativity of their tasks and the ephemerality of their accomplishments. He delights in accidental reminders of vulnerability and indignity such as a fly on the nose, a splattering of mud, a falling roof tile. As Evans and Roberts have stressed, contradiction is the heart of the comic for

Kierkegaard.[15] Here the contradiction is between busy, self-important, calculating consciousness and events that halt it in its tracks, reveal its triviality, and defy its calculation.

If A targets the businessman, the aesthetic critique of seriousness in *Stages on Life's Way* takes a decidedly misogynistic turn.[16] In each of the speeches of "In Vino Veritas," woman is made a joke and denied seriousness. We first hear from the Young Man, who is utterly unfamiliar with love and who plans to keep things that way. To the Young Man, "erotic love is comic," because it is "the greatest contradiction imaginable" (SLW, 33). He identifies a variety of contradictions—that "[t]he psychical at its loftiest finds its expression in the extreme opposite, and the sensual wants to signify the psychical at its loftiest" (SLW, 39), that a selfishly motivated act serves the needs of the species (SLW, 43), that it leads to the birth of an eternal being (SLW, 35-36). But, perhaps most revealing, the Young Man says that "erotic love is comic to a third party" (SLW, 33). This picks up on the suggestion that the negative view of seriousness correlates to a third person view, observing the other without empathizing with the values and goals that endow that person's actions with sense and significance.

Constantin Constantius in turn says that woman is "properly construed only under the category of jest." The contradiction at the root of the comedy here is the disproportion between woman and "the absolute in the ethical requirements." To make a woman—" a little miss of sixteen years"—the object of grandiose ideality is "to inflate her larger than life" and thus to make a jest of her (SLW, 48).

Victor Eremita locates comic contradiction within woman herself. Because woman is "so special, so mixed, so compounded" (SLW 56),

---

[15]C. Stephen Evans, "Kierkegaard's View of Humor: Must Christians Always Be Solemn?," *Faith and Philosophy* 4/2 (1987): 176-86; Robert C. Roberts, "Smiling with God: Reflections on Christianity and the Psychology of Humor," *Faith and Philosophy* 4/2 (1987): 168-75; Roberts, "Sense of Humor as a Christian Virtue," 177-92.

[16]For an in-depth discussion of both the misogyny of "In Vino Veritas" and its self-conscious relationship to Plato's *Symposium*, see Robert L. Perkins, "Woman Bashing in Kierkegaard's 'In Vino Veritas': A Reinscription of Plato's *Symposium*," in *Feminist Interpretations of Søren Kierkegaard*, ed. Céline Léon and Sylvia Walsh (University Park: Pennsylvania State University Press, 1997) 83-102.

romantic consciousness is consigned to meaninglessness. The contradiction on which Victor Eremita focuses is between the idealization of the unmarried woman and the prosaic actuality of the wife. "Formerly empress in the vast outskirts [*Overdrev*] of erotic love and titular queen of all exaggerations [*Overdrivelser*] of giddiness, now Mrs. Petersen on the corner of *Badstrustræde* [Bathhouse Street]" (SLW 57-58). On this basis, Victor Eremita concludes that woman can only appropriately play a negative role, inspiring ideality in man so long as he doesn't enter a positive relation to her. Marriage, insofar as it undergoes the misfortune of being idealized, reveals itself as bourgeois-philistine mentality at its worst (SLW 60).

The Fashion Designer exceeds Victor Eremita by not just describing woman as jest but by using fashion, at cost to himself, to induce women to make fools of themselves. Here, the removed third-person stance associated with a critique of seriousness is radicalized as a malicious assault on the dignity (=seriousness) of persons.

Finally, Johannes the Seducer apparently breaks with the advancing hostility to women seen in the earlier speeches by claiming to speak in praise of woman. But, in a speech echoing Aristophanes' myth of love from Plato's *Symposium*, Johannes a bit more fondly and euphemistically joins the others in evacuating women of all seriousness. Women are the bait the gods use to take captive and weaken men. Seducers are onto this and triumph by stealing the bait without swallowing the hook. But for all his interest in and attention to women, the seducer plays with them, refusing them and his relation to them ultimate seriousness.

While all the symposiasts make a joke of women in some way or other, we should note complexities in their attitudes toward seriousness that emerge in these pages. While there is a boundless, malevolent nihilism apparent in the Fashion Designer, other speakers, especially the first three, make the characteristic move of appealing to a genuine seriousness in critiquing the false. This is especially evident in William Afham's opening reflections on recollection.

> Actually, only the essential can be recollected, for the old man's recollecting, as stated, is basically of an accidental character; the same holds true of analogies to his recollecting. The essential is conditioned not only by itself but also by its relation to the person

> concerned. The person who has broken with the idea cannot act essentially, can undertake nothing that is essential. . . . Despite external indications, anything else he does is unessential. To take a wife is indeed something essential, but anyone who has ever dallied with erotic love [*Elskov*] may very well strike his brow and his heart and his r--- in sheer seriousness and solemnity; it is still frivolity (SLW, 12).

Here, true seriousness is a relation to the essential in contrast to displays of false seriousness by those who actually "dally." The characteristic quality of a relation to the essential is an entire, undivided commitment. William Afham says only he can truly recollect who "pursues one idea, one single idea, is preoccupied only with it" (SLW, 11). Constantin Constantius specifically defines earnestness as "holding fast to th[e] idea" (SLW, 53); and Victor Eremita stands ready, as had William Afham, to give all honor and praise to marriage if it can meet this test of single-mindedness. Alas, Victor says "I wait in vain for the unifying idea that holds these most heterogeneous *disjecta membra* [separated members] of life-views together" (SLW, 64).

There is something deeply disingenuous about such stray and hypothetical positive comments about marriage as Victor Eremita's. When we look more closely at the criterion of assessment the aesthetes are using, we see that no actual marriage could pass the test. For the essential to which absolute fidelity is required is the ideal as opposed to the actual, the pure poetic possibility as opposed to prosaic realities. This explains why a real relation to a flesh and blood woman, who serves as a symbol of finite actuality for both the aesthetes and the Judge, represents a failure of seriousness and even an infidelity to many of the former. This commitment to the unattainable ideal and corresponding repudiation of the seriousness of the actual recalls Denis de Rougemont's *Love in the Western World*.[17] De Rougemont traces a distinctly Western fixation on inaccessible objects of romantic love to the troubador tradition of Provence and ultimately to the Cathar heresy. [18]Are Kierkegaard's aesthetes latter-

---

[17]Denis de Rougemont, *Love in the Western World*, trans. Montgomery Belgion (Princeton NJ: Princeton University Press, 1983).

[18]The Cathars (also called the Albigenses) were a medieval heretical group that

day Cathars? To the extent they are, they display their own distinctive seriousness. On closer inspection, these aesthetes don't represent a one-dimensional refusal of seriousness, but rather they denounce what passes for serious, bourgeois-philistine engagements with actuality in the name of a fidelity to the ideal. The passion of these aesthetes' bitter diatribes against bourgeois-philistine pseudo-seriousness is less an expression of nihilism than of disillusioned idealism.

Judge William's Response to the Aesthetes

Even if we find a seriousness behind the aesthetes' critiques, it is evident that Judge William is in their sights. For he is a man of the office and the marital hearth, the specific targets of the aesthetes' derision. In particular, since Judge William locates the quintessential seriousness of life in marriage, the aesthetes' scorn for woman and love expressed in "In Vino Veritas" goes to the very heart of his life-view. The Judge is aware and determined to respond to such critiques as his title, "Some Reflections on Marriage in Answer to Objections," makes clear. Within the first pages of his essay, he identifies his adversaries as the "clever fellows who have conspired to make marriage ludicrous and to mock what is holy" (SLW, 92). And though his essay was purportedly written prior to the aesthetes' symposium, he responds to the particulars of a number of their speeches.[19] So what is the character and quality of his rebuttal?

Turning the Tables on the Aesthetes. Judge William responds to the critique of calculating, self-interested pseudoseriousness we saw in

---

held Manichaean religious views. Their name derives from the Greek καθαρός (= pure). De Rougemont argues in great detail that the courtly love poetry of southern France originally served as code-language for religious views that couldn't be openly expressed and that negative Cathar attitudes toward embodiment in general and marriage in particular have poisoned Western ideas and imaginings about love ever since. Robert L. Perkins makes a complementary point when he links the aversion toward marriage evident among Kierkegaard's aesthetes to a Platonic disdain for concrete, particular persons as objects of love. See his "Woman Bashing in 'In Vino Veritas'," 87-88, 94.

[19]This is a nice echo of Plato's *Symposium* 205e where Socrates' purported description of an earlier conversation with Diotima contains a reference to Aristophanes' just-delivered speech.

Either/Or, I by joining with it, overbidding it, and turning it back on the aesthetes themselves. Already in the second paragraph of his essay, he praises marriage for miraculously and unpredictably transforming the "little things" in married life into "something significant" (SLW, 90). The *sine qua non* of this miracle is belief, which as in so many of Kierkegaard's writings is set over against calculative understanding: "[W]hile the understanding stands still and the imagination is on a wild-goose chase and calculation calculates wrongly and sagacity despairs, the married life goes along and is transformed from glory unto glory" (SLW, 90).

This early passage sets the tone for the rest of the essay, in which stinging critiques of crass common sense abound. For example, Judge William denounces calculative understanding's native language, probability, and its dearest love, outcome.

> There is a phantom that frequently prowls around when the making of a resolution is at stake—it is *probability*—a spineless fellow, a dabbler, a Jewish peddler, with whom no freeborn soul becomes involved, a good-for-nothing fellow who ought to be jailed instead of quacks, male and female, since he tricks people out of what is more than money and more valuable than money. . . .
>
> There is a phantasm that the person making a resolution chases after the way the dog chases its shadow in the water; it is the *outcome*, a symbol of finiteness, a mirage of perdition—woe to the person who looks for it, he is lost. . . . (SLW, 110)

But does the vigor of the Judge's denunciations necessarily show that he is innocent of the charge of bourgeois-philistine mentality? Could his protestations instead indicate that the aesthetes have drawn blood with their critical depiction of bourgeois seriousness? Rather than damning himself by trying too hard to exonerate himself—as Johannes Climacus points out, *Qui s'excuser, qui s'accuser* (Whoever excuses himself accuses himself) (CUP, 1:529)—Judge William brilliantly (three words seldom seen together!) turns the tables on the aesthetes, accusing them of being the ones mired in calculative reason and its false seriousness. A good place to begin looking at this surprising turn is Judge William's reaction to Goethe's *Aus Meinem Leben* and in particular Goethe's story of a romantic relationship he reconsidered and abandoned.

> I feel as if I were sitting on a conciliation board, far from the boldness of immediacy and far from the high-mindedness of resolution,

> far from the heaven of falling in love and far from the judgment day of resolution; I feel as if I were sitting on a conciliation commission surrounded by fatuous folk listening to a talented attorney defend blunders with a certain poetic ingenuity. (SLW 150)

What a striking reversal! Judge William criticizes the aesthetic icon, Goethe, of "worldly common sense" (*verdslige Forstandighed*), of the very vices of bourgeois-philistine mentality (SLW, 157). And though his essay was purportedly composed before the events recounted in "In Vino Veritas," he directs similar charges against the various symposiasts, using the thin veil of imagining the very views on women and love that appear in their speeches. As William sees it, the Young Man went astray in overestimating the abilities of understanding (*Forstand*), a word charged with pejorative significance at least since Hegel used the German equivalent, *Verstand*, to designate the abstract, atomistic thinking characteristic of both everyday life and prior philosophy.[20] This finite, commonsensical way of thinking simply discredits itself when it seeks to fathom love. William writes, "As soon as the understanding wants to try to explain or think through love, the ludicrousness of it becomes apparent, something that is best expressed by saying that understanding becomes ludicrous" (SLW, 120).

Although Judge William feels compassion for the prematurely reflective Young Man, he is unrestrained in his attacks on the purported connoisseurs of women such as Johannes the Seducer. The sort of comparisons and evaluations these critics direct toward women represent "idiotic seriousness (*den dumme Alvorlighed)*" (SLW, 124). As is typical in Kierkegaard's writings, financial transactions serve as the main and typically pejorative metaphor for such calculative thinking.[21]

---

[20]See, e.g., sec. 80 of *Hegel's Logic*, trans. William Wallace (Oxford: Oxford University Press, 1975) 113-15.

[21]While such pejorative references abound in the authorship, it is also important to note that Kierkegaard and his pseudonyms sometimes use financial metaphors nonpejoratively. For example, the Judge says that through resolution "falling in love is deposited in a trust fund" to be drawn down over the course of married life (SLW 111).

> To put it as mildly as possible, to me such connoisseurs seem like those who sit and change money in the forecourt of the sanctuary; and just as it must be nauseating for someone entering the temple in an exalted frame of mind to hear the jingling of coins, so is it nauseating to me to hear the noise of words such as "slim," "shapely," "svelte, " etc. . . . My joy and my being in love are not that of a horse dealer or the irascible unwholesomeness of a cunning seducer. (SLW, 125)

> For the lover, the most certain of all things is that he is in love, and no meddlesome thoughts, no stockbrokers run back and forth between falling in love and a so-called ideal. . . . (SLW, 160)

He even accuses connoisseurs of women of waiting to marry late in life so as to get "the best in nursing care" for free (SLW, 155).

In an especially significant retort, William reinterprets a saying attributed by Diogenes Laertius to Socrates, "Marry or don't marry—you will regret both." Where A expanded this into a general principle in "Either/Or: An Ecstatic Address," (EO, 1:38-40) apparently hollowing out all significance from life's choices, Judge William sees in it an ironic critique of calculative understanding. The person who would ask Socrates whether he should marry or not, the person who would turn to a third party to aid in assessing the merits and demerits of the potential spouse, shows himself or herself to be a "dunce" who will come to regret either course of action. In what follows, the Judge embraces Socratic irony as the ally of true seriousness in that it cuts down the calculative pseudoseriousness that seeks to replace it.

> There is an irony also in this answer that chastises worldly common sense (*verdslige Forstandighed*) that would make marriage an undertaking like buying a house. . . .
>
> Such things are always pleasant to consider, for if frivolousness in the realm of the erotic is disastrous, then a certain kind of commonsensicality (*en vis Art Forstandighed*) is even more disastrous. But this one saying of Socrates, properly understood, is able to cut down, like death with his scythe, the whole luxuriant growth of commonsensical chatter (*Forstandspassiar*) that wants to talk itself into a marriage. (SLW, 157)

Judge William's appeal to Socratic irony is here especially significant when viewed in light of the broader context of Kierkegaard's writings. From *The Concept of Irony* to the last writings against the established church, Socrates and his irony signify for Kierkegaard a breaking free from and a critical stance toward finite actuality. He is the secular antithesis of bourgeois-philistine mentality even as Christ is its sacred antithesis. To place this appeal to Socratic irony in the Judge's mouth makes no sense if, as commentators would have it, Kierkegaard meant Judge William to be a literary realization of bourgeois-philistine mentality.[22] Whatever the limitations and inadequacies of the Judge and his life-view, he just can't plausibly be seen as one of the busy, calculating burghers that the aesthetes pillory.

Further, the Judge's appeal to Socratic irony helps place him in relation to Kierkegaard's developing views on seriousness. As Michael Theunissen has clearly shown, in *The Concept of Irony*, Kierkegaard tends to set seriousness and irony over against each other as polar opposites.[23] This is especially evident in the section on Hegel's conception of Socrates where Kierkegaard writes, "If we wish to include the qualification of irony, which Hegel so frequently stresses, that for irony nothing is a matter of earnestness, then this can also be claimed for the negatively free subject, because even the virtues he practices are not done with earnestness" (CI, 235). Though even in the dissertation there are indications of a more nuanced, dialectical relation between the two moods,[24] it is only later that Kierkegaard and his pseudonyms develop the formula that "true earnestness is the unity of jest and earnestness" (SLW, 365).[25] By appealing to

---

[22]See, e.g., John Douglas Mullen, *Kierkegaard's Philosophy: Self-Deception and Cowardice in the Present Age* (New York: New American Library, 1982).

[23]Speaking specifically of the dissertation, Theunissen writes:

> In sharp contrast to the negativity and infinity that characterize irony stands earnestness. If the one is the negation of the given (*gegebenen*) and surrounding (*umgebenden*) world, so the other posits them. It attaches itself to the finite and is completely absorbed into it. Thus, the essential distinguishing feature of earnestness is positivity even as negativity marks irony. The expression of earnestness's complete affirmation of finite actuality is pathos.

Michael Theunissen, *Der Begriff Ernst bei Sören Kierkegaard* (Freiburg/Munich: Verlag Karl Alber, 1958) 5; my translation.

[24]See *Der Begriff Ernst bei Sören Kierkegaard*, 17.

[25]For a discussion of this formula, see *Der Begriff Ernst bei Sören Kierkegaard*, 61-

Socratic irony as the ally of true seriousness, by noting that true seriousness involves refusing to take seriously that which isn't worthy of regard as much as it involves taking seriously what is worthy, Judge William places himself squarely within this dialectical view of seriousness. Again, this strongly challenges the caricature of the Judge as a complacently uncritical burgher.

Judge William's Sense of Humor. Although the Judge claims Socratic irony as an ally, it is to humor that he more frequently turns as an antidote to worldly pseudoseriousness. Not only does he reject the aesthetes' image of the serious person as humorless, saying "it is a poor husband who does not become a humorist through his marriage" (SLW, 128), he once again turns the tables on the aesthetes by describing them as the grave and morose ones. The Judge and his wife share a good laugh about posters they encounter all around Sjæland thanking a doctor for curing a family, including an unmarried daughter, of corns. But an amorous aesthete couldn't laugh at such a divergence from the ideal. "A lover would feel offended, because this nasty corn, even after it was removed, has a most disturbing effect on an esthetic romantic view of the beautiful" (SLW, 129). [26]Judge William explains the difference in reactions by saying, "It is precisely marriage's sense of security that sustains the humorous" (SLW, 129). Since the marriage isn't based on the perfect ideality of the spouses, since life together acquaints the two with the vicissitudes of human flesh, such flaws are relativized, distanced and made the object of humor. Here, Judge William's use of the term, "humor," is quite in line with the more developed discussions of humor offered by Kierkegaard's other pseudonyms.

But it is one thing to laugh at others, another to laugh at oneself. In sharp contrast to A, whose final Diapsalm imagines using a divinely granted wish to "always have laughter on my side" (EO, 1: 43), Judge William confesses that, "Generally I am somewhat thin-skinned and cannot very well bear being laughed at. It is a weakness" (SLW, 92). Is he, after all, the insufferable, self-important bore a number of commentators have made him out to be?

62.

[26]Though A does find his own corns funny (EO, 1:28).

In a significant departure from his standard indirectness, Kierkegaard seems to give us a verdict in favor of the Judge at the conclusion of "In Vino Veritas." The final scene appears tailor-made for derisive jollity as the symposiasts conclude their festivities with an early morning stroll. During their walk, they come upon and surreptitiously observe Judge William and his wife enjoying a cup of tea in their garden. If, as the Young Man observed, "erotic love is comic to a third party" (SLW, 33), how much more comic promise must this married couple afford the aesthetes? And yet when the conversation is overheard and the couple walk away, William Afham tells us "the enemy occupation troops retreated without any plunder [*Bytte*]. None of them seemed gratified by this outcome [*Udbytte*]" (SLW, 85).

Why this surprising outcome? Quite clearly because the Judge innoculates himself against the aesthetes' derision by having a sense of humor about himself and his wife. In the overheard conversation, William's (unnamed) wife presses him to take seriously her concern "that if you had not married you would have become much greater in the world" (SLW, 84). But William simply lights a cigar, drums his fingers on the table, hums a song about a husband getting a switch from the woods, and reminds her that "Danish law permits a husband to beat his wife" (SLW, 85).[27] It is hard for present day readers to regard the condescension, interruption and threat of violence we see here as very funny, but his wife is clear that he is jesting and repeatedly presses him to "be serious." His response: "No, you are not going to make me be serious, and you are not going to receive a serious answer; I must either laugh at you or make you forget it, as before, or beat you, or you must stop talking about it, or in some other way I must make you be silent. You see it is a jest, and that is why there are so many ways out" (SLW, 85). With that, the couple kiss and walk away, leaving the aesthetes "without any plunder."

---

[27]There seems to be a connection in Kierkegaard's mind between mockery of pseudoseriousness and cigars. Just as the Judge smokes as his wife frets about him becoming an important man, so Johannes Climacus enjoyed several cigars while deliberating in the Fredricksburg Gardens about how he should go about offering some important service to his society (CUP, 1:186).

As previously with corns and now with worldly accomplishment, humor represents a distancing and relativising of some aspect of life. But what allows one to take this humorous perspective? It is an awareness of something more important, more truly serious. As Roberts points out, "humor is as parasitic upon serious interest as it is upon normal congruity."[28] The contradiction at the root of humor is not only between what we expect and what we encounter but also between what really matters and what doesn't. Evans notes that contradiction is humorous rather than tragic when we are able to take a "superior, somewhat removed perspective" on it. That superior perspective is an expression of a value judgment, of an estimation of what is and what isn't ultimately serious. Evans notes an exception: nihilistic or, in Kierkegaard's terms, demonic humor, that levels all in a wasteland of meaninglessness. But this exception proves the rule in that it shows how essential seriousness is to healthy as opposed to pathological humor.[29]

As William Afham describes watching Judge William and his wife, he twice remarks on the difficulty of distinguishing jest and earnestness in their marriage (SLW, 83). It is difficult because both are present, united in a higher, truer seriousness, a seriousness suffused with focus, commitment, and authenticity but saved from busyness and humorlessness and self-importance by a chastening irony and humor. Already in Judge William, Kierkegaard's mature sense of seriousness as the synthesis of seriousness and jest receives expression—of a sort. But before moving on to look at the questionable aspects of his particular version of this synthesis, we need to look more closely at the Judge's positive comments on the pathos-filled, serious half of the synthesis.

The Case for Seriousness. In making his case for true seriousness—as opposed to defending himself against the charge of false seriousness—Judge William bombards his reader with a welter of positive images and metaphors rather than offering a rigorous, sustained line of argument. (That is why the letters of *Either/Or*, II clearly are philosophically more satisfactory statements of his position.) At times (e.g. SLW, 117-18), he seems simply to throw

[28]Roberts, "Smiling with God," 170.

[29]Evans, "Kierkegaard's View of Humor," 180, 184.

every positive attribute he can think of at marriage (his icon of true seriousness) in a manner reminiscent of Agathon's speech on Love in Plato's *Symposium*. At first glance, the Judge's metaphorical extravagance seems to defy any treatment other than listing, but on closer inspection, the various senses and images coalesce into a sort of web and in many cases trace back to the three distinct etymological associations cited at the start of the essay: weight, truth, and battle. Further, the richness of the Judge's imagistic treatment leads to establishing a variety of links and associations between the three original senses.

Unsurprisingly, the Judge appeals quite early in his essay to the familiar, almost clichéd, but irresistably apt metaphor of "weight of responsibility" in speaking of the ethical life. He writes, "My conviction, then, is my one and only justification, and in turn the guarantee for my firm conviction is the weight (*Vægten*) of the responsibility under which my life, like every married man's life, is placed" (SLW, 91). He immediately shows he is aware of the double-edged character of this image and works to claim the positive associations even while acknowledging the danger of the negative.

> To be sure, I do not feel the weight as a burden but as a blessing; to be sure, I do not feel the bond as binding but as liberating, and yet it is there. The bond? No, the innumerable bonds by which I am bound fast in life as the tree is bound by the multiple branching roots. Suppose everything were to change for me—my God, if that were possible!—suppose I were to feel tied down by being married—what would Laocoön's misery be compared to mine, for no snake, no ten snakes, would be able to wind themselves as alarmingly and tightly around a person's body and squeeze as does the marriage that ties me down in hundreds of ways and consequently would fetter me with a hundred chains. (SLW, 91)

Even before his first explicit references to weight and rootedness, Judge William had already made implicit and philosophically quite significant use of such images. In the opening paragraph of the essay, he implores his "dear reader" not to give his or her life to world travel, foreign language study or discovering a new astronomical system, but rather to marry, "for marriage is and remains the most important voyage of discovery a human being undertakes; compared with a married man's knowledge (*Kjendskab)* of life [*Tilværelse*], any other knowledge of it is superficial, for he and he alone has properly immersed himself in life" (SLW, 89).

Where the focus of attention of the traveller, the linguist, or astronomer is out and away, the married man's movement is inward, an "immersion" in life. Significantly, Judge William here develops the epistemological dimensions of the image of weight. Where there is a lightness to the outward directed objective knower, weight and seriousness resides in the subjective knower, here subjectivity having nothing to do with a relativistic position on truth and everything to do with focused attention on oneself.

And, of course, one's spouse. Judge William, after evoking the image of Ulysses returning home to Penelope after his voyage outward to see "many cities of men," describes marriage as "a unique kind of acquaintance (*en egen Art Bekjendtskaber*)" (SLW, 89). In the Danish, objective knowing is associated with the verb, *at vide*, where *at kende*, the root of *Bekjendtskaber* (acquaintance) is a more personal form of knowing. So, with this opening appeal for marriage, Judge William places himself in the universe of images and ideas that come to full expression in Johannes Climacus's existential epistemology.[30] But he also suggests that this deeper, weightier knowing need not be entirely self-referential, a suggestion that those should welcome who find Kierkegaard and his pseudonyms too asocial and self-absorbed.

One of the starkest contrasts between "In Vino Veritas" and "Reflections on Marriage" is clearly attitude to women. In place of the disturbing misogyny of the aesthetes, Judge William offers a (perhaps equally disturbing) paean to women. What is constant in the two texts, however, is that woman is equated with the actual, the real (SLW, 133,135). Here the etymological association between matter and *mater* (mother) is significant.[31] Judge William's philogy-

---

[30]See Robert L. Perkins, "Kierkegaard: A Kind of Epistemologist," *History of European Ideas* 12/1 (1990): 7-18.

[31]Both terms are related to the Sanskrit root *ma-* (=make). See Charlton T. Lewis and Charles Short, *A Latin Dictionary* (Oxford: Oxford University Press, 1879) 1118. See also Calvert Watkins, *The American Heritage Dictionary of Indo-European Roots* (Boston: Houghton-Mifflin, 1985) 39.

nism is part and parcel of his use of weight as a positive image even as woman as actuality is a stumbling block to the aesthetes.

If we can think of the actual as the heavy and the ideal as the light, we can also think these concepts under the categories of truth and falsity. Where the aesthetes praise the ideal as the true, as the essential worthy of recollection, and use creative forgetting and remembering to correct imperfections in actuality, Judge William values reduplication, a repetition of one's thoughts and words in one's life, or even an existential reduplication in his wife's life of the ideas about marriage he pens (SLW, 96). As noted above, Danish is a language well suited to the Judge at this point. *Ægteskab* (marriage) and *ægtemand* (husband) both derive from the root, *ægte* (genuine). For the Judge, this genuineness amounts preeminently to conviction, truly meaning what one says, and resolution, truly and unreservedly investing oneself in one's actions, and he claims both virtues for himself (SLW, 91, 107). The specific mark of resolution is its sustained, enduring character versus the tentative, playful, and temporary quality of experimental action. "[T]he resolution has the earnestness of perseverence (*Udholdenhedens Alvor*) that sounds through the fleeting and the transitory" (SLW, 118). Thus, a constellation of images of honesty, resolution, existential reduplication, and persistence gather around the root meaning of the Danish word for seriousness, *alvor* (all—true).

The third predominant image of seriousness is that of battle, which as we saw, is associated with the term, "earnest." The Judge calls his argument for the legitimacy of marriage a "battle" (SLW, 102,123) and those against whom he argues "enemies" (SLW, 106); he describes himself as "fighting under the victorious banner of the happy first love" (SLW, 93) and assigns marriage to the literary genre associated with military exploits, the epic (SLW, 117). Further, he claims courage as the distinctive virtue of the married man, first because he boldly undertakes risk (SLW, 116, 165) but also because he is willing to submit himself to the derision of those who hold the married estate in contempt (SLW, 92). It seems, indeed, that the marital is the martial. Just as Socrates claimed but recast traditional Greek notions of bravery when he compared himself to Achilles for refusing to cease practicing philosophy (*Apology* 28c), so Judge

William appropriates the stirring images of battle in his own apology for marriage.

In addition to the three images suggested by the various words for seriousness, Judge William calls upon an additional set of images relating to the experience of meaning and significance. He compares marriage to a book given to the couple by God to read and reread throughout a lifetime (SLW, 95). And in a passage already cited above, he describes marriage as a miracle—a sort of transubstantiation?—"everything revolves around little things (*Ubetydeligheder*) that the divine element in marriage nevertheless transforms by a miracle into something significant (*betydelig*) for the believer" (SLW, 90). Here, Judge William is attentive to a subtle aspect of ordinary usage of "serious." A person who utters nonsense, who jabbers, is not serious but silly. By extension, if human existence is "sound and fury, signifying nothing," then it lacks seriousness.[32] For Judge William, marriage is the essential defense against such a breakdown of sense and seriousness, first because it involves resolution, and without resolution life is just a "waste of time and trouble" and "blather" (*Sladder*) (SLW, 107), and, second, because it is uniquely woman who can work the magic of transforming the insignificant into the significant. Judge William describes his wife as "[she] through whom I feel the meaning of my life, that it has meaning and in many ways" (SLW, 93). He celebrates women's occupation with the apparently trivial, mundane details of life as a sign of their strength and even magic.

> Woman is assigned the less significant tasks, which for that very reason require strength. She chooses her task, chooses it gladly, and also has the joy of continually equipping man with the conspicuous

---

[32]Shakespeare nicely captures this sense of loss of seriousness in Macbeth's cry of anguish on having murdered the king.

> Had I but died an hour before this chance,
> I had liv'd a blessed time; for, from this instant,
> There's nothing serious in mortality.
> All is but toys; renown and grace is dead;
> The wine of life is drawn, and the mere lees
> Is left this vault to brag of. (*Macbeth* II.3.96-101)

This passage is quoted by Vigilius Haufniensis (CA, 146).

> strength. I for my part believe my wife can do wonders; and I more readily understand the greatest feat I read about than the dainty embroidery with which she clothes my earthly life. (SLW, 144)

Judge William specifically defines earnestness as the capacity to grasp and appreciate this miraculous female transformation of the insignificant into the significant. Further, he identifies sympathy and love as necessary preconditions of such awareness (SLW, 140). This assertion complements the "existential epistemology" implicit in the Judge's description of marriage as the true "voyage of discovery." Not only is true knowing serious in the sense of heaviness, of movement inward, of immersion in the actual, it is now identified as a loving, sympathetic, charitable mode of awareness. This interestingly anticipates the epistemological aspects of Kierkegaard's *Works of Love* but also a number of more recent works of moral philosophy, notably Iris Murdoch's *The Sovereignty of the Good*.[33] Further, it stands in the sharpest contrast to the disengaged, unsympathetic, even malicious viewpoint evident in the aesthetes and which I associated with a negative perspective on seriousness. As Judge William asks rhetorically, "Or are jealousy and evil passions alone supposed to make a married man clear-sighted and alert, should not faithful love [*Kjærlighed*] be able to do the same—indeed, be able to keep him alert longer?" (SLW, 140). Though he uses this image of alertness in several other places (SLW, 110, 161), he never develops the image as a main interpretation of seriousness, leaving that task to Kierkegaard, himself, for whom sobriety serves as a major image of seriousness, especially in the late religious writings.[34]

A final significant image in Judge William's defense of marriage is (appropriately!) telos or goal. "Marriage I regard, then, as the highest τέλος [goal] of individual life" (SLW, 101). While no reader of *Fear and Trembling,* which precedes *Stages on Life's Way* in the authorship, can fail to be struck by the portentious associations the term *telos* carries, I want to focus here on the image of height to which the Judge appeals. The image of height plays a significant role in the Judge's letters in *Either/Or*, II, where he speaks frequently of

---

[33]Iris Murdoch, *The Soverignty of the Good* (London: Routledge and Kegan Paul, 1970).

[34]See part 1 of *Judge For Yourself!*

marriage lifting first love up into a higher concentricity, an image he continues to use in "Some Reflections on Marriage" though less prominently (SLW, 161). Most significant for our purposes, however, is the link between height and seriousness. For the serious is the "higher," the more truly important and significant that relativizes, distances, and allows humorous perspective on the "lower," the less important and significant. Accordingly, that which is unequivocally and without qualification serious is the highest; it is the absolute that relativizes all other ends, it is the card that trumps all others. The existence of such a highest telos, such an unqualifiedly serious concern, seems implicit in the formula that true seriousness is the unity of jest and seriousness. It is the source of both the seriousness and the jest, of seriousness by being important and of jest by relativizing that which isn't. But what is this highest *telos*, this ultimately serious concern? This way of putting the question transparently presupposes an answer: God. And especially in the later religious writings, Kierkegaard is quite explicit in explaining seriousness in just these terms.[35] But, as we saw, Judge William identifies marriage as the highest *telos*. Though he surely doesn't so view his comment, it seems a blatant and obvious idolatry (marry-olatry?). Nor is that remark a lone indication that the Judge is elevating marriage to a questionably supreme status. As we have seen, he describes marriage as a sort of miracle, a transubstantiation of the insignificant into the significant. He accuses the husband who fails to believe in this miracle of being worse than a pastor who doesn't believe in God (SLW, 90). And his account of his own church attendance focuses on the mothers and children he worshipfully observes there, entirely to the exclusion of the service itself (SLW, 138-

---

[35]For example, in *Works of Love*, Kierkegaard writes:

> What is the earnestness of life? If you have in truth put this earnest question to yourself, then recall how you answered it, or let me remind you how you answered it. Earnestness is a person's God-relationship. Wherever the thought of God accompanies what a person does, thinks, and says, earnestness is present; in that there is earnestness. (WL, 320)

Michael Theunissen discusses this idea of earnestness as God-relationship at some length. See esp. *Der Begriff Ernst bei Sören Kierkegaard*, 52-58.

40). It seems, indeed, that marriage is the Judge's religion, just as his comment about marriage being the highest *telos* would suggest.

But how clear, how self-conscious is he about his heterodoxy? While in *Either/Or*, II, Judge William seems to have a serene sense of himself as a solid Lutheran, citing Bishop Balle's catechism as his inspiration and sending on the Jutland pastor's "Ultimatum" to A as a summation of all he has said in his letters, there is a much more anxious sense of the religious as a potential threat evident in "Some Reflections on Marriage."[36] It is to this anxious engagement with the religious and its implications for our understanding of seriousness that I turn in the next and final section of this essay.

The Serious and the Sacred

To say that Judge William is anxious about religious issues in "Some Reflections on Marriage" is not to say that he is opposed to religion but rather that he is deeply ambivalent. For, as Vigilius Haufniensis tells us in *The Concept of Anxiety*, anxiety is *"a sympathetic antipathy* and *an antipathetic sympathy"* (CA, 42). The reason for the Judge's sympathy with the religious is not far to seek. As I have argued elsewhere, Judge William's understanding of ethical existence is built on religious foundations.[37] As he sees matters, God creates the task (*Opgave*) by bestowing the gift (*Gave*) first of one's life

---

[36]For a detailed analysis of the parallelisms between Judge William's letters and Bishop Balle's catechism, see Julia Watkin, "Judge William, A Christian?" in *International Kierkegaard Commentary: Either/Or, Part II* (Macon GA: Mercer University Press, 1995) 113-24. The same volume includes three very helpful discussions of the significance of the "Ultimatum." See Robert L. Perkins, "Either/Or/Or: Giving the Parson His Due," 207-32; David R. Law, "The Place, Role, and Function of the 'Ultimatum' of *Either/Or, Part Two,* in Kierkegaard's Pseudonymous Writings," 233-58, and David R. Law, "The Ultimatum of Kierkegaard's *Either/Or, Part Two,* and the *Two Upbuilding Discourses* of 16 May, 1843," 259-90.

[37]George B. Connell, "Judge William's Theonomous Ethics," in *Foundations of Kierkegaard's Vision of Community,* ed. George B. Connell and C. Stephen Evans (Atlantic Highlands NJ: Humanities Press, 1992) 56-70. The term "theonomous" was coined by Paul Tillich to designate an alternative to Kant's stark opposition between heteronomy and autonomy. A theonomous ethic traces obligation back to God but rejects the label "heteronomous" because the self achieves its freedom in its obedient relation to God.

and ultimately of one's beloved, to which the ethical self appropriately responds by choosing oneself "in one's eternal validity" and by choosing the spouse at the marriage altar. While this "theonomous ethic" is most fully worked out in *Either/ Or*, II, it is plainly evident in "Some Reflections on Marriage" as well. William reminds us that "God has instituted marriage" (SLW, 99); he asserts that "if the individual has not in faith placed himself in relationship with God as spirit, paganism haunts his brain as a fantastic reminiscence and he cannot enter into any marriage" (SLW, 100); he describes marriage as "signed in heaven, and then it is countersigned in temporality" (SLW, 112); he rejects the aesthetes' connoisseurship of women, saying that since God chooses the beloved, the lover need not worry about discriminating judgments of relative merit (SLW, 160); and, finally, he specifically traces the seriousness of marriage, the earnestness of the resolution to take a spouse, to God before whom the vows are taken: "[I]s my happiness less because God in heaven guarantees it, and not in jest, as Eros would do it, but in earnestness and truth, as truly as the resolution holds him fast!" (SLW, 165).

While this supportive, reassuring, enabling, and rather domesticated version of God is (almost) the whole story in *Either/Or*, II, in "Some Reflections on Marriage," Judge William has caught a glimpse, anxiously and reluctantly, of the less avuncular face of God. To borrow Rudolf Otto's terminology, after giving us *Either/Or*, II that is heavy on the *fascinans* and almost entirely *tremendum*-free, Judge William has discovered the *tremendum* by the time he writes "Some Reflections on Marriage"—though he does everything he can to get it back in the bottle, to forget it, to return to the religious innocence (disingenuousness?) of the earlier letters.[38] This attempt principally takes the form of a strangely impassioned denunciation of what is for the Judge an entirely hypothetical figure, a "religious exception."[39] While this concept has a richer significance for other

---

[38]Rudolf Otto, *The Idea of the Holy*, trans. John W. Harvey (Oxford: Oxford University Press, 1953) 12.

[39]For a useful statement of the six extremely daunting requirements Judge William lays down for the religious exception, see Sylvia Walsh, *Living Poetically: Kierkegaard's Existential Aesthetics* (University Park: Pennsylvania State University, 1994) 183. Céline Léon identifies nine separate requirements for such an exception

pseudonyms, here it designates primarily a person who is unable and/or unwilling to marry on religious grounds. Though the Judge grudgingly—and inconsistently—acknowledges that such an exception may represent a life that is higher than the ethical (SLW, 169), he spends much of his essay taking back this concession, barring the way to such an existence, criticizing it, limiting it, and even threatening it so as to reassure himself that life "is enclosed in such a way that no one is tempted to want to venture outside, is so constituted that the mere thought of the terror must be enough to crush all foolish and frivolous and inflated and fallacious and neurotic talk about wanting to be an exception" (SLW, 183). But why such hostility toward and concern over a very few melancholy outsiders? Nineteenth century Denmark was hardly in the midst of a monastic revival, so how should we explain the Judge's intensity of feeling?

Like Kierkegaard and the other pseudonyms, Judge William believes that the principle, not the numbers, matter. He perceives in the religious exception a view of God and of humans' relation to God that radically calls into question the irenic compromise between the aesthetic, ethical and religious aspects of life that he has theorized in his writings and more importantly attempted to realize in his life. In denouncing the religious exception, Judge William is, in a real sense, fighting for his life. What exactly, then, is the nature of the perceived threat?

To understand his concern over the religious exception, we need to place that exception against the backdrop of the Judge's broader and quite ambivalent view of religion. After a brief introductory section, Judge William plunges directly into his religious dilemma at the start of the main body of "Some Reflections on Marriage." On the one hand, as we have seen, God is the *sine qua non* of marriage, the giver of the spouse, the witness of the vow, the sustainer of the love. On the other hand, God is so purely spiritual, so universal, and, ultimately, so terrible and awe inspiring that an awareness of God's presence threatens to obliterate the immediate, sensuous dimensions of love that are every bit as essential to marriage.

---

in her essay, "The No Woman's Land of Kierkegaardian Exceptions," in *Feminist Interpretations of Søren Kierkegaard*, 156.

> The difficulty is that as soon as one thinks of God as spirit, the individual's relationship with him becomes so spiritual that the physical-psychical synthesis that is Eros's potency easily disappears. . . . Thus, marriage is theatened with dangers from two sides; if the individual has not in faith placed himself in the relationship with God as spirit, paganism haunts his brain as a fantastic reminiscence and he cannot enter into any marriage; and on the other hand neither can he do it if he has become totally spiritual. . . . (SLW, 100)[40]

Significantly, the Judge presents this dilemma in terms of contrasting and defective versions of seriousness. On the one side is "paganism" which, because it is oblivious to God as spirit, is characterized by "the beautiful jesting earnestness of immediacy" (SLW, 100). On the other side, the thought of God threatens to be "so earnest that the pleasure of love seems to vanish when the God who is the Father of spirits is himself supposed to be the copula" (SLW, 99). The deficiency of the former seriousness is easy to see. Its choices lack substance and staying power. But how can Judge William raise questions about the idea of God being so (= too) serious? When irony and humor chasten pseudoseriousness, they target misplaced seriousness, they expose someone attaching too much significance to something that doesn't merit it. But to raise a concern about the idea of God as being too serious is another matter entirely. If true seriousness is the basis for critiques of pseudoseriousness, on what basis can one critique the truly serious for being too serious?

At first glance, it seems that the Judge employs aesthetic criteria in raising his concern: he worries that "the pleasure of love" will vanish and that the music of life will fall silent (SLW, 99, 111). But it isn't fair just to write the Judge off as an aesthete in disguise. Rather, it is in the name of his distinctive understanding of seriousness that he refuses the alternative and austere seriousness of a purely spiritual existence. As we saw above, Judge William associates seriousness and significance and celebrates woman's ability to

[40]Vigilius Haufniensis also describes this tension between the spiritual and the erotic: "But why this anxiety? It is because spirit cannot participate in the culmination of the erotic. . . . It feels itself a stranger. It says, as it were, to the erotic: My dear, in this I cannot be a third party; therefore I shall hide myself for the time being" (CA, 71).

transform the insignificant into the significant. In sharp contrast, the idea of an entirely transcendent God threatens to evacuate the significance of all that is finite and temporal. It threatens to make a jest of marriage just as ethical seriousness makes a jest of "becoming something much greater in the world" (SLW, 84). As he is forced to admit, "Yet, from the essentially religious point of view, it cannot be denied that it makes no difference whether or not a person has been married" (SLW, 172). (This from the man who earlier in the text celebrated the enduring, even eternal character of his titles, "Husband," "Father," "Head of the Family," "Defender of the Home," "Breadwinner," "Guardian of the Children," in contrast to the ephemeral quality of merely human titles such as king and duke [SLW, 93-94]!)

So Judge William is in a bind. He needs God to establish and sustain marriage but he also needs to guard against that God so relativising the finite and the temporal that it loses sense and significance. He acknowledges that his balancing act, his project of synthesis, is difficult, but he takes it on and claims the biblical image of the burning bush to express his aspirations: "the difficulty is to be able to preserve the qualifications inherent in the erotic so that the spiritual does not burn them up and consume them but burns in them without consuming them (SLW, 100; see also SLW, 166).

This work of accomodation and coexistence parallels and complements the Judge's project of reconciling the aesthetic and the ethical, the immediate and the resolution, that consumed his attention in *Either/Or*, II and continues to engage him here. Though the Judge claims "either/or" as his mantra, he might better choose "both/and," for the guiding vision of all his writings is a happy accommodation of the aesthetic, the ethical, and the religious in a well-rounded, agreeable, responsible and pious life.

And this is why he so resents the religious exception, the person who lives out an exclusive either/or between worldliness and religious faith by renouncing marriage. What is at stake here is not simply a particular person's domestic arrangements. Rather, marriage represents for the Judge a positive, concrete relationship to actuality just as religiously motivated celibacy represents to him its rejection. Thus, "anyone who evades [marriage] crosses out the whole of earthly life in one single stroke and retains only eternity and spiritual interests." (SLW, 101, see also SLW 174, 180).

From the Judge's point of view, such an existence lacks appropriate seriousness. It lacks weight in that it maintains an abstract, disengaged relation to actuality;[41] it lacks courage in that it retreats from the battlefield of life; it lacks truth in that this "religious abstraction" focuses exclusively on a single aspect of the religious—its relativization of the finite—to the exclusion of more positive aspects such as the doctrines of God as creator and as moral lawgiver; and it strips all significance from life in its "fervor of annihilation" (SLW, 171), in its all-encompassing humor toward the finite. In short, by single-mindedly and abstractly focusing on God as the highest *telos,* the "theocentric eccentric" loses sight of all the other dimensions of seriousness. The Judge, having weighed such a self in his balance, finds it too light.

What are we to say of the Judge's critique? First, that it has a deep resonance with much of Kierkegaard's authorship. From *The Concept of Irony* in which he argued that irony must be mastered by a deeper positivity to be healthy, to *Fear and Trembling* in which Johannes de Silentio contrasts the disengagement from finite existence of the knight of infinite resignation with the involvement in the world of the knight of faith, to the writings of Johannes Climacus who contrasts Religiousness A, which humorously revokes time, with Religiousness B, which paradoxically makes time decisive for the self's eternal happiness, Kierkegaard and his pseudonyms repeatedly contrast an alienated otherworldliness to a profound engagement with finite actuality, consistently to the advantage of the latter.

But there is a striking difference between "Some Reflections on Marriage" and those other texts: where the other writings reflect a respect for and appreciation of radical negativity, be it irony or infinite resignation or humor, that frees the self from the bonds of finitude, Judge William rails against religious exceptions for their negative resolutions with an uncharacteristic, immoderate intensity. There is a shrill, harsh, even threatening quality to his harangues that

---

[41]"[T]he abstraction must be regarded as unjustified because it relates itself altogether abstractly to that which it renounces. It does not concern itself with trying to grasp more concretely . . . the beautiful reality [*Realitet*] of falling in love and the true reality of marriage" (SLW, 174).

is never evident in his treatment of aesthetes, with whom he enters into dialog, whom he seeks to understand and advise. In contrast, he delivers an extended diatribe against religious exceptions. Such a self is in "conflict with life" (SLW, 108); it is "a faded glory and as barren as a bachelor's life" (SLW, 109); "the person who has chosen the negative resolution sleeps uneasily at night, expects the nightmare that he chose wrongly will suddenly come upon him, wakes up exhausted to see the barren heath around him, and is never restored because he is continually in suspense" (SLW, 109); he is "a poor wretch or mutineer, . . . an outcast of the race, . . . a stranger to joy, [who] weeps, and perhaps gnashes his teeth" (SLW, 112); "he has ventured out into the trackless infinite space where the sword of Damocles hangs over his head if he looks up toward heaven, where the snare of unknown temptations clutches his feet if he looks toward the ground, where no human help reaches out" (SLW, 179); he is doomed to "this wretchedness—which surely is the deepest, the most agonizing, in which the pain does not cease except in order that repentance can swing its whip over him" (SLW, 181); and in a paroxysm of hostile rhetoric, he compares the exception to "someone whose hands and feet have been cut off and whose tongue has been torn from his mouth" and he requires that the exception "feel himself to be the most wretched of men, the scum of humanity" (SLW, 181).

Though the Judge outdoes himself in describing how frightful such an existence is, he repeatedly accuses the "theocentric eccentrics" of *wanting* to evade life by way of their negative resolutions (SLW, 169, 173). This accusation seems both uncharitable and unfair. For from Abraham to Quidam to Kierkegaard himself, religious exceptions typically experience their particular condition as one that chooses them, as one they would gladly leave behind for the comfort and security of an ordinary life if they could. So why is the Judge, who was so understanding and even sympathetic when analyzing the aesthetes, so harsh and even obtuse in discussing religious exceptions? Clearly, the Judge doesn't just disagree with such individuals but feels hostility and resentment. But why?

At a minimum, the Judge's reaction seems defensive; taking to heart the maxim that the best defense is a good offense, he goes after the religious exception with an intensity that is directly proportionate to the anxiety that the exception induces in him. But the intensity of the attack is so great that one wonders whether this isn't fundamentally a case of projection, the Judge lashing out at a person in whom are realized all his own doubts and misgivings about the reconciliation and accommodation of the aesthetic, ethical and religious.

As Karl Popper points out, such "psychoanalytic" claims aren't subject to decisive confirmation or refutation. Still, this hypothesis about the Judge's defensiveness, his doubts, his lack of conviction is supported not just by the vehemence of Judge William's attacks but also by the evident contradictions in what he says, and especially by the epigram, "The deceived is wiser than the one not deceived" (SLW, 88), an epigram which practically screams his bad faith, his decision to overlook objections to and incoherencies in his life-view.[42] Most compelling, however, is the evident change in the Judge from *Either/Or*, II to "Some Reflections on Marriage." There is really very little change in his message to aesthethes. He remains confident that ethical existence beats out the aesthetic even on aesthetic grounds; it is not only ethically but also aesthetically superior. But where the Judge looked to the religious simply as an ally in the earlier letters, here he is harried by at least some versions of it. As I put it above, he seems to have caught sight of the *tremendum*. Not liking what he sees, he lashes out at individuals who incarnate the *tremendum*, those to whom Flannery O'Connor's maxim, "You shall know the truth and the truth shall make you odd," applies.

Perhaps the best way to get a handle on the change in the Judge's stance toward religion is to note that the letters of *Either/Or*, II are pre-*Fear and Trembling* while "Some Reflections on Marriage" is post-*Fear and Trembling*. While it is plausible to suggest that there was an evolution in Kierkegaard's own thinking about the ethical and the religious over that time period that reflects itself in changes in various writings by the Judge, such an explanation raises all sorts of problems relating to the pseudonymity of the texts. It just doesn't do to explain a change in the Judge by pointing so directly to a change in Kierkegaard. So, I propose instead a rather speculative hypothesis: it is as if the Judge has read and understood *Fear and Trembling* in the

[42]For the Judge's own explanation of his epigram, see SLW, 144.

interval between the earlier letters and "Some Reflections on Marriage" but now is trying to forget what he read there, to convince himself that he can return to his comfortable and familiar life-view.

The parallelisms between "Some Reflections on Marriage" and *Fear and Trembling* are striking: both focus on whether there can be an exception that is higher than the universal, attempt to identify the necessary conditions for being such an exception, ask whether the God-relation is mediated by the universal or is individuated, describe individuals who exist outside the universal as necessarily misunderstood, despised and silent. Further, they use almost identical images for discussing what is at stake in asking such questions: where Johannes de Silentio says if all duty to God is mediated by the universal then "The whole existence of the human race rounds itself off as a perfect, self-contained sphere, and then the ethical is that which limits and fills at one and the same time" (FT 68), Judge William expresses the same idea by speaking of the "gloriousness of life that it is enclosed in such a way that no one is tempted to venture outside" (SLW, 183). Finally, there is a parallelism between Johannes de Silentio and Judge William, both of whom are fascinated by the exception, with the difference, of course, that the former admires and longs to see the exception while the latter bitterly denounces such defectors from the universal.

In fact, the Judge's newfound rhetorical extravagance calls to mind a story Johannes de Silentio tells in *Fear and Trembling* of a pastor who, having preached on Abraham persuades a parishioner to emulate the father of faith by offering his son to God.

> If the preacher found out about it, he perhaps would go to the man, he would muster all his ecclesiastical dignity and shout, "You despicable man, you scum of society, what devil has so possessed you that you want to murder your son." And the pastor, who had not noticed any heat or perspiration when preaching about Abraham, would be surprised at himself, at the wrathful earnestness with which he thunders at the poor man. He would be pleased with himself, for he had never spoken with such emphasis and emotion. (FT, 28-29)

The phrase, "wrathful earnestness," used here perfectly describes Judge William's diatribes against religious exceptions. But Johannes de Silentio's use of it is, of course, profoundly ironic: for to castigate a man for doing what one said to do, for taking one seriously, is transparently not to be serious, no matter how one gesticulates, no matter how loud one raises one's voice.

Now, Judge William isn't caught out in any such obvious hypocrisy. But a parallel exists nonetheless. In both cases, married men of the official class use stern and threatening language to keep would-be exceptions safely confined within the ordinary bounds of social life. But is this really seriousness? Could it be rather an appearance of seriousness that is used to keep at bay real seriousness, just as an appearance of piety is often the best way to neutralize the insistent demands of the sacred? For in *Fear and Trembling* (and in most other texts in Kierkegaard's authorship), we meet an alternative conception of seriousness—that it is to exist as a single individual alone before God, outside the comfortable categories of the universal, aware of one's sin and of one's consequent inability to carry out the demands of ethics. In attacking the exception with "wrathful earnestness" and with evident anxiety, it looks suspiciously as if the Judge is trying to hold at bay, to neutralize, to protect himself from a seriousness that is too serious.

With this suspicious conclusion, I come to the end of this essay not having pinned down the meaning of seriousness but rather indicating that we can go deeper into this central category of Kierkegaard's thought only by moving on to other texts. For the Judge is only *a*, not *the*, realization of seriousness in the corpus of Kierkegaard's writings. That said, the placement of "Some Reflections on Marriage" in the "narrow pass" between the aesthetic and the religious makes it a privileged place to raise questions and identify difficulties in reference to that most protean and equivocal of concepts, seriousness.

6

Morning and Melancholia in "Quidam's Diary"

Vincent McCarthy

> In the Middle Ages a person saved his soul by telling his beads a certain number of times; if in a similar manner I could save my soul by repeating to myself the story of my sufferings, I would have been saved a long time ago.
>
> (Quidam's Diary: Midnight, 14 June)[1]

> The reader who has read Constantin Constantius's little book will see that I have a certain resemblance to that author but nonetheless am very different. (Frater Taciturnus's letter)

If a writer keeps repeating a story, introducing some new twist in each telling, can he eventually convince somebody—perhaps himself—that things had to develop (or unravel) in the way that they did? This is the almost inescapable question that emerges in contemplating the many variations of a doomed engagement in Kierkegaard's pseudonymous writings.

In "Guilty?"/"Not Guilty?" Søren Kierkegaard pseudonymously retold the unhappy love story that had inspired major portions of *Either/Or*, I (1843) and then *Repetition* and *Fear and Trembling* (both 1843). In this large section of *Stages on Life's Way* (1845), he tried to give yet new meaning to the break in suggesting that a self-conscious, suffering, religious direction in the personality blocked normal human fulfillment in a conventional love relationship, but he went on, problematically, to link it to inclosing reserve. Thus "Guilty?"/"Not Guilty?" is a variation of the failed love story in which inclosing reserve is linked to the religious, and in which the religious would be thereby made the impediment to successful love.

---

[1]The section continues: "If my repetition [*min Repetition*] is perhaps not always imploring, ah, it nevertheless preferably ends in this final solace" (SLW, 372). This is one of the few uses of the Danish-English cognate *Repetition*, and where we might expect Kierkegaard's usual term and Danish title for *Repetition*, namely, *Gjentagelse*.

However, everything in the story and even in the telling suggests that inclosing reserve is the sole and sufficient cause for a failed romance, that there is no necessary connection between inclosing reserve and the religious at all. At the same time, we are thrown back on the phenomena and riddle of the repetitions in this work and in the aesthetic authorship, a "story of suffering"[2] that in its very repetitions and variations has continuously intrigued, fascinated and distracted readers.

Emotionally and psychologically, Kierkegaard appears in this work still to be extricating himself from his ill-considered engagement to Regine Olsen in 1841.[3] This may effect the fact and the compostion of Quidam's Diary, but Kierkegaard's private life is not what the work is formally or ultimately about. Instead, it is about understanding the religious dimension of the personality, as revealed in a clash with the aesthetic and ethical. Many readers of Kierkegaard are so struck by the repeated love story that they mistakenly believe that Kierkegaard remained obsessed with it throughout the remainder of his short life. This is not the case. And, despite the exploration of the repeated love tale that the present essay pursues, it should be emphasized at the outset and it bears repeating in the conclusion that, at least theologically and theoretically, Kierkegaard reconciled earthly love and the religious by the time he published *Works of Love* in 1847.[4]

Nevertheless, Kierkegaard's repetition of the love story in *Stages on Life's Way* bears examination for several reasons, among them the tantalizing fact and significance of the repetition itself, the parallels with *Repetition*, and most significantly the distinctive explanation of the love story that the Quidam's Diary section attempts to provide.

---

[2]Johannes Climacus's own way of referring to "Guilty?"/"Not Guilty?" Cf. "A Glance at Danish Literature," CUP, 288-91.

[3]This interpretation, while plausible and perhaps even likely, must nonetheless be recognized as based on grouping several pseudonymous texts together. If Kierkegaard finally does something similar himself, in reviews of the aesthetic authorship, he would doubtless resist this line of interpretation from the subsequent age of Freud. One might counter, invoking the pseudonyms against the author, that Quidam's diary and the love story are, along the lines of the demonic sketched by Vigilius Haufniensis in *Concept of Anxiety*, an unfree self-disclosure crying out for clarification. Still, one knows in advance what a dim view Kierkegaard would take of this. But, *pace Kierkegaard*, we continue.

[4]Specifically in the first series of discourses drawn from the verse "You shall love the neighbor" (Matt 22:39).

The two quotations at the head of this essay go to the heart of the theses that I would like to pursue. For Taciturnus is indeed like Constantin Constantius, author-editor of the pseudonymous 1843 novella *Repetition*. The parallels between the two works are so striking and numerous that I will argue that "Guilty?"/"Not Guilty?" is a reworking of the love tale of *Repetition*—with differences, as Taciturnus notes, but with even more similarities, many of which he passes over.[5] "Guilty?"/"Not Guilty?" may fairly well be called a repetition of *Repetition*.

Indeed, once their similarities and parallels are recognized, the reader may well suspect a literary repetition compulsion on the part of Søren Kierkegaard. Quidam seems to have some sense of this, as he reflects on his own retelling of his story, in the morning and at midnight. Author Kierkegaard is certainly self-conscious on this point, as Frater Taciturnus's quote and other remarks make clear. If indeed "Guilty?"/"Not Guilty?" is something of a literary repetition compulsion, then Kierkegaard may be far less in control of his text than he thought and wished. Does Kierkegaard really enjoy the sovereign control over his pseudonyms and the direction of the authorship that the *Point of View for my Work as an Author* would posit? Or is he perhaps controlled by the love story that was so traumatic for him

---

[5]This article is intended in a sense to be twinned with the article I wrote for vol. 6 of the *International Kierkegaard Commentary: Fear and Trembling and Repetition* (1993), namely, "*Repetition*'s Repetitions," 263-82. In that article, I explored the striking parallels between Kierkegaard's practice of repetition in *Repetition* (1843) and Freud's theory of repetition and repetition compulsion in his *Beyond the Pleasure Principle* (1920). There, repetition automatism, frequently referred to as 'repetition compulsion,' is understood as abreacting to a traumatic experience. (Cf. *The Standard Edition of the Complete Works of Sigmund Freud*, vol. 18.) Kierkegaard's engagement to and rupture with Regine Olsen clearly constituted such an event in his life, and his writings record not only his working out of the affair but his literary transformation and elevation of it. As such, it is finally more than Freudian repetition, while certainly it is also an abreaction along Freudian lines.

Kierkegaard/Johannes Climacus's exploration of the parallels is contained in "A Glance at Danish Literature" within *The Concluding Unscientific Postscript*.

The same IKC volume contains numerous fine essays on *Repetition*. Particularly relevant to the interpretation pursued here are the essays by Stephen Crites ("The Blissful Security of the Moment") and Andrew J. Burgess ("Repetition—A Story of Suffering"). David Gouwens's (also included in the same IKC volume) *Kierkegaard as Religious Thinker: Passions, Virtues, and Praxis* (Cambridge: Cambridge University Press, 1996) relates repetition to hope and virtue in ways that are rich and suggestive.

personally and that he seemingly cannot cease writing about? Does not his unconvincing theory of a religious development linked to and limited by an inclosing reserve effectively distract readers from his main point (namely, the religious) and repeatedly draw their attention to the love affair itself, with which Kierkegaard seems obsessed? The passionate and repeated insistence that the religious has made this love impossible repeatedly fails to persuade. Clearly, despite Kierkegaard's own commonsense realization that biography and authorship cannot be strictly separated, Kierkegaard's personal life intrudes and subverts this text, in a manner that seems to undercut his intentions and that also seems perhaps beyond his control. All this having been conceded, his personal pathology does *not*, in the end, mar the creative transformation of experience or dissolve the more important meaning that the work seeks to impart. In sum, if his tactic of retelling a love story in order to call attention to the religious does not work to explain away his personal trauma, that does not *per se* invalidate his theory of religiously directed melancholia (*Tungsind*) and crisis sparking deeper religious subjectivity.

The problem in Kierkegaard's presentation arises when Taciturnus, the fictional author of a fictional diary, adds inclosing reserve as an essential element in the *Tungsind*-religious link, with its implications for isolation and the inability to sustain an earthly love. His insistence on linking inclosing reserve to the religious does not constitute an argument and it can even lead the reader (and especially one familiar with previous tellings of the love story) to suspect that the religious is being invoked as a dramatic, (self-) glorifying cover for an isolating and debilitating reserve. Quidam would have us accept his retelling of the story as a (romantic) embrace of a once-and-still beloved, through the medium of recollection. Thus, religious impulse and love both survive, and thus there is reconciliation after all. But only in the pseudonym's mind! Indeed, this line of interpretation would bring us back to the aesthetic categories of *Repetition* or even to the young man (A) of *Either/Or*, I. Quidam is beyond the sweet idle melancholy of that young man and into the religious crisis that Constantin foretold for the young man of *Repetition*, as Frater Taciturnus notes in his Letter. In his brooding melancholia, Quidam attempts to justify himself to himself (guilty?/not guilty?), as he tries to puzzle out why he inflicted evident emotional trauma upon himself. His answer does not satisfy himself—the trauma continues, after all; and the answer should not satisfy us. Nonetheless, it contains insights into his predicament and hints at other reasons for the retelling.

Overview of the Diary.

"Guilty?"/"Not Guilty?" purports to be an anonymous diary fished out of Søborg Lake by Frater Taciturnus, stitched together by Hilarius Bookbinder along with the other manuscripts that constitute *Stages on Life's Way* and then brought to the public. Its purported publication history is a tale of distancing, from Frater Taciturnus who is not quiet, from Hilarius who does not laugh, and from Søren Kierkegaard who is more than a little severe (Severinus) with the central character.[6] It is a noisy narrative of "somebody's" self-torment, vacillating between self-accusation and self-justification, a tale of gloom and foreboding. It is not the best of his literary works, although it has moments of literary sparkle and psychological brilliance.[7] "Guilty?"/"Not Guilty?" comprises almost two-thirds of the bulk of *Stages on Life's Way*.[8] Within "Guilty?"/"Not Guilty?" the morning and midnight diary (Quidam's Diary) entries constitute two-thirds of the work, with the remaining a nearly 100-page-long letter to the reader.

The morning and midnight diary entries are placed in a kind of counterpoint. As often in counterpoint, the whole can be less interesting when reduced to its parts: when the upper and lower "lines" are played separately. Nonetheless, the experiment is worth making. For the separate morning and midnight diaries, now intertwined, are supposed to report different years and different stages in the intensification of religious crisis. The morning entries actually stand alone quite well as a separate composition.[9] In contrast, the midnight entries, read alone, are virtually unrelieved

[6]Frater Taciturnus offers to return the document to the author, who will be recognized by the handwriting. Meantime, he has no compulsions about its publications. Frater Taciturnus also estimates that the year of the events related is 1751. Further distancing?

[7]According to Hong, fewer than half the original copies were sold (245 sold; 280 remaindered). The work was well reviewed by P. L. Møller, and Hong quotes Hirsch (writing in 1930) as saying of *Stages* that despite earlier lack of attention it "has become, in Denmark, as well as in Germany, Kierkegaard's most famous and influential poetic work" (SLW "Historical Introduction," xviii). This high estimation was no doubt largely due to "In Vino Veritas."

[8]Sixty-four percent to be exact.

[9]The morning and evening entries give the impression of having been separate compositions subsequently interlaced, each drawing on Kierkegaard's own diaries. The longer midnight pieces ("Solomon's Dream" et al.) are lifted out of Kierkegaard's writing notebooks.

gloom. The ending section, Frater Taciturnus's "Letter to the Reader" is reminiscent of the dull Judge William, but Taciturnus anticipates the critics by announcing his expectation that "two-thirds of the book's few readers will quit before they are halfway through . . . out of boredom they will stop reading and throw the book away" (SLW, 398) and does not overestimate his own writing as he speculates, in the conclusion: "My dear reader—but to whom am I speaking? Perhaps no one at all is left." (SLW, 485).

Those who persevere must have their own reasons. For this interpreter, there is the puzzling relationship between "Guilty?"/"Not Guilty?" and the aesthetic works that preceded it. More substantive is the path that it sketches toward the increasingly inevitable religious moment. For "Guilty?"/"Not Guilty?" is a recapitulation of *Either/Or* and also of *Repetition* but also a clear, deliberate advance beyond the two. If *Either/Or* contains another famous diary, it is that of a seductive lover, not that of a fugitive from earthly love.[10] And if *Repetition* is flight from a young girl and into the poetic, Quidam's Diary stands before increasingly inevitable religious movement—movement that was sensed in *Repetition* but that is clearly gathering momentum in "Guilty?"/"Not Guilty?".

The love story is the central event that took place *before* the diary and that the morning entries attempt to chronicle as recollection in the present tense. But the love story continues as the determining event to stimulate the midnight brooding a year later. It would seem to be a diary reworking of *Repetition*, only this time the "silent confidant" (as the young man entitles Constantin) would formally be the author Quidam himself, overheard by the "silent brother" (Frater Taciturnus), who, ironically, is a more stable ("constant") listener than Constantin, since he does not intrude himself constantly into the story. Nor is there any relationship (of confiding, fleeing, reconciliation) such as characterizes the almost clinical 20th century relationship of "analyst" Constantin and "patient" young man in *Repetition*. Our latinate Quidam writes only to himself about the Quaedam that he never calls by name. If one takes the epistolary novella *Repetition* and the diary

---

[10]It is worth recalling that one of the versions of the Don Juan myth had the (exhausted?) Don Juan enter a monastery at the end of his seducer's career. Is the monkish Frater Taciturnus to be understood as Quidam in Don Juan's monastery?

Although Quidam is no Don Juan or Johannes, one might wish, for her sake, that this young girl too had heard Zerlina in Mozart's "Don Giovanni" before meeting this young man!: "I'd like to but. . . . He may be just tricking me." ("Vorrei e non vorrei. . . . Ma può burlarmi ancor": act I, sc. 3, duet of Giovanni and Zerlina).

novel "Guilty?"/"Not Guilty?" as mirror images of the love story, the latter must be regarded as "through a glass darkly," and this is nowhere more clearly reflected than in the term "Tungsind" that characterizes the latter work. To rejoin the music metaphor above, if *Repetition* is the love story in the key of "Melancholi," "Guilty?"/"Not Guilty?" is the love story in the key of "Tungsind."[11]

Parallelism between Repetition *and "Guilty?"/"Not Guilty?"* Since my thesis is that the one of the meanings of the Diary is as a reworking and development of the love story, I advance the following observations in support of the connection:

First, the title for "Guilty?"/"Not Guilty?" comes from *Repetition* itself. The October 11 letter of the young man asks: "How did it happen that I became guilty? Or am I not guilty?" (R, 200.) What we thought was a rhetorical question in the novella has become the haunting question of the novel. The subtitles of both works are also close: "A Venture in Experiment-

---

[11]I have developed this theory at greater length, if in somewhat different terms, in " 'Melancholy' and 'Religious Melancholy' in Kierkegaard" (*Kierkegaardiana* 10 [Copenhagen, 1977]: 151-65).

Howard Hong's decision to translate "Tungsind" and its various adjectival forms as "depression" and "depressive," "depressing," etc. is seriously misleading. First of all, "depression" has come to have special clinical meanings in the twentieth century and to be associated with the literature and analyses of Freud and his heirs. The Danish twentieth-century term that corresponds to our usage of "depression" is simply the Danish cognate "depression." "Melancholi" and "Tungsind" are not clearly delineated in Danish usage, although "Tungsind" is the darker and more serious stage or form. Nor is Kierkegaard's usage absolutely well defined either. Nonetheless, the general term in *Repetition* is "Melancholi." (*Repetition* is also the principal work where the term "Melancholi" appears, as demonstrated in a McKinnon vocabulary mapping program and confirmed by simple word counts.) "Tungsind" does appear in *Repetition,* but "Tungsind" and its adjectives are the exclusive term in "Guilty?" / "Not Guilty?"

For all the footnotes and apparatus in the new translation of *Stages on Life's Way,* this difference is nowhere noted—not even in the few instances where Hong deviates and translates an adjective as "melancholy." (Cf. SLW, 266, where Ossian is quoted: "Sweet is the sorrow of melancholy," but "Tungsind" is the unindicated Danish term. If "melancholy" is the right term here for "Tungsind"—as it no doubt is—why not elsewhere also?)

An archaic word such as "melancholia" for "Tungsind" might have better delineated the difference and pointed the twentieth-century reader back toward the nineteenth-century romantic context out of which the term comes.

ing Psychology" (*Repetition*) and "A Psychological Experiment" ("Guilty?"/ "Not Guilty?").[12]

The pronoun "I" is "overused" in both books and is excessive even by letter and diary standards.[13] In fact, *Repetition* and *Stages* are literally the most egocentric books in the aesthetic authorship, even though neither "I" is ever named. ("Young man" and "Quidam" are as close as we get, the latter an indefinite pronoun.) Each young man's entries are for a seven-month period (August to February in *Repetition*; January to July in "Guilty?"/"Not Guilty?").[14] Constantin tells the story of a young man's engagement a year before; the morning diary tells of Quidam's engagement a year previous. Both works end with concluding letters by the editor, who meantime has tried to reduce the engagement chronicler to a fiction. *Repetition* is ambiguous about whether the young man is ultimately a fiction, whereas Frater Taciturnu's Letter portrays Quidam as his literary product.

Repetition is about a love story still unfolding. We expect the past tense (since it too is the story of a year ago), but as it unfolds into the concluding pages (and beyond) of the book, we get the present. The morning diary of "Guilty?"/"Not Guilty?" is about the previous year. Where we expect a declared diary entry to be about that day (the meaning of "diary" after all), we get a "diary" of the past in the present tense. For the diary is really about

---

[12]Hong translated "Psychologisk Experiment" as "An Imaginary Psychological Construction," thereby losing the parallel Danish terminology between the two works.

[13]The following is a table of the use of the first-person pronoun in *Stages*, a work of approximately 500 pages in length, of which nearly 300 are "Guilty?"/Not Guilty?""

	jeg	*Jeg*	Total "I"
A. Morning Entries	712	77	789
B. Midnight Entries	1495	135	1630
C. Quidam's Diary (=A+B)	2207	212	2419
D. "Guilty?"/"Not Guilty?"	2476	250	2726
E. *Stages on Life's Way*	3293	337	3630

Not to belabor a point, but from the above it can be seen that most of the occurrences of the pronoun in "Guilty?"/"Not Guilty?" are in the diary entries. The rest of *Stages on Life's Way* is slightly less "I"-centered. In comparison, the next-most "I"-centered work in the aesthetic writings is the 100-page novella *Repetition*.

F. *Repetition*	643	88	731

[14]Except that the young man of *Repetition* makes a reappearance in his surprise May 31 announcement of the young girl's marriage and his (partial) repetition.

the meaning of the events a year ago as they effect the diarist in his morning recollection, in advance of his midnight brooding.

The letters of *Repetition*'s young man might as well be a diary. They are addressed to Constantin as reader but seem written for the author himself. But Constantin, as the formal addressee, has no opportunity to reply (except by publishing them, with commentary, to us as readers), while the writer keeps his distance and furnishes no address. Each work is a love tale placed within several layers of observation: Constantin begins his work as an observer of the love tale and continues, as the tale continues to unfold. Quidam observes his own love tale (a tale of the past, told in the present tense), and then observes himself in the present, in his midnight entries. If one accepts Constantin's attempt to reduce the young man to a fiction, we might even imagine that the love story is Constantin's own, that the letters are to himself ("Dear Diary" instead of "My silent Confidant"), and that his observations are really a retrospective. Of course, this is exactly what happens in the morning and evening diaries of "Guilty?"/"Not Guilty?" which Taciturnus acknowledges as his own creation.

Each book alludes to the religious character of the problem. It only begins to break through in *Repetition*; in "Guilty?"/"Not Guilty?" it is repeatedly referred to. Constantin ends his work with the growing recognition of the religious problem at the root of the young man's melancholy inability to sustain the love relationship; the Diary begins with the *tungsindig* recognition that the religious is at the bottom of Quidam's problems. *Repetition* is about *redintegratio in statum pristinum*, which is how it defines repetition. Taciturnus tells the reader at the end of "Guilty?"/"Not Guilty?" that he has Quidam expect everything to end in a *restitutio in integrum* (SLW, 434). In both works, Kierkegaard's implied thesis is that a wound to the aesthetic life prompts and, by degrees, necessitates confrontation with a higher possibility, namely, the religious. That the particular wound—a love wound—stands behind Kierkegaard's literary works and his own experience is the troublesome link between literature and biography, of course. In the pseudonymous authorship, the wound remains uncured, and perhaps in Kierkegaard's personal life as well. However, in *Works of Love*, Kierkegaard does reconcile religious and human love, theologically and theoretically, as was noted above.

At times, one might almost imagine Quidam as the "young man" of *Repetition*, and thus each of them writing a year after the event, except that the dates of the entries will not allow this interpretation. Because *Repetition* was published first, author Frater Taciturnus had the opportunity to become acquainted with Constantin's work, and so indeed he has, as he acknowledges, *inter alia*, on page 402. But if he wishes to differentiate the two works (SLW, 437), he nonetheless acknowledges the parallels and connections. Needless to say, there is no acknowledged linkage to the love problem of Søren Kierkegaard that is the source of the several pseudonymous tales.

Details from the Diary

Although it may seem hardly possible, Quidam's Diary is even *more* solipsistic than *Repetition*. For *Repetition* was at least addressed to another, and the relationship between the young man and Constantin provides some relief from the ever-present "I." In the Diary, there is no such relief. Neither the author nor the reader has any relief from the self-torturer who writes in the a.m. about today a year ago (misrelation to time?) and then at midnight about his state of mind that day, when the day is done. In the morning, he narrates his way out of a precipitous engagement a year ago, but as if it were today. At midnight, he stews over the aftermath a year later. Where in the authorship do we have a clearer reflection of the divided self that *Either/Or* I first sketched? In the morning we observe a reflective mind obsessed with the unfolding events of a year ago. At midnight we witness a mind brooding on the effects today of events from a year go. It is a kind of split mind or literary schizophrenia. All of this only highlights the crisis—the vague, religious crisis—that has been heating up (since the Diapsalmata) and is now coming to a critical point.

Morning Entries. The morning diary purports to be the "reminiscence diary" of Quidam, written a year after the events narrated (although, with only one exception, in the present tense). In counterpoint to it is the much larger midnight diary, which is "really" today.

It is of course Kierkegaard's own tale repeated and reworked yet again. He told it privately in his journal, indirectly and distortedly in *Either/Or*, repeated it in *Repetition* and has now recounted it twice more in Quidam's Diary. Thus it is an oft-repeated and yet *new* story that we are told each time. And yet it is not Kierkegaard's personal story anymore, by virtue of having been reworked and transformed, from the speculative seduction of *Either/-Or*, I, to the romantic melancholy of *Repetition*, to the *Tungsind*/melancholia of Quidam's Diary. Johannes Climacus's review of it emphasizes "the story of suffering" and the suffering consciousness which distinguishes Quidam from the young man of *Repetition* (CUP: 287-90).

The diary's interlaced and confusing chronicle of unraveling romance and enduring aftereffects mirror the misrelation to time that Kierkegaardian pseudonyms emphasize. Technically, the morning and midnight diaries begin in year 2, five months after the July rupture in year 1. But, even the "one year ago" recollections of the morning diary are not the actual beginnings, for he admits to having seen her a full year before the morning-chronicled love pursuit took place, and perhaps that should be the true year 1. By the time the diary ends, we cannot feel that the story is over. In fact, we might expect a sequel, in January of year 3, that begins "Two years ago . . . "! For the essential problem, whatever it is, is still unresolved, even if implosion seems imminent. In fact, the ending entry, on 7 July, predicts: "The third of January the unrest begins again" (SLW, 396).

The first entry, 3 January, sets out the essential problem, both as it existed "then" (a year ago) and as it exists "today": a young man of powerful religious sensitivity is afflicted by a melancholia (*Tungsind*) that is linked to his religious nature and the unspecified religious direction in which it impels him. It is a lonely, individualizing problem. Meantime he struggles with the more conventional universal-human possibility of marriage. For reasons that neither the Diary nor the authorship ever makes clear or compelling but that is nonetheless a determining "fact," the religious impulse and the romantic instinct are held to be in conflict:

> Should a soldier stationed at the spiritual frontier marry? Does a soldier stationed at the frontier, spiritually understood, dare to marry—an outpost who battles, night and day . . . with the robber bands of a primordial melancholia [*Tungsind*]? (SLW, 195; translation revised: see n. 11 above)

One does not need the midnight entries to see that the relationship is doomed from the beginning. But underlining the doomed quality of the relationship is the midnight entry of 5 January on quiet despair.

His relationship to the young girl[15] is a kind of macho romanticism that proves itself, in hindsight, to be inadequate. She does not understand him, as he recognizes. This was the problem all along. He sees that it makes a married relationship impossible. It never occurs to him that his problem with marriage might be the unrealistic romanticism that leads a young man to single out a young lady who is allowed to be nothing more than the

[15]In her indefiniteness given the parallel indefinite Latin pronoun Quaedam in Taciturnus's letter. See SLW, 737n.519.

projection of sweet-love fancies. Because in his isolation he also fancies himself a very independent individual, it never occurs to him that he is a victim of the unreal social ideas of his age concerning romantic love. The ideas of a bygone age might have been less dangerous. For example, had he contented himself with wearing his lady's colors as in the age of chivalry, they both might have been better off. But now she is to become the occasion of self-growth for him, just as the young girl of *Repetition* played a parallel role in that work. We never come to know either young girl. Quidam even declares that he will not stoop to know her by testing and investigating her nature (SLW, 207)—although we are eventually told that her lack of religious presuppositions (25 January; SLW, 226) removes any basis for the relationship (or at least justifies his conduct to himself in cutting off the relationship, because he feels so cut off). He is *Tungsind*, and she is the symbol of joy (*Glæden*) (SLW, 197, 206).

The doomed engagement takes place quickly on January 12 and immediately begins to unravel. For the prisoner of reflection observes that "Lovers ought to have no differences [*Mellemværende*] between them. Alas, alas, we have been united too briefly to have any differences. We have nothing between us, and yet we have a world between us, exactly a world" (SLW, 216). By January 17, he has a presentiment that it will not work, that it is already over, and that it was over before it began: "it is not with her, it is not with Eros that I must struggle. It is religious crises that are gathering over me. My life-view has become ambiguous . . . " (SLW, 216). By 20 January, he has made his choice: "So I have chosen the religious" (SLW, 222) and three days later he invokes her lack of religious presuppositions as justifying the break that is coming.

By 12 February, he is reading religious books to her, even though he had earlier acknowledged that her lack of religious presuppositions could not be countered by his becoming her religion teacher. He notes that it is not working: she is not attentive. And, meantime, "I myself am growing more and more in the direction of the religious" (SLW, 240).

When he acknowledges his inclosing reserve (*Indesluttethed*) and its being "an elemental flaw" (SLW, 241) he comes closer to stating what is, for most, a more comprehensible grounds for his inability to sustain (or even form) a genuine relationship with the unfortunate young girl. Indeed, here he makes a telling self-disclosure about his inclosing reserve, whose very problem, ironically, is disclosure itself.

The pseudonymn Vigilius Haufniensis considered inclosing reserve in detail in *Concept of Anxiety* (CA, 123-29). There inclosing reserve was described as unfreedom and silence, periodically bursting into unfree disclosure. However, the language of inclosing reserve is, expectably, still self-referential. It does not really reach out to an other. Hence it is monologue, not dialogue.[16] And the reader should nottake the diaries for free communication or dialogue. Recall that neither Frater Taciturnus nor Quidam ever published them. Indeed, admission to inclosing reserve in the monologue-diary is far from being free, self-disclosure to another. No, it is merely self-description to and for oneself, a very unfree disclosure in the manner that Haufniensis described in 1844. And, for all the apparent self-disclosure in recognizing *Indesluttethed* (enclosing reserve) as his problem, there is no hint of real self-transparency.[17] In the end, his invocation of inclosing reserve is more elemental than he realizes. In it resides the fatal obstacle to love, for, as Haufniensis observes, inclosing reserve is demonic. According to Haufniensis, it is, in the ethical sphere, what evil is in the metaphysical. As such, it is the very opposite of marriage, which we will recall from Judge William in *Either/Or*, II, is the very symbol of ethical existence. Yes, inclosing reserve and all that it represents (unfreedom, being locked up in oneself, unable to open to another) would seem to be Quidam's real problem. However, Quidam has grandiosely attributed his inability to sustain a love relationship to the religious.

By 20 February, he is acknowledging the misrelation, sees that she is unhappy and asks her forgiveness for sweeping her into the (mis)relationship. By 28 February, he declares: "Courage and perseverance! I shall reach the religious with her" (SLW, 248).

By 5 March, he observes that there are "no new symptoms," and repeats this in the next two entries, 9 and 20 March. The entry of 25 March has the lovely, melancholy contrast of a young girl 16 summers old and her young man who is twenty-five winters old.

By April, the relationship is coming apart outwardly, and he reassures himself that the religious is the reason. On 17 April he writes "The trouble is that she has no religious presuppositions at all" (SLW, 309), but on 10 April, he sums up the solitariness of his religious thinking when he writes: "Spiritually it is with an individuality as it is grammatically with a sentence:

---

[16]"[F]or monologue is precisely its speech, and therefore we characterize an inclosed person by saying that he talks to himself" (CA, 128). Or, in this case, as one who writes to himself, night and day.

[17]Haufniensis regards transparency as a synonym of disclosure (CA, 127, second footnote).

a sentence that consists only of a subject and a predicate is easier to construct than a periodic sentence with dependent and intermediate clause" (SLW, 297-98). One senses that his notion of spiritual predicates includes only intransitive verbs, that there is no room for subject-object thinking here (or intersubjectivity).Whatever the problem with his solipsistic, or narcissistic, notion of the religious, he sets it up emphatically as the obstacle. 24 April: "[S]he has no sensitivity whatsoever to the motives I consider to be supreme" (SLW, 314). 26 April: "[T]he deepest breathing of my spirit-existence I cannot do without, I cannot sacrifice, because that is a contradiction, since without it I indeed am not. And she feels no need for this breathing" (SLW, 315).

The solitariness of his religious conception comes to expression on 28 April: "[W]hen God speaks he uses the person to whom he is speaking, he speaks to the person through the person himself" (SLW, 316).

By May, there is open talk of rupture, and on 8 May he proposes breaking the engagement, a process that will consume the final two months of entries, as the diary shifts to a weekly chronicle of dissolution.

On 30 May he explicitly links his inclosing reserve and his melancholia. It is repeated in the final morning entry of 7 July: "My life-view was that I would hide my [melancholia] in my inclosing reserve . . . " (SLW, 394). This is nearer to the mark: inclosing reserve hindering the disclosure of his religiously directed melancholy. The important linkage is melancholia and the religious, melancholia as concentrated possibility presaging religious crisis. Still, this linkage does not account for his inability to carry through an engagement and to marry.

Since he has a distorted notion of marriage, it would never occur to him that one of the difficulties might be that he had courted the wrong person. His romantic notion of only one possible beloved precludes this reflection. The reason he could not marry Quaedam may be nothing more than a simple mismatch of Quidam and his Quaedam. But he would have us believe that the fundamental reason is the religious. Yet everything else in his narration would suggest that his emotional isolation, expressed as *Indesluttethed*—is more nearly the reason and that the inability to disclose oneself as one needs to do in a love relationship has no necessary connection to the religious at all, even if the deep inwardness of religious life cannot be readily disclosed to another.

In the end, his inclosing reserve (which Walter Lowrie's translation frequently rendered as "morbid reserve") probably rules out any relationship and would also do so if there were no attendant religious crisis. Indeed, the believable religious crisis is made into the unbelievable reason for the breakup.

In sum, inclosing reserve is the problem in the relationship, not the religious and not melancholia (*Tungsind*). Who was supposed to be persuaded by these repeated attempts: Quidam, his reader, or Kierkegaard himself?

Midnight Entries. Five months after the rupture, Quidam struggles with his oversensitive conscience and his midnight thoughts. If the midnight entries are considered as counterpoint to the morning reminiscences, they are for the most part the same repetitious, gloomy melody, broken only by six thematic, titled pieces (Quiet Despair [5 January]; A Leper's Self-Contemplation [5 February]; Solomon's Dream [5 March]; A Possibility [5 April]; Periander [5 May]; Nebuchadnezzar [5 June]. Only 5 July is lacking.) The pattern of fifth-day midnight entries is one of the most striking structural elements of the diary.

The ghostly diarist worries about Quaedam whom he perceives as pale and suffering. He tells us that he goes to sleep at nine, to rise at midnight for his nocturnal pursuits. "Who would not think me a fool if I told him that now in this current year she preoccupies me more than ever?" (SLW, 217). According to him, he has her life on his conscience and feels like a murderer.

On 2 February he wonders whether he ever loved her, whether he might be too reflective (reserved) ever to love. But this instant of self-clarity vanishes as he asks himself why then all these sufferings and, as he seems ready to accept his suffering as the (romantic) proof that this must have been love, speculatively reflects that his tortured and haunted present is the aftermath of a tragic love.

His repetition compulsion is clearly stated on 7 March: "What is all this for? Why do I do it? Because I cannot do otherwise." But at least to his conscious mind it is no mere *Freudian* repetition compulsion, for he continues: "I do it for the sake of the idea, for the sake of meaning, for I cannot live without an idea; I cannot bear that my life should have no meaning at all. The nothing I am doing still does provide a little meaning" (SLW, 253).

His belief that his religious nature is the root of his inability to have continued or consummated the relationship is repeatedly stated. He dismisses her, this year as last[18], for having no religious presuppositions (7 February; SLW, 236). Yet, he is ambiguous about this too and perhaps gives away the fact that her "nonreligious" nature is not the problem after all, when he comments on 29 April: "If she had become a religious individuality in the proper sense, it would have been frightful for me" (SLW, 318) We are not dealing with the "real" Quaedam in any case—we only see her through Quidam's eyes, and he himself eventually admits that her image is his own creation: "There is one person, one single person, about whom everything revolves. I gaze and gaze so long at this girl—until I draw out of myself what I perhaps would otherwise never have come to see" (7 June; SLW, 364).

On 7 March, he remarks that "Only a relationship with God is the true idealizing friendship" (SLW, 253). But he confesses that, whatever a religious person may be, he himself is not yet one: "I am really no religious individuality; I am just a regular and perfectly constructed possibility of such a person" (20 March; SLW, 257). He declares his need to work himself free of her, even after the rupture and in what is now a year of mourning, in order to turn to "the religious crises" which will then be his task (SLW, 261). However incorrectly he may understand himself, he does have a definite interpretation of his problem and it is that his religious nature, and some impending religious crisis, underlined by Quaedam's lack of religious disposition make a continuation of the relationship impossible. But this is an interpretation *after the fact.* We have no record of his thoughts during the actual time of the rupture. (And we should not be fooled by the morning reminiscence diary.) Everything is "clearer" in retrospect, now that he has settled on a line of interpretation. Having done the incomprehensible deed of breaking off the relationship, he comments on 27 May: "Only religiously can I now become intelligible to myself before God . . . " (SLW, 351). The rupture may intensify his emotional state and thus his separate religious crisis, but the religious is not therefore retroactively the cause. *Post hoc ergo propter hoc* is also fallacious in the realm of the religious.

He seems to come closest to self-transparency when he confesses: "My idea was to structure my life ethically in my innermost being and to conceal this inwardness in the form of deception. Now I am forced even further back

---

[18]But, of course, it was not really last year at all, but merely *last* year as recollected and reported *this* year.

into myself; my life is religiously structured and is so far back in inwardness that I have difficulty in making my way to actuality" (SLW, 351).

If recollections distort, fictional recollections should not be expected to be an exception. Indeed, to some extent recollections always turn out to be fictions as the past, told through a present point of view, is effectively remade. Memory, based in the present, always looks at the past for its own, present purposes. The so-called intentions of the past seem to find much greater clarity too in the present.

The reasons the love story could not endure, however many times Kierkegaard tells it, are ultimately more than unconvincing. The story betrays itself, repeatedly and by its repetitions as having no higher explanation. If this has the effect of undercutting the tragic portrayal of a Quidam unable to marry a Quaedam and reduces it to the probable mismatch of an undefined young girl who agreed, in conventional 19th century fashion, to marry a man she hardly knew but who turns out to be emotionally inaccessible, this does not render it comic either, but only very human, both in its confused, irrational dynamism and in the attempt to render it something more after the fact.[19] But does the unpersuasiveness of Kierkegaard's intended interpretation of the love story necessarily undercut the meaning Kierkegaard wants to give it? Not at all.

For there is no reason to dispute the religious sensibility and divine eros that drives Quidam, only his contention that his brief but haunting romance was made impossible by the religious, rather than by his inclosing reserve. However, Quidam himself seems to sense something of this, or else he would not be struggling with Frater Taciturnus's title: "Guilty?"/"Not Guilty?"

Even if we do not accept Quidam's self-serving romantic analysis of his religious nature precluding a marriage, we should not pass over the more important point that he is clearly trying to make: that he is a religious individuality, struggling with his religious nature and its unclearly seen but definitely sensed directedness. In his letter to the reader, Frater Taciturnus will counsel studying him even in his excess: "Yet it may well have its importance to pay attention to him, because one is able to study the normal in the aberration . . . " (SLW, 398).

---

[19]Taciturnus argues, in his letter, that "the girl is entirely suitable to him, as is meet and proper for the imaginary construction" (*SLW*, 473), but the suitability that he has in mind concerns her dialectical role, not her suitability as love object.

The Six "Short Articles." The fifth-of-the-month entries were originally planned as *seven* insertions into the text, drawn from Kierkegaard's journals[20]. At some point, Kierkegaard dropped the Abelard article (JP, 5:5703, 5609), and so 5 July has no article. The themes of the six, sketching inclosing reserve from various angles (despair, secret disease, secret sin, etc.), are a maudlin series of distractions for the rupture with Quaedam but also Regine Olsen.

5 January (the voice of "Quiet Despair") is about the son who recovers the lost intimacy he had with his now deceased father by imitating his father's voice and saying to himself, as his father once said to him, "Poor child, you are in a quiet despair." Ironically, listening to his father's voice is a source of comfort. But of course the voice is really his own—or perhaps an "impersonal," higher voice that belongs to more than father and son—and it is anything but a message of comfort.

The image conjured up is one of poignant solipsism, of self-referential mastery of loss, indeed of classic Freudian repetition compulsion ("Fort"—"Da")[21] as the son makes the absent father present again through his appropriated voice.

5 February ("A Leper's Self-Contemplation") is a tale of solitude and self-mastery. The disoriented leper Simon calls to and answers himself, reproaching himself for having concocted a salve by which the mutilation of leprosy turns inward. But he renounces its use and therefore voluntarily suffers the fate of external mutilation.

5 March ("Solomon's Dream") is the tale of a son discovering that the father is in despair (thus a kind of mirror image of 5 January). A son steals a glimpse of his father's secret despair, normally obscured by worldly splendor and esteem, and dreams that the worldly achievement is not the blessing upon God's chosen one but an ungodly man's punishment horribly intensified—for both father and son—by the world's misconstrual of worldly station.

5 April ("A Possibility") takes place in Christianshavn, accessed by a narrow bridge, isolated from Copenhagen, a place where "one feels abandoned and imprisoned in the stillness that isolates." The melancholy entry (SLW, 276-88) about a strange, shy, rich and mentally disordered young man who paces oddly, loves children and, in the secrecy of his

---

[20]The "A" *Papirer*: V B 124.

[21]Freud, *Standard Edition of the Complete Works of Sigmund Freud* 18:15.

apartment, collects sketches of children's faces, is almost worthy of an Edgar Allen Poe.

It is the tale of a possibility that haunts and isolates, that renders mad and wise at the same time. The odd conduct of collecting face sketches is exposed: He recovers a (questionable) repressed memory and the attendant guilty of having been led to a whore by his friends and of possibly having fathered a child. Thus, when his employer dies, having made him his heir, the haunted bookkeeper is freed to tend to a "remembered" account. The silent, self-inclosed man feels tortured when his elder cousin teases about a man never knowing for sure how many children he has. When he gives alms to street urchins, he is tormented by the possible and horrible irony of giving alms to his unknown child. It is the tale of a lunatic, a man who pursues in so-called restored health the content of a sickbed fantasy.

5 May ("The Reading Lesson: Periander") is the lesson of a wise man who always acted as a lunatic. He becomes two persons, both wise man and tyrant. Having slept with his mother, killed his wife, alienated and bullied his children and inadvertently brought about the murder of his son, he is a symbol of isolation and alienation. Only in plotting his own death, as escape from life, did he unite wise man and tyrant: Concealing his true identity, he has himself assassinated and buried, and, as part of the plot and to seal anonymity, the assassins themselves are assassinated. His tyranny was his selfish and destructive use of those who carried out his orders; his wisdom consisted in doing away with himself, unknown, unloved, unmourned.

5 June ("Nebuchadnezzar") is the tale of the king of Babylon changed into an ox for seven years, in a dream. It is a story of the defenselessness against the power of God, with a theme of alienation known only to oneself ("My thoughts terrified me, my thoughts in my mind, for my mouth was bound and no one could discern anything but a voice similar to an animal's" (SLW, 361). It too is the tale of a dream that carries over to waking life.

Frater Taciturnus's Letter. In the spirit of our own critical and postmodern era, one needs to be wary of the willfull Taciturnus. For his letter insists on his own interpretation of Quidam's tale, not just about melancholia (*Tungsind*) directed toward the religious but about the role of inclosing reserve, which emerges as problematic and remains so. Taciturnus's interpretation was implicit in Quidam's Diary but already close to the surface; in the letter, it becomes explicit. Taciturnus's first tack is to portray the story as an unhappy love, doomed by misunderstanding between the two principals. But when he writes, "Unhappy love implies that love is assumed and that there is a power that prevents it from expressing itself happily in the lovers' union" (SLW, 405), we should be on guard against Taciturnus's easy identification of "the power." He accounts for the heterogeneity of the couple, or the element of misunderstanding, but viewing the young man in religious categories, the young woman in aesthetic categories (SLW, 420).

Taciturnus describes Quidam as "a demoniac character in the direction of the religious—that is, tending toward it" (SLW, 398). In order to make the same point negatively, he informs the reader that the book is not about the erotic, that he sees as the subject of Constantin Constantius's tale in *Repetition* (SLW, 402). *Repetition* was about a collision within the aesthetic, which then turned a young man into a poet. In "Guilty?"/"Not Guilty?" according to Taciturnus, there is also a collision, but this time, while the girl is once again within aesthetic categories, the young man of this work is "in the power of spirit in the direction of the religious" (SLW, 420). The element of "misunderstanding" becomes the basis for a collision.

To the extent that the issue is the religious, perhaps Taciturnus has not just *Repetition* in mind but the more famous book issued the same day, namely *Fear and Trembling*, with its meditation on Abraham and Isaac. There Abraham is justified by virtue of the religious. Ultimately, it is this point, rather than the Job-like point of *Repetition*, that Taciturnus is pressing here. Indeed, the religious inwardness of Abraham is depicted there as incommunicable. Taciturnus replaces that aspect of the religious with the more problematical category of inclosing reserve.

Quidam's *Tungsind* is nothing less than "the crisis prior to the religious" (SLW, 430). Taciturnus attempts to suggest a necessary link between inclosing reserve and *Tungsind* (religious melancholy/melancholia –'depression' in the misleading Hong translation), which I find unwarranted and unconvincing. He comments that inclosing reserve is a form of *Tungsind* and that *Tungsind* is "the condensed possibility that must be experienced through a crisis in order that he can become clear to himself in the religious" (SLW, 427). In sum: a crisis must be experienced in movement toward the religious, *Tungsind* is that crisis, and inclosing reserve is a form of *Tungsind*. If one accepts this unqualified linkage, then Quidam's moral quandary and emotional-psychological impediment are both absolved by being linked to the religious. However, if the link of *Tungsind* and the religious holds (that is, *Tungsind* as Kierkegaard means it and not with the connotations of the twentieth-century term 'depression'), the link of inclosing reserve and the religious emerges as very dubious indeed.

In his commentary, Taciturnus goes on to state that Quidam's reserve is the "condensed anticipation of the religious subjectivity" (SLW, 428). This might allow for the possibility that, once the religious crisis is over and religious subjectivity achieved (if achieved), Quidam might be able to come out of his reserve. But nowhere does Taciturnus suggest anything of the kind. And, in fact, the character of Quidam would not hold out this hope either. Were we to imagine him as having completed and resolved his religious crisis, we cannot imagine him as *outwardly* changed. We can only imagine that he would remain as reserved as ever and have to find some new reason for his isolating reserve. Taciturnus's psychological experiment never systematically explores inclosing reserve. And while Taciturnus maintains that "there is no real healing for him except religiously within himself" (SLW, 428), he does not suggest that inclosing reserve is itself ever healed or overcome.

Taciturnus observes that, after a more lenient way fails (SLW, 448), the young man created a deception in order to try to exit from the relationship. Yet Taciturnus's letter, and the whole of "Guilty?"/"Not Guilty?" with it, is another level of deception, the attempt to argue that the religious can now account for a the end of a romantic mismatch in a way that the melancholy aesthetic categories of *Repetition* could not. In the process, the linkage between the darker melancholy of *Tungsind* and a religious crisis is an important point in Kierkegaard's developing religious psychology. But the invocation of the religious, while dialectically an advance, leaves the secret of inclosing reserve intact. The interlacing of the religious, inclosing reserve, and unhappy love is perhaps successful from a dramatic and literary point of view and with a nineteenth-century audience. But it fails to convince those of subsequent times that things had to end as they did.

In the appendix to his letter, Taciturnus remarks that, "From the point of view of the aesthetic, every *heautontimoroumenos* [self-tormentor] is comic" (SLW, 465). This realization probably pained Kierkegaard as much as it pains each of his reflective readers. While he was willing to render himself comic and be laughed at in a persona, a comic role not of his *conscious* making was something to flee, through repeated attempts to tell the story in a way that would make sense and convince somebody (quidam), perhaps Kierkegaard himself and most of all.

Kierkegaard's "arguments" fail here, as Quidam/Taciturnus gives us a new variation of a failed love story. Because it fails, we are cast back upon the phenomena and variations of the repeated love story, where we may hear "Guilty?"/"Not Guilty?" 's distinctive message.

Conclusion

Kiekegaard's various meditations on impeded or impossible earthly love suggest numerous questions about the object/Object of human desire. In the human desire for a beloved, is there some dawning revelation of a greater dynamic of desire? In the insufficiency of the object/s of human desire, is there a pointer or a pointing toward a greater Object? If so, does the Object represent a spiritual oasis in the desert of desire, or only a spiritual mirage? Kierkegaard surely believes in the spiritual oasis, yet, through his pseudonyms, he conducts his readers only through earthly mirages.

Is Kierkegaard's story of failed personal fulfillment—transformed into literature, told repeatedly in different modes, and claiming to point beyond itself—merely the desperate attempt to justify himself for his irrational conduct in the mundane business of breaking a rashly conceived engagement? Or is it recollection of an older religious truth, triggered by personal trauma and approached from different angles ("The Seducer's Diary," *Repetition*, *Fear and Trembling*, "Guilty?"/"Not Guilty?") as the trauma is reenacted in literary variations? Is it ultimately a revelation about the nature and telos of desire that sees beyond itself and its initial object?

Kierkegaard would no doubt be dismayed to have his reader bog down in psychoanalytic reductions, at the price of missing the intended meaning of the work. But his repetitions and variations throughout his authorship—both of the love tale and possible justifications—gainsay easy acceptance and send us repeatedly to the personal love story hiding openly in the literary variations. His pseudonyms, their tales and their analyses prompt a scrutiny and a skepticism that take Kierkegaard seriously and yet hold him, as willful interpreter of his own works, at arm's length. Kierkegaard's intentions are clear, even without the interpretations given by pseudonyms. His suggestion of religious crisis manifested in emotional life is rich, nuanced and suggestive. But his theory that inclosing reserve is a symptom of religiously directed melancholia (*Tungsind*) is never argued, only asserted, and is finally to be rejected. This means that the rupture cannot be ascribed to the religious, while it can still be assigned to inclosing reserve. And inclosing reserve is reduced thereby to an attendant danger in the religious, not viewed as an attendant condition.

Strictly speaking, Kierkegaard has in a sense guarded himself and his work from the biographical diversion he causes, through his use of pseudonyms. Indeed, if one is disappointed that the opposition of earthly love and heavenly love seems extreme and unreconciled at the end of "Guilty?"/"Not Guilty?" one most not forget that Frater Taciturnus is, despite his monk's name, only an *aesthetic* pseudonym, who consequently does not have the religious perspective that could and should be able to reconcile earthly and heavenly love. Recall too that *Stages on Life's Way* was published in 1845, only four years after the breakup with Regine Olsen. Kierkegaard's fixation on the event is amply attested to in the published aesthetic writings of 1843–1845, an obsession which increasingly subverts the text by compelling the careful reader to ask to what extent it undercuts or weakens his larger theory of religious subjectivity. But the larger theory is ultimately unshaken.

Works of Love, published over his own name in 1847, makes clear that Kierkegaard recognized that love of the other is at the center of the Christian message and of the religious life, Christianly understood. Yet the force of his fixation in the aesthetic writings is to make us wonder whether or not he ever successfully reconciled the two in practice, or whether the inclosing reserve he cites remained a personal emotional obstacle in moving from the theory of religious living to practice in Christianity.

7

Suspended Reflections: The Dialectic of Self-Enclosure in Kierkegaard's "Guilty?"/"Not Guilty?"

Darío González

Even though the distinction between "immediacy" and "reflection" is a recurrent motif in many of Kierkegaard's works, it is doubtless that the last section of *Stages on Life's Way* shows one of the most conspicuous forms of that confrontation, namely the opposition between a lost immediacy and a "self-enclosed" reflection. Presented as the result of an act of writing which has been totally determined by the movement of reflection, "Guilty?"/"Not Guilty?" is a diary that begins and develops twice. Day after day the author evokes, during the morning, events that took place one year before, and writes, during the night, the diary of the current year. Morning and night, the diary refers to the encounter of an essentially reflective narrator and a feminine character who seems to be situated outside the reserved and reflective structure of the narration, as if her "immediacy" merely consisted in her capacity to reemerge as an object of reflection from the dark background to which she is confined. Given this peculiarity, the contradiction defined by immediate and reflective existence is here originally linked to the tension between aesthetic and religious categories. As Frater Taciturnus points out in the "Letter to the Reader" that accompanies the diary, the feminine character is "aesthetically immediate" (SLW, 432), she lacks "religious presuppositions" (SLW, 399), while the male's character is "ethical dialectical" (SLW, 432) or, according to another definition, "a demonic character in the direction of the religious" (SLW, 398). But neither those presuppositions nor the demonic presentiment of the religious are a sufficient qualification of what Kierkegaard would call the religious "stage" of existence: the stage of the "fulfilment" (SLW, 476) as opposed to that of the "desired ideality of aesthetics" (CA, 17n). Instead, we see that self-enclosed reflection still involves a merely "desiring" relationship with its object.

The very fact that immediacy and reflection, far from being complementary moments in a continuous process, are here opposed to each other as dramatic characters, makes it possible to illustrate a dialectical relationship which simply does not coincide with a "dialectic of reflection" able to incorporate immediacy as one of its elements. The importance of Kierkegaard's strategy in "Guilty?"/"Not Guilty?" becomes clear when one goes back to the meditations on marriage that compose the previous section of *Stages*. The author of that section knows that, although "reflection is immediacy's angel of death" (SLW, 157),"the immediacy of falling in love" is still allowed to stand in the domain of reflection (SLW, 158). This statement makes perfect sense given a conception according to which the immediacy of love can be dialectically comprehended under the ethical category of marriage, even if it is true that "without resolution there is no marriage" (SLW, 166) and resolution in turn presupposes reflection (SLW, 157). At the same time, the notion of "resolution" operates on an ethical level as corresponding to a religious conception: the resolution "is a religious point of departure", "a religious view of life constructed upon ethical presuppositions" (SLW, 162). The resolution of marriage is here the link between the immediacy of falling in love and the only kind of immediacy "that is *ebenbürtig* (of equal standing)", namely the "*new* immediacy" of the religious (SLW, 162). Thus, the difference between the second and the third major parts of *Stages* is not merely the one between an ethical and a religious view of life but, first of all, the essential difference between two topologies, two manners of conceiving the articulation of the spheres. It is not only that the author of the second part sees life with ethical eyes. He can do it only because, in addition, he is able to recognize in every stage of existence the achievement of a previous one.

In contrast, it would be hard to say that the third part of the book simply exemplifies the religious point of view. Not even the central character of "Guilty?"/"Not Guilty?" is unequivocally defined as a religious personality. Once again, the distance between his view of life and a strict conception of the religious can be measured according to the manner in which he "reflects" on love.[1] In the terms used by the author of the second part of *Stages*, the

[1]Accordingly, the difference between the second and the third parts of *Stages* consists in the distinctive role that the *aesthetic* element performs in each case. This

narrator of the third part is not able to fend off the "spiritual temptation" to kill the immediacy of love by means of reflection (SLW, 157). He has lost the "clairvoyance" that the lover should preserve in these cases despite the risk of falling into a sort of "desperate reflection" (SLW, 158)[2]. His capacity of reflection is infinite, while, in the religious, "reflection is discharged into faith" (SLW, 162). His reflection consists in doubting, and all his doubt allows him to do in a religious domain is to "discover religious crises" in the perils of life (SLW 257). Although it is said that he is determined in an ethical-dialectical fashion, his reflection is far from making possible any form of resolution. The character is "ethically" constructed only in order to emphasize the ethical dimension of his "silence" and the necessity of a "teleological suspension of the ethical principle of speaking the whole truth" (SLW, 230), a phenomenon that Kierkegaard presents here under a very precise denomination: *Indesluttethed,* "self-enclosure" or "inclosing reserve". As already noted, that is indeed the most extreme form of the confrontation between immediacy and reflection in "Guilty?"/"Not Guilty?": "He is inclosingly reserved—she cannot even be that"; "all inclosing reserve is due to a dialectical reduplication that for immediacy is altogether impossible" (SLW, 427). Considered as the suspension of an ethical demand, self-enclosure is in this story the only category that indicates, albeit negatively, the presence of an intermediary stage between the aesthetic and the

---

interpretation involves, as we have seen, the opening of a fundamental discussion concerning the significance of the theory of the stages. A very concise presentation of this problem can be found in Harvie Ferguson, *Melancholy and the Critique of Modernity. Søren Kierkegaard's Religious Psychology* (London & New York: Routledge, 1995) 114-15:

> If the "theory of the stages" is identified as "Kierkegaard's thought," rather than the complex of relations generated within the aesthetic, then . . . the spheres become ordered according to a developmental scheme, driven by a process of *aufheben,* in which the lower is preserved in being elevated into a new higher relation. . . . But, if their pseudonymity is seen as central to their meaning, then these same works can be read as demonstrating the modern tendency towards the progressive "aestheticization" of experience. It is aesthetic immediacy, undergoing a series of self-generated internal transformations, which creates the mere illusion of "movement" into "higher" and more developed stages. But all stages, in reality, remain aesthetic stages, and the aesthetic pseudonyms become trapped in a process of "experimenting" in which they are in fact drawn farther and farther away from "actuality."

[2]Howard and Edna Hong translate *fortvivlede* (literally, "desperate") here by "preposterous."

religious. But that implies that both the aesthetic and the religious are now mere possibilities of existence, two forms of "ideality" that constantly diverge from each other. Arguably, the erotic incidents evoked in the diary are only an excuse for the exposition of religious notions such as "suffering" and "repentance". But the central character in the story "is unable to take himself back in repentance", and therefore "at the extreme point he becomes suspended (*bliver hængende*) in a dialectical relation to actuality" (SLW, 447).

On different levels, this *suspension* is precisely what characterizes the dialectic of self-enclosure in "Guilty?"/"Not Guilty?". Inasmuch as the narrator is not able to invoke any actual religious experience as a ground for his reserve, the content of his self-enclosure is nothing but the very confrontation of ideal possibilities. Self-enclosure is here "a strictly formal qualification and therefore can just as well be the form for good as for evil" (SLW, 230). The narrator can easily state what is *not* the object of his concern: "It is not with her, it is not with Eros that I must struggle" (SLW, 216). But it is also significant that the final version of the text does not include the continuation of this very sentence as indicated in the drafts: It is not with Eros that I must struggle, "but with God; it is a religious battle that gathers over me; it is my view of life that demands a rebirth" (SLW, 572). His true suffering consists in the fact that he must struggle with himself and with a "view of life" that applies to none but to himself: "My life-view was that I would hide my depression in my inclosing reserve" (SLW, 394).

The peculiar profile of the reflective character in "Guilty?"/"Not Guilty?" is only understandable with regard to the fact that he has to deal with an *immediate* personality that resists the impact of reflection, in spite of the fact that reflection itself is "utterly inexhaustible" (SLW, 240). Here the individual's reflection unfolds, so to say, within its own limits, and that is also why it assumes the form of self-enclosure which is characteristic of the demonic personality (SLW 230). On the one hand, the "direction of the religious"—which, as already observed, is not religious existence as such—seems to constantly confuse itself with the retracting movement of reserve. On the other, the ontological value of immediacy is so radical that it perverts every attempt to totalize human experience in terms of pure reflection. It is not surprising that, in spite of being himself "in the direction" of the religious, the central character of "Guilty?"/"Not Guilty?" doubts that his reflective and religious orientation can be universally applied to others. There is at least one, namely his beloved, who should perhaps be preserved in her innocence, which is to say in her pure immediacy:

> For me, without much knowledge of people, it has been my comfort and likewise my victory over life, my relief from the differences in life, that one may require the religious of every individuality. And yet here I have run up against an individuality from whom I am not sure I dare to require this, to whom I might be doing a wrong thereby. (SLW, 239)

Albeit indirectly, this passage tells us something important about the role of aesthetic immediacy in the case of an individual who is already able to reflect on his own existence according to religious categories. The aesthetic element which collides with the narrator's religious orientation is not primarily his erotic impulse nor is it the beauty of the beloved[3]—not the aesthetic "ideality" in any sense—but a much more emphatic sense of the "immediate" dimension of individual life, a dimension that seems to involve at once both the girl's innocence before her encounter with love and an undetermined condition of existence prior to every ethical or religious determination. The narrator's doubt about his own culpability, as indicated by the title, expresses his concern about the right to introduce religious presuppositions into somebody else's life. In its deepest sense, however, the doubt affects the necessity of passing from one "sphere" to another, which is perhaps the fundamental problem posed by Kierkegaard in *Stages*. Once again, what promotes this doubt is the presence of an "immediate" creature whose very existence, although it is conceptually associated with one of the stages, might bring into question the whole dialectic of the spheres considered as a dynamic process. Such a creature is the feminine character, the "young girl" that the narrator confesses to "fear" more than anything else in the world (SLW, 266). This doubt concerning the universality of existential categories can be understood in connection to the reservation made in "The Seducer's Diary", where Kierkegaard writes that "the word *existence* already says too much" as far as the woman's being is concerned (EO, 1:431). Paradoxically, to situate the woman's being outside the scheme dominated by the notion of existence makes it possible to consider her as a being who is constantly demanding a revision of that scheme.[4] But the

---

[3]"She is lovable, it is true, but this does not essentially mean anything. If she were lovelier than an angel, that would not concern me; a girl's beauty does not essentially concern me" (SLW, 266).

[4]The problem is some times explicitly presented as a challenge for philosophical thinking: "Is it a perfection in a woman, this secret rapport she has with time; is it an imperfection? Is it because she is a more earthly creature than the man, or

reservation about the woman's existence in *Either/Or* is actually made by a reflective character who is, moreover, defined according to aesthetic principles, while in "Guilty?"/"Not Guilty?" the woman's existence comes to challenge the whole "life-view" of a reflective personality which is also qualified as being "ethical-dialectical". If the doubt is deeper in this last case, it is perhaps because the aesthetic element, which here is partially indicated by the narrator's encounter with the feminine figure, makes itself present in the text in a very particular fashion. Thus, although the existence of the young girl never becomes a decisive element in the story, now her image appears with all the force of something that has been negated in a previous moment.

I say "her image" advisedly. In fact, according to the psychological description of the male character in "Guilty?"/"Not Guilty?", his experiences concerning the woman's existence correspond to a sort of imaginary irruption rather than to a process of reflection. The woman does not cease "appearing" before his eyes, and yet he is not able to understand the meaning of her presence in the whole of his own experience. The sentence that the narrator regularly repeats in his midnight diary: "Today I saw her" (SLW, 242, 335, 391) is less the recording of an actual experience than the suggestion of an impossible encounter: "Today I saw her. Yet this seeing does not help me much, for I dare not believe what ordinarily is considered to be the surest of all—my own eyes" (SLW, 368).[5] The immediacy of her presence

---

because she has more of eternity within her? Please do answer; after all, you have a philosophical mind" (EO, 2:307).

[5]This contradiction might be explained as an expression of the "aesthetic split" that Bradley R. Dewey correctly recognizes in the Seducer's self:

> On the one hand, Johannes seems to possess a participant "agent-self" which carries out specific acts in the world of flesh and blood—moving about living rooms, speaking, touching. But Johannes also possesses another self which "hovers," invisible, near the agent self, directing its activities and reveling in the pleasureful stimuli it thus receives. If the hovering self gets too closely involved with the activity itself—i.e., identifies too closely with the agent self—it loses the aesthetic distance it needs to direct the action and enjoy the stimuli.

Bradley R. Dewey, "Seven Seducers: A Typology of Interpretations of the Aesthetic Stage in Kierkegaard's 'The Seducer's Diary' ", in *International Kierkegaard Commentary: Either/Or, I*, IKC 3, ed. Robert Perkins (Macon GA: Mercer University Press, 1995) 185. In fact, the aesthetic distance kept by the "hovering self"—as a pure observer—simultaneously avoids the encounter between the object of its reflection and the "real" object with respect to which it acts.

is here so extreme that, from the point of view of reflection, she is nothing but a phantasmal image of herself. In a way, this phenomenon constitutes the very possibility of an effective erotic relationship. That is why the author of "The Seducer's Diary" describes it in a positive manner:

> The image I have of her *hovers* indefinitely somewhere between her actual and her ideal form. I now have this image before me, but precisely because either it is actuality or actuality is indeed the occasion, it has a singular magic. I feel no impatience, for she must live here in the city, and at this moment that is enough for me. This possibility is the condition for the proper appearance of her image—everything will be enjoyed in slow drafts. (EO, 1:334; my emphasis)

At this point the seducer admits to *knowing* that he is in love, and this is the "interesting" condition which he wants to stress as being differentiated from mere falling in love (EO, 1:334). The experience alluded to in "Guilty?"/-"Not Guilty?" focuses on the same intermediary space where the beloved's "image", as the seducer would say, *hovers* between actuality and ideality. "Interesting" love is the passion which positively develops in the *inter-esse* of love[6], a dimension which is at once that of the presence and that of the radical absence of the beloved. But the narrator of "Guilty?"/"Not Guilty?" does not even know if he is in love: "perhaps I am sleepless because I cannot know for sure whether I love or do not love" (SLW, 232). Paradoxically, he suffers from all the symptoms of an unhappy love, that kind of love in which, according to the "Reflections on Marriage" contained in the same book, the woman "has her supreme reality, and here her meaning is so doubtful that she signifies nothing positive but is negatively the occasion for

[6]Kierkegaard himself suggests that the Danish word *Interesse* (interest) is also to be understood in the sense of *inter-esse* (being between) (JC, 170), a notion that he then uses in his definition of existence's "actuality" in the *Postscript*: "Actuality is an *inter-esse* (between-being) between thinking and being in the hypothetical unity of abstraction" (CUP, 1:314). Actuality here is not the synthesis of being and thinking but the space in which that synthesis fails. Setting aside the content of this formula, it is clear that the notion of "inter-esse" applies to the different situations in which a certain *suspension* is to be indicated. Even on the level of his literary strategies, Kierkegaard insists on the fact that the "imaginary construction", which is characteristic of *Repetition* and "Guilty?"/"Not Guilty?", demands the opening of an intermediary space, a *Mellemværende* (a "being-in-between") that "encourages the inwardness of the two [characters] *away from each other in inwardness*" (CUP, 1:264).

the arousal of the unhappy lover's ideality" (SLW, 146). However little attention Kierkegaard seems to pay here to the technical language of philosophy, it is important to observe that, in unhappy love, the woman has *Realitet* (reality), not *Virkelighed* (actuality). She becomes real only to the degree in which the unhappy lover "fears" her, she is as real as an "occasion" for unhappiness is supposed to be, but she does not transcend the level of mere possibility. Thus, she hovers somewhere between actuality and ideality, more as an obstacle to their conciliation than as a synthesis of them. That is precisely the ontological status of the "immediacy" which reflection has to deal with in this case. Here reflection constitutes the relation to something that is already and by itself an undetermined *relationship* between two terms, namely between an actual "form" and an ideal one.

The structure of reflection as a second-degree relationship can be considered as characteristic of Kierkegaard's dialectics, particularly in those contexts where the religious point of view is concerned. This aspect will be familiar at least to the reader of his later works, as it is the case of *The Sickness unto Death*. More broadly, it is important to take note of the general application of such a structure in order to understand, for instance, the internal economy of Kierkegaard's references to woman and the feminine in the so called aesthetic works. Beyond their narrative dimension, the feminine figures alluded to in *Either/Or*, *Repetition*, and *Stages* are in every case emblems of a certain understanding of the aesthetic existence in itself. Moreover, they indicate how and to what degree the aesthetic penetrates the other "spheres" of existence both on a descriptive and on an epistemic level. Beginning with the first lines of *The Concept of Irony*, the feminine designates the gender of the *phenomenon* as opposed to an observer who "brings the concept along with him" (CI, 9). Already in this case the relation between the phenomenon and the observer takes the form of a dramatic scene in so far as the phenomenon presents itself as an *image*. Only to this extent can it be said that the phenomenon in question—Socrates' existence—*is* irony. But it is crucial to realise that here the image does not merely illustrate a conceptual content. It is not, either, a simple object that the observer would incorporate into a process of reflection in order to comprehend it or to conceptualize it. Even the image of irony represented by Socrates "floats" between ideality and actuality (CI, 128).[7] Although it can

[7]It is also in virtue of this ambiguous position that irony, far from being definitively given as a complete phenomenon, consists in continually "coming back"

be the "occasion" of a passage from the one to the other, the image might also indicate the mere possibility of a relation, or even of the *misrelation* between ideality and actuality.

The particular significance of the story "Guilty?"/"Not Guilty?" consists in the fact that now the dialectic of imagination clearly interferes with the reflective process that structures the narration. The most obvious example of this interference is given by the inclusion in the diary of six independent and apparently digressive stories: "Quiet Despair" (SLW, 199-200), "A Leper's Self-Contemplation" (SLW, 232-34), "Solomon's Dream" (SLW, 250-52), "A Possibility" (SLW, 276-88), "The Reading Lesson" (SLW, 323-28), and "Nabuchadnezzar" (SLW, 360-63). The "Letter to the Reader" later informs us about the strategical meaning of these entries: they have been inserted into the diary "in order to throw light upon [the narrator's] inclosing reserve", as if he were "searching for an expression for his own reserve" (SLW, 429). There is, however, something equally important to take into account. In several of these stories, as we will attempt to show, the allusion to a *visual image* seems to mark the site where the reflective structure of the diary can no longer be understood as an exercise of self-consciousness. In other words, reflection loses its subjective centre and succumbs to the "hovering" presence of an external image. It is no chance that the whole piece is presented in the "Letter to the Reader" as an *experiment* that, far from applying to an actual personality, only refers to a *Quidam*, somebody who "does not exist outside" the author's imaginary construction (SLW, 403). If the narrative architecture of Quidam's diary is already digressive in itself, we could say that some of those interspersed stories embody even more precisely the internal law of the digression.

In the story entitled "Quiet Despair", Kierkegaard immediately passes from an anecdote on Jonathan Swift's madness to a series of rather enigmatic remarks concerning the relationship between "a father" and "a son". The link between these two parts consists in their common reference to a mirror and to an exclamation made before it. "Committed to the insane asylum he himself had established when he was young", the old Swift, it is said, "often stood in front of a mirror with the perseverance of a vain and lascivious woman, if not exactly with her thoughts. He looked at himself and

---

as a sort of uncanny spectrum of itself: "The ironic nothing is the dead silence in which irony walks again and haunts" (CI, 258). The transition from the Socratic to the Romantic form of irony is just the historical confirmation of that fact (see CI, 197).

said: Poor old man!" (SLW, 199). Then a different narrative fragment repeats the motif:

> Once upon a time there were a father and a son. A son is like a mirror in which the father sees himself, and for the son in turn the father is like a mirror in which he sees himself in the time to come. Yet they seldom looked at each other in that way. . . . Only a few times did it happen that the father stopped, faced the son with a sorrowful countenance, looked at him and said: Poor child, you are in a quiet despair. Nothing more was ever said about it, how it was to be understood, how true it was. . . .
>
> Then the father died. And the son saw much, heard much, experienced much, and was tried in various temptations, but he longed for only one thing, only one thing moved him—it was that word and it was the voice of the father when he said it.
>
> Then the son also became and old man. . . . Then he did not look at himself in the mirror, as did the aged Swift, for the mirror was no more, but in loneliness he comforted himself by listening to his father's voice: Poor child, you are in quiet despair. For the father was the only one who had understood him, and yet he did not know whether he had understood him; and the father was the only intimate he had had, but the intimacy was of such a nature that it remained the same whether the father was alive or dead. (SLW, 199-200)

"Quiet despair", as it is known, is an expression that Kierkegaard himself attributes to his father in a journal entry (JP, 1:740). Setting aside every possible connection between this story and the author's biography, what is noteworthy here is that the relation between the characters is in every case mediated by the "image" that each one of them sees and recognizes in the other's face. Then, by reflecting on himself, the son finds nothing but the image of himself which is expressed in the father's exclamation. But precisely because it is contained in an obscure and undeveloped exclamation about which "nothing more was ever said", the "true" image of the self never reaches the level of verbal communication. Now the ineffable image of the self is the point of departure of a new kind of reflection that, as we have said, unfolds according to the dialectic of "inclosing reserve". Again and again the movement of reflection rediscovers that image without being able to express its meaning. This movement, of course, is not simply self-reflective if "self-reflection" implies the individual's transparent relationship to himself or herself. Inasmuch as an individual, according to Kierkegaard's metaphor, becomes a "mirror" for another's recognition, the first of the two individuals (the son) is captured in a reflective movement that starts and ends with the image of himself which has been seen by the other. The centre of such a reflection, the point at which it begins and to which it returns, is not the "I" but the image itself. As in the story of Swift, the son is so paradoxically reflective that he is not even capable of pronouncing this "I" and needs to refer to himself as a second person: "Poor old man", "poor child, *you* are in quiet despair!"

Even if it is possible to say that this story exemplifies the narrator's "searching for an expression for his own reserve", it would be wrong to read it simply as a causal explanation (or search for an explanation) of his reserved temperament. The author's perspective is not "psychological" in this narrow sense. What is at issue here is not the biographical reference to an "event" which would immediately allow us to understand a certain aspect of his personality, but the psychological *structure* of that which Kierkegaard calls "inclosing reserve", a structure that is to be described as a basic possibility of existence. If the insertion of this story succeeds in "throwing light" upon the character's self-enclosure, it is simply because it indicates that which self-enclosure structurally *hides*: depression, melancholy (SLW, 394, 427). "Given the fact that inclosing reserve is essentially reflection" or, as it is more properly said in the "Letter to the Reader", "is due to a dialectical reduplication" (SLW, 427), the secret link between reserve and melancholy can be explored in those moments when the reserved individual suddenly perceives the emptiness of his own reserve: "His inclosing reserve contains nothing at all but is there as the frontier, and it holds him, and at present he is depressed in his reserve" (SLW, 428). The same can be said of the whole text, when the diary is viewed as a metaphor for self-enclosure: "It deals with nothing. . . . It contains nothing" (SLW, 397). Self-enclosure's fundamental emptiness is what makes possible the digressive style that characterizes the text. But this very emptiness appears to be the focal point from which melancholy emerges as the uncanny truth of the individual's reserve. That is also the point at which the subjective capability of reflection collides with the representation of an image that, far from being reduced to "nothing" in the digressive course of reflection, appears to be ineffably significant for the comprehension of the self as a totality.

A second example can help us point out the function of this ineffable image. The fourth and longest digressive entry included in the diary is called "A Possibility". The character is now a bookkeeper who shows "a decided partiality for children" (SLW, 279). The relation between a father and a son, which was a given fact in "Quiet Despair" as much as in the third and the fifth stories, "Solomon's Dream" and "The Reading Lesson", has here the value of a "mere" possibility. Under the suspicion that, without knowing it, he could be the father of a child, day after day this bookkeeper spent his time in studying the face of every single child that crossed his path. In each case, "he paused with the child, spoke with him, and during all this regarded the child as attentively as if he were an artist who painted nothing but children's faces" (SLW, 280). In fact, as the good bookkeeper that he was, he recorded the results of his observations by sketching the faces and introducing variations in the portraits according to physiological and physiognomic criteria (SLW, 281). The whole story is presented as the description of a case of insanity, which is also a recurrent theme in the last part of *Stages*. Whether the innocent victim is Jonathan Swift in his asylum (SLW, 199) or Don Quixote proposing to populate all Spain with knight-errants (SLW, 402), madness implies that a noncentered reflection remains active even if the identity of the "I" is irrevocably lost. But the problem that Kierkegaard focuses both in "Quiet Despair" and "A Possibility" is less the transition from sound reason to madness than the proliferating solitude of reason within the limits in which "inclosing reserve" holds it. The bookkeeper does not cease "calculating" in order to find the lost element that would allow him to reconstruct his past. This excess of calculation gives by itself the measure of his insanity. "A possibility" describes, in a way, the reverse and complementary movement to that indicated in "Quiet Despair". If it is true that "a son is like a mirror in which the father sees himself" (SLW, 199), it goes without saying that the character of "A Possibility" is looking for a "mirror" where to recognize an image of himself that, so far, is merely a "possible" and phantasmal image. His insecurity is not substantially different from that expressed by the son in the first story: "For the father was the only one who had understood him, and yet he did not know whether he had understood him" (SLW, 200). The son confirms this very insecurity by repeating the father's exclamation: "Poor child, you are in quiet despair!". This experience, in turn, parallels the one alluded to in *Either/Or*, where another unfortunate character (once again, a bookkeeper) goes mad "in his despair over having ruined a business firm by stating in the account book that seven and six are fourteen", and then keeps "repeating to himself day and day out, 'Seven and six are fourteen'" (EO, 1:32). What is interesting here is that the "repeated" calculation indicates again and again the site of a *lacking* element, as if the lost magnitude that makes the difference between "six" and "seven" corresponded to some unknown object. What all these characters "repeat" is actually the allusion to something that they themselves have never experienced as a fully achieved phenomenon. As a figurative expression for the emptiness of self-enclosure, the bookkeeper's wrong calculation is a sort of infinite reflection on nothing or, at most, a reflection concerning an element which is to be recorded as an "X" in the account book of recollection.[8] This is clearly the problem of the unhappy character in "A Possibility":

> And just as at the base of every scientific investigation there is an *X* that is sought, or, looked at from another side, just as the inspiration for the scientific investigation is an eternal presupposition, the certainty of which seeks its corroboration in the observation, so also did his troubled passion have an *X* that was sought. (SLW, 282)

> But whether he tried to penetrate to the source of that recollection by way of specific historical research or by way of the enormous detour of ordinary human observations and, supported only by treacherous theories, wearily tried to change that unknown *X* into a denominated quantity, he did not find what he sought. (SLW, 286)

As far as self-enclosure is concerned, this "X" does not merely designate an internal representation that the individual is not able (or willing) to submit to verbal exchange but, rather, the individual's incapability to reflect on a determined content. That is also how the demonic and self-enclosed personality is defined in *The Concept of Anxiety*: "The demonic does not close itself up with something, but it closes itself up within itself, and in this lies what is profound about existence, precisely that unfreedom makes itself a prisoner" (CA, 124). Already in this text the content of self-enclosure is indicated as an "X":

> The demonic is inclosing reserve, the demonic is anxiety about the good. Let the inclosing reserve be *x* and its content *x*, denoting the most terrible, the most insignificant, the horrible, whose presence in life few probably even dream about, but also the trifles to which no one pays attention. What then is the significance of the good as *x*? It signifies disclosure. Disclosure may in turn signify the highest (redemption in an eminent sense) as well as the most insignificant (an accidental remark). (CA, 126-27)

The reading of this passage can help us to understand how, in *Stages on Life's Way*, Kierkegaard can state that Quidam's melancholy, which is the

---

[8]The metaphor is taken from *In vino veritas*: "But recollection's bookkeeping is a curious thing" (SLW, 11).

only denomination for the mysterious content of his reserve, "in turn is the condensed possibility that must be experienced through a crisis in order that he can become clear to himself in the religious" (SLW, 427). It is not that his melancholy operates as a necessary condition for him to become a religious personality. But the "abstract form" of melancholy expresses at the same time the structure of human freedom and, consequently, the condition for an individual's relation to "the good". Both in the "Psychological Experiment" carried out in "Guilty?"/Not Guilty?" and in the "Psychologically Orienting Deliberations" that constitute *The Concept of Anxiety*, Kierkegaard is describing a basic structure that does not correspond with a specific "sphere" of existence. Although "x" designates in every case the unknown variable in the experiment, this variable appears to be a constitutive element both in an aesthetic and in an ethical-religious conception of life, both in self-enclosure and in self-manifestation, and here again, both in aesthetic digression and in religious earnestness. In all of these cases, moreover, it is crucial to observe that "x" expresses the point at which the privacy of every individual life collides with the ideality of language. To this extent, the author of *The Concept of Anxiety* seems to have been much more explicit: while unfreedom is linked to self-enclosure, "freedom is always *communicerende* (communicating)"; in this case "language, the word, is precisely what saves, what saves the individual from the empty abstraction of inclosing reserve" (CA, 124). Under the dramatic form of the story "Guilty?"/"Not Guilty?", however, Kierkegaard tells us something else. Language does not only constitute here the possibility of the individual's self-manifestation but, at the same time, it makes possible the individual's encounter with the words of others. Given the very possibility of this encounter, "x" is also the undetermined trait that the individual irrevocably lacks in every attempt to compose an image of himself or herself, a trait that only the voice of others would possibly be able to convey.[9] Language is

[9]This conception can be understood as the point of departure for a different view of the ethical and the religious. The idea of a word that primarily belongs to others is linked to a meditation on the essence of God's word. In this sense, as Kierkegaard would suggest, the word is in and by itself *the mirror* in which the person should look at himself or herself. The metaphor appears in the Epistle of James 1:22-24 and is originally developed by Kierkegaard in different contexts (JP, 4:3902, 4:4562; FSE, 9-51). For an interesting application of this motif and an analysis of its consequences in Kierkegaard's dialectic of reflection, see H. E. Baber and John Donnelly's reading of *The Sickness unto Death*, "Self-Knowledge and the Mirror of the Word", in

something more than the transparent medium which allows the individual's existence to unfold in an ethical direction and, consequently, "to speak the whole truth". Inasmuch as the single individual speaks a language which bears the abstract mark of an undetermined content, the suspension of "the ethical principle of speaking the truth" is already contained in language as a basic possibility.

In "Guilty?"/"Not Guilty?", language still presents the structure of an "ethical" ideality insofar as the ethical is "the sphere of requirement" (SLW, 476). The narrator's self-enclosure becomes "dialectical" precisely because he is constantly being confronted with the requirement to speak, to confess, to repent.[10] But here it becomes clear that the "suspension" of the ethical is related to a dramatic situation in which the individual finds himself still "suspended in a dialectical relation to actuality" (SLW, 447). The importance of this "experiment" or "imaginary construction in thought" consists in the fact that its author introduces again and again on different levels a "variable" that expresses that suspension: a "hovering" image, the uncertain recollection of an obscure past, an undetermined element with regard to which reflection itself remains suspended.

International Kierkegaard Commentary: The Sickness unto Death, IKC 19, ed. Robert L. Perkins (Macon GA: Mercer University Press, 1987) 161-84.

[10]Even if the diary, as already noted, is here a symbol of the narrator's self-reflective temperament, his self-enclosure seems to be structured according to his virtual relationship with an observer (the author of the "Letter to the Reader"). Moreover, when Kierkegaard compares the characters of "Guilty?"/"Not Guilty?" and *Repetition* in the *Postscript,* he stresses the fact that Quidam is the equivalent to both Constantin Constantius and the Young Man (CUP, 1:290). It is not that the structure of the relation between the Young Man and his "silent confidant" should now be recognized as an internal characteristic in Quidam's reflective personality, but it is obvious that the figure of the *absent confidant* performs an important role in "Guilty?"/"Not Guilty?": "Just suppose a third person (*en Trediemand*) had witnessed this situation!" (SLW, 387); "If there were one person to whom I could turn, I would go to him and say: *Bitte, bitte* [Please, please], put a little meaning for me into my confusion" (SLW, 359); "Is there nevertheless no third party (*ingen Trediemand*)? No. Everything is dark; the lights are out all over. . . . If a third party did think about my love relationship, or someone else—for when all is said and done I am perhaps the only one who thinks about it and I am not even a second party on the subject" (SLW, 223). As the Young Man himself points out in the first section of *Stages,* "reflection is always a third party" with respect to the lovers, even when only one of the lovers is the one who reflects (SLW, 33-34).

8

Living the Possibility of a Religious Existence: Quidam of Kierkegaard's Stages on Life's Way

Louise Carroll Keeley

In "Guilty?/Not-Guilty?" Kierkegaard's method of indirection gives way to intentional obfuscation. Like Chinese boxes receding one into another, this text is designed to conceal. Nor is this surprising when one considers what it undertakes: an imaginary psychological construction about inclosing reserve punctuated by parables that always feature some kind of thematic hiddenness to reinforce the parable's form. Even the impossibly chatty Frater Taciturnus, whose name seems ironic when one considers the sheer volume of words at his disposal, becomes genuinely taciturn when it comes to his real meaning: "Not even what I am writing here is my innermost meaning" (SLW, 386) he brags. Or is this meant, perhaps, neither as a taunt nor as a final observation, but as an invitation to consider what that real meaning might be?

I will argue that *possibility* is Kierkegaard's real thesis in "Guilty?/Not-Guilty?." More exactly: Kierkegaard proposes *the possibility of a religious existence as it is experienced as a possibility* by Quidam of *Stages on Life's Way*, who admits "I am really no religious individuality; I am just a regular and perfectly constructed possibility of such a person" (SLW, 257). "An actual religious individuality I am not" Quidam confesses, though "I am a superbly constituted possibility for it" (SLW, supplement, 581). Quidam exhibits possibility by remaining always in it. Hence the pseudonym's style of infuriating inconclusiveness mirrors Quidam's inner irresolution. As Quidam straddles the disjunction between guilty/not guilty, he hovers "right over the head of the contemporaries" (SLW, supplement, 657). Whether tortured and confounded, or momentarily at ease—what he proves unwilling to do is to tether possibility to necessity so as to make a religious affirmation that is grounded in *actuality*. Instead, he remains throughout "a demoniac character in the direction of the religious—that is, tending toward it" (SLW, 398).

Kierkegaard, of course, does not support the continual elongation of possibility. Quite the opposite: in a later text, *The Sickness unto Death*, he characterizes possibility unsecured by necessity as one form of despair. But even *Stages on Life's Way* already points the way beyond the self-indulgent wavering of the obsessive Quidam. The way it suggests begins with *inclosing reserve*, passes through *repentance*, and ends in *religious transparency*. That is, Kierkegaard begins with possibility and then counsels a movement from *possibility* through *necessity* to *actuality*. Although Quidam never undertakes the movements himself, stalled as he is in sheer possibility, the way through repentance to religious transparency is urged indirectly. Thus Walsh is correct that Quidam is "not an authentic religious personality" although he does point the way for one.[1] Curiously, it is the pilgrimage that Quidam did *not* take—but *might* have—that is the real spiritual teaching of *Stages on Life's Way*.

The order of my argument will reflect the prominence of these three themes. First, the *inclosing reserve* of Quidam will be studied to determine its nature and rationale. Curiously, inclosing reserve is the preserve of possibility. Fueled by imagination, reserve's inclosure provides the perfect site for possibility's excessive development. Second, I will consider how *repentance* introduces the counterweight of necessity into Quidam's venture into unrestricted possibility. Repentance itself can never be mandated, if by that move one seeks to circumvent freedom. But the penitent does discover, like a nugget at the bottom of the self, the unnegotiable data of human guilt. It is not the decision to repent that is necessary; rather, in repentance something necessary and ineradicable about the self and its disposition toward evil is discovered. Repentance begins when one consents to this necessity. Third, I will address the summons to *religious transparency* and the consequence which such a move has for Quidam's relationship with self, others, and God. Religious transparency is the decision to live that consent which begins in repentance but does not culminate there. In Kierkegaard's view, religious transparency means seeing oneself as one really is and consenting to be that self before God. Here consent is both an admission and a disclosure as well as a readiness to be scrutinized by God—not in fear that one will be found lacking (though all are lacking), but in trusting surrender to the loving gaze of God. *What Kierkegaard professed to be unable to do*

[1]Sylvia Walsh, *Living Poetically: Kierkegaard's Existential Aesthetics* (University Park: The Pennsylvania State University Press, 1994) 213, n. 12.

with Regina, what Quidam was unable to realize with his beloved—namely, to achieve a full and intimate disclosure of the self—it is this that all must do before God.

Inclosing Reserve: The Interiority of Excessive Possibility

In Frater Taciturnus' imaginary psychological construction, everything is arranged to produce the impression of a formidable inclosing reserve (*Indesluttedhed*). Even the setting and a serendipitous discovery conspire to make the impression: from an inclosed and receding lake, a locked box is fished out which, forced open, yields papers whose dates suggest that they were placed there many years ago. The Frater confesses that "the box was locked, and when I forced it open the key was inside: inclosing reserve [*Indesluttedhed*] is always turned inward in that way" (SLW, 189). If the key is indeed inside, Quidam's lengthy, obsessive, and preoccupied musings which fold in and overlap so repeatedly, ought to contain some discoverable meaning. The excruciating interior dialogue in Quidam that refuses—despite the taciturnness that the pseudonym's name implies—to be quieted down or settled, must contain some account of itself. But Quidam makes it difficult to fish out.

Quidam's story is long, infuriatingly repetitious, self-absorbed, obsessive, and—by his own admission—boring.[2] Still, it is "the exposition of this nothing" (SLW, 347) which most interests him and which he seems incapable of bringing to a close.[3] When the diary does taper off, Quidam sounds the same theme again: "It contains nothing, but . . . sometimes it is the hardest life that deals with nothing" (SLW, 397). Obviously, Quidam's diary deals with *something* in one sense; his engagement to his beloved and its subsequent wreckage are carefully documented with facts, observations, timetables, and details as well as vividly nuanced recollections. Why then does he recast it as "nothing"—especially after he has belabored and

[2]"My suffering is boring," he confesses (SLW, 347)—and his account of it sometimes reduplicates that content! The Frater notes another difficulty: "How fatiguing it must be to be inclosingly reserved, I can best see in the fact that it is fatiguing to think it" (SLW, supplement, 629).

[3]The chatty Frater seems equally disinclined to bring his remarks to an end. When he does, he reiterates the obvious—["I have spoken"] (SLW, 494), even as he concedes the likelihood that "there is no reader who reads all the way through" (SLW, 494).

reworked both the precipitating events and his ongoing reflection upon them in such a tightly wound but inconclusive way?[4]

The answer lies in Quidam's refusal to give substance to his life by consenting to the necessity in it. As things stand, he is right to characterize his accounting as a "nothing" for it records only a long string of possibilities which elicit no definite affirmation from him. This entourage of possibilities carries Quidam away from himself just when what is needed is to turn back. He is adrift without a reliable compass. In a storm at sea, "the compass still points due north. But on the sea of possibility the compass itself is dialectical, and the deviation of the magnetic needle cannot be distinguished from the reliable pointing" (SLW, 299). Worse still, it is as if Quidam himself has never consented to *be* anything definite—unless *waverer* can make a credible claim in this regard.

Nonetheless, there *is* something definite about Quidam that he acknowledges backhandedly even as he withholds full consent. This acknowledgement is evident in the requirement that he keep his inner self inclosed or boarded up. Obviously, he would never insist upon such a requirement unless he had an intimation, whether justified or not, that there was something about him that needed to be kept under wraps. What preoccupies him inwardly he never ventures to express outwardly: thus the striking incommensurability between his inner and his outer sides: "It is true, my outer being is entirely different from my inner being" (SLW, 235). This discrepancy is the mark of inclosing reserve.[5] If the deception is accom

---

[4]Kierkegaard's account of Quidam's double-reflection helps explain the young man's confusion: "This imaginary construction [*Experiment*] (" 'Guilty?'/'Not Guilty?' ") is the first attempt in all the pseudonymous writings at an existential dialectic in double-reflection. It is not the communication that is in the form of double reflection (for all the pseudonymous works are that), but the existing person himself exists in this" (SLW, supplement, 654). Add to this Quidam's self-observation (surely an understatement): "An individuality like me is not nimble" (SLW, 195).

[5]Kierkegaard's observations in this regard are wide-ranging. He offers the simple observation, for example, that "it is the art of the inclosingly reserved person to seem calm although he is agitated" (SLW, 358). But he underscores the incommensurability most memorably when he uses examples. Three in particular stand out: the mussel, the Latin teacher, and the fear of being buried alive. The mussel's predicament is not apparent to anyone else: "So it is with a mussel that lies on the seashore; it opens its shell searching for food; a child sticks a twig in between so that it cannot close up. Finally the child gets tired of it and wants to pull out the twig, but a sliver remains. And the mussel closes up, but deep inside it suffers again

plished resourcefully enough, others can be easily duped. But Quidam cannot convincingly fool himself.

The "anonymous experimental subject"[6] which Frater Taciturnus constructs presents particular interpretive difficulties. He is characterized by inclosing reserve but tends in the direction of the religious. It is difficult to understand what makes such a person religious, or even if he *is* genuinely so at all. Granted, Kierkegaard elsewhere designates religiousness as a new immediacy not commensurable with public disclosure, but Quidam's secrecy seems more suspect.[7] One might think that he has something to hide. At any rate, how should one understand this hybrid combination of inclosing reserve and religious directionality?

Kierkegaard has seeded the question in the preceding section where Judge William espouses his ethical observations on marriage. The Judge's criteria for the religious exception are such that they disqualify Quidam.

---

and cannot get the sliver out. No one can see that there is a sliver, for of course the mussel has closed up, but that it is there the mussel knows" (SLW, 388). The Latin teacher, thought boring and strange by his students, gives an intimation of hidden passion in his recounting of the interiority of the subjunctive mood when it describes a lover waiting expectantly for his beloved; thereupon "he fell silent, then cleared his throat, and said with the usual pedagogical gravity: Next" (SLW, 205). Finally, the fear of being buried alive and the anxious search for a way to insure against it provides a vivid picture of the most torturous incommensurability imaginable: being alive, but buried as if dead (SLW, 376). Frater Taciturnus hints that the parables dated the fifth of each month provide glimpses into the state of inclosing reserve. "He [is] essentially* inclosingly reserved. . . . *The significance of the portions entered the fifth of each month" (SLW, supplement, 630). I have focused on only one of the entries which I think is the most important one—namely, "A Possibility." Stephen Dunning identifies what is common to all six parables: "These parables have been subjected to great hermeneutical gymnastics by interpreters, most often in efforts to show that they are cryptic autobiographical statements." But Dunning argues that "The role of these parables . . . is to illustrate in narrative form several varieties of the contradiction within withdrawnness between inwardness and external appearances or behavior. . . . Thus inner states of melancholy, sickness, guilt, madness, wisdom, and terror are hidden by, respectively, external liveliness, health, royalty, charity, madness, and frightening behavior. The common thread that connects the six parables is the incommensurability of inner and outer." See Stephen Dunning, *Kierkegaard's Dialectic of Inwardness: A Structural Analysis of the Theory of Stages* (Princeton NJ: Princeton University Press, 1985) 126-27.

[6]Walsh, *Living Poetically*, 173.

[7]"Faith is not the first immediacy but a later immediacy" (FT, 82).

Most notably, the requirement that the exception be a married man—the very status which Quidam renounces—assures his elimination as a candidate. But it is not surprising that the experimental persona does not meet the ethical Judge's assessment of what a religious exception should be if, as Frater Taciturnus claims, Quidam is no longer operating within that contextual sphere. Moreover, it is significant that what the Judge does say about the religious exception—though tentative and as if squinting, points beyond the secure confines of the ethical to a religious sphere which he can intimate but not grasp. It seems appropriate, then, to begin with the ethical understanding of what makes a religious exception.

Fittingly, the author of "Some Reflections On Marriage" identifies himself by station and not by name as "a married man." Happily accommodated by the universal in marriage, a name seems superfluous, even if his identity *is* widely known. As Judge William explores the safe expanse of marriage, he stops occasionally to ask about those others who seem not to fit the specifications of the universal so exactly. Eccentrics, anomalies, exceptions—what sense can a married man make of these? The married judge's musings are brief but suggestive:

> If in his quest for the resolution the lover encounters anomalies, finds that he has become singular, not in the sense that this singularity promptly comes off in the washing of resolution, but singular in such a way that he does not dare to trust that he is a universal human being, in other words, if he encounters repentance, then it may last a long time, and if he is really in love, as is indeed assumed, then he can regard himself as someone selected to be examined by life, for when he is questioned by love up one side and by repentance down the other side about the same thing, his examination can become much too rigorous.
>
> But I shall not pursue this here. . . . (SLW, 164)

Universality and singularity are the chief dialectical categories in the judge's rhetorical toolbox. The former accommodates the vast majority, including the judge; for these, marriage provides the frame within which the individual's singularity is best and most happily expressed. Thus "the authentic prototype of marriage" produces partners best described as "contiguous angles on the same base" (SLW, 168-9). But the advocate of marriage is aware of and disconcerted by the predicament of those others whose singularities do not fit snugly into the universal. If anyone "does not dare to trust that he is a universal human being" (SLW, 164), the judge warns, he is destined to be rigorously examined. Punctuating the strenuous "*longitude of time*" (SLW, 101), the examination pits love and repentance against one another. The individual must answer repeatedly to love (which longs to express itself in the universal) but also repentance (which answers that one's singularity is so constituted that such an expression of love can never be suitably managed). As love and repentance declare repeatedly their inability to negotiate a compromise, the anomaly comes more and more into view. Appropriately, it is here that the married man breaks off, aware that his categories are insufficient to account for this exception—and ill-prepared to abandon them in favor of the religious interpretation that can.

The experimental Quidam of "Guilty?/Not-Guilty?" exhibits the very features that the judge foresaw but could not explain. Marriage is the prospect most welcome to him, but the movement toward penitence seems to caution sternly against such an undertaking. Indeed, for most of the diary he backpedals. The marriage proposal, once made in earnest, is now repented of in angst. Stuck, as he is, on the cusp of the ethical tending toward the religious, repentance seems to trump love's claim to possession. But Kierkegaard—if not the Frater!—affirms the more difficult truth of their unity.[8]

What are the anomalies that Quidam claims are operative in his case and to what degree do they compromise his status as a "universal human being" (SLW, 164)? Do Quidam's anomalies entail the forfeiting of the universal and the occupancy of the category of the singular? If so, is this a singularity oriented in the direction of the divine (like Abraham in *Fear and Trembling*) or in the direction of the demonic (as *Fear and Trembling's* merman, in one of his three expressions, illustrates)? Is Quidam guilty, not guilty, both, or

---

[8]This is certainly Kierkegaard's position in *Fear and Trembling*. In the dialectical variations of the merman story, the merman who wins "Agnes *and* repentance" is the merman religiously conceived. See Louise Carroll Keeley, "The Parables of Problem III in Kierkegaard's Fear and Trembling," in *International Kierkegaard Commentary: Fear and Trembling and Repetition*, IKC 6, ed. Robert L. Perkins (Macon GA: Mercer University Press, 1993) 127-54. The quidam has some intimation of this, even if he can't quite manage it himself: "I suspect that the religious crisis is to bring it into what I have begun here" (SLW, 222); that is, into his relationship to her. He is even more explicit later: "It would have been better if I could have remained faithful to her; it would have been greater if my spiritual existence had countenanced everyday use in a marriage, and I would have understood life more surely and easily. This is the order of rank. Next comes what I do" (SLW, 396). More poignantly, even Kierkegaard acknowledges this truth: "If I had had faith, I would have stayed with Regine. Thanks to God, I now see that" (SLW, 505).

neither? Once the direction of his singularity is determined, the role of repentance in re-positioning Quidam in relationship to God and also to himself and his beloved will be considered.

Inclosing reserve is the formal qualification which best describes Quidam's inner life. But what is inclosing reserve? Sometimes Quidam alludes to what it is by using familiar diagnostic expressions (a flaw, for example) that he connects somehow to his depression.[9] Frater Taciturnus, Quidam's pseudonymous creator, concedes that he has allowed this to happen: "in order to throw light upon his inclosing reserve, I have inserted into the diary a few entries in which he seems to be searching for an expression for his own reserve" (SLW, 429). But the Frater is vigorous in his contention that this never succeeds: "he never expresses himself directly—that he cannot do—but indirectly" (SLW, 429); "with regard to his reserve, nowhere does he explain what it implies" (SLW, 427); "he himself cannot even say what it contains" (SLW, 428); "he does not and cannot say what *is making* him reserved" (SLW, 428); "he never says what his reserve contains, but only that it is there" (SLW, 428).

For obvious reasons, the content of the quidam's inclosing reserve is never disclosed; after all, to disclose its content is to overcome concealment—the very feature of reserve which must be preserved if it is to persist in *being* reserve. Moreover, if "the language of inclosing reserve is a language only in silence" (SLW, 427), as the Frater contends, then any speaking about it invariably misleads. But even if the Frater is right on this point, something of its formal structure can be discerned. Effectively it reduces Quidam to "a closed book" (SLW, supplement, 621), especially in relationship to "her."

Quidam is less shy about discussing the *consequences* of his inclosing reserve since they are such by virtue of making an impact in the world. But even here he is constrained by a constitutional reluctance. Thus he speaks of "a vast misrelation" (SLW, 244) between them that is exacerbated by her devotedness in the face of his agitation and withdrawal. What is immediacy for her is dialectical for him, such that the misrelation is apparent only to

---

[9]Frater Taciturnus explains: "His inclosing reserve is essentially a form of depression" (SLW, 427). Quidam confirms: "What is my sickness? Depression. Where does this sickness have its seat? In the power of the imagination, and possibility is its nourishment" (SLW, 391). The Frater is insistent upon the connection of depression with possibility: "Here, then, lies the significance of his depression. It is the concentration of possibility" (SLW, 424).

him. Her "buoyancy in the world" contrasts with his "buoyancy in dancing over abysses" (SLW, 222). Most notably, his refusal to begin by "initiating her into my sufferings" (SLW, 197) gives pause, for it undermines marriage's ethical charge that the partners be disclosed to one another. Thus inclosing reserve is "in conflict with the ethical commitment in marriage" (SLW, supplement, 615). In Quidam's view, marriage does not require that the partners share irrelevancies, mundane annoyances, or superfluous details about their lives. But it *does* mean that one "must not hide something about which he can say, 'I cannot disclose that to her'" (SLW, supplement, 615). And Quidam is confident that this is precisely his predicament with reference to his beloved and his inclosing reserve.

Though Frater Taciturnus insists that Quidam is unable to express his inclosing reserve directly, there is nothing to prevent the Frater himself from offering some observations on it. These observations will prove decisive for our understanding of inclosing reserve.

The first point that the Frater makes is baffling but suggestive: inclosing reserve is "the frontier, the frontier of understanding that posits the misunderstanding" (SLW, 428). A frontier suggests the edge—not, perhaps, of the discoverable, but of what has been thus far discovered—the furthest point, newly arrived, beyond which one has not yet ventured. When it is the *understanding's* frontier that is at issue, as Frater Taciturnus claims is the case with inclosing reserve, something beyond understanding is the territory which awaits exploration. This unexplored domain just past the reaches of the understanding is, understandably, terrifying. Just as Johannes de Silentio conceded his own reluctance to venture there even as he applauded the courage and passion of Abraham who did, so too does Quidam stall on the cusp or frontier of something new; as the Frater puts it, "it (the frontier) holds him" (SLW, 428).

At this juncture, Frater Taciturnus proves genuinely helpful: "his reserve is neither more nor less than *the condensed anticipation of the religious subjectivity*" (SLW, 428; emphasis added). That is, "inclosing reserve is and remains the intimation of a higher life" (SLW, 428) or "the anticipation of a higher life" (SLW, 428). But this intimation of a higher life is one from which one would draw back, mindful of its terrors and ill-prepared to surrender the controlling authority of reason. But the way back has been compromised by the prominence of the governing intimation such that "there is no real healing for him except religiously within himself" (SLW, 428). Here the holy terror of Abraham, who knew well the cost of such a venture, is experienced by Quidam *as a prospect*. And this is precisely the Frater's next point.

Frater Taciturnus implies that it is possibility that explains Quidam at the deepest level. *Quidam inhabits the possibility of a religious existence and this is precisely his crisis*: "His inclosing reserve is essentially a form of depression, and his depression in turn is the condensed possibility that must be experienced through a crisis in order that he can become clear to himself in the religious" (SLW, 427). He adds that "this is the most abstract form of the state of reserve—when it is the anticipation of a higher life in the condensation of possibility" (SLW,428).

Quidam's attempts to express inclosing reserve are never direct: "Therefore they must also be understood indirectly. One of them is titled 'A Possibility' . . . " (SLW, 429). Given the fact that the Frater singles out "A Possibility"as one of the entries in question, it makes sense that the others are its companion stories featured on the fifth of every month. These include " Quiet Despair" (January 5); "A Leper's Self-Contemplation" (February 5); "Solomon's Dream" (March 5); "The Reading Lesson" (May 5); and "Nebuchadnezzar" (June 5); But it is "A Possibility" (April 5) that Frater Taciturnus identifies as "*for him the crucial category, which therefore must be pursued to an extreme*" (SLW, 429; emphasis added).

The entry "A Possibility" is important because it suggests both a dialectical and a thematic unity underlying *Stages on Life's Way*. Despite the elaborate artifice which Hilarious Bookbinder constructs to suggest that the many papers composing *Stages on Life's Way* are discrete and unrelated, "A Possibility" hints otherwise. Its main character seems strangely reminiscent of another, much younger character in an earlier section. Both sound the same theme: the dangerous possibility of new life. One fears it as a prospect (heading into the future); the other laments it as a possibility (looking backwards into the past). But neither the prospect nor the possibility can ever be established as certain. But this is the predicament of Quidam as well—it is the terrifying possibility of new religious existence that preoccupies and terrifies him.

In "In Vino Veritas," a young man, inexperienced in eros, offers this caution: erotic love, though ludicrous, gives pause nonetheless for it issues forth in new life. The young man informs the other banquet-goers that he refrains from erotic activity thereby avoiding the consequence of creating new life, "such an enormous consequence as the one of which we speak . . . a consequence of which no one knows whence it comes or if it comes, whereas it nevertheless, if it comes, comes as a consequence" (SLW, 44). In his view, caution dictates chastity (or at least abstinence) if "new life" (SLW, 43) is what one seeks to avoid. Many pages later "A Possibility" recounts the ongoing agony of a kindly but mentally disordered gentleman who worries that he might have fathered a child in his youth. How this came about—or, more accurately, *might* have come about, is reminiscent of "In Vino Veritas" and its dinner banquet. The diarist describes how this "quiet, reserved, somewhat shy . . . person unacquainted with the world" (SLW, 282-3) undertook "an excursion to the woods [which] ended with an unusually splendid dinner party" (SLW, 283). But surely this sounds like the young man of "In Vino Veritas"! After the party the man and his companions —who, like the participants of the first banquet were "men of the world" (SLW, 283), opted for a new destination: they "visited one of those places where, strangely enough, one pays money for a woman's contemptibleness. What happened there, even he himself did not know" (SLW, 283). Thereafter, the subject of "A Possibility" is beset by anxious thoughts concerning the "consequence" of erotic activity: the "possibility was that another being owed its life to him" (SLW, 284). The implication seems to be that the young man and the kindly but obsessed elderly man are one and the same. *What concerns them both is a possibility of new life.*

But this is also the situation of Quidam of "Guilty/Not-Guilty," although in his case it is the possibility of a new religious life for himself that gives pause. Presumably, this "consequence," like the former one, requires some association in love. At any rate, the "medley of pseudonymous authors"[10] of *Stages on Life's Way* is less diverse and more unified than it seemed at first glance. The key to their unity is their exploration of possibility.

Frater Taciturnus is quite direct when it comes to the question of what should be done next: "From the standpoint of this possibility, one can struggle ahead to religious transparency; this is what he has to do. But this he does not know . . . " (SLW, 428). Instead, Quidam prefers to remain put in possibility, which is rooted in and kept alive by the power of imagination. That is, confronted with the prospect of a genuinely religious existence, Quidam continues to hold fast to the possibility. What eludes him is the decisiveness which is the mark of the religious person.

The possibility which preoccupies Quidam most is the possibility of his guilt. But to the extent that he is preoccupied with the minutiae of this question any real religious development is halted. Quidam's plight reveals

---

[10]Julia Watkin, *Kierkegaard* (London: Geoffrey Chapman, 1997) 47.

how what *seems* a religious preoccupation can undermine *real* religious development. But this can be difficult to see for one caught up in the preoccupation itself. What is needed first—as a prelude to religious transparency—is repentance.

Repentance: The Recovery of Necessity through the Affirmation of One's Guilt

Possibility infinitizes; it carries one away from the movement in place that genuine self-development requires. This is the predicament—self-imposed, but disturbing nonetheless—of Quidam throughout most of the diary. If Quidam wants to rectify that imbalance he can do so only by re-tethering possibility to necessity. The necessity to be restored as the limiting factor of possibility is the affirmation of oneself as guilty. Guilt finitizes and finitizes *radically* : it says, in effect, that Quidam is this definite individual whose shortcomings, weaknesses, and guilts pertain to him essentially. Here necessity very definitely does not mean that some deed was *fated*, as if Quidam had no choice about it at all. But it *does* mean that guilt itself is inescapably part of who he is. Repentance "goes back" to acknowledge this necessity, but it does so with the subsequent intention of going forward in freedom and grace.

Repentance is "the central problematic of his diary."[11] But Quidam never enters wholly into repentance. Instead he remains perched on the brink of repentance but seems confused about what he ought to repent. This is surprising given the considerable effort that he expends in accusing himself, assessing those self-accusations, and repeatedly evaluating these findings. So intent is he on discovering specific guilts that he might have incurred in the past that would explain the misrelation between them that he misses the consequent guilt which follows from his decision to engage in inclosing reserve. This consequent guilt has to do with the impoverished nature of his relations with other human beings, including but not limited to the beloved. Furthermore, he overlooks altogether that residual guilt which resists human mastery and is common to all. In this respect he is like the one who misses the haystack while rummaging about in it for the needle.

Quidam's main fixation is whether or not he has specific faults, especially in relation to "her." He fixes upon specific offenses as being determinative of guilt, as if these acts, and these alone, were the source of

[11]Stephen N. Dunning, *Kierkegaard's Dialectic of Inwardness*, 129.

any personal culpability. Once identified, he questions further whether they can be satisfactorily handled in such a way as to allow him to go forward in marriage. He worries, for example, that his primordial depression is the root cause of his guilt and the source of the misrelation between them. Although the onset of the depression seems not to have been in his control, Quidam remains disconsolate and guilty nonetheless. Even after he acknowledges that he started the relationship in good faith and hence cannot hold himself accountable for the start, he persists nonetheless in his unhappy tabulations.[12]

Moreover, this obsessive preoccupation with uncovering specific guilts means that his focus remains fixed upon himself. Thus his status is essentially contradictory: he is religiously absorbed *in himself*. He is so concerned to justify himself that he fails to see that it is God who must do it.

To the extent that Quidam remains stuck in inclosing reserve, a consequent and very specific guilt does follow which he should concern himself with, but does not.[13] Quidam's fascination with the self is so intense that the claims which others make upon him are neglected. Quidam's inclosing reserve has isolated him outside all worthwhile human involvements. He is so preoccupied with himself that he has no energy left over for others. This is obvious in relation to "her." Granted, she does figure prominently—even this is an understatement—in his *thoughts*, and she preoccupies him more intensely this year than she did a year ago. But when his relationship to his beloved is considered in any context that is not merely theoretical, it does not turn out to be much of a relationship. Put simply: he fails her.[14] This is

---

[12]Quidam declares: "I dare to testify on my own behalf that I entered into the relationship with the most honest will" (SLW, 373). But a few pages later he amends his understanding: "Am I guilty, then? Yes. How? By my having begun what I could not carry out. . . . Now I understand more clearly why it was impossible for me. What then is my guilt? That I did not understand it sooner" (SLW, 380-81).

[13]He does have some awareness of guilt—"I have indeed acted shabbily toward a human being" (SLW, 350)—but not much of it is directed *toward* that other.

[14]See Harvie Ferguson, *Melancholy and the Critique of Modernity: Soren Kierkegaard's Religious Psychology* (New York: Routledge, 1995) 113. Ferguson chides Quidam for using his beloved "as a kind of spiritual trial essential to his own inner development" because it is his "devaluation of his loved one." See also Céline Léon, "The No Woman's Land of Kierkegaardian Exceptions" in *Feminist Interpretations of Soren Kierkegaard*, ed. Céline Léon and Sylvia Walsh (University Park: Pennsylvania State University Press, 1997). Léon observes a pattern here: Kierkegaard's "production, in strict parallel with the author's biography, limits itself to aborted relationships, fictitious moves, engagements that lead nowhere. Although there is no dearth of fiancés—the Young Man of *Repetition* (1843), Quidam of *Stages on Life's*

especially true the further away in time he gets from the original engagement. By the time the diary peters out, his "relationship" to her is as cerebral, infinitizing, and insubstantial as possibility itself. The gaze of inclosing reserve spotlights the self with such intensity, but the beloved remains outside its circle of illumination. But surely this does not meet even the minimalist standards of ethics which require that the beloved be concretely—and not merely theoretically—cherished. And as Kierkegaard makes clear later on in *Works of Love*, this is very definitely *not* the religious ideal.

The existence to which Quidam holds fast is something altogether unworldly and seems to require that he remain alone, with no beloved in view, forsaking rather than forsaken. But Quidam never budges from his professed belief, however indefensible in experience, that his faithfulness to her never wavers. In his last diary entry he observes: "in faithfulness to her, my resolution is with all my power to remain faithful to the ideas and to my spiritual existence" (SLW, 396). What is this "spiritual existence" for the sake of which he is willing to sacrifice so much?

The spirituality of Taciturnus' tortured Quidam is suspiciously dismissive of the claims of others—of those whom Kierkegaard elsewhere calls one's neighbors, but also those persons one loves preferentially: "I have not had much to do with people in a more intimate sense," Quidam confesses: "My spiritual existence has occupied me too much" (SLW, 314). In fact, worldly involvements of any sort are outside the purview of this putative spirituality. Quidam notes, without hesitancy, that the spiritual existence he advocates entails the languishing of the outward person, the renunciation of finitude's comforts, and the avoidance of deeds which, enacted in the world, are thought petty. Is this the sort of spiritual existence that Kierkegaard genuinely means to recommend: withdrawal from the world, renunciation of its offerings, closure rather than openness to its joys?

The answer must be a decisive "no." While the Frater is uncharacteristically quiet on this point, his pseudonymous counterpart—Johannes de

---

Way (1845), and Kierkegaard himself—none of the engaged parties ever actually walk to the altar" (Léon, 147-48). Léon's designation of Quidam as "no more than a knight of 'resignation'" (Léon, 163) and *not* a knight of faith entails this pointed rebuke with respect to his treatment of his beloved: "In brief, all along he was saying no to the *girl*. By saying yes to her in eternity, he says no to her in this life. Where the *girl* is concerned, despite Quidam's protestations to the contrary, *his* alternative becomes *her* destiny—a no-win situation that consists of either being lied to within marriage, or being forsworn out of it (SLW, 402)" (Léon, 164-65).

Silentio of *Fear and Trembling*, whose name implies some unspoken connection to the Frater—speaks eloquently on this matter. De Silentio describes a faith which entails a deepened joy, a reinvigoration of the finite, and a recovery there of the beloved. But all of this is realized as the culmination of a double movement of infinite resignation and of faith; it is only after Abraham has waived his claim to his beloved son Isaac that he receives him back again in the paradoxical movement of faith. Is there some comparable double movement that Quidam does not make which accounts for his confusion and pain? Is the joylessness of Quidam a sign that his religious development remains incomplete? Given the Frater's observation that "a religious person is always joyful" (SLW, 470), one must suspect that Quidam's joylessness is an indication that he is not.

Léon inquires into whether or not Abraham's expectations for *this* life are shared by Quidam as a way to assess their respective positions with regard to the question of the double movement of faith: "A highly significant feature of *Fear and Trembling* is Johannes de Silentio's conviction that Abraham believed all along that he would get his son back and *in this life* (my emphasis). Therefore, if we are to pursue the comparison with the story of Abraham and Isaac, as the very importance of *Fear and Trembling* enjoins us to do, the question must be asked as to when (if?) Quidam expects to get back what he is relinquishing."[15] Léon concludes that Quidam is "no knight of faith, no Abraham"[16]:

> Quidam is unwilling, or unable, to hope for the removal of his temporal cross, "his thorn in the flesh." . . . Indeed at no point does Quidam's faith appear to be the extraordinary faith of the knight of faith who could say: "I have faith that I will get her—that is, by virtue of the absurd" (i Kraft af det Absurd); by virtue of believing that "for God all things are possible" (For Gud er Alt muligt). . . . In his despair, he is no more than a knight of "resignation"; that is, an individual determined "to make the eternal suffice, and thereby to be able to defy or ignore suffering in the earthly and the temporal" . . . (SUD, n. 70). Put another way, Quidam has just enough faith to be a knight of resignation who is ready to sacrifice a beloved being, but not enough to be a knight of faith (Troens Ridder) who believes, like Abraham, that the Lord will give him back that individual.[17]

---

[15]Léon, "The No Woman's Land," 157.
[16]Léon, "The No Woman's Land," 164.
[17]Léon, "The No Woman's Land," 163-64.

Quidam can be understood as a knight of infinite resignation both in his willingness to resign himself to the loss of his beloved and in his self-understanding as to what that resignation means religiously. But is this really what Quidam was intended to model? If it is, "Guilty?/Not Guilty?" is nothing more than an illustrated repetition of the same movement of infinite resignation that *Fear and Trembling* had already featured. One might wonder what the point is of such a duplication. Instead, perhaps Quidam is not a mere redundancy after all but the figure who intimates the reality of a second set of movements, less prominent textually than *Fear and Trembling's* featured ones, but by no means less significant.

Although the double movement of infinite resignation and faith proper are the premiere categories of *Fear and Trembling*, they are shadowed by two analogous but inverted movements that mirror them. These two categories are the movement of repentance and the consciousness of the forgiveness of sins. It is my contention that Quidam's spiritual development can be charted more accurately if these categories are made foreground and the more familiar ones are allowed to recede. In this case Quidam is not a mere version (either failed or not) of Abraham—a kind of spiritual subset of a type already described. Instead, in this reading he is like Abraham in that he, too, has a double movement to make but unlike him in that he stalls at the prospect of making it. Perhaps Quidam models the human indecisiveness which the Father of Faith overcame.

When these pairs (of double movements) are plotted, they show some proportionality in their structures. The movement of infinite resignation: the movement of faith proper as the movement of repentance: the consciousness of the forgiveness of sin. In infinite resignation the knight resigns himself to the loss of "the whole substance of his life" (FT, 43) insofar as this in concentrated in "one single desire" (FT, 43). Resignation entails something definite about the knight's *future* when it ordains that he must *waive all claim* to this desire. Repentance, by contrast, orients the penitent in the direction of the *past* and requires, as a first step, that one *reclaim* it in its entirety as one's own. The movement of faith proper is a paradoxical affirmation by virtue of the absurd that promises *restoration* in this life of one's desire. Consciousness of the forgiveness of sins can only happen by a comparable paradoxical movement but in its case what is offered is a *taking away*.

It remains true, however, that these categories are Quidam's not by virtue of any successful maneuvering through them on his part, but rather as a way that still awaits his transit. In the diary, Quidam remains stalled on the cusp of repentance. Although Quidam strains to identify specific guilts, his real expertise lies in his ability to make guilt dialectical. Not only do specific offenses pile up, contributing to the accumulating heap of guilt, but guilt itself becomes resourceful in perpetuating itself. The irresoluteness of Quidam is his fundamental difficulty: "the demonic in Quidam of the construction is actually this, that he is unable to take himself back in repentance, that at the extreme point he becomes suspended in a dialectical relation to actuality" (SLW, 447). This means, in common language, that it is "a *dubium* about which a man might debate with himself forever."[18] And this is where he gets stalled: every "dubium" seems to exact from him a further scrutiny and to exacerbate the "dialectical agony" (SLW, 451): "He can have a murder on his conscience; the whole thing can be a gust of wind" (SLW, 447). The Frater summarizes the difficulty: "When repentance is posited, guilt must be assumed as clearly and certainly substantiated. But the difficulty arises precisely when this becomes dialectical" (SLW, 447). He adds this clarification: "The dialectical form of the repentance here is as follows: he cannot begin to repent, because what it is he ought to repent of seems to be undecided as yet; and he cannot find rest in repentance, because it seems as if he were continually about to act, to undo everything, if that were possible—That he gives way to this is the demonic" (SLW, 451).

All of this is the work of the imagination when possibility steers its course. Quidam infinitizes guilt by continually obsessing over it. This wavering, obsessive, irresolute pondering of guilt sometimes lapses into a form of self-torment and self-torment "is, viewed religiously, reprehensible . . . self-torment is a sin like other sins" (SLW, 468). There is no rock that the quidam does not turn over in his effort to understand his guilt; nor does he ever quit finding new rocks to turn over. But this is where he makes his mistake. If neither the enumeration of specific guilts nor the dialectical perpetuation of them are the real task set before him then engagement in dialectical guilt turns out to be an *impediment* to repentance.[19] If the constant

---

[18]Louis Mackey, *Kierkegaard: A Kind of Poet* (Philadelphia: University of Pennsylvania Press, 1971) 89.

[19]Kierkegaard identifies other impediments to repentance in his authorship, including doublemindedness, perverse egocentricity, and scrupulosity. Whoever is afflicted by scruples walks, as it were, on stones: every piece of reality becomes the occasion for one's condemnation. Unlike scrupulosity, dialectical guilt does not confer an equivalence in evil upon every encountered reality. Instead it isolates one

reckoning and re-reckoning of Quidam's guilt means that he never gets beyond the specter of possibility, how can he hope to achieve a genuine religiousness that is grounded in actuality?

Quidam's excruciating interior dialogue is fueled by an excessive preoccupation with possibility and a corresponding neglect of necessity. But this unwieldy synthesis is identified later in *The Sickness unto Death* as the despair of possibility due to lack of necessity. As the double reflection of Quidam is tensed to its breaking point and he is dispirited by thought's vicious refusal to quit, he must resolve to stop. The stoppage which I have in mind is not so much a break with reflection as with the possibility that continually fuels its. If Quidam can re-tether possibility to necessity, its dialectical counterpart, he can then recover that relation to reality that had been forfeited when possibility's overdevelopment had first gotten underway. The way back to necessity goes through repentance and it begins with an acknowledgment of one's radical guilt: "over against God we are always in the wrong."

But this is where Quidam balks. To the extent that Quidam continues to equivocate over his guilt he "does not, in fact, fully achieve the religious."[20] Quidam's repentance remains dialectical: that is, his guilt is assessed in terms of external criteria or results. But this is repentance ethically conceived: "Until he divorces the question of his guilt from the girl, however, his repentance remains merely ethical, partially external and partially internal, a 'dialectic' in which he never becomes free of reality."[21] If "for the religious individual, guilt is a presupposition rather than a problem, and one that is known inwardly rather than on the basis of external evidence,"[22] then Quidam's repentance is not fully religious.

Moreover, affirmation of one's radical guilt can never be achieved through human understanding: he must "let go of comprehension as his avenue of approach."[23] Quidam's inclosing reserve has already been

---

piece of reality and then subjects it to endless interpretation. Furthermore, in its case there is some cause for alarm: the disputed event is, objectively regarded, ambiguous. It may well stand in need of repentance. Whereas the scrupulous conscience suffers from the *certainty* of its conviction (even though this "certainty" is a mistaken apprehension), Quidam is bothered by the *ambiguity and doubt*. In both instances, the result is akin to treading water: one constantly gets no further.

[20]Dunning, *Kierkegaard's Dialectic of Inwardness*, 138.

[21]Dunning, *Kierkegaard's Dialectic of Inwardness*, 136.

[22]Dunning, *Kierkegaard's Dialectic of Inwardness*, 135.

[23]Dunning, *Kierkegaard's Dialectic of Inwardness*, 140.

described as leading to the frontier of the understanding. But now he must pass beyond, just as Abraham did when he made the paradoxical movement of faith beyond reason and the infinitizing perspective of resignation. In Quidam's case, repentance undertaken religiously would overleap the calculative mindset altogether and affirm fundamental or radical guilt. When coupled with the consciousness of the forgiveness of sins, a new, paradoxical and religious immediacy is achieved. But this, of course, is what Quidam has so far refused: he is tending in the direction of the religious but has not yet made these requisite double movements. Just as infinite resignation finds its paradoxical inverse in the movement of faith proper, so repentance finds its paradoxical fulfillment in the consciousness of the forgiveness of sin. But as long as Quidam persists in understanding repentance ethically, he will never venture into these paradoxical depths.

But what would it mean to venture deeper into genuine religiousness? The major moves can be summarized as follows. First, Quidam must break his attraction to repentance conceived in so perversely dialectical a way. He can begin by renouncing all reckoning of guilt that purports to be exhaustive in its accounting. Instead, he must make an affirmation of fundamental guilt so radical that it defies enumeration. In so doing, he is moving out of an ethical notion of repentance and into a religious one. Thereafter, Quidam needs to acknowledge that repentance has its paradoxical counterpart in a consciousness of the forgiveness of sin. This is not so easy to do, in large part because it means leaving the safety of the rational behind. After all, that God should forgive sins can never be demonstrated but only believed.

Because persuasion relies upon the categories of reason and this religious venturing goes into the paradox, Quidam will be unable to talk himself into this venture. (Perhaps this is the real significance of Frater Taciturnus' name: at a certain point, talking just doesn't help.) "And there's the rub. Taciturnus, and Quidam with him, can never fully enter into the religious, the joy of resting over deep waters, so long as they insist upon understanding *why* they must tread a path of guilt and repentance."[24] Instead, Quidam is invited to follow Abraham's dangerous lead although new movements, previously described, have been specified to fit his case.

If Quidam were to make both the movement of repentance and the paradoxical affirmation of the forgiveness of sin, a further surprise would follow: "*the moment must come when one lets the act of repentance go.* For

---

[24]Dunning, *Kierkegaard's Dialectic of Inwardness*, 139.

one single moment this has a deceptive similarity to forgetfulness. But to forget guilt is a new sin. This is the difficulty. To hold firmly to guilt is the passion of repentance" (SLW, 452; emphasis added) but it gets itself something else to remember, too—namely, the merciful and unconditional love of God. The degree of intimacy that one achieves in this respect—that is, the depth of one's perception that God is Love— will correlate exactly with the development of religious transparency.

The Actuality of Religious Transparency: Being Positively Trustworthy with God

There is no evidence in the text that Quidam ever makes such a paradoxical affirmation. Indeed, it is precisely here that he stalls: he lives the possibility of a religious existence but not yet the religious existence itself. Nevertheless, Kierkegaard maintains that "the whole exposition tends toward *the forgiveness of sin*" (SLW, supplement, 644) to underscore that it is here that true repentance arrives, even if Quidam does not. [25]

If Quidam knows that repentance plus the consciousness of the forgiveness of sins is higher than repentance alone *why does Quidam not do*

---

[25]Kierkegaard affirms the consciousness of the forgiveness of sin in *Three Discourses on Imagined Occasions,* released under his own name one day before the publication of *Stages on Life's Way.* A confession, a wedding, and a service at a graveside are the featured occasions. Given the fact that there are three occasions evocative of three discourses and that *Stages* features a similar triangulation, it is tempting to assume a straightforward match. If so, "In Vino Veritas" would correspond to the confessional discourse, "Reflections On Marriage" to the discourse on the occasion of a wedding, and "Guilty?/Not-Guilty?" to the graveside discourse. There is no dispute about the correspondence of the middle parts: "that the second part of each work (Judge William on marriage and the discourse at a wedding) is a counterpart of the other is readily seen." See Howard and Edna Hong, "Historical Introduction" to SLW, xi. But there *is* dispute about the proper alignment of the flanking sections and whether their correspondence is direct or inverted. Thus the Hongs assume a straightforward serial order but note that Emanuel Hirsch had once "considered the other parts to be related in serial order, but later he discerned that the substance in each of the others indicates a relation in reverse order of first and third." See SLW, "Historical Introduction," xi. If Hirsch's correction is right then the confessional discourse is the counterpart of "Guilty?/Not-Guilty?." Given Kierkegaard's insistence that "the whole exposition tends toward *the forgiveness of sin,*" (SLW, supplement, 644), I think that there is good reason to argue for the inverted alignment of the first discourse paired with the third section of *Stages.*

what he knows to be highest? In effect, he is analogous to the weary pilgrim who cannot bring himself to walk like everyone else if this means giving up the gait which expresses his mortification so vividly:

> Suppose a pilgrim had been wandering for ten years, taking two steps forward and one back, suppose that he finally saw the holy city in the distance and was told: That is not the holy city—well, presumably he would keep on walking. But suppose he was told: That is the holy city, but your method is completely wrong; you must break yourself of the habit of walking in this way if you want your journey to be pleasing to heaven! He who for ten years had been walking in this manner with most extreme effort! (SLW, 223)

Perhaps the torment and difficulty of walking in such a way is exactly what Quidam likes. Compared with other pilgrims whose ways seem smoothed from the outset, this pilgrim's assurance that his undertaking has more merit is presumed on the basis of its relative arduousness. But such a presumption is mistaken. It indicates that the pilgrim remains stuck in a comparative framework whereas what is wanted is a sense for the Absolute. To assume that the relative ease of someone else's journey lends weightiness to one's own posits a comparison between oneself and others. But the true pilgrim remains intent upon *God*, making comparison an unholy diversion. In Kierkegaard's view a comparative analysis of one's relationship with God is always fraudulent—especially when one presumes a Pharisaic advantage.

It is worth noting that the pilgrim's gait is itself incommensurable, consisting of a series of lopsided strides. In this respect the pilgrim Quidam is thoroughly unlike the celebrated dancer of *Fear and Trembling* who reconciles the sublimity of the leap with the most ordinary pedestrian motion. Instead, this weary pilgrim seems intent upon an arduous journey, arriving on his own terms or none at all. In Quidam's case, the very difficulty must satisfy some desire on his part to earn a relationship to God. But if the forgiveness of sins dispenses with all human earning and accents God's unconditional love instead, then it is to God's grace rather than his own efforts that he should attend.

Quidam relates the story about the pilgrim immediately after he has posed this question to himself: "*Might it be possible, might my whole attitude to life be askew, might I have run into something here in which secretiveness is forbidden?*" (SLW, 222; emphasis added). The question is an important one given the care with which he has managed inclosing reserve thus far. If secretiveness is indeed forbidden then Quidam has veered dramatically off course and repentance is in order. But surely secretiveness before God is wrong. More exactly, although one can never manage to *be* secret before God (since God is not bound by human reluctance), the very effort to cover up itself presupposes a lack of trust. Instead, Quidam has been urged to "struggle ahead to religious transparency" (SLW, 428) and give up all opacity before God. To do this requires trust.

In fact, religious transparency is something akin to having a trustworthy relationship with God. It is significant that the finest statement of the concept appears in the confessional discourse which, I believe, is the companion piece to this one. Kierkegaard writes: "A person can actually strive in all honesty to become more and more transparent to himself, but *would he dare to present this clarity to a knower of hearts as something positively trustworthy between himself and him?*" (TDIO, 33; emphasis added).

Transparency seems to be achieved by degrees and it begins with being honest with oneself. In ordinary discourse, one speaks of such a requirement matter-of-factly, as if it were easy to accomplish once decided upon. But Kierkegaard is fascinated by the strenuousness of self-disclosure when the self, in a conscious decision, gives consent to being itself.

When the self is seized by some fear or thought or anxiety that terrifies it, its natural tendency is to block it out. This settles the anxiety but it does so at the price of delimiting the self. One agrees, in effect, in this negotiated compromise with the self, to live within the narrowest straits of the self in order to stave off these anxious thoughts. The movement toward transparency begins when one resolves to reclaim the surrendered portions of the self where these anxieties make their home. What this means in concrete terms is that one allows one's anxiety to penetrate one to the quick:

> For example, once I was seized by the thought that it must he horrifying to be buried alive. Instantly it became clear to me that this might happen to me . . . in time and temporality one must be prepared to suffer everything. . . . At first I tried to find some means or other of protecting myself. I once jotted them all down, and someone who is not very scheming would surely be astonished at the cunningness of my calculations. But then my depression impounded my cleverness and now I had to think up just as ingenious objections, until it was clear that there was no certainty at all in the whole wide world; even if I had all the cleverness of the world, even if all mankind were to do everything for me, there was no protection against it possibly happening to me. What then? (SLW, supplement, 614)

The person who takes the first step toward transparency allows his fear to be absorbed without moving to redirect it elsewhere. But as Kierkegaard's dangling question makes clear, the result is not altogether satisfying: "What then?" (SLW, 614).

The next step is to find "a religious reassurance" by bringing one's terror—or whatever it is that is dark or opaque in the self—into intimate association with God. In this move one forgoes the selective reduction of the self and consents to be oneself whole, before God:

> So I practice thinking the thought and include my conception of God's love. Gradually I become intimate with it, intimate with the thought that it might happen to me, but also with the thought that God is still love and that everything will turn out for the good and that one dies only once, even if one is buried alive. Now and then I am visited by the thought. It lasts but a minute, the very same minute I am reoriented in my religious view, and the whole thing does not disturb me at all; but I do nevertheless have the thought. With respect to the person who wants something finite, the point is to keep the terrors away; with respect to the religious, the point is to be receptive to the terrors, to open oneself to them. (SLW, supplement, 614)

The religiously developed person has become intimate with the terrible, "intimate with the thought that what he most fears will happen to him, but he also becomes expert in practicing this thought in his assurance of God's love" (SLW, 375). God makes transparency possible, but the self must consent to the Light's illumination of it. In so doing the self trusts God enough to let God disclose who it really is, what it really thinks, and what it fears most deeply without deceit, evasion, or excuse. In religious transparency the whole self is effectively seen through, its actuality disclosed from the inside out.

Quidam concedes that it was precisely this transparency that he had been intent on avoiding: "My idea was to structure my life ethically in my innermost being and to conceal this inwardness in the form of deception. Now I am forced even further back into myself; my life is religiously structured and is so far back in inwardness that I have difficulty in making my way to actuality" (SLW, 351). But making his way back to what is actual is his religious task and this means to "become intelligible to myself before God" (SLW, 351) and to choose "a relationship of confidence" (SLW, 351) with God. This choice to be on utterly trustworthy terms with oneself and with God is religious transparency. In Quidam's case, "this is what he has to do" (SLW, 428), though he has not yet successfully done it. Hence he lives the possibility of a religious existence as it is experienced as a possibility, but the task is to make it actual.

9

The Ethical and Religious Significance of Taciturnus's Letter in Kierkegaard's Stages on Life's Way

John J. Davenport

> And the closer I came to the moment which was to mark the great change in me, the more I shrank from it in horror. But it did not drive me back or turn me from my purpose: it merely left me hanging in suspense.[1]

" 'Guilty?'/'Not Guilty?': A Story of Suffering" or Quidam's Diary, as it has come to be called, is the central piece in *Stages on Life's Way*. Frater Taciturnus, Kierkegaard's pseudonym, begins by telling us how he accidentally retrieved the diary from a box lost in "the depths" of Søborg Lake: "The box was locked, and when I forced it open the key was on the inside: inclosing reserve is always turned inward in that way" (SLW, 189).[2] Taciturnus proceeds as if this Diary were a true story, but he indicates at the end of his introduction that it is really an "imaginary psychological construction" that is supposed to facilitate study of a particular kind of "passion carried to its extreme," which is not found in "the many inadequate manifestations of the psychical states that actuality offers" (SLW, 191). Thus the Diary is mainly an exercise in what Kierkegaard calls experimental psychology: it is meant to explore what states of thought and passion are possible for human beings, which in turn depends on the ontological relation between the categories of aesthetic, ethical, and religious existence.

---

[1]St. Augustine, *Confessions*, trans. R. S. Pine-Coffin (New York: Penguin Books, 1961) viii.11.175.

[2]Compare this to C. S. Lewis's view in *The Problem of Pain* (London: Collier/Macmillan, 1986) "that the damned are, in one sense, successful rebels to the end; that the doors of hell are locked on the inside" (127).

But while the Diary itself is a work of endless richness (and many riddles) it is Taciturnus's subsequent "Letter to the Reader" that deals directly with the philosophical themes motivating Kierkegaard in the Diary. In fact, Taciturnus's "Letter" is as important for understanding Kierkegaard's conception of the existential categories as anything he wrote.[3] Of the many topics treated in Taciturnus's reflections, I will consider a few of the most important: what they imply about the structure of human volition and character; what they say about religious consciousness, repentance, and their relation to ethical resolve; and what they tell us about the limits of philosophical study of these matters. I will leave almost entirely out of this account how the story in the Diary and the commentary in the "Letter to the Reader" may reflect the circumstances of Kierkegaard's own relationship with Regine Olsen.[4]

---

[3]Yet commentary on the "Letter" is scanty in the secondary literature. Gregor Malantschuk, one of the greatest Kierkegaard scholars, says that Taciturnus only "has an auxilliary function with respect to Quidam," and gives him half a page: see Malantschuk, *Kierkegaard's Thought*, trans. Howard V. Hong (Princeton NJ: Princeton University Press, 1971) 278.

[4]In his introduction to the first English translation of *Stages on Life's Way* (New York: Schocken Books, 1967; reprinted from the Princeton University Press 1940 original) Walter Lowrie wrote that "Quidam's Diary is in every detail the story of S.K.'s unhappy love," and he is angry with Kierkegaard for writing it (13). The Diary and the Letter undoubtedly do hint at the problems that led Kierkegaard to believe he could not marry Regine, in fairness to her, and they reflect his own personal and continuing distress over this decision. Taciturnus at one point even says: "He does not love. For he lacks the immediacy in which there is the first basis of the erotic. If he could have become hers, he still would have become a spirit who wants to do everything to indulge her—but not a lover" (SLW, 436). I question Lowrie's judgment that Quidam's story was meant to parallel Kierkegaard's in every detail, if only because the commentary in the Letter makes it abundantly clear that too close a parallel would not be at all complimentary to Regine (which would not be in accord with the love for the girl that Quidam professes). In any case, Taciturnus stresses again and again that what matters is not whether the story is "true" in the historical sense (SLW, 440), but whether it reflects what is possible for finite existing persons. If somebody asks "whether my imaginary construction is a real-life story, whether it is based on something actual," then he responds, "Yes, certainly, it is based on something actual, namely, on the categories" (SLW, 445). This seems to be Kierkegaard's way of telling critics to focus on what the imaginary construction shows about existential ontology (which is my aim), and not on whether it is autobiographical to any significant extent. I am willing to listen to others who will nevertheless argue, doubtless with some justification, that

I. Passion versus Consequentialism: Kierkegaard, Williams, and Frankfurt

Taciturnus begins by telling us that we should pay attention to Quidam, difficult as he is to understand, "because one is able to study the normal in the aberration;" Quidam's state of despairing tension is an aberrant form of religiousness, or a case of someone on the brink of "normal" religiousness, who thereby sheds light on the true structure of faith and the paradox that "it is the most difficult of all, even though absolutely accessible and absolutely enough for everyone" (SLW, 398). In particular, we are told that Quidam's love for the girl is "unhappy" not in the aesthetic but in the religious sense.

What does this mean? Romantic love cannot be unhappy in the aesthetic sense for Kierkegaard unless first it is absolute in the sense of being *the* love of one's life, the one love to which one is prepared to devote oneself entirely, because it can last a lifetime. When this kind of romantic love is blocked by contingent circumstances, then we have unhappy love in the purest aesthetic sense. "Unhappy love implies that love is assumed and that there is a power that prevents it from expressing itself happily in the lovers' union" (SLW, 405). If we consider famous cases of unhappy love, such as Abelard and Héloise, "we shall promptly see that the passion is immediate and that the contradiction is from the outside" (SLW, 407). This is the same in other passions that can be celebrated in poetry:

> In his enthusiasm for his native land, the patriotic hero does not relate himself to himself, or the enthusiasm does not relate itself to itself, but relates itself to a surrounding world and therein also to a relationship of erotic love, to a relationship of veneration. This is how poetry must understand it. The esthetic hero must have his opposition outside himself, not in himself. (SLW, 407)

Without this kind of pure immediacy, there is no aesthetic *heroism* and we sink from poetry into the lowest kind of attitude, in which there is no pure passion for anything intrinsically valuable in the world, but only a base "commensensicality" (SLW, 406), an impure consequentialism that cares for nothing but the total quantity of goods it can get. Thus an age that disbe-

---

Kierkegaard still meant (and perhaps could not help but mean) to reveal something about himself to literary codebreakers among his audience. In this, perhaps, he was not entirely true to his own principles. But this aspect of the text, even if it is legitimate territory, is both beyond my competence and not my current interest.

lieves in erotic love "as an absolute passion" (SLW, 405), preferring the kind of romanticism portrayed in "The Seducer's Diary," cannot believe that an earnest unhappy love is possible (SLW, 401). Such a sophisticated generation cannot appreciate the pure romance of *Romeo and Juliet*: "the grocer boy, a matter-of-fact philosopher, a pawnbroker, or whatever other representative of common sense one would use" will regard the play from an ironic distance (SLW, 407-408). Kierkegaard's disgust at a utilitarian public that cares for nothing unconditionally—or in a way that might demand sacrifices in quantitative results—is especially clear here:

> What, then, can be the consequence when people reject poetry and yet have no higher passion? This, of course—that people go astray with half-baked ideas and are made happy in fancies and self-delusions, and this generation becomes the most expeditious but not the most judicious, the promising and prevaricating generation without parallel. (SLW, 408)

A short digression into contemporary moral psychology will help clarify the ethical significance of Kierkegaard's distinctions here. What Taciturnus means by a "higher passion" of the unconditional kind required for good poetry is similar to what Bernard Williams, in one of his best essays, has called "ground projects."[5] Williams explains the notion as follows:

> Some desires are admittedly contingent on the prospect of one's being alive, but not all desires can be in that sense conditional, since it is possible to imagine a person rationally contemplating suicide, in the face of some predicted evil, and if he decides to go on in life, then he is propelled forward into it by some desire (however general or inchoate) which cannot operate conditionally on his being alive, since it settles the question of whether he is going to be alive. Such a desire we may call a categorical desire.[6]

A man's "ground projects" in this sense will "to a significant degree give a meaning to his life," but they need not "be very evident to consciousness," and they certainly do not have to be as reflectively ordered, consistent, and rational as a Rawlsian "life-plan."[7] They can be "immediate" in Kier-

---

[5]See Williams, "Persons, Character, and Morality," *Moral Luck* (Cambridge UK: Cambridge University Press, 1981): 1-19.

[6]Williams, "Persons, Character, and Morality," 11.

[7]Williams, "Persons, Character, and Morality," 12. Williams's language also suggests that the motivation involved in ground projects must be teleological, in the sense that the agent feels pulled towards the desired end, as in appetitive *conatus*—

kegaard's sense. As Williams explains, the nexus of such projects grounds our life-meaning because these are the projects we would be willing to die for:

> There is no contradiction in the idea of a man's dying for a ground project—quite the reverse, since if death really is necessary for the project, then to live would be to live with it unsatisfied, something which, if it is really his ground project, he has no reason to do.[8]

For Williams, the meaningfulness of human lives depends on having such absolute purposes, and this becomes central to his account of what is wrong with utilitarianism. Williams argues that in order for a direct utilitarian who wants to maximize desirable outcomes to begin, he or she must first have other "first-order projects" in terms of which desirable outcomes will, in part, be defined.[9] These will often include "the obvious kinds of desires for things for oneself, one's family, one's friends, including basic necessities of life, and in more relaxed circumstances, objects of taste. Or there may be pursuits and interests of an intellectual, cultural, and creative character."[10] First-order desires of these kinds may not always constitute ground projects; perhaps they usually do not, since one cannot coherently care about too many things in the absolute way. We can even imagine a person whose *only* project is that of maximizing happiness in himself and others. This would be a peculiarly empty person, one with no passion for other first-order goals at all.[11] But most people are not like this:

---

but this is not essential to the notion of a ground project. In defining this notion, we need not assume a neo-Humean theory of motivation. It might very well be possible for us to *give ourselves* ground projects in a more active way, or to posit ground projects for ourselves, on grounds whose recognition by the agent does not itself constitute a sense of *conatus*.

[8]Williams, "Persons, Character, and Morality," 13.

[9]Note that the term "first-order" as Williams uses it refers to the end or *telos* desired: a project is first-order if its defining aim is something other than the satisfaction of desires themselves, or the cultivation of desires, or anything else that mentions first-order desires in its description.

[10]J. J. C. Smart and Bernard Williams, *Utilitarianism: for and against* (Cambridge UK: Cambridge University Press, 1973) 110.

[11]This individual could allow that others' happiness would be measured in part by the pursuit and satisfaction of their first-order projects, but his own happiness would have no other cause than success in maximizing happiness in general, and thus he has no first-order satisfactions that could enter into the determination of what states of affairs would maximize overall happiness. Such a being would be

instead they are "taken up or involved in any of a vast range of projects" aimed at things other than happiness *per se.*[12]

There are different basic kinds of "projects" to be distinguished, corresponding to how fundamental a role they play in our lives. Williams uses the term "commitment" for one broad species of project, namely "those with which one is more deeply and extensively involved and identified."[13] Commitments are lasting pursuits that give intelligible shape to a sustained course of activity requiring some perseverance, which provide much of the personal meaning our lives have for us: "It may even be that . . . many of those with commitments, who have really identified themselves with objects outside themselves, who are thoroughly involved with other persons, institutions, or activities or causes, are actually happier than those whose projects and wants are not like that."[14] "Commitment" in this sense is quite similar to what Harry Frankfurt has called "caring," by which he means a volitional attitude that guides our actions and endows us with stable purposes over an extended period, giving narrative shape to a life that would otherwise be "merely a succession of different moments."[15] Frankfurt writes:

> A person who cares about something is, as it were, invested in it. He *identifies* himself with what he cares about in the sense that he makes himself vulnerable to losses and susceptible to benefits depending upon whether what he cares about is diminished or enhanced. . . . Insofar as the person's life is in whole or part *devoted* to anything, rather than being merely a sequence of events whose themes and structures he makes no effort to fashion, it is devoted to this.[16]

---

altruistic in so pure a way (involving a kind of total self-emptying) that he would no longer look like an altruistic *person* at all, but rather like a kind of mechanism.

[12]Smart and Williams, *Utilitarianism*, 112. Williams adds that commitments "can make sense to a man (can make sense to his life) without his supposing that it will make him *happy*," and this seems right. For even if having commitments is conducive to happiness, it may be that the sort of commitments most conducive to happiness will not themselves be commitments to the pursuit of one's own happiness, but to other things. On this topic, see Joel Feinberg's discussion of psychological egoism in *Reason and Responsibility*, 4th ed. (Belmont CA: Wadsworth, 1978).

[13]Smart and Williams, *Utilitarianism*, 116.

[14]Smart and Williams, *Utilitarianism*, 113-14.

[15]Harry Frankfurt, "The Importance of What We Care About," in *The Importance of What We Care About* (Cambridge UK: Cambridge University Press, 1988): 80-94, 83.

[16]Harry Frankfurt, "The Importance of What We Care About," 83.

Like Williams on commitments, Frankfurt thinks cares need not arise from distinctively moral judgments; they can be entirely *aesthetic* in Kierkegaard's broad sense of that term. Significantly, Frankfurt also relates caring in his sense to love. Among different modes of caring, he writes, "the most notable . . . are perhaps the several varieties of love."[17] At other points, even closer to Kierkegaard, Frankfurt uses the language of "love" as a stand-in for every mode of "caring" or committed dedication.[18]

An ability to be committed or to care in these senses will be essential for many of the most meaningful and fulfilling activities open to us in human life. Engaging in what Alasdair MacIntyre has called "practices" requires this kind of devotion,[19] and as Charles Taylor has similarly argued, developing intimate human relationships of friendship and conjugal love requires the staying power of noninstrumental care for the other.[20]

Given this gloss on caring or commitment in general, we may think of "ground projects" as one species of commitment, i.e. an especially profound kind that involves our basic reasons for living. Thus ground projects are manifested in what Kierkegaard would call "infinite" passion, and this puts some limits on the type of goals one can pursue as ground projects: as Taciturnus says, "It is a contradiction to be willing to sacrifice one's life for a finite goal" (SLW, 410).[21] Ground projects will also help determine what other less central or fundamental commitments are volitionally possible for a person. But a person need not have clearly articulated her ground projects in a self-conscious manner: thus it is possible to live them in what Kierke-

---

[17]Harry Frankfurt, "The Importance of What We Care About," 85.

[18]Harry Frankfurt, "The Importance of What We Care About," 89-90. He also speaks of "the varieties of being concerned or dedicated, and of loving" (93). Also see Frankfurt's papers "Autonomy, Necessity, and Love" and "On Caring" in his new book, *Necessity, Volition, and Love* (Cambridge UK: Cambridge University Press, 1999).

[19]See Alasdair MacIntyre, *After Virtue*, 2nd Ed. (Notre Dame IN: University of Notre Dame Press, 1984) chap. 14.

[20]See Charles Taylor, *The Ethics of Authenticity* (Cambridge MA: Harvard University Press, 1991) 52-53.

[21]Paul Tillich argues similarly that although it is possible to have idolatrous "unconditional concern" for an object, goal, or ideal that objectively lacks unconditional value, eventually the inadequacy of such an object of concern will tend to undermine unconditional concern for it: see Tillich, *The Dynamics of Faith* (New York: Harper & Row, 1957) 64, 96-98.

gaard calls immediacy, and he thinks infinite passion will first arise in this form.

Whether they are pursued in pure immediacy or involve reflective evaluation, however, the infinite commitment of the will that characterizes ground projects is incompatible with a utilitarian attitude towards one's subjective ends. As Williams argues, a man's "decisions as a utilitarian agent are a function of all the satisfactions which he can affect from where he is: and this means that the projects of others, to an indeterminately great extent, determine his decision."[22] Of course sometimes our projects do have to give way when they conflict with the more important projects of others, and we have to be sensitive to this. But loyalty to our deepest commitments cannot vary with every change in the social context that may alter the net effects that are likely to follow from our pursuing them, given how others may react. As Williams asks,

> [H]ow can a man, as a utilitarian agent, come to regard as one satisfaction among others, and a dispensable one, a project or attitude around which he has built his life, just because someone's else's projects have so structured the causal scene that this is how the utilitarian sum comes out?[23]

To expect someone to abandon his ground projects for such reasons would, as Williams says, be "to alienate him in a real sense from his action and the source of his actions in his own convictions."[24] The point here is not that a morally responsible agent can never recognize reasons to change his or her ground projects, or be open to changing them,[25] nor that his or her ground projects require the agent to ignore all possible consequences of actions,[26]

---

[22]Smart and Williams, *Utilitarianism*, 115.

[23]Smart and Williams, *Utilitarianism*, 116.

[24]Smart and Williams, *Utilitarianism*, 116.

[25]Such an agent, whose ground projects are completely unresponsive to reasons (including considerations about consequences), would a fanatic in the serious sense of that term. Fanatics are a proper subset of those who display infinite passion in Kierkegaard's sense, but it is possible to display such passion without being fanatical as well (so displaying such passion does not entail fanaticism).

[26]On the contrary, ground projects and other existentially less fundamental cares or commitments almost always guide action *in part* through determining the relevance and importance that different kinds of consequences should have in our considerations, or through guiding our sense of how to make this determination. And as Williams points out, principles can be nonconsequentialist without requiring us to do certain things or pursue certain causes "whatever the consequences,"

but rather that a human life cannot have a narrative structure without some commitments that are regarded as worthwhile for their own sake, along with related principles that will direct one's attention to more particular sorts of outcomes than total or average happiness.

Finally, this implies a subtler point of even more general significance: to have ground projects is generally to care about something in a manner that cannot be explained simply in terms of optimizing results or bringing about the best states of affairs; to care is generally to be constrained in *the way* results may be pursued, and even more importantly, to see intrinsic value in certain types of action, attitude, attentiveness and determination in pursuing our ground project. This is especially clear if the ground project aims at inward ends, such as cultivating certain aspects of our own personality, developing talents, or altering our character (whether in desirable or undesirable directions). Ground projects usually direct us towards realizing some state of affairs, but this is hardly all they do: if we could permanently secure that state of affairs simply by pushing a button on a superpowerful machine, then the ground project could not play the role that it does in giving our life narrative shape. But since what consequentialist principles directly enjoin is the maximizing of some state of affairs (S), as opposed to directly enjoining certain forms of action or attitude, consequentialist concerns to maximize S cannot replace a ground project that involves caring about S. As Williams was the first to note, the consequentialist version can even require the agent to do something counter-to-S if this will cause other agents to take steps that will maximize S-states,[27] whereas *caring* about S will not usually have this implication.

Instead, genuinely caring about something or someone rules out resorting to strategies of betrayal to benefit them. For example, if someone cares about his children, she will not (unless her judgment is impaired), consider doing them some real harm on the assurance that others will then give them some compensating benefit that greatly outweighs the harm. Beyond a certain point (which only prudence in the classical sense can ascertain), to care is to refuse to calculate consequences any further, to

---

however extreme: instead, such principles can be limited in scope such that they do not apply in certain sorts of highly bizarre situations (Smart and Williams, *Utilitarianism*, 90-91).

[27]Smart and Williams, *Utilitarianism*, 89.

bracket some possible outcomes as irrelevant, and to rule out decisively certain particular ways of producing cared-for outcomes.[28]

This is most clear with respect to ground projects, as Taciturnus helps us see in contrasting two politicians. The first has only a finite passion for his goal, though (comically) he wants to be heroic, considers himself inspired, and deceives himself into believing that he is willing to sacrifice his life. "But he is sagacious enough to perceive—something that is hidden from the more simple—how important his life is for the state, that if he lives a long time no one is going to be in want, but inspiration this is not" (SLW, 411). The other dies for his cause without trying to calculate the consequences of his absence on the public good.[29] It is for lack of such persons, Taciturnus says, that "modern politics does not inspire its devotees to sacrifices" (SLW, 410).[30] For

---

[28]This helps answer George Connell's complaint that "Judge William's concept of love" is inconsistent with the kind of mature evaluation of potential partners necessary for a viable marriage, and requires an immediacy that is "too fragile to survive in the world of reflection within which every normal, adult human being lives"—see Connell, *To Be One Thing: Personal Unity in Kierkegaard's Thought* (Macon GA: Mercer University Press, 1985) 179. As the Judge insists, commitment or love is compatible with ethical reflection on what or who is worth caring about, and why, as long as the evaluation is not simply consequentialist, but itself starts from some absolute principles or purposes to which one is undialectically devoted. When the Judge speaks of reflection that destroys love, he has in mind the kind of consequentialist calculation that reduces all relationships to contracts for mutual advantage.

[29]Imagine, to make the point vivid, that Abraham Lincoln had been unwilling to risk assassination by issuing the Emancipation Proclamation because he could foresee that his absence would let extremists on both sides make the Reconstruction into a violent struggle with debilitating social consequences. Or imagine that Nelson Mandela had been unwilling to risk ending his life in obscurity in a forgotten prison because he feared that then no one else would be able to lead the resistance to apartheid. The risk involved in this kind of calculation is the perversion of every pure motive. We cannot remain true to our commitments if we try to factor in accommodations for every possible turn of chance. This does not mean that we should be careless with our lives, fear nothing, or throw them away needlessly (as perhaps Alexander Hamilton did in his duel). But to be willing *to die for something* means being willing, past a point, not to consider some of the possible consequences of dying for it; in other words, it means restricting the possible consequences to which we will be sensitive in deciding how to act.

[30]This comment on nineteenth-century Europe cannot but prompt the thought that probably one of the reasons for fascism's quick rise to popularity as an

> All inspiration has its source in the passion of infinity, where every Tom, Dick, and Harry, together with all their sagacity, vanish as nonentities. . . . There is no inspiration in faith in oneself, even less in faith in one's bit of shopkeeper shrewdness. All inspiration has its source in one's passion or, deeper, in faith in a providence, which teaches a person that even the death of the greatest man is a jest for a providence that has legions of angels in reserve, and that he therefore should go resolutely to his death and leave his good cause to providence and his posthumous reputation to the poet. Just as one seldom sees an unhappy lover these days, likewise does one seldom see a martyr in the political world. . . . (SLW, 411)

Taciturnus's comments on unhappy love thus rely on this first ethical insight, which is foundational for the rest of his account: living for ground projects implies at minimum the implicit rejection of consequentialism. Thus the critique of calculative practical reasoning found throughout Kierkegaard's work.[31] What Kierkegaard means by "heroism" or "knighthood" is, furthermore, the infinite passion of absolute commitment to a particular *kind* of ground project, namely one that is perceived by the agent as being *noble* in some sense—whether aesthetic, ethical, or religious.[32] But as we will see, aesthetic, ethical, and religious heroes are distinguished not only by the kind of nobility they attribute to their ends, but also in the structure or form taken by their infinite passion for these ends.

---

ideological movement in the early twentieth century was the fact that its leading exponents at least seemed to evince genuine pathos. When it has been starved of resolute commitment and decisiveness in the state, a people may be too eager to embrace a leader who displays infinite passion without worrying about what exactly his or her goal is—or by tacitly assuming that it must be passion for a noble rather than an ignoble goal. Kierkegaard is sensitive to this kind of error: he recognizes that passion, care, or commitment is a precondition for virtue, but not virtue itself; equivalently, aesthetic heroes need not be ethical heroes.

[31]To cite just one example, later in Taciturnus's Letter we get an extended critique of Börne's suggestion that in big towns like Paris, statistics on crime and poverty will prevent people from viewing crime as sin, because crime is then recognized as an inevitable ailment of the body politic (SLW, 479-80). Taciturnus also praises Copenhagen as being "large enough to be a fair-sized city, small enough so that there is no market price on people," a town that (unlike the hustle of Paris) maintains "the more tranquil temperament that lets the single individual feel that he, too, still has some significance" (SLW, 487).

[32]See for comparison Kierkegaard's early discussion of dying for a passion, JP, 5:5100. I am indebted to Robert Perkins for this reference.

II. Forms of Unhappy Love

In light of the foregoing, we can better understand the different levels Kierkegaard distinguishes within the aesthetic sphere of human existence. The baseline level is a life without specific cares or commitments, and thus without any authentic engagements in practices or full self-investment in intimate relationships. Such a life is perhaps most often one of banal materialism. Thus Taciturnus says that "a generation of armchair life-insurance salesmen" will not understand why poetry can't celebrate their contemporaries (SLW, 412), and he refers to "bourgeois-philistines" who fail to grasp that tragedy lies in the power of external obstacles to prevent the fruition of "the infinity of immediacy" (i.e. an unselfconsciously pure or unconditional commitment) (SLW, 414). But the aestheticism of volitional mediocrity and carelessness can still involve reflection of a sort, namely speculative detachment that prevents involvement and leads one to view all pursuits as bets that should be hedged. Reflection of this kind, which Taciturnus calls "finite reflection" (SLW, 414), resolves all practical questions by a mediation that shuns unqualified commitment to anything—noble or ignoble—in favor of a mixture of half-measures and compromises that neutralize the existential risk of anything disturbing our comfortable complacency. This is what Kierkegaard has in mind when Taciturnus writes, for example, that "The same reflection that corroded love will also corrode the infinite passion of politics" (SLW, 410). As George Pattison says, for Taciturnus, "reflection has corroded the passion of the great lovers of the past" and "when love itself has been drained of passion in favor of prudential self-interest, it can be of no further use to poetry."[33] The tendency towards such neutralizing reflection was also Kierkegaard's chief complaint against his culture in his essay on "The Present Age:" it results in "the age's absence of passion, the short-term nature of its enthusiasm, its calculating prudence, its lack of action and decision, its craving for publicity, its indolence, its mercenary interests. . . . It is an age of envy, idle chatter, and levelling,"[34] which domesticates even religious doctrine to the point where

[33]George Pattison, "Art in an age of reflection," in *The Cambridge Companion to Kierkegaard*, ed. Alastair Hannay and Gordon Marino (Cambridge UK: Cambridge University Press, 1998) 76-100, 97.

[34]Pattison, "Art in an Age of Reflection," 96.

it loses all power to rouse the spirit, or to challenge us out of a life of numb but polite vacuity.

As this suggests, the baseline or lowest-level aestheticism need not be (even if it often is) an especially *hedonistic* existence, concerned only with one's own material pleasures; it need not even be egoistic or aimed (in decision-theoretic terms) at maximizing the satisfaction of one's own subjective preferences. As long as it is existentially uncommitted, or lacking in absolute devotions that could conflict with the habit of consequentialist maximizing, one's life will lack narrative unity.[35] Such a life may have no ground project other than the tacit and unrecognized hope never actively to form any ground projects, or never to face honestly the question of what is worth dying for.[36] For example, referring to the section on "The Rotation Method" in *Either/Or* Volume I, Malantschuk aptly describes "that caricature of human life who makes his appearance when one no longer

---

[35]Lewis's imaginary senior devil, Screwtape, writes that a vague feeling of half-conscious guilt, experienced as a "dim uneasiness," can tempt a human being into bad faith, into fleeing from the source of the discomfort and losing himself in distractions. If properly cultivated, Screwtape says, this leads the patient not to a life of indulgent hedonism, which still requires some real pleasures, however inordinately pursued, but rather to a state of listless numbness and timewasting: "All the healthy and outgoing activities which we want him to avoid can be inhibited and *nothing* given in return, so that at last he may say, as one of my own patients said on his arrival down here, 'I now see that I spent most of my life in doing *neither* what I ought *nor* what I liked.' The Christians describe the Enemy as one 'without whom Nothing is strong.' And Nothing is very strong: strong enough to steal away a man's best years not in sweet sins but in a dreary flickering of the mind over it knows not what and knows not why, in gratification of curiosities so feeble that the man is only half-aware of them." See C. S. Lewis, *Screwtape Letters* (London: William Collins Sons, 1979) letter #12, 56. Kierkegaard would regard this state of complete self-dissolution as the nadir of aestheticism, the polar opposite of nobility within the aesthetic category, lacking not only goodness, but also the greatness which amoral heroes can sometimes attain.

[36]This is how I characterized aestheticism in my earlier essay, "The Meaning of Kierkegaard's Choice between the Aesthetic and the Ethical," *Southwest Philosophy Review* 11/2 (August 1995): 73-108. I compared the state of the aesthete to Frankfurt's "wanton" who lacks higher-order volition and thus lacks resolute cares. I am now modifying that description to take into account the possibility of aesthetic heroism, which is a limiting form of aestheticism approaching the ethical. Aesthetic heros reject consequentialism in their passionate attitude, but have not embraced the ethical demands which alone can provide a firm foundation for lasting commitment of the will.

believes in anything permanent and therefore ventures nothing for his convictions. One gets along in life by shrewd calculations. Prudence teaches one never to tie oneself seriously to anyone; doing so may bring difficulties and hinder the serious enjoyment of life."[37]

Relative to such unheroic mediocrity, "fully definitive pathos" (SLW, 408) for an end whose value is not (at least initially) understood in terms of its ethical nobility will be a higher form of aesthetic existence. Pure erotic love is the paradigm case. Even in its heroic infinitude, however, this kind of love or devotion remains within the aesthetic sphere for Kierkegaard primarily because the passion *itself* is not reflexive, unlike some commitments that involve the agent taking a deliberate attitude towards her own projects. Because of its *immediacy* or undialectical structure, then, erotic love cannot encounter any opposition from within the agent's own psychology or operative motives. The immediacy of aesthetic pathos is thus not simply naivete: it too is "not entirely without reflection; as poetry sees it, it has relative reflection by having its opposition outside itself" (SLW, 412). The lovers can reflect on each other, on the prospects for their relation, on external factors keeping them apart, but not on their devotion itself. Similarly, earnest unhappy love is classified as aesthetic because the collision is between pure eros and uncongenial external circumstances.

This also helps to distinguish unhappy aesthetic love from another sort of "unhappy love" in which the hero does not directly and primarily care for his beloved, but perversely enjoys the feeling of strong passions that can be heightened by outward frustrations, allowing him to revel in his lamentations.[38] We find this attitude in the imaginary author of "The Seducer's

---

[37]Gregor Malantschuk, *Kierkegaard's Way to the Truth*, trans. Mary Michelsen (Minneapolis: Augsburg Publishing House, 1963), 32.

[38]Thus Lewis's Screwtape writes: "[I]f you had been trying to damn your man by the Romantic method—by making him a kind of Childe Harold or Werther submerged in self-pity for imaginary distresses—you would try to protect him at all costs from any real pain; because, of course, five minutes' genuine toothache would reveal all the romantic sorrows for the nonsense they were and unmask your whole stratagem" (*Screwtape Letters*, letter #13, 59). By contrast, Kierkegaard conceives earnest unhappy love in a way that implies the possibility of a different kind of romanticism which, while it remains aesthetic, is still the expression of unselfish and ordinate passion. Quidam is different than both of these: he is neither a Madame Bovary nor a Romeo. It is important to realize that when Taciturnus contrasts Quidam's state with genuinely tragic unhappy love, he does not thereby mean to place him in the category of perverse romanticism. The perverse romantic

Diary" in *Either/Or* Vol.I, which is the foil for Quidam's Diary. In quite a different way, Quidam is also mad enough "to want to be an unhappy lover, although he may not even be one" (SLW, 401-402). This shows that Quidam's state cannot be that envisioned in the aesthetic paradigm of unhappy love, which requires that "it must not be in love's power to remove the obstacle" (SLW, 405). From the aesthetic perspective, to *want* to be in unhappy love is a pragmatic contradiction: it would amount to wanting one's love to be frustrated by external events, which is incompatible with infinite passion for the beloved, i.e. the precondition for any kind of unhappy love. The problem is how Quidam can love in earnest (as opposed to the perverse simulacrum of eros) yet simultaneously want this genuine romantic love to be unhappy.

Taciturnus suggests that this is possible only if what prevents the fulfillment of Quidam's love is an inward condition that coexists with romantic eros towards his beloved. But not just any sort of inward obstacle will do here. Harry Frankfurt has argued that it is possible for persons, in virtue of their capacity for what he calls "higher-order will," to be volitionally opposed to various desires on which they may nevertheless compulsively act.[39] For example, the "unwilling addict" is a person who acts on a compulsive desire for some drug (e.g. heroin) while nevertheless authoritatively (or in her true self) willing *not* to act on this desire.[40] Such an addict has in one sense a strong passion for her drug of choice, but this compulsion does not constitute caring for the drug in Frankfurt's sense, or a commitment to taking it in Williams's sense. Although she might feel like dying if deprived of it, and although she may spend her waking hours doing nothing but pursuing it, this is against her true wishes: she seeks a life without the drug, and thus dependency on it is not her ground project, not what makes

---

and Quidam are both beyond the aesthetic type of unhappy love, but in different ways.

[39]Harry Frankfurt, "Freedom of the will and the concept of a person," *Journal of Philosophy* 68/1 (January 1971); repr.: *The Importance of What We Care About*, 11-25.

[40]Frankfurt, "Freedom of the will," 17-18. In this paper, Frankfurt describes the higher-order attitude that represents the true self simply as a second-order desire not to act on the desire for the drug, but he modifies this account in later papers to make clear that the authoritative higher-order attitude may require a more complex description. Debate about this description still continues in contemporary theories of autonomy, but for our present purposes what is important is the idea that one can identify with or reject first-order motives, not simply in the sense of evaluating them negatively or positively, but in the sense of being *resolved* for or against them.

her life worth living, but precisely the opposite.[41] An agent's commitments or cares, including the existentially fundamental ones that rank as ground projects, may be quite unreflective or immediate in Kierkegaard's sense, but they presuppose at least tacit consent from the higher-order will. Thus Quidam's inward obstacle cannot be an inward unwillingness to be in love with his beloved, for love cannot remain an infinite passion if alienated from the agent's self. If Quidam viewed his eros simply as an addiction to be overcome, as a random *conatus* alien to his inner self (as might someone who had earnestly vowed celibacy) then it would not be romantic love at all in the sense that Kierkegaard means: it would not involve any authoritative or identity-defining commitment to physical, emotional, and spiritual bonding with the beloved.

Nor can Quidam's problem be the inverse case in which the agent is firmly resolved to pursue his romantic love for his beloved, but finds himself overcome by other conflicting desires that he earnestly but futilely tries to resist (e.g. alcohol or gambling). In this case, the factors that interfere with the lovers' ability to consummate their love in lasting union happen to be internal to one (or both) of their psyches, but *qua* interfering factors they are analogous to external impediments such as a jealous ex-lover, an unfriendly authority, separation by geographic distance, and so on. For by hypothesis, the psychological obstacles to romantic love envisioned here are in the *volitional* sense just as "external" to the lovers' agency as the more familiar outward factors that conspire to keep true lovers apart: for the compulsions and bad habits frustrate their efforts to requite their love in just the same way as would a disease. The infinite passion of immediate and unsullied erotic love can be real despite being made "unhappy" by psychological problems in the lover, but only if the lover is an unwilling victim of these problems (and striving unsuccessfully against them) in a way analogous to Frankfurt's unwilling addict. If this were Quidam's state, then he would be in unhappy love, but he could not be said to *want* it to be unhappy: rather the love would be unhappy only because it was blocked by some psychic state of his that he most adamantly did *not* want, or (in Frankfurt's language) with which he did not identify.

---

[41]Indeed, if her "unwillingness" to be an addict is strong enough, then reliable evidence that she will never be able to break the cycle of addiction may even motivate suicide as the one way to escape a life of addiction, viewed as a life not worth living. Of course Kierkegaard would not say this, but see Korsgaard, *The Sources of Normativity* (New York: Cambridge University Press, 1996) 161-62.

This is clearly not what Taciturnus means when he says that Quidam's love "has its obstacle within itself" (SLW, 413). Rather,

> Simultaneously he holds on firmly to his love, and he has no obstacles from the outside; on the contrary, everything smiles favorably and threatens to be changed to terror if he does not follow his wish, threatens him with a certain loss of his honor, with the death of his beloved—thus he simultaneously holds on firmly to his love and maintains that despite everything he will not, cannot make it concrete. (SLW, 414-15)

In Quidam, unlike Frankfurt's unwilling addict, there is a conflict *between ground projects* themselves: he "identifies" in Frankfurt's sense with both of his projects, despite their incompatibility. In other words, Quidam is in the state which Frankfurt calls volitional "ambiguity."[42] His love is an unqualified commitment, which remains irrevocable even after breaking the engagement, but it conflicts with another hidden commitment that he cannot avoid. As Pattison says, "He realizes that he cannot go through with the marriage for reasons that never become clear but concern a secret guilt that involves his father."[43] The precise content of the commitment motivated by this guilt is not directly revealed in the Diary, but it is an obstacle to the requital of love because it commits the agent to a kind of secrecy incompatible with the complete opening of self to the other sought in marriage. It suffices here to note that the general form of this problem does not require that the hidden commitment itself be *religious* in the sense of being a commitment to God (for in most cases such a commitment is not incompatible with the commitment of conjugal love).[44] It could be a conflict with another aesthetic or ethical project that inwardly blocks the fulfillment of happy love. As Taciturnus says, the tension arises because of "a higher

---

[42]See Frankfurt, "Identification and Wholeheartedness," in *Responsibility, Character, and the Emotions*, ed. Ferdinand David Schoeman (New York: Cambridge University Press, 1987); reprinted in *The Importance of What We Care About*.

[43]George Pattison, "Art in an Age of Reflection," 88.

[44]And Taciturnus even says that love can "happily" undergo infinite reflection and become religious (SLW, 414). In Kierkegaard's own case, of course, the conflicting commitment may have been a religious one, i.e. not to involve Regine in a family he believed was cursed for his father's sin, or to follow a divine will that he believed barred him from marriage. But I do not think Kierkegaard's considered conviction is that only such a more unusual sort of religious commitment requiring solitude or spiritual privacy could be behind the tension in inwardly unhappy love (although he sometimes seems to write this way).

passion" than the infinite but immediate pathos known by poetry, which makes one's passion itself dialectical:

> Admittedly, unhappy love . . . has its dialectic, but it has it outside itself, not in itself. That which is intrinsically dialectical in itself contains the contradiction in itself. . . . In poetry, therefore, love does not relate to itself but it relates to the world, and this relationship determines whether it becomes unhappy. Therefore as soon as passion's sonority ceases to sound from the one, as soon as there is a conflict in passion itself—indeed, even if a higher passion announces itself in a new sonority—as soon as the concurrent sound of doubleness is detected in it, the poet cannot become involved with it. (SLW, 406)

The conflict is thus between two infinite or unqualified passions themselves, and this produces a different kind of reflection in the agent, which Taciturnus calls "infinite reflection" (SLW, 412-14). In Quidam's story, "the difficulties do not arise because love collides with the world but because love must reflect itself in the individuality" of the agent (SLW, 413). In contrast to the "finite reflection" of the lowest-level prudential aestheticism, the passionate reflection motivated by the inward conflict of pure commitments is "infinitely higher than immediacy, and in it, immediacy relates itself to itself in the idea. But this 'in the idea' signifies a God-relationship of the widest scope, and within this scope there is a multiplicity of more specific determinants" (SLW, 414). In other words, inwardly unhappy love tends towards religious consciousness.

III. From Aesthetic to Religious Pathos: Disentangling Taciturnus's Logic

But if my analysis of Quidam's inward form of unhappy love has been accurate, it may be hard to see why this should necessarily bring him towards religious consciousness. Why cannot he simply subsist in an inwardly conflicted volitional state? That he can continue in such a state for any time of course already indicates something fundamental about the structure of the human spirit, even though spirit is still only emergent in the aesthetic stage of existence. In part, I think the answer lies in the fact that such a conflict awakens what we might call *deep freedom* in the agent, i.e. not freedom to form this or that particular intention to perform a finely individuated action (abstracted out of the subjective narrative of which it is part), but rather freedom with respect to ground projects, or in Frankfurtian terms, with respect to the higher-order will that commits us authoritatively to some set of ends and to the motives and reasons for action involved in such caring. In immediacy, this freedom is not self-conscious, even if it is there nascently or *in potentia*: for this reason, the poetic hero "is not free in his passion" (SLW, 414). By contrast, Quidam discovers his freedom in the deep sense, not just with respect to outward action in the world, but with respect to his own pathos, his own cares, and the volitional character they compose. Thus his anguish: either way he goes, he apparently will have failed to be true to the values that define his self.

Hamlet's predicament is similar to Quidam's in this sense. Hamlet is not an aesthetic hero, since he lacks external obstacles to his goal of exacting just vengeance, but he does not pursue that goal decisively. This could be explained by assuming that Hamlet is a coward falling *below* aesthetic heroism and lacking an infinite passion for justice, and this could be in either of two ways: "if the plan remains fixed, Hamlet is essentially a loiterer who does not know how to act; if the plan does not remain fixed, he is a self-torturer who torments himself for and with wanting to be something great. Neither of these involves the tragic" (SLW, 453). The only other alternative is that Hamlet's passion for justice is genuine, but stymied by an inward conflict with a higher passion, in which case he transcends aesthetic heroism. Taciturnus suggests that the higher pathos behind his misgivings may be religious, leading him to repent of the plan even before carrying it out (SLW, 453-54).[45] The religious man becomes heroic not through any external success but through his invisible "relation with God" (SLW, 459), "in the interior being" (SLW, 454). If he suffers in this relation, it is because of obstacles internal to his will.

But it is still not entirely clear why Taciturnus believes that such an inward conflict will cause the individual to "become more and more religiously absorbed in himself," or why it should put him into "the state of suspension in which the religious has to consolidate itself" (SLW, 426). He says that Quidam's problem is that he remains in this suspension, ostensibly because he does not know if his beloved will recover permanently and

[45]Notice the structural parallel between this portrayal of Hamlet and the portrayal of Abraham in *Fear and Trembling*. Abraham cannot simply be a tragic ethical hero; either he is a murderer (and thus unethical) or he is a religious hero, who remains ethical only through his faith in a divine dispensation. Likewise, Hamlet cannot be an aesthetic hero: either he is "essentially a vacillator" (SLW, 453), below any heroism, or he is a religious figure whose authentic passion is checked by "religious doubts" (SLW, 454).

completely from his rejection, but inwardly because "he cannot find rest in the ultimate religious resolution" (SLW, 426) which alone Taciturnus thinks can heal such an inward conflict: "there is no healing for him except religiously within himself" (SLW, 428). He has broken the engagement and thus chosen the commitment opposed to the erotic (while nevertheless still loving his beloved), but he cannot fully accept or be completely reconciled to this decision until he knows its outward result on his beloved. He remains in this "demonic" unreconciled state because he hangs on to the idea that he might be "less guilty" if only "she came out of all this all right" (SLW, 427). This hesitation on the brink of religious consciousness is one possible form of what Taciturnus calls "inclosing reserve." In Quidam's case this is a 'defense mechanism,' a way in bad faith of preventing the emergence of religious consciousness: he is "depressed in his reserve," but it is so inclosing that it conceals the source of the depression: "he does not and cannot say what is making him reserved" (SLW, 428).

We must beware of a possible misreading at this point. It can seem (especially since Kierkegaard's pseudonyms themselves were not always clear on this) as if Quidam's depression or reserve is itself the inward obstacle that makes his love unhappy. Commentators have often suggested this. Pointing out an important parallel, Paul Sponheim says

> *Repetition* takes with the *Stages* the theme of a broken engagement—broken because there is no possibility for the sharing marriage requires. In *Repetition,* it is a young man's poetic spirit, which renders the beloved's image more precious than her actuality, which constitutes the obstacle. In the *Stages,* it is the state of melancholy that bars the way to the openness of marriage.[46]

But this is potentially misleading, because the melancholy or inclosing reserve itself results from a prior conflict between erotic love and another unnamed infinite passion in the individual: it is the symptom and not the cause of the problem. Or rather (since it is a form of spirit, not causally determined) inclosing reserve is Quidam's way of dealing with the more basic clash in his passions, and thus reserve becomes the *form taken by* the dialectic of these passions. In this form, the passion that is an inward obstacle to erotic love is not fully understood or articulated:[47] "Even if her

[46]Paul Sponheim, introduction, *Stages on Life's Way* (New York: Schocken Books, 1967), ix.

[47]We cannot say that it is "repressed," for then he would try to proceed with

lightheartedness . . . had been capable of making him a happy married man, this was not what he was supposed to be. But of this he does not dream and merely feels his misery so deeply that he is incapable of being what everyone is capable of—being a married man" (SLW, 430-31). The passion that marks him as not meant for marriage remains unspecified but presupposed in the imaginary construction.

It is clear that the resulting melancholy is not simply depression in our contemporary sense (even though Quidam sometimes implies a comparison between himself and persons we might consider clinically depressed[48]). It is an existential crisis that does not result from any experience of ineffectiveness in pursuit of external affairs and goals. As opposed to the crisis of aesthetic life found in the depression of "poets, artists, and thinkers," Taciturnus says, "the depression of my character is the crisis prior to the religious" (SLW, 430). But Taciturnus has still not fully clarified why the form of Quidam's inner conflict should necessarily point towards a religious resolution, whether he resists it or not.

To understand this we must first grasp that for Quidam the inward conflict of his passionate commitments is also experienced as an *ethical* dilemma. A passage deleted from the draft of the "Letter" is clear on this point: "he has in fact established an ethical point of view before he becomes engaged" (SLW, 623; *Pap.* V B 148:34). He began the engagement in earnest response to eros for the girl, but despite being "resolute" in it, he is ethically committed to her honor, and so the love cannot be requited before marriage (SLW, 435). As Taciturnus says, "For a thinker, a girl's honor is the idea and consistency" (SLW, 432). But his conscience also forbids him to marry her: "He is sure of one thing—that it will be the ruination of the girl to be united with him" (SLW, 435). What this shows is that the hidden passion that forbids marriage, in conflict with his erotic project, is an ethical passion, one the agent pursues because he sees it as an ethical requirement. Yet since this is only dimly articulated, as we see in the Diary he thinks of it like a divine interdiction; in foreboding, he has an obscure dread of the result if he marries her. Therefore for her sake "he breaks the engagement." But after her response that she "wants to die" (SLW, 434), even if this was

erotic love despite the disturbance of the repressed passion.

[48]For example, in the Diary Quidam says "many a time no one is more cunning at hiding what he wants to hide than a mentally disordered person, and . . . many a word from him contains a wisdom of which the wisest need not be ashamed" (SLW, 279).

not meant seriously, "he is obliged to think that he has crushed her" (SLW, 435). He is guilty of breaking his pledge, of betraying her erotic love, and now potentially guilty of murder, depending on whether or not she recovers (fully and inwardly) from the affair. Although he cannot really understand her aesthetic suffering, his is an essentially ethical suffering: it is "responsibility and guilt" (SLW, 432). Because he began the engagement, the inward conflict of his passions has become an ethical dilemma: apparently whichever way he goes he will be guilty. Even worse, in both directions the exact nature of his violation will remain uncertain: he cannot be sure what will happen to her if he marries her, or if he doesn't. Therefore if he looks for a religious resolution to his dilemma, he cannot view it in the way that Taciturnus later describes (anticipating the end of the *Postscript*) as the childish view

> that sin is something particular, and this particular the forgiveness of sin then takes away. But this is not forgiveness of sin. Thus a child does not know what forgiveness of sin is, for the child, after all, considers himself to be basically a fine child. If only that thing had not happened yesterday, and forgiveness removes it and the child is a fine child. (SLW, 481-82)

The given circumstances of Quidam's dilemma mitigate against falling into this error and encourage him to see his dilemma not as an accidental and unfortunate conflict of passions that might in other circumstances have harmoniously coexisted, but rather as a symptom of an essential problem, i.e. the radical insufficiency of the unaided human will relative to the demands of absolute ethics. Thus in commenting on the themes of *Repetition* and *Stages on Life's Way* in the *Concluding Unscientific Postscript*, Kierkegaard's pseudonym Climacus argues that the proper interpretation recognizes in the broken pledge a "teleological suspension of the ethical," but unlike the one in *Fear and Trembling* where "the person tested comes back again to exist in the ethical" (CUP, 1: 266). Instead, in Quidam's narrative,

> The teleological suspension of the ethical must have an even more definite religious expression. The ethical is then present at every moment with its infinite requirement, but the individual is not capable of fulfilling it. This powerlessness of the agent must not be seen as an imperfection in the continued endeavor to attain an ideal. . . . The suspension consists in the individual's finding himself in a state exactly opposite to what the ethical requires. . . . Thus the individual is suspended from the ethical in the most terrifying way, is in the suspension heterogenous with the ethical,

> which still has the claim of the infinite upon him and at every moment requires itself of the individual. (CUP, 1:266-67)

This fairly describes the result of Quidam's dilemma: he is pushed towards recognizing that radical "heterogeneity from the ethical," or "*sin* as a state in a human being," is an unavoidable condition in *his* existence (whether or not he recognizes it in all human lives).

Taciturnus does not emphasize what is stressed in the discussion of sin-consciousness in other pseudonymous works (such as *The Concept of Anxiety*, the *Postscript*, and *Sickeness Unto Death*): namely that even *recognizing* one's state as sinfulness in the categorical sense is itself a leap, which already involves a nascent relationship with a personal divinity, rather than merely becoming aware of one's comprehensive failure in relation to the ethical standards and ideals in terms of which one cannot but judge one's life. The sense of unworthiness that Kierkegaard has in mind is too complete or total for even the most severe ethical guilt; it involves a sense of *interpersonal* alienation from the eternal that one cannot intelligibly have in relation to abstract precepts, universal principles, or ideal paradigms. So although the relationship is radically negative—a feeling of absolute alienation—sinfulness nevertheless thereby acquires the subjective quality of a unique or uniterable relation to something not only eternal but also *personal.*

In fact, from the Christian perspective of the discourse published as the companion to Quidam's Diary (i.e. "On the Occasion of a Confession"), the direct individual relationship with God that constitutes faith must always begin in this negative way. This is the paradox: "without purity no human being can see God and without becoming a sinner no human being can come to know him" (TDIO, 15, cf. 28). This certainly doesn't mean that we have to commit some particular sin to approach God, but rather that our eyes have to be opened to our existential sinfulness. Beyond the first eye-opener, when we come to know good and evil, there is the second eye-opener when we see our nakedness before the divine. Thus "the direct relation is at the outset a broken relation" (TDIO, 19-20). It begins in "the stillness in which every human being becomes guilty," no matter how long or short the list of their particular transgressions (TDIO, 14). Seeking God therefore at first means losing God in a positive way; the seeker first becomes sensible of his infinite distance from Him, before "the seeker himself is changed" so that God can draw near, so near that "he himself can become the place where God in truth is" (TDIO, 23).

Two special features of Quidam's unhappy love push him towards such a beginning of religious consciousness. First, when he discovers that his basic commitments are in inward conflict, he understands these commitments in terms of their ethical significance (and not simply the aesthetic importance or nobility of their goals). This means that their joint unsatisfiability becomes a genuine ethical dilemma not only regarding what to do, but regarding what to care about most. But Taciturnus seems to imply not only that Quidam experiences his inner tension ethically, but that a volitional conflict necessarily tends to be experienced this way. We might ask instead if an agent finding a conflict within himself between two passions that are immediate and infinite in Kierkegaard's sense could not experience this aesthetically, for example, as simply a terrible psychological misfortune. Note, however, that if an agent continues to live this way, this leaves her few viable options:

(1) she can become psychologically paralyzed by the dilemma and pursue neither commitment;
(2) she can live with the cognitive dissonance of the dilemma, pursuing both commitments in an alternating and mutually self-defeating sequence; or
(3) she can try to resolve the conflict by wholeheartedly following one commitment against the other.

In Kierkegaard's view, human persons are by nature teleologically oriented towards the last of these alternatives: (1) and (2) will seem unsatisfactory, and cannot be sustained. But once the agent moves towards a resolution in wholeheartedness, the decision between alternatives cannot be made arbitrarily. In searching for criteria to ground such a decision, the agent will reflect on the meaningfulness and value of his or her commitments, both to himself and others. In this process Kierkegaard believes the force of ethical requirements will come to be felt. Though these will not be the only salient considerations, the agent seeking to resolve inward volitional conflict cannot do so effectively in the long run without interpreting his or her cares in terms of their ethical merit and their potential effects on others. This is part of the argument in *Either/Or* Volume II that forming authentic commitments or ground projects will inevitably involve the agent in making choices understood in terms of ethical criteria.[49] If so, then Quidam's way of taking

[49]Note that this view faces a possible counterargument that nothing prevents the aesthete from continuing to judge his or her commitments and their conflicts

his dilemma is simply a mark of his maturity as an ethical agent. But his ethical consciousness is not yet embedded in a fully religious life-view.

It is the second feature of Quidam's situation that pushes him from the perspective of ethical humanism towards the wider religious perspective: he cannot effectively calculate the guilt that he cannot avoid, nor does he know how to contain it within definite limits. In this sense, his situation is worse than King David's, who can try via a messenger to abort the order sending Uriah to certain death (SLW, 450). But whether or not his messenger arrives in time, King David is guilty of something specific: namely, having intended to murder Uriah, before repenting of it. Quidam's guilt is less determinate, and his case is more comical because it was only good intentions that led to his potential guilt: "Inspired solely by sympathy, he takes an extreme risk, and just look, he has a murder on his conscience, or rather, he enters into dialectical agony" (SLW, 451). Thus Quidam's dilemma becomes an image for a problem that is deeper than any particular and apparently avoidable violation of ethical ideals. If even pure ethical passion can lead to indeterminate guilt, we have not an isolated failure, but a sign that humanity's existential condition is one of essential "heterogeneity" relative to the ethical in general. For the anguish of his unavoidable yet indeterminate guilt to move Quidam towards religious faith, he must therefore "be able to grasp the ethical with primitive passion in order to take offense properly" (SLW, 430), that is, to be offended by the apparent impossibility of escaping guilt, which in turn is the precondition for recognizing sinfulness as a state of radical separation from the eternal.

The story therefore has an ontological point. Taciturnus, like Climacus following him in the *Postscript*, holds that

> There are three existence-spheres: the esthetic, the ethical, the religious. The metaphysical is an abstraction, and there is no human being who exists metaphysically [or *sub specie aeterni*]. The metaphysical, the ontological, is, but it does not exist. . . . The ethical sphere is only a transition sphere, and therefore its highest expression is repentance as a negative action. The esthetic sphere is the sphere of immediacy, the ethical the sphere of requirement (and

---

only in nonethical terms. This view, which seems to follow from positions defended by Bernard Williams and Nietzsche, requires a more extended answer. I try to give this answer in another essay: see the discussion of "authentic aestheticism" in "Towards an Existential Virtue Ethics," which will appear in the collection titled *Kierkegaard after MacIntyre*, ed. John Davenport and Anthony Rudd (Chicago: Open Court, 2001).

> this requirement is so infinite that the individual always goes bankrupt), the religious the sphere of fulfillment, but, please note, not a fulfillment such as when one fills an alms box or a sack with gold, for repentance has specifically created a boundless space (SLW, 476-77)

that is, a space one can never finish traversing in this life. Lest the stories of Abraham and Job give us the wrong impression, Taciturnus emphasizes that the narrative of a religious hero cannot (for us as existing mortals) have a truly final outcome in the same way as the quest of an aesthetic hero. Divine forgiveness is a miraculous reprieve, an absurd (or humanly impossible and incalculable) possibility of reconciliation with the ethical, but it is not as temporally discrete an event as the happy ending of a fairy tale. Religious existence has temporal duration and requires perseverance, just like pathos in the first immediacy, but unlike the latter, faith is not requited or fulfilled in a temporally discrete end point.

Thus Taciturnus can delineate the existence-stages by reference to the different kinds of outcomes towards which they are oriented. "The esthetic result is in the external and can be shown," when the hero succeeds in his quest for some noble end, or dies trying (SLW, 441). By contrast, the ethical demands absolute justice, projecting an ideal of its immediate realization relative to which any temporal process of striving for justice can only be an approximation (SLW, 441). When the eternal ethical ideal is represented in aesthetic fashion as an external achievement in time, "one sees in the total thought of the ethical a world order, a Governance, providence. This result is esthetic-ethical and therefore can be shown in the external to a certain degree" (SLW, 442). But this Kantian ethical teleology, with the cosmic fulfillment of rigid ethical law as its eschatological vanishing point, is only an image for the *inward* synthesis of ethical ideality and immediacy that is the result of religious existence. This result—the justification of the person through repentance and the forgiveness of sins—also produces an agreement between the ideal demand of justice and temporal existence, but only inwardly, and only *after* the recognition of sinfulness has separated the individual from the first immediacy of his passions. The religious fulfillment which puts him back into relation with the ethical is therefore not like the external achievement at the end of an aesthetic hero's quest: the religious is not the "first immediacy" (SLW, 399). Thus "[t]he religious outcome, indifferent towards the external, is assured only in the internal, that is, in faith" (SLW, 442). And because the individual can never take the positive achievement of this inward result for granted, but must strive in faith to maintain it, "the result lies in the internal and . . . is continually postponed" (SLW, 442). The religious *telos* is thus not a "result" or an "outcome" in the ordinary sense. Religious faith strives towards an ideal synthesis between the ethical and *inward* immediacy (in the existing state of the will).

The repentance in which religious consciousness begins is also not a phase we can move past, or a finite task we can finish and be done with, as in Hegelian theologies (SLW, 451).

> But if healing is to begin for the existing person, the moment must come when one lets the act of repentance go. For one single moment this has a deceptive similarity to forgetfulness. But to forget guilt is a new sin. This is the difficulty. To hold firmly to guilt is the passion of repentance . . . [yet] to let go of it, to remove it so it is not just as present at every moment, is necessary for healing. (SLW, 451-52)

Quidam's problem is that he prefers to remain obsessed with his repentance, just in order to avoid fully and wholeheartedly repenting. Rather than accept the essential guilt of human life that is revealed by his dilemma, and that is only resolvable through grace, he clings to the hope of averting his potential guilt with respect to the girl by his own mortal efforts, i.e. by reversing his break with her, or by some other strategy. He focuses on the fact that he is in a kind of "superposition" between being guilty or not guilty for a *particular outcome* (her fate) when instead his spiritual growth depends on seeing the problem in terms of the total guilt essential to the human condition.[50] Hence "he cannot find rest in repentance, because it seems as if he were continually about to act, to undo everything, if that were possible.—That he gives way to this is the demonic" (SLW, 451). The term "demonic" is used because this state involves rebelliousness,[51] a lingering refusal fully to accept grace. To recognize the absolute need for it, given the human impossibility of fulfilling the universal demands of the absolute ethics (as

---

[50]This is also what Taciturnus means, as best as I can make out, when he writes that Quidam's "aberration is due to his letting her actuality disturb his integrating of himself in repentance, with the result that he cannot find peace in his repentance because she makes it dialectical for him" (SLW, 436).

[51]But it is an unselfconscious rebelliousness, a halting and halfhearted resistance to the required self-surrender before God, a form of spiritual stalling and delaying that tacitly prefers self-torment to submission—as opposed to the absolute and resolute determination to make such rebellion permanent, which is the end point of the demonic taken in the direction of evil, the Nietzschian despair that Anti-Climacus calls "defiance."

opposed to the more contextualized demands of a given *sittlichkeit*), requires a level of horror for which he still isn't prepared, a final despair of spiritual self-sufficiency for which he still lacks the courage: this is what Taciturnus means in saying that "the deep dark night of his soul should become still darker, for then he will recover" (SLW, 424).

We aren't given the final result of this inward struggle with God, and this for two closely connected reasons. First, religious existence for human beings in time must be "negative" in the sense of always remaining an unfinished task, always suffering in the impossibility of assuming that one's salvation is completed "in positive infinity, which usually is reserved for the deity and eternity and the deceased" (SLW, 444). Religious existence "is never finished, at least not in time, nor can it be represented as such without deception" (SLW, 445). Thus a genuine religious speaker must be concerned with his own guilt, rather than with fundamentalist millenarian bombast: "he lets heaven remain closed, in fear and trembling does not feel that he himself is finished" (SLW, 464). Second, for us, each existing person's story can be interpreted only as a fragmentary narrative, and imaginary constructions (as opposed to grand metaphysical systems) should give us no more: "To complete an individuality and put down a summary answer, that is for the great systematic thinkers, who have so much to traverse; to allow it to come into being in all its possibility is what interests one who composes imaginary constructions" (SLW, 436). Taciturnus's sort of ontological psychology thus respects its own limits as a finite endeavor in human self-understanding. Ultimate outcomes are for God, beyond human calculation.

In summary, Taciturnus's "Letter" maps out Kierkegaard's inner teleology of the human will. On this view, it is our nature to care, to form commitments, and until some of our projects have an unconditional significance for us—or are pursued with infinite passion—we have not willed anything earnestly: "lost in something abstract . . . they actually do not live, but merely waste their lives" (SLW, 659; *JP* VI 6410). Using a metaphor to which Kierkegaard frequently returns, we are afraid to soar and have not used the spiritual wings within us: instead of "lofty flight in willing," we have "won the security of the pedestrian on the highway of mediocrity" (TDIO, 20). But once we establish ourselves through commitments to ends we think are noble in themselves, the highest ethical definition of nobility cannot but take on a dramatic relevance for us. As Harry Frankfurt argues, the caring person inevitably becomes interested in knowing "what conditions must be satisfied if something is to be suitable or worthy as an ideal or an object of love," that is, *what is worth caring about, and why*.[52] In particular, we come to care about criteria and grounds for caring: "if *anything* is worth caring about, then it must be worth caring about what to care about."[53] Nor can we intelligibly base our identity on ground projects whose significance is wholly solipsistic.[54] Kierkegaard holds that as commitment becomes infinite, we cannot fully understand the significance of our ground projects without referring them to the background of absolute ethics, the final or widest existential horizon implicit in all social ethics or *sittlichkeit*. But once this happens, the pressure builds to recognize that our failure to commit ourselves to the infinite good and to follow through on our commitments are not contingent or accidental failures, but a sign of sinfulness. And then the transition to the religious stage through repentance is at hand.

IV. Conclusion: Suffering

This explanation of Taciturnus's analysis is sufficient to show why Kierkegaard sees such a close connection between religious faith and suffering. Lowrie writes, "for S.K., suffering is the religious category—not accidentally (as when suffering occurs in the aesthetic sphere and mars pleasure, or in the ethical sphere and obstructs striving) but essentially, and that not only in the beginning but throughout."[55] That suffering is *essential* to religious consciousness distinguishes it because "suffering in relation to esthetic and ethical existence is accidental; it can be absent and there can still be an esthetic or ethical existence" (CUP, 1:288). Ethicoreligious life is related to suffering in a number of interrelated ways for Kierkegaard,[56] but not all suffering has specifically religious significance. Taciturnus takes pains to emphasize that properly religious suffering is not the kind of self-inflicted torment we find in the heroes and heroines of what I have called

---

[52]Frankfurt, "The Importance of What We Care About," 91.

[53]Frankfurt, "The Importance of What We Care About," 92.

[54]See Charles Taylor's argument that authentic self-definition demands attention to interpersonal standards and ethical criteria without which ground projects cannot make sense: "Inescapable Horizons," *The Ethics of Authenticity*, chap. 4.

[55]Lowrie, translator's introduction to *Stages on Life's Way*, 11. On this distinction, also see the end of the "Speculative Sermon" from the draft of *Stages*: SLW, 640; *JP* I.625.

[56]See the excellent discussion of this theme in David J. Gouwens, *Kierkegaard as Religious Thinker* (Cambridge UK: Cambridge University Press, 1996) 162-72.

perverse romanticism (SLW, 468).[57] Whereas aesthetic heroes pursue "great and quantitatively conspicuous" aims, and fear the powers of fate that undermine such grand purposes, the religious hero fears guilt, and suffers from the radical guilt required for repentance (SLW, 462). Thus "[t]he suffering is within the individual himself; he is no esthetic hero, and the relationship is with God" (SLW, 459). In Quidam's "Story of Suffering," the hero's anguish approximates to religious suffering, because he suffers from indeterminate guilt, but his suffering is not quite fully religious, since it is partially self-torment (SLW, 472), by which he keeps himself from wholeheartedly repenting.

This suffering signifies the fact that the religious hero lives in "second immediacy," and because of this, his commitments are not first or primarily to results in the external world: he continues care about his neighbor and to act, but on a different basis than the passions of first immediacy.[58] As Malantschuk notes, in the third of the *Edifying Discourses in Various Spirits*, Kierkegaard formulates the law: "to relate oneself absolutely to the Eternal and relatively to the temporal. It is hereby decisively affirmed that the goal of human life lies beyond the temporal. . . . He who takes this position in earnest is bound to suffer in this world, and thus suffering becomes the characteristic mark of the religious life."[59]

Faith may require suffering because it requires continued repentance, dying to immediacy, and being prepared for martyrdom in witnessing to Christ. But there is a further relation between suffering and religious consciousness in Kierkegaard's interpretation, and it is here that a potential problem becomes apparent. Kierkegaard links Christian existence to a particular theological answer to the problem of evil, namely one version of the Irenaen view that the temporal world is a "vale of soul making," in John Hick's famous phrase. By itself this is a theodicy, a metaphysical theory, but

---

[57]He also suggests that Quidam's beloved may have fallen into this perversion, since "she . . . exaggerated as much as possible and tormented herself with wanting to be an unhappy lover on the largest possible scale" (SLW, 466).

[58]This is apparently what Kierkegaard means by saying that, while the aesthete's fault is to live abstractly, and this is condemned by the ethical (which brings one back to concrete responsibilities), the religious hero living in patient expectancy lives in the true abstraction, the right sort of abstraction (SLW, 660; JP VI 6410, Pap X1 A 377). In other words, religious abstraction is the opposite of worldliness, but without disengaging from life or ceasing to care, as in aesthetic abstraction.

[59]Gregor Malantschuk, *Kierkegaard's Way to the Truth*, 58.

it motivates the existential response to evil that Kierkegaard makes essential to Christian religiousness: namely, humble submission to the trials and difficulties of mortal life as tests necessary for the growth of spirit, and hence as guided by divine providence, which must be dealing justly with us. This was certainly Kierkegaard's own response to "physical, psychical, and spiritual" problems which made him feel that he was denied the possibility of ordinary married life.[60] Commenting on the sermon at the end of *Either/Or II*, Malantschuk writes,

> In anguish when he was at the point of revolting against God, Kierkegaard consoled himself with these thoughts about man's wrong and man's guilt in relation to God. These reflections may help others in the same situation. There are times and occasions when a man considers himself or others to be suffering innocently in this world. It is also true that in their mutual relationships men can be more guilty or less guilty. But in our relation to God we are always—no matter what happens—unrighteous and guilty. To think otherwise is the same as trying to abolish God or to revolt against him.[61]

Kierkegaard seems right that religiousness in general requires a sense of being answerable to "a higher ethic than social morality,"[62] whose demands we will never perfectly fulfill. He may also be right that transition to the religious requires the leap of sin-consciousness. But in addition, he insists that because of our radical moral inadequacy, the sufferings caused by *all moral and natural evil* are just and for our spiritual good (while still trying to alleviate pain).[63] We can be asked to accept this as an unfathomable mystery, but Kierkegaard seems to me instead to regard acceptance of this

---

[60]Malantschuk, *Kierkegaard's Way to the Truth*, 55.

[61]Malantschuk, *Kierkegaard's Way to the Truth*, 60.

[62]Malantschuk, *Kierkegaard's Way to the Truth*, 60.

[63]Compare C. S. Lewis's view that "The creature's illusion of self-sufficiency must, for the creature's sake, be shattered; and by trouble or fear of trouble on earth . . . God shatters it, 'unmindful of His glory's diminution' " (*The Problem of Pain*, 97). And "the old Christian doctrine of being made 'perfect through suffering' is not incredible" (105). "If the world is indeed a 'vale of soul making,' it seems on the whole to be doing its work" (108). Yet although there is much merit in the notion of corrective or remedial suffering, and even more in the idea of martyrdom in the struggle to remain true to the highest ideals, Lewis himself came later (after his wife's death) to see that as an explanation for all natural evil, this is quite inadequate.

theodicy as the only existentially adequate medicine for the rebelliousness evinced in the doubts and anger commonly occasioned by experiencing the problem of evil firsthand in our lives.

Here I think Kierkegaard badly erred, and this error infects the analysis of some of the main themes in his authorship(s). In my view, the pathos that arises from the existential problem of evil (the problem *as experienced*, rather than merely contemplated as a conceptual puzzle to be solved by analytic ingenuity) is not in itself rebelliousness, but originally one of the deepest expressions of precisely the ethical volition that is a prerequisite for genuine faith. If this is right, it is possible to reject Irenaen theodicies without being in rebellion against God or cutting oneself off from Christian religiousness. Indeed, at the risk of sounding heretical, I think this may not only be possible but even necessary today. In post-Holocaust historical time, we may have to rethink the notion of divine sovereignty over the world that Kierkegaard took for granted and look for a different theodicy if commitment to Christianity is to remain existentially possible. Or so it seems to this single individual.

10

The Concept of Fate in Stages on Life's Way

Grethe Kjær

It is generally agreed that Søren Kierkegaard's existential concepts must be interpreted differently according to which of his pseudonyms is using them. In other words, they can vary in content, but this content is closely connected with the view of life that the pseudonym in question represents. This also holds true for the concept of fate, and in a work such as *Stages on Life's Way*, with its many pseudonymous figures, there is rich opportunity to see how this word can constantly change meaning and to consider the consequences implied in the pseudonyms' different presentations of it.

Through the ages, fate, itself inexplicable, has been the explanation of the inexplicable, whether this has been viewed as blind chance, unavoidable fate, or the in some way determined necessity. For the ancient Greeks, it was the unfathomable power to which not only men but also the gods were subordinate. From the standpoint of metaphysics fate has been regarded as the unity of necessity and chance, and so it appears to human beings as the historical—or, as Goethe in *Wilhelm Meister* more poetically expresses it: "Das Gewebe dieser Welt ist aus Notwendigkeit und Zufall gebildet" ("The web of this world is woven by necessity and chance").[1]

Fate in the stringent metaphysical sense of the word is to be found in the authorship first and foremost in the writings of the psychologist Vigilius Haufniensis. He views fate as the unity of the two apparent opposites, necessity and chance, and he says about this:

---

[1]Goethe lets *ein Unbekannter* express this view of life when Wilhelm Meister asserts his belief in a "Macht, die über uns waltet, und alles zu unserm Besten lenkt." See Goethe, *Wilhelm Meisters Lehrjahre,* Ein Roman, herausgeg. von Goethe, Erster Band, Cap. 17, S. 172; Goethe's *Neue Schriften,* Dritter Band (Berlin, 1795). Translation by the editor.

> Fate may also signify exactly the opposite, because it is the unity of necessity and the accidental. This is something to which we have not always paid attention. People have talked about the pagan *fatum* (which is characterized differently in the Oriental conception and in the Greek) as if it were necessity. A vestige of this necessity has been permitted to remain in the Christian view, in which it came to signify fate, i.e., the accidental, that which is incommensurable with providence. However, this is not the case, for fate is precisely the unity of necessity and the accidental. This is ingeniously expressed in the saying, fate is blind, for he who walks forward blindly walks as much by necessity as by accident. A necessity that is not conscious of itself is *eo ipso* the accidental in relation to the next moment.(CA, 96-97)

In *The Concept of Anxiety*, Vigilius Haufniensis looks at the concept of fate first and foremost from a psychological angle. The main stress is upon the contrast-filled doubleness contained in the word "fate," making it the object of anxiety. Therefore, according to Kierkegaard, the concept of fate belongs, precisely as the object of anxiety, to paganism, paganism not only in antiquity but also in the modern world. In his search for an explanation of existence, a final cause, a final authoritative instance, a person will eventually encounter fate as an explanation. But fate itself is and remains inexplicable, an ambiguous something, which is and is not, and on which a person feels himself dependent, without, however, being able to come into any real relation to it. A person's anxiety therefore becomes an anxiety about "nothing," or, as Vigilius Haufniensis says: "in fate the anxiety of the pagan has its object, its nothing. He cannot come into a relation to fate, because in the one moment it is the necessary, and in the next it is the accidental" (CA, 97). Nevertheless, the pagan through the oracle seeks to come in contact with fate; but the tragic thing is that the oracle's replies are just as ambiguous as fate, and the relation to the oracle also becomes one of anxiety.

The same applies to what Kierkegaard calls modern paganism. When a person does not have a view of life that contains faith in something eternal within or outside himself, he will, when he is put in unforeseen or menacing situations, begin to seek some explanation of existence or to get light shed upon the future. He seeks "a relation to spirit as something external," a relation to something which is not spirit and yet to which he wishes to stand in a spiritual relationship (CA, 96-97). That is, the person wishes to come in contact with the unknown cosmic powers which are presumed to rule the world, and he tries, just like the Greeks, to consult them in some way or other, for example, through astrology, palmistry, fortune telling or omens;

but the answers will always be ambiguous just as the answers of the ancient Greek oracles were, precisely because these powers, like fate, are nothing.

But the two aspects of the concept of fate also make possible other views, and these, as already mentioned, can be encountered in the different pseudonymous authors, some putting the main emphasis upon what is chance, others upon what is necessary, while, in Kierkegaard's upbuilding writings, one finds a criticism of the confusion of fate with providence within the Christian view of life.

Stages on Life's Way is especially interesting since it contains a broad spectrum of different conceptions of fate, among other things because one finds represented in this one book all three stages of existence. These stages are mentioned briefly by Frater Taciturnus, author of the third and final section of the book, in the following manner:

> There are three existence-spheres: the esthetic, the ethical, the religious. . . . The esthetic sphere is the sphere of immediacy, the ethical the sphere of requirement (and this requirement is so infinite that the individual always goes bankrupt), the religious the sphere of fulfilment, but, please note, not a fulfilment such as when one fills an alms box or a sack with gold, for repentance has specifically created a boundless space, and as a consequence the religious contradiction: simultaneously to be out on 70,000 fathoms of water and yet be joyful. (SLW, 476-77)

The concepts "fate, chance" are, according to Frater Taciturnus "esthetic categories" (SLW, 441-42), and therefore one would expect to find them only in the first section of the book in "In Vino Veritas," where one encounters people who represent different forms of the aesthetic view of life and who are all "consistent to the point of despair" (CUP, 1:298).

The concept of fate does not belong within the ethical view of life, for "The ethical asks only about guilty or not guilty, is itself man enough to be a match for men, has no need for anything external and visible, to say nothing of something as ambiguously dialectical as fate and chance" (SLW, 442). So, too, the word "fate" appears only twice (!) in "the married man's" (alias Judge William) essay "Some Reflections on Marriage in Answer to Objections." In the first instance he calls being "unhappily married" the "worst of fates" for a woman (SLW, 142), and in the second a particular ironic view of woman is mentioned in which there is "sympathy for her presumably unhappy fate" in not being married (SLW, 145; cf. 58). Thus here the Judge uses the word fate about a human being's lot in existence.

Now one could of course expect, when the ethicist so decisively rejects fate and chance, that these concepts would not appear at all, or at any rate would not be taken seriously in the book's third section "Guilty?"/"Not Guilty?" where the author describes a person, Quidam, who is on the way to the third stage, the religious. But this is not the case. It is not merely the experimenter Frater Taciturnus—who declares that he is not religious himself—who uses the words; also Quidam, who says about himself that he has "religious presuppositions" (SLW, 195), speaks about "fate and chance" as realities, which he however thinks he can "abolish" (SLW, 400; see also 249).

On closer examination it also appears that Quidam, when he uses the word "fate," gives it an entirely special meaning, since he understands by it something personal, the inherited characteristics and particular influences of a special kind in childhood and youth that can acquire so decisive an influence that if some particular event occurs they can make the person an "exception."

But before we go on to deal with the special significance of the word fate as we encounter it in "Guilty?"/"Not Guilty?" we will take a closer look at how one of the aesthetes, Victor Eremita, views fate, shedding light upon it not merely on the basis of his speech at "The Banquet," but taking into consideration his statements in *Post-Scriptum* to *Either/Or*, which is written in the same year as "In Vino Veritas." For Victor Eremita, fate is first and foremost synonymous with a necessity that lies in the factual nature of existence for which he does not make much of an attempt to find an explanation. The only breach of this necessity is due to "chance," which often plays tricks on people—perhaps merely because it is a necessity that one has not foreseen. It is the unpredictable fate that—although not lacking a certain humor—is the deciding factor in human existence. Of his own relation to fate he says:

> I ascribe it all to fate and for that reason am circumspect enough not to draw any conclusions from that, because fate is a very touchy character and one must be extremely cautious in association with it. I have, therefore, always tried to place myself on a firm footing in relation to it. If it meets me on my way, if it takes care of me, well, then I thank it, even though I would rather thank a human being. But I do not go a step out of my way in order to meet it on the next street; I do not cling to it when it leaves me. (EO, 2:417-18)

His hardened attitude to the phenomena of life also comes to expression in his statements about woman, which, however, are marked by a kind of "sympathetic irony" (CUP, 1:298, see also SLW, 145). For he finds her fate especially tragic because, hidden from herself, it is both ridiculous and pitiable, fixed as it is partly by nature and partly by society. He describes her life briefly thus: "Formerly Empress in the vast outskirts [*Overdrev*] of erotic love, and titular queen of all exaggerations [*Overdrivelser*] of giddiness, now Mrs. Petersen on the corner of Badstuestræde [*Bathhouse Street*]" (SLW, 57-58). She has not even influence on the negative significance she can acquire for the man. She acquires this when she through "the courtesy of fate" can "make her appearance before him at the right moment," after which she does best to "be unfaithful to him, the sooner the better" (SLW, 62-63).

Through his consistent negative-ironic attitude to existence Victor Eremita approaches the demonic—his view of life is despair. What is said in *The Sickness unto Death* applies to him: "The determinist, the fatalist, is in despair and as one in despair has lost his self, because for him everything has become necessity." The demonic in Victor Eremita consists of his despairingly maintaining that all existence is subject to an inevitable necessity, he "has no God, or, what amounts to the same thing, his God is necessity; since everything is possible for God, then God is this—that everything is possible" (SUD, 40).

In the second section of the book, "Some Reflections on Marriage in Answer to Objections," Judge William, as representative of the ethical view of life, uses the opportunity to settle accounts with the misleading views of woman and marriage expressed by the speakers at the dinner party. This, however, occurs indirectly, stated as general observations, since he, "according to the design of the work, cannot be assumed to know" what was said at the dinner party (CUP, 1:298). His contribution on "divine dispensation" [*Tilskikkelse*] (SLW, 115-16) is thus in fact a refutation of Victor Eremita's fatalistic outlook on life. Instead of talking about fate and chance, the ethicist talks about "divine dispensation." He makes his decision confident that a person is granted freedom's possibility to make a choice—but he also knows that there is something called "divine dispensation" to which he must submit. For in the words "divine dispensation" lie both the concepts of necessity (as something a person cannot himself alter) and of chance, but at the same time it also expresses that everything a person experiences is "divinely dispensed," that is, sent the person by a higher power, by Governance. One cannot fathom the "secret" of divine dispensation, but one can learn to come to terms with it and take up one's responsibility; and the more positive and concrete a person's decision is, "the more it has to do with a relation to the divine dispensation. This gives it the ideality of humility, meekness, and gratitude" (SLW, 115-16).[2] Yet it can also be the case that a person's decision is so proud, so abstract, so inhuman, that it does not intend to take "divine dispensation" into consideration, but interprets all the latter's "argument" as "extrajudicial" (cf. Quidam's remark about abolishing fate and chance, SLW, 400n.).

As previously mentioned, Quidam, who is intended to illustrate a development "in the direction of the religious" (SLW, 420), has a special interpretation of the concept of fate as the conditions that are to be found partly in heredity and partly in external circumstances (corresponding to necessity and chance). It is worth mentioning that already at the beginning of Kierkegaard's authorship we find a similar view, namely in A's piece on "The Tragic in Ancient Drama Reflected in the Tragic in Modern Drama." In the classical Greek tragedies, the individual cannot liberate himself from his connection with the race, and its guilt can thus also become the particular individual's inescapable fate. Although the particular individual "moved freely," he nevertheless rested in "substantial determinants, in the state, the family, in fate" (EO 1:143). A maintains, unlike his contemporaries, who automatically make "the individual responsible for his life," that it also holds true in our time that "Every individual, however original he is, is still a child of God, of his age, of his nation, of his family, of his friends, and only in all this does he have his truth" (EO 1:145 translation revised).

But even though there can be a "sadness and a healing" (EO 1:145) in the old Greek view that there is something inevitable that one is involved in without any individual guilt, what is inherited or taken over from the race can be of such a nature that it can prevent the individual from fulfilling the ordinary ethical demands required by society, so that he becomes an "exception." For example, the individual may be unable to marry in a society that requires marriage and regards it as "central in temporality," as Judge William puts it (SLW, 170-71). In his observations concerning the justifiable exception he argues that it is not enough that the person concerned, at the same time as he recognizes "the reality of marrying" *in abstracto*, declares that "he is unhappy, unfit for this joy, for this security in existence; he is depressed, a burden to himself, and feels he must be that to others." No,

[2]Cf. "It is not according to the external divine dispensations that we can judge of God's grace or displeasure" (J. P. Mynster). Christian Molbech: *Dansk Ordbog* (Copenhagen, 1833) col. 509, under *"Tilskikkelse."*

"having experienced" is lacking, "First of all something has to happen" (SLW, 175-76)—it must have actually become manifest that there is something that makes a marriage impossible.

This is also the case with the examples of exceptions we encounter in works like *Either/Or*, *Repetition*, and not least in *Stages on Life's Way*. In the aesthete A's sketch for a modern *Antigone*, Antigone has discovered the secret that lies behind the tragic fate of the race, a secret that she cannot share with anyone, why she is unable to marry. In *Repetition* "the young man" perceives, after he has got engaged, that he poetically transforms his love into recollection, and therefore he is not suited for marriage. Both Antigone and the young man have to see, through what has happened to them, that they are prevented from marrying because of a special fate, so that they are placed outside the universal as exceptions. But the special thing about the young man in *Repetition* is that he wishes it to be clear that it is because of a psychological peculiarity and not because of any guilt that he cannot marry the girl. He wishes to be in the right, as Job was. Constantin Constantius says about this, however, that "Fate has played a trick on him and let him become guilty" (R, 304). This statement immediately raises the question: can fate make a person guilty? Can it force a person into such circumstances that he can lose his freedom and yet nevertheless be declared guilty? Or, as Constantin Constantius puts it: can the individual lose himself in event or fate in such a way "that freedom is taken up completely in life's fractions without leaving a remainder" (R, 315)? For the young man, the problem is solved through freedom emerging again in repetition; he submits to his fate and through doing so thereby receives himself again on a higher level as poet.

It is such questions that also Quidam later comes to ask himself. Yet whereas for Constantin the important thing first and foremost was to make clear psychologically how repetition could come about, the task for Frater Taciturnus in *Stages on Life's Way* is, with the help of an "experiment" to try to get to the bottom of the difficult problem: when is it a matter of fate and when is it a matter of guilt? In other words, where does a person's guilt begin, when circumstances in life come into play over which the individual has no control and which therefore acquire the character of necessity or fate?

Quidam, after having experienced something like the two other above-mentioned characters, namely a love affair with a subsequent engagement, becomes clear that he is the victim of an unhappy fate that will prevent him from marrying. But when he becomes engaged, in his idealism he believes that a person has a possibility of freedom to "lift himself above" his given conditions (CA, 73). Only he knows that the melancholy from which he suffers cannot be removed,[3] but he also knows that he is able to hide it, to incapsulate it in himself, something he considers necessary, since it has its origin in part in secrets he cannot tell anyone. In return, he has, precisely through the bitterness of melancholy, won his way to a joy of life which he looks forward to being able to share with his future wife.

What becomes the stumbling block for Quidam is "the wedding" (SLW, 355), in which the lovers with God as witness promise to share everything. Here, the secret of his melancholy becomes an insuperable obstacle. He sees no way out other than to attempt to get the girl unharmed out of the relationship into which he has himself knowingly and deliberately brought her. It now becomes his task to do this in the most considerate manner. Of course he knows that he is making the girl unhappy, but it takes him by surprise that she implores him for the sake of God and his deceased father to remain with her, and that she declares that it will be her death if he leaves her. Out of respect for the girl, he feels obliged to take this statement seriously, and thereby she causes him to have "a murder on his conscience" (SLW, 432).

With this, things take a new turn: can he become guilty of the girl's death? He must face this possibility. Yet his guilt must, he thinks, nevertheless depend on whether the girl really dies. He "must wait for information from actuality about what he has really perpetrated" (SLW, 450). He believes that it is the girl who "determines his fate"—as if he would be "less guilty because she came out of it all right, less guilty even if she had dealt wrongly with him" (SLW, 426-27). But according to Frater Taciturnus, his fate is already determined. The girl becomes his fate only in the sense that he, through falling in love with and becoming engaged to her, has had to realize that with his personal background he is not capable of fulfilling the universal ethical and marrying. He must realize that he is an "exception." But can this make him guilty, when the cause of his not being able to go through with a marriage is a secret that was forced on him and a melancholy whose origins lie partly in something inherited and partly in the conditions in which he has grown up?

---

[3]Cf. Kierkegaard's statement: "I have never at any moment in my life been deserted by the faith: one can do what one wills—except one thing, otherwise unconditionally everything—except one thing, lift the melancholy in whose power I was" (PV, 80, translation revised).

He had wanted to have it in his power to be able to express himself in the universal any moment he wished—now he feels his proud existence "crushed." Governance has caught him, and he is "forced back into this solitary understanding" that "my choice is not free. Here I am sensible of freedom only when in necessity I submit to necessity and in the submission forget it" (SLW, 351 translation revised).

What fate actually means for Kierkegaard is what the contents of Quidam's diary deals with, namely, how the consequences of inevitable conditions in a person's life can become that person's fate. There can scarcely be any doubt that Quidam's description of his period of engagement corresponds, to a certain extent, to Kierkegaard's own experience of his situation surrounding the broken engagement with Regine Olsen. "A few entries," the so-called "interpolations," which Frater Taciturnus on the fifth of every month has "inserted into the diary" in order to throw light on Quidam's inclosing reserve (SLW, 429), all contain references to experiences in Kierkegaard's youth—to what became Kierkegaard's own fate.

The "Quiet Despair" (SLW, 199-200) thus emphasizes the close relationship and the unspoken understanding between father and son, and this probably is also meant to indicate melancholy as something hereditary. In "A Leper's Self-Contemplation" (SLW, 232-34, cf. 507), Kierkegaard outlines the two possibilities that he thought in his earliest youth that he faced: either to put up with his melancholy and his inclosing reserve and take refuge in God—or go out in society as a mocker of existence, a possibility he has partially realized for a time (cf. SLW, 235) and through which he made himself popular in certain circles.

"Solomon's Dream" principally describes the shocking discovery Kierkegaard made in his early youth, that it was his father's secret guilt and not his piety that made him stay close to God, and that God's blessings towards him were felt more like a curse—a postponement of punishment. "The horror of the dream is this contradiction"; but added to this is, for Kierkegaard, the fear of how things will go with him when the only man he "had admired for his strength and power was tottering" (SLW, 250-52, cf. 507-508). What inherited tendencies did he himself contain—could they be so strong that they could lead him astray? It is the anxiety about such consequences, reflecting itself in the next story "A Possibility" (SLW, 276-88 cf. JP, 5: 5622, 5624, 5656), that possibly discloses something of the father's secret, but possibly also refers to Kierkegaard's own escapade.

The most horrifying interpolation is, however, "The Reading Lesson" (SLW, 323-28), which is given the date of Kierkegaard's birthday and therefore must be regarded as especially significant. It has to do with a revelation of a scandalous and gruesome family situation, a son's showdown with his father and their final decision to "divide their estate not as father and son make division in love but as deadly enemies make division" (SLW, 327).

The last interpolation "Nebuchadnezzar" (SLW, 360-63) is, in my opinion, the most difficult to understand. Possibly it is Quidam's (Kierkegaard's) pride and confidence in his own powers that is depicted by the "Babel" Nebuchadnezzar has built. Like Quidam, by wanting to make himself lord of "fate and chance" Kierkegaard has himself tried to usurp a power which belongs to God alone. He has "taken his gold and silver vessels and destroyed his temple." Later, it says: "A voice was suddenly heard and I was transformed as swiftly as a woman changes color."[4] He is changed into a beast in the field, which may symbolize that Kierkegaard, after the broken engagement, is excluded from the possibility of making himself understood to other people. In the same way as Quidam he feels himself caught by "Governance," and "misunderstanding and again misunderstanding are the heavy iron bars" before his window (SLW, 351).

The melancholy described here—with all its conditions that Kierkegaard could partly hide but not abolish, and perhaps also other sufferings, partly of a psychic and partly of a physical nature—Kierkegaard experienced for many years as a heavy, almost unbearable, fate. It could tempt him to protest against the whole of existence, to demand the position of the printing "error" that wants to mutiny against the author (God) and that out of spite demands to remain as evidence that he is a "second-rate author" (SUD, 74).

Here we are at the heart of the problem: how would it be possible for a person to "make clear" to himself, "to what extent it is fate or to what extent it is guilt"? (CA, 120). How can a person be guilty of something, that as its deepest root contains conditions over which he has no control, psychological defects, for example? A person can apply his will to "work against" his weakness, but the problem remains: "shall he persecute himself, as it were, and perhaps go mad over his inability to overcome it, or shall he humble himself under it" (JP, 1:905; cf. JP, 4:4586)?

This does not affect the validity of the freedom that a person possesses, as the pseudonym Vigilius Haufniensis asserts; he is convinced that there never could be in a person's life such a "more" of unhappy conditions that

---

[4]Possibly it is God's voice he hears. Cf. "Then (so it goes in those old tales) the command was given to him: 'Let go of this object!' " (FSE, 78).

these would be able to form a direct transition to sin, insofar as this transition takes place through a leap that can be carried out only by the single individual himself (CA, 72-73 see also 108-109). But the question still remains: when such conditions become a serious hindrance to the single individual in fulfilling the universal ethical demand made to a person by society, where then does the individual's responsibility and guilt begin, and when can he be said to be a justifiable exception?

As late as 1844, Kierkegaard writes in a Journal entry: "It is and always will be the most difficult spiritual trial [*Anfægtelse*] not to know whether the cause of one's suffering is mental derangement or sin. Freedom, which is otherwise used for the struggle, in this case becomes dialectical with the most dreadful contrasts" (JP, 4:4586). It is especially this problem that "Guilty?"/"Not Guilty?" is about. What happens with Quidam is precisely that his dialectic can certainly help him to see that he is guilty, but how far? On June 18 he writes in his Diary:

> Am I guilty, then? Yes. How? By my having begun what I could not carry out. How do you understand it now? Now I understand more clearly why it was impossible for me. What then is my guilt? That I did not understand it earlier. What is your responsibility? Every possible consequence for her life. Why every possible one, for this certainly seems to be an exaggeration? Because here it is not a matter of an event but of an act and an ethical responsibility, the consequences of which I do not dare to arm against by being courageous, for courage in this case precisely means opening oneself to them. What can serve as your excuse? That my total individuality predisposed me to something in which I had been corroborated on all sides, which, if I had sought a confidant, I would find confirmed—namely, "That a depressed person should not torment his wife with his sufferings but like a man should inclose them within himself." What is your consolation? That I, in acknowledging this guilt, also sense a Governance in it all. (SLW, 380-81, translation revised)

In view of the way the situation has developed, Quidam thinks that he has done the best he could do for the girl. But he has also come to a deeper understanding of himself as exception, as the printing error that nevertheless has its "meaning," or as the "weed that grew apart from the useful grain—then it would indeed stand on the side, would indeed be a weed, and would indeed be disgraced, but suppose that nevertheless it was called Proud Henry" (SLW, 397).

This statement, which concludes the diary, does not seem to indicate that Quidam feels that he really has something to repent. In his "Letter to the Reader," Frater Taciturnus tries to explain why Quidam, in spite of his self-knowledge, "is unable to take himself back in repentance." This is, he says, because Quidam "becomes suspended in a dialectical relation to actuality" (SLW, 447), and thinks that "he must wait for information from actuality about what he has really perpetrated" (SLW, 450), namely, whether the girl will die because of the broken engagement or escape unhurt (SLW, 198, 450, 394). As long as Quidam still wishes to keep himself in a state of suspense regarding what he has done wrong, "repentance" is "dialectically prevented from constituting itself" as Frater Taciturnus puts it, and Quidam thereby approaches the demonic (SLW, 446). Yet, according to Frater Taciturnus, it is "not the dialectical that makes a person demonic—far from it, but it is remaining in the dialectical" (SLW; 436-37). Perhaps it also holds true for people generally, "that the dialectical is found most frequently but amounts to nothing at all" (SLW, 447). But it signifies precisely that for every responsible person there can arise situations where that person must consider the following question: How far am I responsible in this particular situation? Where is the limit concerning what I am able to do by my strength of will and what I am unable to do because of hindrances that lie in unalterable conditions? The pseudonym Johannes Climacus expresses it thus: "Where then, is the boundary for the single individual in his concrete existence between what is lack of will and what is lack of ability; what is indolence and earthly selfishness and what is the limitation of finitude? . . . Let all the dialecticians convene—they will not be able to decide this for a particular individual *in concreto*." Dialectics can take a person only as far as the point where "the objective uncertainty" must "force out the passionate certitude of faith," so that "in absolute subjection the conflict about right and wrong collapses in absolute worship" (CUP, 1:490-91).

Being the experienced psychological observer he is, Frater Taciturnus can see, although he himself is not religious, that it is this that must happen to Quidam. He must give up wanting to be in the right, experience his own "destruction" before God (SLW, 450). But Frater Taciturnus does not let us know whether Quidam ever reaches "repentance"—he does not wish to give the reader a result, but to let an individuality "come into being in all its possibility." Therefore it is not unthinkable that Quidam "once more become dialectical. If that happens, he remains demonic" (SLW, 436).

"Repentance" generally, is a special problem for Frater Taciturnus, whose own view of existence is "the unity of the comic and the tragic"

(SLW, 483). He is, however, of the opinion that "only the person who in repentance exhausts the dialectical, only he repents" (SLW, 476). Repentance must precede the forgiveness of sins which means, "one has become another person." How this can happen, and how the second immediacy becomes different from "the first immediacy," is for Frater Taciturnus one of the "most difficult questions" (SLW, 483-84).

In addition, if one looks at repentance "in the direction of sympathy" it must prove embarrassing that one person can be saved through repentance while another apparently is shipwrecked "despite his good intentions." "Life certainly must still have laws; the ethical order of things is no hullabaloo in which one person escapes unscathed from the worst and another scathed from the best" (SLW, 478-79). Is it a question of fate or possibly of a predestination? In order to cast light on his problem, Frater Taciturnus produces as an example a gambler gripped by repentance so that he gives up gambling completely. He has been near the precipice, but repentance holds him fast so that his intention seems to succeed and he is possibly saved. But one day a suicide is dragged out of the Seine and it turns out to be a friend of his, also a gambler, who had thus in vain fought a despairing battle to resist his impulse. The first-mentioned gambler had loved him because he was a better person than himself; he is unable to pass the judgement without further ado, that "He did not want to be saved." He also knows that the same thing could still happen to him. If he hopes for his own salvation, he must humble himself under the explanation that it must then be due to predestination. But in his sympathy for the other man he finds this hard to accept:

> Yet on the other hand he himself cannot be saved by chance; that is thoughtlessness. And if he says that the other gambler went down despite his good intentions, then he himself goes down; and if he says that consequently the other was unwilling, then he shudders, because he still saw the good in him and because it seems as if he is making himself better. (SLW, 477-78, translation revised)

Frater Taciturnus lets the problem of repentance and forgiveness of sin lie, because it "is extraneous to the task the experiment has assigned itself, for its Quidam is only a demonic figure oriented to the religious" (SLW, 484 translation revised); in addition, he asserts that this problem goes beyond his understanding and his capacities.

On the other hand he is clear that when Quidam in spite of everything sees his own destruction as produced by "the hand of God," he no longer ascribes his misfortune to fate but to Governance. Expressed in religious categories which for Frater Taciturnus is of course "a strange tongue," it can signify that

> providence, which is infinitely concerned about each and every person, equips an individuality, to whom it gives unusual powers in relation to actuality. "But," says providence, "lest he do himself too much harm, I tie this power up in depression and thereby hide it from him. What he is capable of doing, he will never find out, but I will use him; he is not going to be humiliated by any actuality—to that extent he is more pampered than other men, but within himself he is going to feel destroyed as no other person feels it." (SLW, 450)

"Experimenting," Frater Taciturnus sees this as a possibility (SLW, 450 translation revised). He has let Quidam experience what, according to Judge William, is the beginning of being an exception, namely, he "must feel himself to be the most wretched of men, the scum of humanity" (SLW, 181).[5] But the Judge admits that it goes beyond his comprehension whether

> out of this wretchedness . . . a sense of being blessed can develop, whether in this dreadful nothingness there can be any divine meaning, what faith it must take to believe that God could intervene [*gribe ind*] in life this way, that is, in such a way that it manifests itself as such to the one suffering and acting, for if God actually is the one who intervenes, then he has well provided for the rescue of the annihilated ones, except that at the critical moment the one apprehended [*den Grebne*], the one selected, cannot know about it. (SLW, 181-82)

* * * * *

Just as Quidam has misunderstood his situation and believed that his misfortune is due to an inevitable fate, so also, according to Vigilius Haufniensis, has one allowed a "vestige of this necessity" to remain "in the Christian view, in which it came to signify fate, that is, the accidental, that which is incommensurable with providence" (CA, 97).

For the particular individual it will depend on his personal belief, whether he will presuppose a fate or a providence, for, to a certain extent,

---

[5]"Then he sinks down, desperate in all his wretchedness, when that single word, that final, that ultimate word, so ultimate that it is not within human language, is not forthcoming, when the testimony is not with him, when he cannot tear open the sealed dispatch that is only to be opened out there and that contains the orders from God" (SLW, 181).

the "Christian providence . . . corresponds to fate in such a way that it is the unity of necessity and the accidental, so that for providence the accidental is, and yet in such a way that for providence nothing is accidental" (CA, 199).

The question thus becomes one of whether a person dare believe that everything that happens to him is due to God's providence, to divine dispensation, and is not merely caused by necessity or chance. But it was clear to Kierkegaard that belief in a providence would always be very difficult for people. In 1846 he writes:

> A *Providence* [*Forsyn*] is no easier to understand (to grasp) than redemption [*Forløsningen*]—both can only be believed. . . . Providence and redemption are categories of despair—that is, I would have to despair if I dared not believe it, yes if I were not commanded to believe. Thus they are not the occasion of despair—they keep despair away. (JP, 3:3628)

11

The Relation of Kierkegaard's Stages on Life's Way *to* Three Discourses on Imagined Occasions

Andrew J. Burgess

On 29 April 1845, one day before publishing *Stages on Life's Way*, Kierkegaard put out a set of discourses, *Three Discourses on Imagined Occasions* (hereafter *Three Discourses*). The double event continues a pattern of matching pseudonymous writings with religious discourses under his own name, starting with the pairing of *Either/Or* with *Two Upbuilding Discourses* in 1843. Once again he puts out two works almost simultaneously using radically different literary styles, and once again he employs a different publisher for each book. Still, this time the tie between the two members of the pair seems closer than before, because the one book describes three stages, while the other consists of three discourses.

Is there a connection and, if so, what is it? The traditional view, developed by Emanuel Hirsch and Howard Hong, focuses on parallels between the three parts of *Stages on Life's Way* and the corresponding discourses in *Three Discourses*. In this essay I will critique that view and the three-stages schema on which it relies, and I will argue that the fundamental either/or built into *Stages on Life's Way* also creates for the two books a larger either/or that includes them both.

The Hong and Hirsch Proposals

During the past century two proposals have been offered relating the three stages in *Stages on Life's Way* to *Three Discourses* in terms of thematic parallels. Both proposals originate with Emanuel Hirsch, and both have been taken up by Howard Hong in his prefaces to the new Princeton edition of Kierkegaard's works. The two proposals first turn up in the two volumes of Hirsch's classic work *Kierkegaard-Studien*. The first proposal comes from the first volume of the work, in a part published separately in

1930,[1] and Hong adopts it in his definitive 1993 English language edition of *Three Discourses* (TDIO, x). This view matches the discourses in order with the three stages on life's way: that is, the first part of *Stages on Life's Way*, the banquet symposium, parallels the first discourse, the confessional; the second part, the advice on marriage from a married man, the wedding discourse; and the third part, " 'Guilty?'/'Not Guilty?'" and its commentary, the graveside discourse. Three years later, however, in the second volume of the same work, Hirsch changed his mind and reversed the order of the stages, so that while the middle part of *Stages on Life's Way* continues to match the wedding discourse, the banquet symposium stands in parallel with the graveside discourse and " 'Guilty?'/'Not Guilty?'" with the confessional discourse.[2] This is a position Hong had cited, evidently with approval, in his introduction to the 1988 edition of *Stages on Life's Way* (SLW, xi), but he later abandoned it (TDIO, x). For the sake of simplicity I call the first proposal, which keeps the stages in *Stages on Life's Way* order, the "Hong proposal," since this is his later view; while the second proposal, reversing the order, which was Hirsch's later view, I call the "Hirsch proposal."

Hong states his proposal briefly but effectively in the introduction to *Three Discourses* (TDIO, x). The first discourse, at a confessional, "with an emphasis on stillness, wonder, and seeking God," is the "counterpoint" to the first part of *Stages on Life's Way*, "with its banquet and speechmaking on erotic love." The second discourse, at a wedding, "deepens and rectifies Judge William's panegyric on marriage in *Either/Or II*, and in the second part of *Stages*." The third discourse, at a graveside, "on the earnestness of life evoked by the earnest thought of death, constitutes an unambiguous sharpening of the implicit ethical and religious earnestness in Quidam's " 'Guilty?'/'Not Guilty?'" in Part Three of *Stages on Life's Way*." Hong explains how Kierkegaard worked alternately on the two manuscripts, so that *Three Discourses* is thus "not only chronologically the companion piece to *Stages* but is also its counterpoise in content."

The parallels drawn in the Hong proposal do not all have the same strength. Although there is a close parallel between the wedding discourse and *Stages on Life's Way*'s advice from a married man, the other two parallels are not distinctive. On the basis Hong cites, why should not the first

---

[1]Emanuel Hirsch, *Kierkegaard-Studien*, I-II (1930–1933; repr.: Valduz/ Leichtenstein: Topos, 1978) I, 150 [278]. The first page numbers are for the original ed.; the page numbers in brackets are for the reprint ed.

[2]Hirsch, II, 150-65 [752-67].

discourse be paired with Quidam's reflections rather than the third? The confessional discourse shares its stillness also with the quiet of Quidam's meditations, and, if Frater Taciturnus is right, Quidam, if not yet seeking God, is nonetheless moving in a religious direction. Likewise, on the basis of the motifs Hong points out, why should not the third discourse be paired with the "In Vino Veritas" banquet symposium in *Stages on Life's Way*? The earnestness evoked by the thought of death in the graveside discourse would also provide a sharp counterpoint to the flippant banqueters.

The Hirsch proposal, on the other hand, keeps the close parallel between the middle stage and the middle discourse, but abandons the two other looser parallels. He pairs the first discourse with the third part of *Stages on Life's Way* and the third discourse with the first part of *Stages on Life's Way*. In this way Hirsch is able to achieve a closer match between one of the pairs than the Hong proposal, but at the cost of a less intuitively compelling order, since he reverses the order in which the discourses match the parts of *Stages on Life's Way*. Hirsch's explication of his proposal is stimulating and worth considering even where it sometimes fails to convince, as it does in treating the contrast between the aesthetes' "In Vino" banquet symposium in *Stages on Life's Way*, all frivolity, with the graveyard discourse, with its earnestness evoked by the thought of death. Here Hirsch points to several places in the banquet speeches at which the revelers mockingly refer to death.[3] In his speech Constantin Constantius, for example, recommends that one needs to be earnest enough to relate unhappy love to death "for the sake of the jest" (SLW, 53). If the woman can die of love, he speculates, she may perhaps also be revived again; and if so she will become an entirely different human being who thus can love for the first time. "Oh death, how powerful you are," he concludes; "the most powerful emetic, the strongest laxative could not purge so clean" (SLW, 54). In their speeches Victor Eremita and Johannes the Seducer also make similar satiric references to the convention of dying for love (SLW, 60, 79). The difficulty with Hirsch's case here, however, is that the references to death are so completely incidental that a person will never be struck by any such parallels with the graveyard discourse unless some commentator comes along and insists upon them.

By contrast, Hirsch also makes another, and more effective, tie than Hong's, between Quidam's "Story of Suffering" and the confessional

---

[3]Hirsch, II, 157 [759].

discourse.[4] Quidam is obsessed by the question whether or not he is guilty. The title of his diary—" 'Guilty?'/'Not Guilty?' "—tells his story. The confessional address thereby answers to his moral suffering, although it is not an answer he is aware he is seeking or one he is yet prepared to find.

Each of the two proposals thus has at least one problem it cannot resolve. The drawback with the Hong proposal is that two of the three parallels do not work well enough to be effective, while the drawback with the Hirsch proposal is that, in addition to having a rather weak parallel between the *Stages on Life's Way* banquet and the graveside discourse, he does not alert the reader to the reversal of the order of the discourses in relation to the stages. On balance, the Hong account is the stronger of these two proposals, since, if readers look for parallels they will at least expect to find them in normal order.

In addition to the difficulties specific to each of the two proposals, the proposals also share another shortcoming, that the parallels they find, even when they are relatively strong, are sometimes positive and sometimes negative. That is to say, to be a close parallel here sometimes means that the two things in parallel are much alike, and sometimes that they are much unlike. For Hirsch, for example, the ideas in the Judge's reflections on marriage in *Stages on Life's Way* agree closely with the religious categories used in the wedding discourse in *Three Discourses*, only that these categories do not yet fit his personal existence.[5] Yet the parallel Hirsch draws between the way the aesthetes in the banquet symposium flippantly refer to the fact of death, on the one hand, and the earnest way death is kept in mind in the graveside discourse, on the other, is a comparison between directly opposite situations. The first parallel is of situations that are closely similar in kind, the second of situations radically different in kind. Using both cases as parallels is confusing.

The general difficulty with both proposals is that neither way of drawing the parallels seems much better than the other. Both proposals work somewhat, but neither proposal can present a decisive argument against the other. Both proposals suggest intriguing parallels, but that is not enough. Neither of them is compelling enough that the reader is likely to hit upon it when reading *Three Discourses* after reading *Stages on Life's Way*. Moreover, the two proposals tend to cancel each other out; since the two

---

[4]Hirsch, II, 162-65 [764-67].

[5]Hirsch, II, 161n.2 [763n.2]; cf. I, 155n.2 [283n.2].

proposals exclude each other, yet seem about equally plausible, the plausibility of each proposal undercuts the plausibility of the other. Nor is there any way in principle to exclude a third, fourth, or even a fifth or sixth proposal, based on the other possible permutations matching the three parts of *Stages on Life's Way* with the three discourses. One might, for example, match the Judge's stern reflections with the confessional discourse, the aesthetes's symposium about women with the wedding discourse, and Quidam's diary with the graveyard discourse. Several proposals are suggestive and not easily written off.

The value of such thematic investigations as Hirsch and Hong present is that they encourage readers to look at the texts more closely than before and to pay attention to the intricate interweaving of motifs the books contain. What they do not demonstrate is how *Three Discourses* must be related to *Stages on Life's Way* in any particular way. For that, new data or a different approach may be called for.

The Issue of Chronology

Two recent studies of Kierkegaard manuscripts, one on *Stages on Life's Way* and one on *Three Discourses*, report several findings that revise the traditional chronology assumed for the production of these two works and thereby bear directly upon the question of their relation to each other.[6] These findings are: (1) except for the final "Letter" by Frater Taciturnus, the drafting of *Stages on Life's Way* precedes that of *Three Discourses*; and (2) although the dates for the drafting of Taciturnus' "Letter" and *Three Discourses* cannot be fixed with precision, there does not seem to be a time when the threefold structure of the one book might have influenced the structure of the other.

(1) The writing history of the two books shows that Kierkegaard wrote *Three Discourses* after drafting all of *Stages on Life's Way* except the final "Letter to the Reader." Thus, whatever their thematic continuities, the one

---

[6](1) Søren Bruun, Leon Jaurnow, and Jette Knudsen, "Tekstredegørelse," *Kommentar til Stadier pas Livets Vei*, vol. K6 of *Søren Kierkegaards Skrifter* (Copenhagen: Gad, 1999). I am indebted to Niels Jørgen Cappelørn and Jette Knudsen for providing me with advance drafts from this material. (2) Niels Jørgen Cappelørn and Jette Knudsen, "Tekstredegørelse," *Kommentar til Opbyggelige Taler 1843, Opbyggelige Taler 1844, Tre Taler ved tænkte Leiligheder*, vol. K5 of *Søren Kierkegaards Skrifter* (Copenhagen: Gad, 1998).

book follows most of the other in time. Hong's suggestion that Kierkegaard may have written the two manuscripts alternately during the same period (TDIO, x) would thus only be true for Taciturnus's final "Letter" and not for the rest of *Stages on Life's Way*. This finding suggests that any parallels should be looked for between the three discourses and this letter, not between the discourses and the whole book.

In their commentary on the new edition's textual history of *Stages on Life's Way*, Søren Bruun, Leon Jaurnow, and Jette Knudsen at the Søren Kierkegaard Centre in Copenhagen establish that the first two parts of the book—the banquet symposium and the letter on marriage by the Judge—were complete already by November, 1844, and the best estimates are that he finished drafting the third part, Quidam's diary, about December 1844 or January 1845. Since Frater Taciturnus's "Letter to the Reader" presupposes the details of Quidam's diary, Kierkegaard could not begin to draft Frater Taciturnus's "Letter to the Reader" until after that date.[7] That makes January or February 1845, rather than 1844, as has sometimes been assumed (SLW, 621-46), the earliest possible time for beginning his drafting Taciturnus's "Letter." On the other hand, there is evidence to indicate that Kierkegaard began serious drafting of *Three Discourses* near the middle of February of that year. A reference in Kierkegaard's journals (TDIO, 133-34) to a sermon preached on February 9, 1845, on the same text as Kierkegaard's first discourse, suggests that this is when he began writing this discourse; and according to the first editor of Kierkegaard's papers, H. P. Barfod, the first substantial drafts of *Three Discourses* came from a packet marked February 10, 1845 (manuscript 1).[8] This set of circumstances suggests that, except for the "Letter to the Reader," Kierkegaard had finished drafting *Stages on Life's Way* before he began major drafting of *Three Discourses*. Only the "Letter" in the last section of *Stages on Life's Way* might have overlapped with the drafting of *Three Discourses*.

(2) Although the dating of the manuscripts of Taciturnus' "Letter" and *Three Discourses* leaves room for much flexibility, specifying a point at which each of the three stages might have been correlated with its corresponding member of the three discourses, or vice versa, runs into several problems. Even during that period, perhaps part of February and into March, 1845, when Kierkegaard may have been drafting both *Three Discourses* and

---

[7]Bruun, Jaurnow, and Knudsen, K6 82.

[8]Cappelørn and Knudsen, K5 393.

the "Letter" in *Stages on Life's Way*, the threefold shape of the one book does not seem to have influenced that of the other.

The problem for the view that the structure of *Stages on Life's Way* influenced the structure of *Three Discourses* is that Kierkegaard wrote down the main ideas for *Three Discourses* early in this period, before *Stages on Life's Way* is likely to have had three parts. The first drafts of *Three Discourses* are in the packet (manuscript 1) dated 10 February 1845. Here the titles of the three proposed discourses ("at a confessional"/"at a wedding ceremony"/"at a burial," in that order, are already given, along with the texts for the first and third discourses (the second was later changed), together with parts of the introductions to the first and third discourses. That packet is very small, but its contents do indicate that the arrangement, scripture texts (except for the text of the second discourse), and imagined occasions he selected for the three discourses were already set down at this point in time .

But was there a time before 10 February 1845, when Kierkegaard could have been influenced by the threefold structure of *Stages on Life's Way* to put out a set of three discourses? The problem here is that at that time *Stages on Life's Way* may not yet have become a book with a threefold structure. As Hong explains (SLW, viii-ix), *Stages on Life's Way* was originally written as two separate manuscripts, "The Wrong and the Right," containing "In Vino Veritas" and the reflections of Judge William, and " 'Guilty?'/'Not Guilty?'" containing Quidam's diary and Frater Taciturnus's letter to the reader. Not until after he was well into writing Taciturnus' "Letter" does Kierkegaard even refer to the notion of three spheres. The first clear indication that he has decided to put the two books into one appears in a table of contents that covers all of *Stages on Life's Way*. The manuscript containing that table of contents (manuscript 28) was likely written in February.[9] The basis for this dating is that this manuscript (SLW, 517) refers to a letter Kierkegaard's proofreader, Israel Levin, sent out in February to a long list of people asking them to provide samples of good handwriting for use in a proposed textbook for reading handwriting. Although the preface to *Stages on Life's Way* speaks of the pseudonymous editor Hilarius Bookbinder learning about this request in the newspapers (SLW, 4), Kierkegaard himself evidently received such a letter from Levin, since he wrote a reply saying that he would not be able to help (LD, 183, letter #123).

---

[9]Cappelørn and Knudsen, K6 84.

the second volume of *Either/Or*, and adding some points about the religious stage from *Postscript*. In the process, one obvious source for information on the stages, *Stages on Life's Way* itself, easily gets overlooked. If the works of Kierkegaard's authorship were imagined to line up along Kierkegaard Street, *Either/Or* would stand at one end of a block as a twin-towered landmark and the familiar *Postscript* skyscraper would dominate the other end. Between the two would loom the massive *Stages on Life's Way*, strange and unknown. The literati, after sampling the choice parts of *Either/Or*, would move on for a quick visit to *Fear and Trembling*, while the aspiring philosophers would make obligatory stops at *Philosophical Fragments* and *Concept of Anxiety* before settling in at *Postscript*; but most would pass by *Stages on Life's Way* without really noticing it.

Reading *Stages on Life's Way* can be a powerful antidote to an overly simplistic grasp of what stages are. The variety in the pseudonymous authorship of the book creates diversity in how the notions of stages are presented, and the overall concept of stages in the book complements both *Either/Or* and *Postscript*, as a brief description will show.

Either/Or begins a familiar pattern in Kierkegaard's works, contrasting "the aesthetic" with "the ethical," that is to say, the life of the completely detached observer with that of the (at least occasional) participant. In volume one of the book Mr. A, the aesthete, is a purely detached observer, so detached, he says, that he even declines to accept that role (EO, 1:39). In volume two, on the other hand, the ethicist, Mr. B, exhorts Mr. A at least to choose to be what he is, because in that way he will cease to be purely an observer (EO, 2:211).

This same either/or between the observer and the participant persists in *Postscript*, though in another way than in *Either/Or*. The alternative is posed on the first page of *Postscript*'s main text. Here the either/or is between the participant in faith and the one who "is not in a relationship of faith but is objectively in a relationship of observation and as such is not infinitely interested in deciding the question" (CUP, 1:21). This either/or divides the book into two parts, a one chapter discussion of the "objective problem" of the truth of Christianity, and the rest of the book discussing the "subjective problem."[12] Unlike Mr. B, Johannes Climacus, the pseudonymous author of

---

[12]See Andrew J. Burgess, "The Bilateral Symmetry of Kierkegaard's *Postscript*," *International Kierkegaard Commentary: Concluding Unscientific Postscript to "Philosophical Fragments,"* IKC 12, ed. Robert L. Perkins (Macon GA: Mercer University Press, 1997) 337-38.

Postscript, does not characteristically describe this opposition in terms of a disjunction between the aesthetic and the ethical. Instead he sometimes refers to the latter alternative as "the ethical-religious" (CUP, 1:119, 198, 202), and later on he speaks of "the ethical and the ethical-religious" (CUP, 1:396, 426, 434, 467, 481). The "ethical-religious sphere" he describes as "the upbuilding in the sphere of Religiousness A" (CUP, 1:561; cf. CUP, 1:519). On the other hand, the alternative to the ethical-religious is almost always simply the aesthetic, although he does also speak of "the esthetic-ethical" (CUP, 1:347). In this way *Postscript* continues the basic disjunction laid down in *Either/Or* but develops it in new directions.

Unfortunately *Postscript*'s references to three stages can easily obscure this structurally fundamental either/or. Commenting on *Stages on Life's Way*, Climacus himself warns against this difficulty: "despite this tripartition," he says, "the book is nevertheless an either/or. That is, the ethical and the religious stages have an essential relation to each other" (CUP, 1:294). Because the same Danish word may be translated as "an" or "one," the contrast is formulated more sharply in Danish than in the English translation. In effect what the passage says is that there are *three* stages but only *one* either/or, between the aesthetic and the ethical-religious. *Postscript* thus continues *Either/Or*'s dichotomy between the observer and the participant, only here the Hegelian speculative philosopher, rather than Mr. A, represents the observer and has difficulty putting his thought into practice.

Stages on Life's Way differs from both *Either/Or* and *Postscript*, in that it includes not just one either/or, but several. In fact, each person in *Stages on Life's Way* conceives the various stages in terms of that person's distinctive enthusiasms and preconceptions, as well as the stage that person occupies. Borrowing a favorite term from Climacus, one may say that *Stages on Life's Way* conceives of the stages "subjectively," that is to say, in terms of the particular "subject" who is living in each stage. Moreover, a person can, and usually does, live at the same time in more than one stage at once, in overlapping "existence-spheres" rather than stages (SLW, 476-77).

The basic strategy of *Stages on Life's Way* is to present ideas not as positions, motifs, theories, or stages, but instead as ideas instantiated in flesh and blood individuals. As Climacus acknowledges, *Stages on Life's Way* lets ideas contend in terms of existing individuals rather than abstract standpoints (CUP, 1:295). When *Stages on Life's Way* sets out to refute one position with another, it does not just let the ideas collide but brings the people holding both positions together and lets them work the matter out. If necessary, as in "In Vino Veritas," the book has to get the participants mildly drunk to get the discussion going, but it does not bring ideas together unless it can imagine specific persons holding them and sharing them with each other. The reason the textbook notion of stages often sounds so artificial is that commentators take ideas from one part of the book and put them together with ideas from another, abstracting from the particular dramatic settings within which characters hold those ideas.

On the other hand, what helps make *Stages on Life's Way* effective in demolishing stereotypes about the stages is its cast of idiosyncratic personalities, especially the characters representing the aesthetic, and the diversity of views they have on how the stages are organized. Gone is Mr. A, the main aesthetic figure in *Either/Or I.* In his place are Victor Eremita, the editor of *Either/Or*; Johannes the Seducer, also from *Either/Or*; Constantin Constantius, the narrator in *Repetition*; a "young man," who is not identified, but who may be the young man with whom Constantius corresponds in *Repetition*; and the "Fashion Designer," a crank whose plan is to make women ridiculous by means of changing fashions. These five meet by arrangement at a banquet symposium, but, although they are all identified as aesthetes, none of them agrees much with any of the others. Almost the only point on which they all agree is also where they most differ from Mr. A, regarding the relation of the aesthetic to the ethical. Beyond that the five have little in common. At least one of the banqueters, Johannes the Seducer, could well be described as a sensualist, but that term surely would not apply to the "young man," who idealizes women. Defining the aesthetic turns out to present unexpected problems. Moreover, even if someone could devise a definition that would classify the "young man" as an aesthete along with the other four, it would not necessarily cover the situation of Mr. A in *Either/Or*. Thus, although *Stages on Life's Way* enriches the concept of the aesthetic, it also makes the task of defining it harder than before.

Further complicating the presentation is the way the figures in *Stages on Life's Way* understand the stages terminology in terms of their own various outlooks on life. The way Mr. B draws the distinction between the aesthetic and the ethical in *Either/Or* does not work in *Stages on Life's Way*. Unlike Mr. A in *Either/Or* I, all five banqueters in *Stages on Life's Way* are committed to a goal in life, a feature they share with the "ethical" person, as Mr. B understands that term in *Either/Or*. On that basis even Johannes the Seducer can argue that his life "expresses an idea" (SLW, 78), although the idea he instantiates is only that every marriage ought to start out with the wife being seduced by someone like himself (SLW, 79). Constantin Constantius puts the matter differently when he proposes that woman needs to be understood not in terms of the aesthetic but rather of the jest, which is an "embryonic ethical category" (SLW, 48). A person committed to the aesthetic life needs to be "sufficiently earnest to hold fast to this idea—and that much earnestness we ought to have at all times—for the sake of the jest" (SLW, 53). At face value what Constantius suggests here is that aestheticism, too, has an ethical basis, so that, in a sense, the aesthetic here arises out of the ethical. In all these banquet speeches, however, irony is piled upon irony, so that a reader must be careful not to accept everything the speakers say.

The second part of *Stages on Life's Way* adds new interpretations of the relationships among the stages. Mr. B, here called "Judge William," takes a different stance toward the religious than he did in *Either/Or*. *Either/Or II* leaves open the possibility of a religious stage that follows the ethical, when it concludes with a sermon that the Judge had heard and admired, but in *Stages on Life's Way* he disputes whether that possibility is ever realized. Although Judge William is willing to admit in *Stages on Life's Way* that he knows "a life that is higher" and which is in "the direction of the religious, in the direction of spirit" (SLW, 169), he sets such stringent conditions for this religious "exception" to the ethical to be justified in what he does that in the end Mr. B does not know whether the conditions are ever in fact met (SLW, 183).

Unexpectedly, Judge William, the champion of the ethical, is also the person who points out a case where the ethical is not needed for getting to the religious. Just before Judge William's discussion of the religious exception to the ethical, which he thinks is unlikely to exist, he brings up another kind of example that certainly does exist: the feminine. Whereas a masculine soul reaches the religious through reflection and "through an ethical development," he says, a "feminine soul" does not, but "swiftly as a bird she comes from aesthetic immediacy to the religious" (SLW, 166). Nor can these remarks be dismissed as merely the isolated musings of Judge William, since a year later Kierkegaard himself takes a similar stand when reviewing the novel *Two Ages*.[13]

Although the part of *Stages on Life's Way* dealing with the third or "religious" stage takes up fully two thirds of the book, the central figure of

---

[13]Lee Barrett, "Kierkegaard's *Two Ages*: An Immediate Stage on the Way to Religious Life," *International Kierkegaard Commentary: Two Ages*, IKC 14, ed. Robert L. Perkins (Macon GA: Mercer University Press, 1984) 53-55.

those pages provides only a marginal example of what the religious is supposed to be. That figure, Quidam, is the subject of the diary " 'Guilty?'/'Not Guilty?': A Story of Suffering," actually written by Frater Taciturnus as a kind of psychological experiment. Taciturnus describes Quidam as a person living "in the direction of the religious" (SLW, 398) but not there yet. Quidam does not, for example, qualify as a "justified exception" to the ethical, in Judge William's terms, because for that he would have had to be married before he gave up his beloved (SLW, 177-78).

Taciturnus's words about Quidam, that he lives "in the direction of the religious," are only part of his statement. By themselves they could be misleading, perhaps suggesting that Quidam has only to continue down his present path to become completely religious. The full statement by Taciturnus is that Quidam is a kind of "demoniac character in the direction of the religious" (SLW, 398). In this case what is demonic about him is that "he is unwilling to relate himself to himself in his religious idea but understands her in esthetic categories and cheats the ethical a little as if he were—if he is guilty—less guilty because she came out of it all right . . ." (SLW, 427). He is not "demonic in the direction of evil . . . but neither is he purely religious" (SLW, 433). In the terminology *Concept of Anxiety* adopts a year earlier, he is demonic in the sense that he "is in the evil and is in anxiety about the good" (CA, 119).

In *Stages on Life's Way*, to be a demoniac means to have chosen a side path that just keeps leading one further and further astray. Of course, *Stages on Life's Way* does not mean to suggest by this analysis that the path of life consists of one great thoroughfare plus a few side streets that may distract from it. The course *Stages on Life's Way* lays out is much more like a maze than a superhighway, and no one can avoid getting caught in one or another of the innumerable paths of the demonic. Even someone not personally involved, such as Frater Taciturnus, can see that no one escapes (SLW, 479). The Judge identifies Johannes the Seducer as demonic (SLW, 148). Quidam is thus by no means alone in pursuing the demonic. How far the realm of the demonic extends is not otherwise specified in *Stages on Life's Way*. Climacus in *Postscript* later includes the Fashion Designer within the diversity of the demonic, because that person has "demonic despair in a state of passion" (CUP, 1:298).

Even the image of a maze fails to do justice to the complexity of the book, because the book's characters do not agree on where their journeys begin or end. Through all the twists and turns of its argument, *Stages on Life's Way* critiques any effort to chart the human journey in a simple way.

Stages on Life's Way uses the categories of the aesthetic, the ethical, and the religious not to assign each member of the human race to one of three discrete classes, or to identify each part of a typical human life with one of three stages. Instead, *Stages on Life's Way* builds a great theatrical stage on which the typified personalities it creates, many of them aesthetic, ethical, and religious in different senses and at different times, can come into mutual contact and act out the human drama, conversing with and confronting each other.

In *Stages on Life's Way* the nature and order of the stages are themselves in dispute. What one character in *Stages on Life's Way* calls aesthetic, another calls ethical, and what one calls ethical, another calls aesthetic. Thus neither the term "stage" used in the title of the book, nor the term "existence-sphere," expresses the full complexity of the situation; for, although the latter term allows for an overlapping of the spheres, it does not express how what is ethical for one person is aesthetic for another. The order of stages, too, is in dispute, so that whereas in one sense the aesthetic may precede the ethical, in another the ethical may precede the aesthetic, and in one key passage the ethical is dropped out between the aesthetic and the religious. To add to all this, the demonic remains a possibility at every point along the way. The potential complications are endless.

It is true that the characters in *Stages on Life's Way* do share some common concepts of the aesthetic and the ethical that they do not share with the authors of *Either/Or*. Above all, none of them tries to take the stance of a pure observer such as Mr. A. Thus even when someone like Frater Taciturnus keeps to a role as observer, he does not thereby deny that he is also a participant in the drama; instead he sees himself as participating in a particular way. Climacus draws attention to this difference between the two books by noting that in *Either/Or* the aesthete is only "an existence-possibility" whereas in *Stages on Life's Way* the aesthete is existing (CUP, 1:295).

Nonetheless, the diversity of viewpoint in *Stages on Life's Way* stands in the way of identifying the basis of its structure. The four parts of the book present incompatible accounts of what the stages are and how they fit together, yet it makes a great deal of difference which part is selected as the guide to the structure of the whole book.

The Letter by Frater Taciturnus

For the purpose of the present essay, I am selecting Taciturnus's final "Letter to the Reader" as the key to the literary coherence of *Stages on Life's*

Way. After all, who else is in a position to interpret the entire book? Only Taciturnus has an interest in presenting categories for the book as a whole. Moreover, manuscript study has shown that until Kierkegaard wrote the Taciturnus letter he had not yet planned to put together the two halves of *Stages on Life's Way* into one volume with the kind of structure it eventually received.

True, the book claims not to privilege any viewpoint but to leave that kind of decision up to the reader. In this respect the book follows the lead of *Either/Or*, which also sets out to leave the alternatives open. Like *Either/Or*, however, *Stages on Life's Way* does operate within an overall structure; and just as the either/or in the book by that name is set by Mr. B rather than Mr. A, even though Mr. B is not nearly as memorable a writer, so, too, Frater Taciturnus, rather than the glittering cast of characters that precedes him, best defines the categories operative throughout *Stages on Life's Way*.

Insofar as the book is one work, rather than—as it sometimes seems—a collection of reflections from various sources, *Stages on Life's Way* is Taciturnus's book. Looking at the book in that way provides the basis for answering three questions: (1) What is the definitive understanding of the stages in *Stages on Life's Way*? (2) What is the basic either/or built into the book? and (3) What is the relation between *Stages on Life's Way* and *Three Discourses*?

The Stages in Stages on Life's Way, *according to Taciturnus*

Only one paragraph in *Stages on Life's Way* (SLW, 476) takes up the stages explicitly, and the term there is "spheres" rather than "stages," but that paragraph defines Taciturnus's viewpoint. This is also the viewpoint that Kierkegaard uses to tie together the two previously drafted volumes of the book into one work, and it contains concise formulations for each of the three stages or spheres.

The ethical. To make sense of Taciturnus's key paragraph about the three spheres, the best place to begin is with the ethical sphere, because that is where he differs most from one's usual expectations. For Taciturnus, the ethical is the "sphere of requirement (and this requirement is so infinite that the individual always goes bankrupt) . . . " (SLW, 476). The ethical is an ideal that is never fully realized in human life. Earlier in the letter Taciturnus speaks of the ethical as the "life-view that judges him," and he indicates that when the ethical becomes clear to someone the person is "shipwrecked" (SLW, 435). What people usually mean by the ethical is guidelines for living, perhaps on the order of the kind of advice the Judge gives in his essay of reflections on marriage. Taciturnus seems well aware of this understanding of the ethical, but he prefers to define it in terms of what he thinks of as its "highest expression . . . repentance as a negative action" (SLW, 476). Properly speaking, the ethical poses an infinite requirement, according to Taciturnus, and when that requirement is watered down in everyday usage the distinctively ethical is lost.

From this definition of the ethical it follows that Taciturnus does not expect to be able to find unequivocal examples of the ethical among people's actions. No one fulfills the infinite demands of the ethical. The hallmark of the ethical in a person is not moral rectitude but repentance.

Although Taciturnus's understanding of the ethical differs from that of the others in *Stages on Life's Way*, he does have allies among the pseudonyms of other Kierkegaard books. Even the Judge, writing the second volume of *Either/Or*, has sympathy for the view, since he includes at the end of his letters a sermon he had recently heard by a Jutland pastor, on the theme "The Upbuilding That Lies in the Thought That in Relation to God We Are Always in the Wrong." Whether the Judge actually understands this text is doubtful, but he thinks that it is saying just what he had been trying to express in his letters to Mr. A (EO, 2:338). On the other hand, Vigilius Haufniensis, the author of *Concept of Anxiety*, grasps the point exactly: "Ethics points to ideality as a task and assumes that every man possesses the requisite conditions. Thus ethics develops a contradiction, inasmuch as it makes clear both the difficulty and the impossibility" (CA, 16). Haufniensis goes on, no doubt after perusing the apostle Paul as well as a few Lutheran dogmaticians, saying: "What is said of the law is also true of ethics: it is a disciplinarian that demands, and by its demands only judges but does not bring forth life" (CA, 16; Gal. 3:19, 21, 24). Similarly, for Johannes Climacus in *Postscript* the infinite ethical demand is what drives the ethical-religious life. The two concepts are different but belong together, and that is why Climacus repeatedly uses the expression "the ethical and the ethical-religious" in *Postscript* when he is sketching the various expressions of religiosity (CUP, 396, 426, 434, 467, 481). An absolute standard is needed to uphold the everyday understanding of the ethical, just as hard currency has to back up paper money; ". . . the comparative, conventional, external, bourgeois conception of the ethical is useful enough in ordinary dealings. But if it is forgotten that the hard currency of the ethical must be present in the inwardness of the individual . . . then that generation . . . is nevertheless poverty stricken ethically . . ." (CUP, 1:546.

The religious. Of the religious sphere Taciturnus says little, beyond that it is "the sphere of fulfillment" (SLW, 476). He does lay out "an issue for the religious: the forgiveness of sin" (SLW, 481); but he soon admits the issue turns out to be "beyond both my understanding and my capacities" (SLW, 484), evidently because such forgiveness presupposes that the person forgiven "has become another person" (SLW, 483). Here Taciturnus is evidently defining the religious as what Climacus will later call "the religious in the strict sense" (CUP, 1:519), that is to say, "Religiousness B" or Christianity.

The aesthetic. If no person instantiates the ethical in everyday life, and the religious is beyond Taciturnus's understanding, what remains for him to write about? All that is left is the sphere of the aesthetic, or, more generally, of the aesthetic-ethical. Quidam's diary "lies essentially within the esthetic" (SLW, 455). Taciturnus sees himself with no alternative but to combine the ethical with the aesthetic in the story he writes for Quidam. He argues that, since the ethical as such demands that good triumph and evil be punished with boundless speed, the only way for him to write a diary covering more than an instant of time is to combine the aesthetic with the ethical. "The total thought of the ethical has been retained and the boundless speed has been slowed down by esthetic categories (fate, chance), and now at the end one sees in the total thought of the ethical a world order, a Governance, providence. This result is esthetic-ethical . . ." (SLW, 441-42).

The implication of Taciturnus's understanding of the stages is that everything in the book, from start to finish, belongs in either the aesthetic or the aesthetic-ethical sphere. Taciturnus even thinks of his own essay in that way and is careful not to go beyond those bounds.

The Either/Or in Stages on Life's Way, according to Taciturnus

Taciturnus presents his character Quidam as caught between two alternatives, the aesthetic-ethical and the ethical-religious. This is not the same set of alternatives with which Mr. B faces Mr. A in *Either/Or*, between choosing one's course in life or just continuing to drift. Quidam has long since made the kind of choice Mr. B called for in *Either/Or*. In the diary in *Stages on Life's Way* Taciturnus presents Quidam with another, more difficult choice.

Taciturnus sets up the situation for Quidam in terms of stages: "The stages are structured as follows: an esthetic-ethical life-view under illusion, with the dawning possibility of the religious; an ethical life-view that judges him; he relapses into himself, and he is just where I want him to be" (SLW, 435). Quidam is torn between two alternatives, the aesthetic-ethical that he is, and the ethical-religious that he is to become. In Taciturnus's "experiment" Quidam finds himself judged by an infinite ethical demand, that is, "the ethical," and he cannot accept it and "relapses into himself."

But what is "aesthetic" in Quidam's case? He does not simply observe his ethical crisis, as Mr. A might have done, but feels it intensely and cannot escape it. The clue comes in Taciturnus's phrase that he "relapses into himself." His diary is for himself alone, and he locks it in a trunk that he sinks into the middle of the deepest lake in the land. When the diary is accidentally discovered it is "a sigh from below, a sigh *de profundis* . . . a sigh from the inclosed lake, a sigh from an inclosed soul . . ." (SLW, 188-89).

What is true of Quidam is also true, in one way or another, of each of the other characters in *Stages on Life's Way*. Happily they are not all as apt to brood as he is, but none of them cares much about having readers. The person who records the banquet symposium in the first part of the book is William Afham, a highly elusive figure, who identifies himself as "the pure being that is everywhere present but yet not noticeable, for I am continually being annulled" (SLW, 86)—a delightful spoof on an Hegelian concept. The reader he writes for is not indicated, and his remarks about the solitariness of recollection (SLW, 14) suggest that his recollections are for himself alone. The individual speakers at the symposium are distracted by the spectacular banquet setting from giving much serious attention to each other's opinions. Constantius, in fact, forbids any discussion and commands them that they "forget every speech as soon as it is delivered" (SLW, 47-48). Taciturnus, who writes the last two thirds of *Stages on Life's Way*, describes his opinions in detail but says little about those whom he expects to be his readers. Although he concludes his work with a long "Letter to the Reader," he doubts that by the end anyone is left (SLW, 485, 494), nor does he greatly care whether there is since, as he reflects, "I have forever and a day for myself and can talk with myself about myself undisturbed and without inconveniencing anyone" (SLW, 485). The only author in the book who pays much attention to the reaction of the reader is Judge William, in part two of the book, but even the Judge in *Stages on Life's Way* is not as involved with his potential reader as he was in *Either/Or*, since in the earlier book he directed his arguments personally to his young friend Mr. A, whereas here he sets out merely "to persuade one individual" (SLW, 95).

Although not all the characters in *Stages on Life's Way* are equally "aesthetic" in this sense, they are all completely put off by the infinite demands of the ethical. This is as true of the Judge and Quidam as it is of the aesthetes at the banquet. Even for Quidam it is an open question whether his behavior was guilty or not guilty, while by the standards of the ethical he would have to be judged totally guilty.

The Relation between Stages on Life's Way and Three Discourses

The answer to the question about the relation between the two books follows from the fundamental conflict of life-views between the aesthetic-ethical, on the one hand, and the ethical-religious, on the other. As Taciturnus sees it, to understand a life-view one must not only enunciate the principles involved but also lay out the forms of life in which those principles are embedded. "Quidam's Diary," as well as the other parts of *Stages on Life's Way*, explore variations of the aesthetic-ethical alternative, but they lack any way of representing concretely the ethical-religious alternative that begins with the consciousness of total guilt. This latter task would call for a different kind of book, perhaps one beginning at the confessional: a book, in fact, such as *Three Discourses*. Moreover, since no one like Taciturnus or William Afham could possibly write that kind of book, Kierkegaard himself might have to do it, writing under his own name.

Nothing brings out the contrast between the aesthetic-ethical and the ethical-religious in the two books more sharply than the difference in the two ways of relating to the reader. The aesthetes's ostentatious disinterest in the reader's response in *Stages on Life's Way* is the polar opposite of *Three Discourses*'s care for "that single individual" [*hiin Enkelte*], the reader or listener who appropriates what the writing or discourse says and applies it to oneself. The kind of love Kierkegaard feels for one of his readers, Regine, he here shares with them all. The book, he says, "quietly waits for that right reader to come like the bridegroom and to bring the occasion along with him. Let each do a share—the reader therefore more" (TDIO, 5). Much of the wording of the preface is nearly the same as what is used in each of the six books of upbuilding discourses published during the two previous years. What is distinctive in this particular preface is the emphasis on the shared responsibility of the author and reader. Both the reader and the book have a part. "Here there are no worldly 'mine' and 'thine' that separate and prohibit appropriating what is the neighbor's." For this reason the dedication can speak of appropriation as both "the *book's* joyous *giving of itself*" and as "the *reader's* even greater . . . triumphant *giving of himself*" (TDIO, 5). The author and the reader share responsibility for the discourses. The reader's share of the responsibility for communication, however, is "more" than the speaker's, because the author explicitly declines to speak with authority and thereby leaves it up to the reader to take on some of the author's responsibility too.

Defining the Order of the Discourses in Three Discourses

The remaining question is the reason for the order of the discourses in *Three Discourses*. The Hong and Hirsch proposals offer detailed answers to this question, even though they do not agree with each other. What is the answer if *Three Discourses* represents the ethical-religious side of an either/or?

Answering this question using Taciturnus's stages terminology involves drawing upon different parts of his letter. The first discourse has to be ethical, since the highest expression of the ethical is represented by repentance (SLW, 476), and *Three Discourses* opens with a discourse at the confessional. Since the ethical-religious spans from the ethical to the religious, the third discourse might possibly represent the religious, although for Taciturnus the religious is the realm of forgiveness, and the third discourse makes no reference to that theme. Still, that is only what Taciturnus leads one to expect in a discourse that is not explicitly Christian. Finally, if the first discourse is ethical and the third religious, the second, wedding discourse, should be aesthetic, to fill out of the set. That identification might surprise the aesthetes at the banquet in *Stages on Life's Way*, but not the Judge, since the Judge once wrote an essay in *Either/Or* on "the aesthetic validity of marriage." Following Taciturnus, then, the order of the discourses comes out as ethical, then aesthetic, and then religious.

The problem with this analysis is that it depends largely on guesswork, with little textual foundation. Taciturnus provides only a few random bits of support, and Kierkegaard himself rarely applies the full set of the three stages categories to interpret his explicitly religious discourses. On occasion Kierkegaard does use these categories, for example in a journal entry referring to the middle section of *Upbuilding Discourses in Various Spirits*, but in that case he keeps to the standard order of the stages: aesthetic, ethical, and then religious (JP, 5:5970; cf. JP, 5:5975). Moreover, when other pseudonymous writings apply the set of stages categories to the religious sphere, the terms may not be used in Taciturnus's sense. If, for

Reading Stages on Life's Way and Three Discourses Together

In many ways *Stages on Life's Way* and *Three Discourses* are a matched set. The two books belong together, with *Stages on Life's Way* representing the aesthetic-ethical and *Three Discourses* the ethical-religious.

Stages on Life's Way differs from *Either/Or* in that *Stages on Life's Way* does not draw as sharp a distinction between the aesthetic, or observer, and the ethical, or participant. Unlike Mr. A, Taciturnus chooses to be what he is, and in fact he continually reminds himself of this task. Taciturnus also sees that the real danger for Quidam is not that he should become an observer of his own case (that is, become "dialectical") but that he might continue on as an observer indefinitely. "It is," Taciturnus says, "not the dialectical that makes a person demonic—far from it, but it is remaining in the dialectical" (SLW, 436-37).

Even though Taciturnus grasps the three "existence-spheres" or stages (SLW, 476-77) far better than anyone else in the book, he is still limited in what he can understand, and he knows it. For him the problem is that his detached observer status sometimes prevents him from getting the point of what he sees (SLW, 484-87; cf. CUP, 1:291). From his bird's-eye viewpoint he can see what is going on far below, but he cannot always make personal sense of it. For Taciturnus understanding a stage of life may be compared to seeing a sports event. The photographer up in the blimp is able to record every detail of what happens in a stadium, but without inside information the camera cannot interpret the action or distinguish the parts of the game from preliminaries. Similarly, the person who observes a stage of life may see every detail and yet not be able to make anything out of it. Taciturnus's letter supplies the video shots from the sky camera, and from that viewpoint *Three Discourses* is simply a detail in the comprehensive picture created by *Stages on Life's Way*. On the other hand, Taciturnus would grant that *Three Discourses* has its place too; it is like the talk of the players in the huddle, and for them the blimp might be just a distraction.

One difference between the two books comes in the kinds of readers each book looks for. *Stages on Life's Way* fosters a reader who is an observer of other's lives and of his own. For such a reader *Three Discourses*, as well as *Stages on Life's Way* itself, is mainly an occasion for analysis and classification. *Three Discourses*, on the other hand, waits for "that single individual" who will put the ideas into practice and appropriate them for oneself. Such a reader will take the ideas of both *Stages on Life's Way* and

Three Discourses and adopt some of them as a personal challenge. Does this mean that the reader of these books must make a choice, whether to become an observer or "that single individual"? If that is the situation, the choice has already been made in favor of "that single individual." Does this result mean, then, that the reader of these two books should simply observe the two books and classify their similarities and differences? If that is the situation, a choice has been made nonetheless, in favor of Taciturnus's kind of reader.

The relationship of *Stages on Life's Way* to *Three Discourses* is a "repetition" (in the sense of the term Kierkegaard uses in his book of that name) of the relationship between the first and second volumes of *Either/Or*. While Kierkegaard's text leaves the issue open between Mr. A and Mr. B, the way the book is written favors Mr. B; for, although there may at first seem to be nothing abstractly impossible about the notion of a pure observer, there is something absurd about Mr. A thinking he is one in practice. Likewise, the design of *Stages on Life's Way* and *Three Discourses* gives priority to "that single individual" over the mere observer. Even though both Taciturnus's observer and "that single individual" are readers in some sense or other, the latter is a better fit for what Kierkegaard's rhetorical theory says a reader should be.

Fortunately Kierkegaard has provided the reader with two books rather than just one, and he has left some ambiguity in how they go together. According to *Stages on Life's Way* the two books complement each other, while according to *Three Discourses* they present a choice between two opposing kinds of reading. In this way Kierkegaard has left it up to the reader to distinguish each book from the other and then, if possible, to learn how to read them together.

Previous Volume Consultants

Volume 1. *Early Polemical Writings*
Julia Watkin, University of Tasmania

Volume 3. *Either/Or, Part I*
David Gouwens, Brite Divinity School

Volume 4. *Either/Or, Part II*
Edward F. Mooney, Sonoma State University

Volumes 3 and 4. Title Consultant for *Either/Or*, I and II
George Connell, Concordia College

Volume 6. *"Fear and Trembling" and "Repetition"*
Abrahim H.Kahn, University of Toronto (*Fear and Trembling*)
David Goicoechea, Brock University (*Repetition*)

Volume 7. *"Philosophical Fragments" and "Johannes Climacus"*
Lee Barrett, Lancaster Theological Seminary

Volume 8. *The Concept of Anxiety*
Vincent A. McCarthy, St. Joseph's University

Volume 12. *Concluding Unscientific Postscript to "Philosophical Fragments"*
Merold Westphal, Fordham University

Volume 13. *The Corsair Affair*
Burce H. Kirmmse, Connecticut College

Volume 14. *Two Ages*
Merold Westphal, Fordham University

Volume 16. *Works of Love*
Lee Barrett

Volume 19. *The Sickness unto Death*
Louis Dupré, Yale University

Index